HOUGHTON MIFFLIN

Spelling and Vocabulary

Senior Author
Shane Templeton

Consultants
Donald R. Bear
Rosa Maria Peña

 HOUGHTON MIFFLIN   BOSTON

Acknowledgments

For each of the selections listed below, grateful acknowledgment is made for permission to excerpt and/or reprint original or copyrighted material as follows:

UPWORDS®, SCRABBLE®, and BOGGLE® are registered trademarks of Hasbro Inc. Used by permission of Hasbro Inc. All rights reserved.

Select definitions in the Spelling Dictionary are adapted and reprinted by permission from the following Houghton Mifflin Company publication: Copyright © 1994 THE AMERICAN HERITAGE STUDENT DICTIONARY.

Excerpt from *Digging the Past,* by Bruce Porell. Copyright © 1979 by Bruce Porell. Adapted and reprinted by permission of HarperCollins Publishers.

Excerpt from "Grandpa's Miracle," by Eve Bunting. Reprinted by permission of the author.

Excerpt adapted from *How Do They Find It?,* by George Sullivan. Copyright © 1975 by George Sullivan. Published by The Westminster Press, Philadelphia, PA.

Excerpt from *Kon-Tiki: The Classic True Adventure of Crossing the Pacific by Raft,* by Thor Heyerdahl. Copyright 1950, © 1960, 1984 by Thor Heyerdahl. Adapted and used by permission of Dillon Press, an imprint of Silver Burdett Press, Simon & Schuster Elementary and Gyldendal Norsk Forlag, Norway.

Excerpt from "The Mural," by Emilia Durán, in *Celebrations* from *Houghton Mifflin Reading,* by Durr et al. Copyright © 1986 by Houghton Mifflin Company. Reprinted by permission of Houghton Mifflin Company. All rights reserved.

ISBN-13: 978-0-618-31161-3
ISBN-10: 0-618-31161-0

11 12 13 14 15 - WC - 12 11 10 09

Contents

Contents

Contents

Contents

7

Contents

Student's Handbook

How to Study a Word

❶ Look at the word.

- What are the letters in the word?
- What does the word mean?
- Does it have more than one meaning?

❷ Say the word.

- What are the consonant sounds?
- What are the vowel sounds?

❸ Think about the word.

- How is each sound spelled?
- Did you see any familiar spelling patterns?
- Did you note any prefixes, suffixes, or other word parts?

❹ Write the word.

- Think about the sounds and the letters.
- Form the letters correctly.

❺ Check the spelling.

- Did you spell the word the same way it is spelled on your word list?
- Do you need to write the word again?

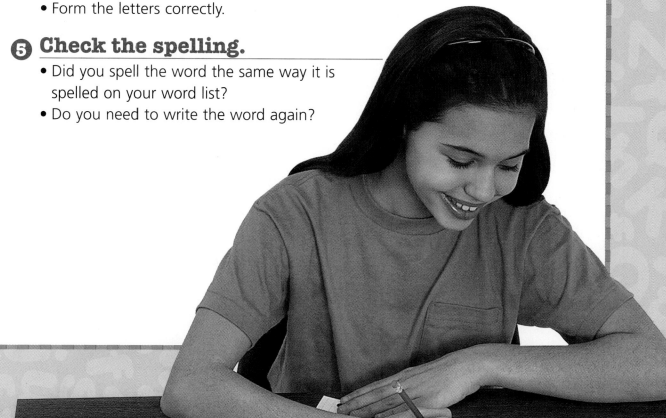

Activities and Games

Word Sorts with Partners

1. Choose 15 to 20 Spelling Words that can be sorted into two or more categories.
2. Write each category on a small card. Then write each Spelling Word on a card.
3. Trade category cards and word cards with a partner. Try to sort each other's words into the correct category. Review and discuss each other's work.

CHALLENGE Have your partner try to guess the categories and sort the words. Discuss the word sort together.

Sorting Ideas

- by vowel sounds (**Example:** |ou| as in *foul* from |ô| as in *vault*)
- by spelling patterns for one vowel sound (**Example:** th*eme*, pr*each*, and sl*ee*ve for |ē|)
- by the way *-ed* and *-ing* are added (**Example:** sli*pp*ed from *modeling*)
- by prefix or suffix
- by syllable pattern (**Example:** VC|CV from V|CCV)
- by the way one syllable pattern is divided (**Example:** VC|CV, VCC|V, V|CCV)

Winner's Circle

Players: 4

You need: a game board with 4 paths, word cards with Spelling Words, 4 marking pens of different colors, spinner, 4 game markers

How to Play

1. Make a game board like the one shown.
2. Each player chooses a colored pen and then uses that marking pen to make 5 word cards. Players place their cards face down near them.
3. Players choose a path and place their game marker on their *Start* space.
4. Player 1 spins and moves the number of spaces shown. The player with the cards written in the same color as the space where Player 1 landed turns over the top card and reads the word aloud. Player 1 spells that word. If correct, Player 1 stays on the space. If incorrect, Player 1 moves back one space. When players land on their own color, they do not have to spell a word.
5. Players take turns until a player reaches the *Winner's Circle*.

Roll and Spell

Players: 2 to 4, a caller

You need: paper, pencils, spelling cube, list of Spelling Words

How to Play

1. Make a paper cube, and write a spelling category or a sound on each side. The categories or sounds should match the Spelling Words in the list.
2. Player 1 rolls the cube. The caller reads a word from the list that matches the pattern rolled. Player 1 spells the word aloud. If correct, Player 1 writes the word.
3. The game ends when a player correctly writes five words.

Short Vowels

|ă|

craft

|ă| Sound

_____

_____

|ĕ| Sound

_____

_____

_____

|ĭ| Sound

_____

_____

_____

_____

_____

_____

|ŏ| Sound

_____

_____

|ŭ| Sound

_____

_____

_____

_____

Read and Say

Basic

READ the sentences. **SAY** each bold word.

1. depth	The **depth** of the water is too shallow for diving.
2. craft	I sailed my **craft** into the harbor.
3. plunge	Who will **plunge** into the pool?
4. wreck	The old car was a **wreck**.
5. sunk	The boat was **sunk** by the storm.
6. film	We need **film** for the camera.
7. strict	My teacher is **strict** but fair.
8. bomb	The **bomb** exploded near the city.
9. switch	Will you **switch** places with me?
10. length	The **length** of the pool is thirty feet.
11. prompt	Be **prompt** for school, not late.
12. pitch	The batter hit the first **pitch**.
13. else	Somebody **else** looks like you.
14. cliff	Rocks fell from the edge of the **cliff**.
15. pledge	I **pledge** to study harder.
16. scrub	Please **scrub** the tub until it is clean.
17. brass	The door has a shiny **brass** knob.
18. grill	He will cook on the **grill**.
19. stung	Joe was **stung** by a bee.
20. plump	My puppy is **plump** but not too fat.

Think and Write

Each word has the **short vowel pattern**, a short vowel sound spelled by a single vowel and followed by a consonant sound. Each word has one of these short vowel sounds:

|ă| cr**a**ft |ĕ| d**e**pth |ĭ| f**i**lm |ŏ| b**o**mb |ŭ| pl**u**nge

• What letter spells each short vowel sound?

Now write each Basic Word under its short vowel sound.

Review		Challenge	
21. swift	23. bunch	26. habitat	28. tepid
22. tense	24. grasp	27. intact	29. magnetic
	25. ditch		30. deft

Independent Practice

Spelling Strategy Remember that a short vowel sound is usually spelled *a*, *e*, *i*, *o*, or *u* and is followed by a consonant sound. A short vowel sound spelled by one vowel and followed by a consonant sound is the **short vowel pattern**.

Word Analysis/Phonics Complete the exercises with Basic Words.
1. Write the word that begins with a silent consonant.
2–3. Write the two words that end with the |ch| sound.
4–6. Write the three words that end with double consonants.

Vocabulary: Context Sentences Write the Basic Word that completes each sentence.
7. The divers sailed in a sturdy _____.
8. The old ship had _____ long ago.
9. Would they _____ into the water?
10. The crew carried waterproof cameras and plenty of _____.
11. Ann was _____ by a jellyfish.
12. Kevin had to _____ mud from the treasures he found.
13. Everyone was told to be _____ for the next morning's dive.

First Dive!

Challenge Words Write the Challenge Word that matches each definition. Use your Spelling Dictionary.

14. quick and skillful
15. moderately warm
16. area where animals or plants live or grow
17. not damaged or impaired
18. having the power to attract

Spelling-Meaning Connection

bomb
bombard

How can you remember that *bomb* ends with a silent *b*? Think of the related word *bombard*, in which the *b* is pronounced.

19–20. Write *bomb* and *bombard*. Underline the letter that is pronounced in one word and silent in the other.

Word Analysis
1. _____
2. _____
3. _____
4. _____
5. _____
6. _____

Vocabulary
7. _____
8. _____
9. _____
10. _____
11. _____
12. _____
13. _____

Challenge Words
14. _____
15. _____
16. _____
17. _____
18. _____

Spelling-Meaning
19. _____
20. _____

Entry and Guide Words

1. _____
2. _____
3. _____
4. _____
5. _____
6. _____

Word Hunt

7. _____
8. _____
9. _____
10. _____
11. _____
12. _____
13. _____
14. _____
15. _____
16. _____
17. _____
18. _____
19. _____
20. _____
21. _____
22. _____

Dictionary

Entry and Guide Words **Entry words** are the words a dictionary defines. They are listed in alphabetical order. Two **guide words** at the top of each page show the first and last entry words on that page. Use guide words to help you find words quickly in a dictionary.

jasmine | jeopardize

jel·ly·fish |jĕl′ ē fĭsh′| *n.* Any of numerous sea animals having a soft, often umbrella-shaped body. *Many jellyfish have tentacles that can cause a sting.*

Practice **1–6.** Write the six words from the list below that belong under the guide words *swell | swivel*. Write them in alphabetical order.

swept	sweet	swing	switch
swift	swine	sword	swipe

Review: Spelling Spree

Word Hunt Write the Basic or Review Word that you find in each of the longer words below.

7. elsewhere
8. swifter
9. grilling
10. pitchfork
11. strictest
12. ditches
13. aircraft
14. cliffhanger
15. filmstrip
16. lengthwise

17. bomber
18. scrubber
19. switchboard
20. brassy
21. intense
22. plumpness

WHOA!

✓ How Are You Doing?

List the spelling words that are hard for you. Practice them with a family member.

Proofreading and Writing

Proofread for Spelling Use proofreading marks to correct nine misspelled Basic or Review Words in this report.

Example: The boat's ~~lenth~~ *length* is thirty feet.

Diving Instructor's Report

After making a plege to avoid dangerous objects, the student divers swam to a dept of twenty feet. Then the buntch of swimmers separated into pairs.

Jim got stuck while trying to plundge into an old boat that had sonk to the ocean floor. Jim's partner couldn't reach far enough to graps his arm. With a swift kick, she swam for help. Meanwhile, Jim was stunk by a stingray. After a promt rescue, I gave Jim a strict lecture. He promised not to explore a reck again.

Pool Rules
No splashing
No running

Write a List

Create a list of water-safety rules. Try to use five spelling words. You might want to make your list into a poster.

Proofreading Tip   **Check each word. Put a check mark over each word as you look at it.**

Basic

1. depth
2. craft
3. plunge
4. wreck
5. sunk
6. film
7. strict
8. bomb
9. switch
10. length
11. prompt
12. pitch
13. else
14. cliff
15. pledge
16. scrub
17. brass
18. grill
19. stung
20. plump

Review
21. swift
22. tense
23. bunch
24. grasp
25. ditch

Challenge
26. habitat
27. intact
28. tepid
29. magnetic
30. deft

Proofreading Marks
¶ Indent
∧ Add
⊙ Add a period
⸜ Delete
≡ Capital letter
/ Small letter
∼ Reverse order

Expanding Vocabulary

Spelling Word Link

plunge
switch

Using a Thesaurus Where can you find an exact word to replace a vague word? Where can you find synonyms, words with the same or similar meanings? Use a thesaurus! Look at this entry.

main entry ...part of speech   definition

fall *v.* to come down suddenly from a standing position. *Hal tripped and fell.* ◄········ sample sentence

subentry ······► **plunge** to dive swiftly and with force. *Tina plunged into the waves.*
tumble to fall with a rolling motion. *Apples tumbled from the crate.*

1. _____

2. _____

3. _____

4. _____

Read pages 255–256 to learn how to use your Thesaurus. Then use your Thesaurus to find the four subentries given for the word *change.* Write the subentries.

Show You Know! Write the subentry that best replaces *change* in each speech balloon.

5. Let me just **change** the lens on my camera. Now smile!

6. See, they *did* **change** diving equipment over the years!

7. Maybe if I **change** poles, I'll catch something.

8. My big brother tries to **change** my manners when we're with his friends.

5. _____

6. _____

7. _____

8. _____

Real-World Connection

Science: Underwater Exploration All the words in the box relate to underwater exploration. Look up these words in your Spelling Dictionary. Then write the words to complete this article.

Sunken Wreck Found!

The __(1)__ Anya Meer and her assistants, exploring the depths of the Indian Ocean in a __(2)__, made an amazing discovery when they were only one __(3)__, or six feet, from the sea floor. Their __(4)__ equipment indicated that a very large object was nearby.

Then they saw it: a three-masted Spanish __(5)__ that had sunk in the 1500s. It had been __(6)__ for nearly five hundred years. The crew decided to __(7)__ the ship's __(8)__, which included a trunk filled with pirates' treasures.

Spelling Word Link

wreck

oceanographer
submarine
salvage
fathom
cargo
submerged
sonar
galleon

1. _____
2. _____
3. _____
4. _____
5. _____
6. _____
7. _____
8. _____

Try This CHALLENGE

Yes or No? Write *yes* if the underlined word is used correctly. Write *no* if it is not.

9. <u>Sonar</u> is used to track planes.
10. Tom tried to <u>salvage</u> his valuables from the fire.
11. An <u>oceanographer</u> studies lakes and ponds.
12. The divers were <u>submerged</u> for nearly an hour.

9. _____
10. _____
11. _____
12. _____

★★ Fact File

Captain William Kidd captured French ships for the English in the late 1600s. Accused of robbing friendly ships too, Kidd and his exploits inspired *Treasure Island* by Robert Louis Stevenson.

Long Vowels

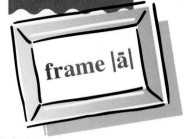

frame |ā|

|ā| Sound

_____

_____

_____

_____

|ē| Sound

_____

_____

_____

|ī| Sound

_____

_____

|ō| Sound

_____

_____

_____

|yōō| Sound

_____

_____

Read and Say

Basic

READ the sentences. **SAY** each bold word.

1.	*theme*	Greed was the **theme** of the story.
2.	*quote*	They each read a **quote** by Lincoln.
3.	*gaze*	We like to **gaze** at paintings.
4.	*pace*	Amy walks at a slow **pace**.
5.	*preach*	Dad tries not to **preach** to me.
6.	*strive*	He will **strive** to do his best.
7.	*trait*	Friendliness is a **trait** I admire.
8.	*mute*	Jay was **mute** with fear.
9.	*sleeve*	She tore her **sleeve**.
10.	*roam*	Deer **roam** throughout the forest.
11.	*strain*	He had to **strain** to finish the race.
12.	*frame*	The picture is in a wood **frame**.
13.	*league*	Jill plays in a baseball **league**.
14.	*soak*	Please **soak** that dirty pan in hot water.
15.	*grease*	Try to clean the **grease** off the oven.
16.	*throne*	The king sat on his **throne**.
17.	*fume*	Do you smell the **fume** from the fireplace?
18.	*file*	Her paper is in the **file**.
19.	*toast*	They had **toast** with jam for breakfast.
20.	*brake*	The **brake** on each wheel helps stop the bike.

Think and Write

Each word below has a long vowel sound, which can be spelled vowel-consonant-e or with two vowels written together.

|ā| g**a**z**e**, tr**ai**t |ē| th**e**m**e**, pr**ea**ch, sl**ee**ve |ī| str**i**v**e**

|ō| qu**o**t**e**, r**oa**m |yōō| m**u**t**e**

• What patterns do you see for these long vowel sounds?

Now write each Basic Word under its long vowel sound.

Review	23. brain
21. greet	24. code
22. boast	25. deal

Challenge	28. refute
26. microphone	29. pertain
27. emphasize	30. coax

Independent Practice

Spelling Strategy Remember that a long vowel sound may be spelled vowel-consonant-*e* or with two vowels written together.

Word Analysis/Phonics Complete the exercises with Basic Words.

1–2. Write the two words that end with the |s| sound.

3–5. Write the three words that begin with the consonant cluster *sl* or *str*.

6–8. Write three words by adding two missing letters to each group of letters below.

      6. pr _ _ ch   **7.** _ _ ote   **8.** leag _ _

Vocabulary: Classifying Write the Basic Word that belongs with each group of words.

9. cereal, juice, _____
10. robe, crown, _____
11. gas, smoke, _____
12. picture, wire, _____
13. wash, rinse, _____

Challenge Words Write the Challenge Word that fits each clue. Use your Spelling Dictionary.

14. to prove to be wrong
15. to urge persistently
16. to stress something
17. to relate to
18. used by a singer at a concert

Spelling-Meaning Connection

Did you know that *mute* and *mutter* are related in spelling and meaning? Both come from a Latin word meaning "silent." Don't let the different vowel sounds confuse you!

19–20. Write *mutter*. Then write the Basic Word that is related to *mutter* in spelling and meaning.

mute
mutter

Word Analysis

1. _____
2. _____
3. _____
4. _____
5. _____
6. _____
7. _____
8. _____

Vocabulary

9. _____
10. _____
11. _____
12. _____
13. _____

Challenge Words

14. _____
15. _____
16. _____
17. _____
18. _____

Spelling-Meaning

19. _____
20. _____

Find a Rhyme

1. _____
2. _____
3. _____
4. _____
5. _____
6. _____
7. _____
8. _____
9. _____
10. _____
11. _____
12. _____
13. _____
14. _____

Change the Word

15. _____
16. _____
17. _____
18. _____
19. _____
20. _____
21. _____
22. _____
23. _____
24. _____
25. _____

Review: Spelling Spree

Find a Rhyme Write a Basic or Review Word that rhymes with the underlined word.

1. He's a neighbor I _____ whenever we <u>meet</u>.
2. Marty read a _____ from Pat's very long <u>note</u>.
3. Our handshake will <u>seal</u> the terms of our _____.
4. My brother likes to <u>boast</u> about Mom's tasty French _____.
5. The palace has many chairs but only one <u>lone</u> _____.
6. Add that office _____ to the ever-growing <u>pile</u>.
7. Ballplayer <u>McTeague</u> belongs in a major _____.
8. The horse's unusual <u>gait</u> may be an inherited _____.
9. You must always _____ for your business to <u>thrive</u>.
10. Mary, in a <u>daze</u>, didn't notice my stern _____.
11. We will leave, I <u>assume</u>, if we smell a bad _____.
12. Put a cover on the _____ so that the splattering will <u>cease</u>.
13. My pet <u>peeve</u> is a torn _____.
14. The beauty of the <u>flute</u> leaves me _____.

Change the Word Write a Basic or Review Word by adding one vowel or consonant to each word below.

Example: tank *thank*

15. fame
16. them
17. ode
18. ram
19. ace
20. bran
21. oak
22. peach
23. rake
24. stain
25. boat

✔ **How Are You Doing?**

Write your spelling words in ABC order. Practice any misspelled words with a family member.

Proofreading and Writing

Proofread: Spelling and End Marks End every sentence with the correct mark.

DECLARATIVE: Today we are giving speeches in class.
INTERROGATIVE: What topic did you choose?
IMPERATIVE: Do not mumble when you speak.
EXCLAMATORY: What a wonderful speech that was!

Use proofreading marks to correct four misspelled Basic or Review Words and two incorrect end marks in these guidelines.

Example: ~~Pleese~~ *Please* save your questions until the end? ⊙

How can you give a good speech.

- Choose your theem.

- Perhaps begin with a quote.

- Smile pleasantly as you great the audience?

- Do not gaz down at your notes.

- Finally, pase yourself. Strive to end on time.

Basic

1. theme
2. quote
3. gaze
4. pace
5. preach
6. strive
7. trait
8. mute
9. sleeve
10. roam
11. strain
12. frame
13. league
14. soak
15. grease
16. throne
17. fume
18. file
19. toast
20. brake

Review

21. greet
22. boast
23. brain
24. code
25. deal

Challenge

26. microphone
27. emphasize
28. refute
29. pertain
30. coax

Write a Speech

Write and present a short speech to inform others about something that interests you. Try to use five spelling words. You might want to draw or cut out pictures to illustrate your talk.

Proofreading Tip

Proofread for one kind of error at a time. Check that you have used correct end marks.

Proofreading Marks

¶   Indent
∧   Add
⊙   Add a period
⌷   Delete
≡   Capital letter
/   Small letter
∩   Reverse order

21

Expanding Vocabulary

Spelling Word Link

quote

Building a Word Family for *quote* Words, like people, can have families—groups of words related in spelling and meaning. Add each word part or ending below to make a form of *quote*. Use your Spelling Dictionary to find the meaning of each new word. Then write a sentence for each word you built.

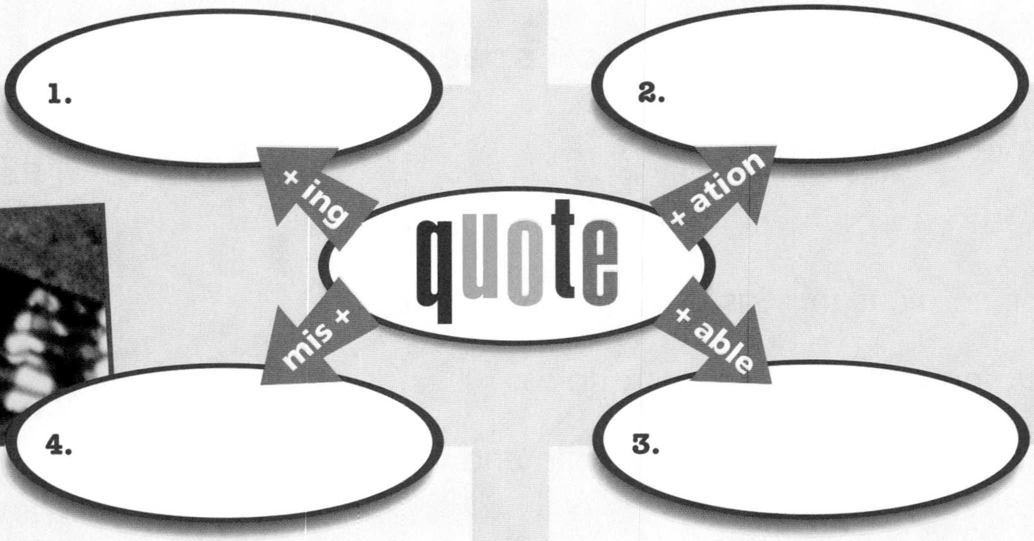

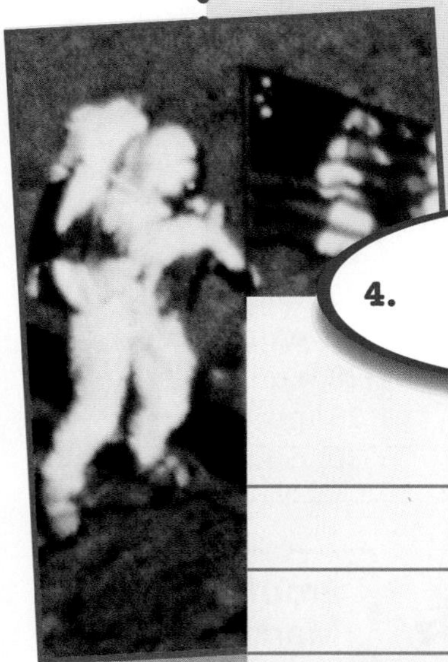

1.

2.

+ ing

+ ation

mis +

+ able

quote

4.

3.

"That's one small step for man, one giant leap for mankind."

Neil Armstrong

"I have a dream that my four little children will one day live in a nation where they will not be judged by the color of their skin but by the content of their character ."

Martin Luther King, Jr.

Real-World Connection

Language Arts: Public Speaking All the words in the box relate to public speaking. Look up these words in your Spelling Dictionary. Then write the words to complete this paragraph.

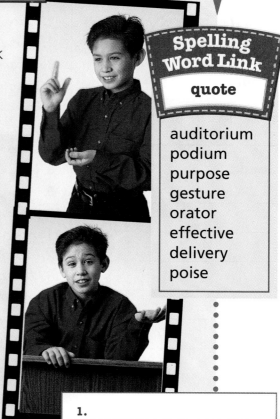

Spelling Word Link

quote

auditorium
podium
purpose
gesture
orator
effective
delivery
poise

Body language can be an __(1)__ part of speech making. Whether your __(2)__ is to inform or entertain, both the physical and the spoken __(3)__ of your speech are important. Stand straight and look out at your audience; every good __(4)__ does. Try using a hand __(5)__ to help you stress a point. Practice your movements. When you finally walk up to that wooden __(6)__ to speak, you may be nervous—especially if you are speaking in a large __(7)__. However, with a little experience, you will gain self-confidence and __(8)__.

Try This CHALLENGE

Clue Match Write a word from the box to match each clue.

9. You do this in a pantomime.
10. People gather here.
11. Dancers have this.
12. Abraham Lincoln was a good one.

Fact File

Martin Luther King, Jr., the main leader of the United States civil rights movement in the 1950s and 1960s, was a powerful orator. His famous "I Have a Dream" speech was a stirring plea for racial equality.

1. _____
2. _____
3. _____
4. _____
5. _____
6. _____
7. _____
8. _____

9. _____
10. _____
11. _____
12. _____

More Vowel Spellings

|ī| cycle
|ĕ| sweat

|ē| Sound

_____

_____

|ī| Sound

_____

_____

_____

_____

|ĕ| Sound

_____

_____

_____

_____

_____

_____

|ĭ| Sound

_____

_____

|ŭ| Sound

_____

_____

Read and Say

Basic

READ the sentences. **SAY** each bold word.

1. cycle — How fast can you **cycle** to the store?
2. sweat — I **sweat** when I ride fast.
3. rhythm — Listen to the **rhythm** of the drums.
4. rely — You can **rely** on me whenever you need help.
5. pleasant — That singer has a **pleasant** voice.
6. routine — What is your daily **routine**?
7. cleanse — Always **cleanse** a cut to kill the germs.
8. shove — Do not **shove** anyone in line.
9. reply — I will **reply** to your letter.
10. meant — We **meant** to call you earlier.
11. sponge — Wash the car with soap and a **sponge**.
12. apply — I will **apply** for that job.
13. threat — The rain was a **threat** to our picnic.
14. myth — We read a Roman **myth** in class.
15. deny — I will not **deny** what I said.
16. leather — The bag is made of soft **leather**.
17. rhyme — That poem does not **rhyme**.
18. thread — Sew it with strong **thread**.
19. meadow — The cows are grazing in the **meadow**.
20. ravine — The **ravine** beside the road was deep.

Think and Write

Each word has a long or a short vowel sound with a less common spelling pattern.

|ē| rout**ine**　　|ĕ| sw**ea**t　　|ŭ| sh**ove** (o-consonant-e)
|ī| c**y**cle　　　|ĭ| rh**y**thm

• What are less common spelling patterns for the |ē| and the |ī| sounds? for the |ĕ|, the |ĭ|, and the |ŭ| sounds?

Now write each Basic Word under its vowel sound.

Review
21. breath
22. measure
23. typical
24. deaf
25. crystal

Challenge
26. endeavor
27. oxygen
28. dynamic
29. realm
30. trampoline

Independent Practice

Spelling Strategy Keep in mind these less common spellings when you try to spell a new word with these vowel sounds:

|ē| *ine* |ī| *y* |ĕ| *ea* |ĭ| *y* |ŭ| *o*-consonant-*e*

Word Analysis/Phonics Complete the exercises with Basic Words.

1. Write the word that ends with the |j| sound.
2–3. Write the two words that begin with the |r| sound spelled with two letters.
4–5. Write the two words that have the |z| sound spelled *s*.

Vocabulary: Synonyms Write the Basic Word that is a synonym for each word below.

6. contradict
7. use
8. danger
9. answer
10. gorge
11. depend
12. perspire
13. pasture

Challenge Words Write the Challenge Word that matches each definition. Use your Spelling Dictionary.

14. a kingdom
15. energetic; vigorous
16. to make an effort
17. a device for acrobatics
18. a colorless, odorless, tasteless gas

Word Analysis
1. _____
2. _____
3. _____
4. _____
5. _____

Vocabulary
6. _____
7. _____
8. _____
9. _____
10. _____
11. _____
12. _____
13. _____

Challenge Words
14. _____
15. _____
16. _____
17. _____
18. _____

Spelling-Meaning
19. _____
20. _____

Spelling-Meaning Connection

Clean and *mean* are related in spelling and meaning to *cleanse* and *meant* even though they have different vowel sounds. **Think of this:** I did not *mean* what you think I *meant*.

> mean
> meant

19–20. Write *mean* and *meant*. Then underline the two letters in each word that are the same but that spell different vowel sounds.

Parts of an Entry

1. _____
2. _____
3. _____
4. _____

Hidden Words

5. _____
6. _____
7. _____
8. _____
9. _____
10. _____
11. _____
12. _____
13. _____
14. _____
15. _____
16. _____
17. _____
18. _____
19. _____
20. _____

How Are You Doing?

Write each spelling word in a sentence. Practice any misspelled spelling words with a partner.

Dictionary

Parts of an Entry Look at some of the different kinds of information you can find in a dictionary entry:

pronunciation   part of speech   adjective forms

entry word····▸ **pleas•ant** |plĕz′ ənt| *adj.* **pleas•ant•er, pleas•ant•est** **1.** Pleasing: *a pleasant climate.* **2.** Pleasing

definition ····▸ or favorable in manner; amiable: *a pleasant person.*

sample phrase ···

Practice Use your Spelling Dictionary to complete these exercises.

1. Write the entry word for *meadow.* Show the syllables.
2. Look up *ravine.* Write the abbreviation for the part of speech of the entry word.
3. Write the first definition of *apply.*
4. Write the sample phrase given for the second definition of *deny.*

Review: Spelling Spree

Hidden Words Find two Basic or Review Words hidden in each sentence. Write the words in order.

Example: My mom gave <u>me a dow</u>ny pillow and a fan<u>cy clear</u> vase.
    meadow   cycle

5–6. Did you leave the shovel in the garden yesterday?
7–8. Does this weather report mean that we will get rain?
9–10. This device gives a measurement of your breathing rate.
11–12. I have an idea for using the old tire lying in the attic.
13–14. While at her aunt's house, Emily cleans every room.
15–16. Reporters were plying us with unpleasant questions.
17–18. My sisters both read many stories, poems, and rhymes.
19–20. I am applying my thoughts toward solving that problem.

meadow cycle

Proofreading and Writing

Proofread for Spelling Use proofreading marks to correct nine misspelled Basic or Review Words in this editorial.

Example: We can no longer ~~denie~~ *deny* this problem!

Rocky Mountain Times

Editorial

Bikers Beware!

If you like to cicle to the ravene, you won't find the trip pleasant anymore. What was once a routene ride past a pond and a medow may now be a thret to your safety. Water that sparkled like cristal is now dulled by trash. Its odor may make you hold your breath. In the grass you'll see tires, cans, and even a spunge. This is no longer a tipical day in the country. The rithim of a smooth ride is a lost joy.

Basic

1. cycle
2. sweat
3. rhythm
4. rely
5. pleasant
6. routine
7. cleanse
8. shove
9. reply
10. meant
11. sponge
12. apply
13. threat
14. myth
15. deny
16. leather
17. rhyme
18. thread
19. meadow
20. ravine

Review
21. breath
22. measure
23. typical
24. deaf
25. crystal

Challenge
26. endeavor
27. oxygen
28. dynamic
29. realm
30. trampoline

Write to Compare and Contrast

Write two paragraphs comparing and contrasting a racing bicycle and a tricycle. How are the two cycles alike? How do they differ? Try to use five spelling words.

Proofreading Tip   **Check for words that have silent letters.**

Proofreading Marks

¶	Indent
∧	Add
⊙	Add a period
૪	Delete
≡	Capital letter
/	Small letter
∼	Reverse order

Expanding Vocabulary

Number Prefixes A **prefix** is a word part at the beginning of a word that adds meaning to the word. For example, *bicycle* means "a cycle with two wheels" because the prefix *bi-* means "two." Knowing number prefixes can help you figure out many new words. Use your Spelling Dictionary to look up each word in the box. On the chart, fill in the number of each prefix and list each word under the correct prefix.

uni- =	*bi-* = 2
1.	7. bicycle
2.	8.
tri- =	*quad-* =
3.	9.
4.	10.
octo- =	*dec-* =
5.	11.
6.	12.

Show You Know! Answer the questions below, and add each bold word to the correct box on the chart. Use your Spelling Dictionary if you need help.

13. If the word root *ped* means "foot," how many feet does a **quadruped** have?
14. How many track and field events are in a **decathlon**?
15. How many horns does the mythical **unicorn** have?
16. How many books, movies, or plays are in a **trilogy**?
17. How many musicians belong in an **octet**?
18. If a centennial celebrates one hundred years, how many years does a **bicentennial** celebrate?

13.

14.

15.

16.

17.

18.

Real-World Connection

Recreation: Bicycling All the words in the box relate to bicycling. Look up these words in your Spelling Dictionary. Then write the words to complete this paragraph from a cycling handbook.

Spelling Word Link

cycle

reflector
lever
terrain
sprint
tandem
puncture
maintenance
kilometers

Cycle Racing

Prepare your bike before every race, whether you enter a short, 800-meter __(1)__ or a longer race covering ten __(2)__. Oil and tune every gear and __(3)__ a day ahead; good __(4)__ can be a factor in winning the race. Carry a tire repair kit in case bumpy __(5)__ causes a __(6)__. Make sure that your bike has at least one red __(7)__ for safety. If two of you are riding a __(8)__, these preparations are doubly important!

page 6

Try This CHALLENGE

Yes or No? Write *yes* or *no* to answer each question.

9. Are kilometers the same as miles?
10. Can terrain refer to a desert?
11. Could a tack puncture a tire?
12. Can a marathon be called a sprint?

1. _____
2. _____
3. _____
4. _____
5. _____
6. _____
7. _____
8. _____

9. _____
10. _____
11. _____
12. _____

★★★ Fact File

A recumbent is an unusual kind of bicycle. The rider leans back and extends the legs forward to pedal. A recumbent called the HPV (human-powered vehicle) can go over 55 miles per hour.

Spelling |ou|, |oo̅|, |ô|, |oi|

|ou| spr**ou**t |oo̅| bl**oo**m

|ou| Sound

_____

_____

_____

_____

_____

|oo̅| Sound

_____

_____

_____

_____

|ô| Sound

_____

_____

_____

_____

|oi| Sound

_____

_____

_____

Read and Say

Basic

READ the sentences. **SAY** each bold word.

1. bloom — What a huge **bloom** that plant has!
2. sprout — My plant has a new **sprout**.
3. droop — Don't let the vine **droop** over the doorway.
4. crouch — I must **crouch** to cut the rose.
5. annoy — Loud noises **annoy** me and hurt my ears.
6. vault — Our money is safe in the bank **vault**.
7. squawk — A sudden **squawk** from the hen startled me.
8. avoid — Please **avoid** being late for the start of class.
9. sought — Mom **sought** an answer to my question.
10. naughty — Our **naughty** puppy often gets in trouble.
11. mound — Plant the seeds in that **mound** of dirt.
12. groove — The sliding door moves along a **groove**.
13. foul — The **foul** odor came from the dump.
14. hoist — Let's **hoist** the sails on the boat.
15. gloom — A sad movie can fill me with **gloom**.
16. trout — Nancy caught a **trout** in the lake.
17. noun — A **noun** can name a person or a place.
18. roost — The bird's **roost** was high in a tree.
19. clause — A **clause** is a group of words.
20. appoint — Will you **appoint** me team captain?

Think and Write

Each word has the |ou|, the |oo̅|, the |ô|, or the |oi| sound.

|ou| spr**ou**t |ô| v**au**lt, squ**aw**k, s**ough**t, n**augh**ty
|oo̅| bl**oo**m |oi| av**oi**d, ann**oy**

• What are spelling patterns for the |ou|, the |oo̅|, the |ô|, and the |oi| sounds?

Now write each Basic Word under its vowel sound.

Review	23. haul	Challenge	28. taut
21. scoop	24. loose	26. bountiful	29. turquoise
22. moist	25. hawk	27. adjoin	30. heirloom

Independent Practice

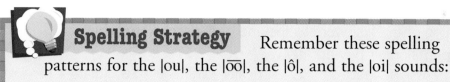

Spelling Strategy   Remember these spelling patterns for the |ou|, the |o͞o|, the |ô|, and the |oi| sounds:

|ou| *ou* |o͞o| *oo* |ô| *au, aw, ough, augh* |oi| *oi, oy*

Word Analysis/Phonics Complete the exercises with Basic Words.
1. Write the word with the |kw| sounds.
2–3. Write the two words that rhyme with *loom*.
4–5. Write the two words with double consonants.

Vocabulary: Definitions Write the Basic Word that matches each definition below.

6. to begin to grow
7. to bend or sag downward
8. to raise or haul up
9. a pile of earth or rocks
10. a bird's perch
11. dirty, unpleasant
12. a freshwater fish
13. to leap over

Challenge Words Write the Challenge Word that fits each clue. Use your Spelling Dictionary.

14. to be next to
15. opposite of *loose*
16. light bluish green
17. synonym for *abundant*
18. something that was your great-grandmother's

Spelling-Meaning Connection

annoy
annoy**ance**

You can add the suffix *-ance* to the verbs *annoy* and *avoid* to make the nouns *annoyance* and *avoidance*. **Think of this:** If you *annoy* someone, you are an *annoyance*.

19–20. Write *avoidance*. Then write the Basic Word that you see in *avoidance*.

Word Analysis
1. _____
2. _____
3. _____
4. _____
5. _____

Vocabulary
6. _____
7. _____
8. _____
9. _____
10. _____
11. _____
12. _____
13. _____

Challenge Words
14. _____
15. _____
16. _____
17. _____
18. _____

Spelling-Meaning
19. _____
20. _____

Word Addition

1. _____
2. _____
3. _____
4. _____
5. _____
6. _____
7. _____
8. _____
9. _____
10. _____
11. _____
12. _____
13. _____
14. _____
15. _____
16. _____

Hink Pinks

17. _____
18. _____
19. _____
20. _____
21. _____
22. _____
23. _____
24. _____
25. _____

Review: Spelling Spree

Word Addition Write a Basic or Review Word by adding the beginning of the first word to the end of the second word.

Example: flood + power   *flower*

1. grant + behoove
2. hasty + joist
3. next + haughty
4. found + sail
5. veil + fault
6. crisp + pouch
7. appeal + joint
8. class + pause
9. scare + loop
10. awake + devoid
11. ripple + boost
12. sewer + bought
13. glare + broom
14. square + hawk
15. annex + joy
16. haste + maul

Hink Pinks Write a Basic or Review Word that answers the question and rhymes with the given word.

Example: What do you sing at lunchtime?
noon _____   *tune*

17. What is an escaped fowl? _____   goose
18. What is wrong with a group of tired chickens? coop _____
19. What is a pile of radios? sound _____
20. What flower is worn by a new husband? groom _____
21. What is seen on the face of an unhappy fish? _____ pout
22. What is a bird-watching hike? _____ walk
23. What is a person who searches for new buds? _____ scout
24. What is a wet lifting machine? _____ hoist
25. What is a circus performer who uses only one part of speech? _____ clown

How Are You Doing?

Write each spelling word as a partner reads it aloud. Did you misspell any words?

Proofreading and Writing

Proofread: Spelling and Commas A compound sentence is made up of two simple sentences joined by a conjunction, such as *and, but,* or *or.* Use a comma before the conjunction.

Cate wants to plant a garden, but she needs seeds.

Use proofreading marks to correct four misspelled Basic or Review Words and two missing commas in these instructions.

Example: Meg dug a hole with the ~~skoop~~ *scoop* and she planted the seeds.

Directions: Fill your garden with sunny yellow marigolds.

After the last frost, you can plant marigold seeds outside in

lose soil but you must avoide shady areas. Lightly mound

the soil over the seeds. Keep the seeds miost. They will

sprout in about ten days and they should blume soon after.

Marigolds

Write a Story

Write a one-page story beginning with this sentence: *When Pat planted her garden, everything went wrong.* How did Pat solve the problems? Try to use five spelling words and at least one compound sentence. Share your story with a classmate.

Proofreading Tip **Be sure to use a comma to separate the parts of any compound sentences.**

Proofreading Marks

¶ Indent
∧ Add
⊙ Add a period
⌐ Delete
≡ Capital letter
/ Small letter
∿ Reverse order

Expanding Vocabulary

Spelling Word Link

vault

wound
desert

Homographs Words that have the same spelling but different meanings are called **homographs**.

vault¹ |vôlt| A safe for valuables.   **vault²** |vôlt| To jump or leap over.

Some of the homographs below differ not only in meaning but also in pronunciation. Use your Spelling Dictionary to help you fill in the chart.

Word	Pronunciation	Sentence
vault¹	|vôlt|	The jewels are in the **vault**.
1.	2.	He will **vault** over the fence.
3.	4.	Harsh words can **wound** people.
5.	6.	She **wound** the yarn into a ball.
7.	8.	The **desert** is hot and dry.
9.	10.	Please don't **desert** the team!

Work Together On your own and on another sheet of paper, write three sentences, using one word from each homograph pair. Illustrate your sentences if you like. Then trade papers with a classmate and read each other's sentences aloud. Which homographs are used? Did you pronounce them correctly?

Real-World Connection

Recreation: Gardening All the words in the box relate to gardening. Look up these words in your Spelling Dictionary. Then write the words to complete this paragraph on gardening.

Spelling Word Link

sprout

lettuce
cucumber
scallion
zucchini
cauliflower
asparagus
parsley
radish

Plan your vegetable garden with eating in mind! If you like leafy green salads, be sure to plant some __(1)__. The small red-skinned __(2)__ and the __(3)__, a young onion, are also good in salads. Don't forget the __(4)__, which is good for pickling. Curly-leafed __(5)__ can be used to flavor many dishes. Green-skinned __(6)__, a type of squash, and __(7)__, which is related to the cabbage, are also popular crops. If you grow tender spears of __(8)__, leave plenty of space between the plants.

1. _____
2. _____
3. _____
4. _____
5. _____
6. _____
7. _____
8. _____

Try This CHALLENGE

Write a Menu Blurb Write a brief description of a restaurant's newest salad creation. Name the salad, and make it sound so delicious that everyone will order it. Create an entire menu if you like.

★★★ Fact File

The Hanging Gardens of Babylon, one of the Seven Wonders of the Ancient World, probably were built by King Nebuchadnezzar II for his wife. The gardens did not hang but rose on terraces.

Spelling Vowel + |r| Sounds

|ûr|

earth

|ûr| Sounds

_____

_____

_____

_____

_____

_____

_____

|ôr| Sounds

_____

_____

_____

_____

|är| Sounds

_____

_____

_____

_____

|îr| Sounds

_____

Read and Say

Basic

READ the sentences. **SAY** each bold word.

1. *fierce* — The angry cats had a **fierce** fight.
2. *sword* — The king carried a sharp **sword**.
3. *court* — We played on the clay tennis **court**.
4. *snarl* — Some dogs **snarl** at people.
5. *thorn* — The bear had a **thorn** in its paw.
6. *earth* — The bird swooped down to **earth**.
7. *skirt* — My aunt wore her wool **skirt**.
8. *chart* — I made a **chart** of the food groups.
9. *urge* — I **urge** you to be kind.
10. *yarn* — Her cat plays with a ball of **yarn**.
11. *whirl* — The dancers **whirl** around the stage.
12. *mourn* — They **mourn** for their lost pet.
13. *rehearse* — We will **rehearse** the play today.
14. *curb* — Park the car by the **curb**.
15. *earnest* — He made an **earnest** promise to return.
16. *starch* — The **starch** made my shirt stiff.
17. *purse* — I left my **purse** at the store.
18. *birch* — I peeled some bark from the **birch**.
19. *pierce* — That pin will **pierce** the balloon.
20. *scorn* — Please don't **scorn** your friend.

Think and Write

Each word has one of these vowel + |r| sounds:

| |ûr| | sk**ir**t, **ur**ge, **ear**th | |är| | ch**ar**t |
| |ôr| | th**or**n, c**our**t | |îr| | fi**er**ce |

• What are three spelling patterns for the |ûr| sounds? What are two spelling patterns for the |ôr| sounds? What are spelling patterns for the |är| and the |îr| sounds?

Now write each Basic Word under its vowel + |r| sounds.

Review
21. pearl
22. stir
23. torch
24. pour
25. scar

Challenge
26. circumstances
27. turmoil
28. absurd
29. forfeit
30. sparse

Independent Practice

Spelling Strategy   Remember these spelling patterns for these vowel + |r| sounds:

|ûr| *ear, ur, ir* |ôr| *or, our* |är| *ar* |îr| *ier*

Word Analysis/Phonics   Complete the exercises with Basic Words.

1. Write the word that begins with the |s| sound spelled *sw*.
2–4. Write the three words with the |k| sound spelled *c*.
5–8. Write the four words that have a final |s| sound.

Vocabulary: Analogies   An **analogy** compares word pairs that are related in some way. Write the Basic Word that completes each analogy.

Example: Fast is to **quick** as **start** is to **begin**.

9. *Flower* is to *daisy* as *tree* is to _____.
10. *Shirt* is to *pants* as *blouse* is to _____.
11. *Rejoice* is to *celebrate* as *grieve* is to _____.
12. *Cactus* is to *spine* as *rose* is to _____.
13. *Sewing* is to *thread* as *knitting* is to _____.

Challenge Words   Write the Challenge Word that is a synonym for each word. Use your Spelling Dictionary.

14. confusion   16. ridiculous   18. conditions
15. penalty   17. uncrowded

mourn
mourning

Spelling-Meaning Connection

How can you remember the difference in spelling between *morning* and *mourning*? Think of the meaning. The word *mourning,* which means "the expression of sorrow for a person who has died," is related in spelling and meaning to *mourn*.

19–20.   Write *mourning*. Then write the Basic Word that you see in *mourning*.

Word Analysis

1. _____
2. _____
3. _____
4. _____
5. _____
6. _____
7. _____
8. _____

Vocabulary

9. _____
10. _____
11. _____
12. _____
13. _____

Challenge Words

14. _____
15. _____
16. _____
17. _____
18. _____

Spelling-Meaning

19. _____
20. _____

Spelling Table

1. _____
2. _____
3. _____
4. _____
5. _____
6. _____
7. _____
8. _____

Word Detective

9. _____
10. _____
11. _____
12. _____
13. _____
14. _____
15. _____
16. _____
17. _____
18. _____
19. _____
20. _____
21. _____
22. _____
23. _____
24. _____
25. _____

Dictionary

Spelling Table How can you find a word in the dictionary if you do not know how to spell it? A **spelling table** can help. It shows the ways that a sound can be spelled.

SOUND	SPELLINGS	SAMPLE WORDS
|ûr|	ear, er, ir, or, our, ur	learn, herd, girl, word, journey, turn

To find \|mûrth\|, you would look up the word with each spelling of the \|ûr\| sounds until you found *mirth*.

Practice Write the word that has each pronunciation below. Use the Spelling Table on pages 279–280 and your Spelling Dictionary.

1. \|dĭ stûrb′\| 3. \|rē′ sûrch′\| 5. \|jûr′ nē\| 7. \|kŏn′ sûrt′\|
2. \|swûrl\| 4. \|dĭ zûrv′\| 6. \|pûr′ fyo͞om′\| 8. \|kûr′ ĭj\|

Review: Spelling Spree

Word Detective Write a Basic or Review Word for each clue.

9. wild and mean
10. has peeling bark
11. mark left after an injury
12. provides light
13. what you do with a spoon
14. feel grief
15. found on a rosebush
16. graph or table
17. found in an oyster shell
18. what actors must do
19. spin rapidly
20. what mean dogs do
21. makes shirts stiff
22. a homophone for *pore*
23. rims a street
24. used to make sweaters
25. what arrows do to targets

✓ **How Are You Doing?**

List the spelling words that are hard for you. Practice them with a family member.

Proofreading and Writing

Proofread for Spelling Use proofreading marks to correct eight misspelled Basic or Review Words in this legend.

fierce
Example: *Robin Hood had a ~~fearce~~ concern for the poor.*

The Legend of Robin Hood

Robin Hood would steal the purce of a rich person and give the money to the poor. He wore disguises—a mask or even a scirt—to carry out his deeds. His skill with both a bow and arrow and a sord was a threat to any enemy. With his followers he lived close to the erth in Sherwood Forest. He tried to stir the common folk, to erge them to unite. He was loyal to the king but ernest in his fight against some members of the cort. His skorn for greedy and dishonest citizens was his claim to fame.

Write an Ad

Robin Hood needs members for his merry band. Write a help-wanted ad describing the job and its qualifications. Try to use five spelling words.

Help Wanted

merry Men

Proofreading Tip

Say each word aloud to yourself.

Proofreading Marks

¶ Indent
∧ Add
⊙ Add a period
⌇ Delete
≡ Capital letter
/ Small letter
∽ Reverse order

Expanding Vocabulary

Spelling Word Link

urge

Building a Word Family for *urge* Add each suffix or ending shown to make a form of *urge*. Use your Spelling Dictionary to find the meaning of each new word.

1. _____

+ ing

5. _____   + ent + ly   **urge**   + ed   2. _____

+ ency   + ent

4. _____   3. _____

Complete each speech balloon with a form of *urge*.

YOUR HELP IS ___(6)___ NEEDED! TWENTY-SEVEN LIVES ARE AT STAKE! PLEASE! THIS IS A MATTER OF UTMOST ___(7)___!

No. 7

WHY WERE YOU ___(8)___ ME TO HELP? SAVING LIVES IS ___(9)___, NOT THIS!

I ___(10)___ YOU BECAUSE EACH OF MY CATS HAS NINE LIVES!

6. _____

7. _____

8. _____

9. _____

10. _____

Show You Know! Write a sentence for each form of *urge* that you built. Use another sheet of paper.

Real-World Connection

Language Arts: Legends All the words in the box relate to legends. Look up these words in your Spelling Dictionary. Then write the words to complete the paragraph on this book jacket.

TALES OF ARTHUR

If a story is all true, it's history. If it mixes fact and ___(1)___, it's a ___(2)___. Its main male character, the ___(3)___, or its main female character, the ___(4)___, is a person who really lived but whose deeds have been exaggerated. One legendary hero is King Arthur, who ruled the ___(5)___ of Britain and was guided by Merlin, a ___(6)___ with great powers. The tales in this collection tell of the ___(7)___ adventures of Arthur and his knights and their ___(8)___ for a holy cup. Read one and you'll want to read on!

Spelling Word Link

sword

legend
quest
hero
heroine
perilous
fantasy
sorcerer
kingdom

Try This CHALLENGE

Yes or No? Write *yes* or *no* to answer each question.

9. Is a textbook about the history of England a fantasy?
10. Is King Arthur a heroine?
11. Would fighting an angry dragon be perilous?
12. Could a queen rule a kingdom?

1. _____
2. _____
3. _____
4. _____
5. _____
6. _____
7. _____
8. _____

9. _____
10. _____
11. _____
12. _____

Fact File

In one of the legends about the sword Excalibur, young Arthur proves his right to the English throne by pulling Excalibur from a stone. In another tale the Lady of the Lake gives Arthur the sword.

41

6 Review: Units 1–5

|ă|

craft

craft	wreck	strict	bomb	sunk
grill	plump	prompt	pledge	brass

Spelling Strategy   Remember that a short vowel sound is usually spelled **a**, **e**, **i**, **o**, or **u** and is followed by a consonant sound. A short vowel sound spelled by one vowel and followed by a consonant sound is the **short vowel pattern**.

Write the word that completes each sentence.
1. After the accident, the car was a total _____.
2. Teachers expect you to be _____ with your homework.
3. The jeweler displayed earrings made of silver and _____.
4. This peach is firm and _____.

Write the word that fits each meaning.
5. went below the surface
6. demanding strong discipline
7. artistic skill or ability
8. an explosive weapon
9. a formal vow
10. a cooking device

1. _____
2. _____
3. _____
4. _____
5. _____
6. _____
7. _____
8. _____
9. _____
10. _____

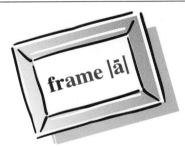

frame |ā|

strive	mute	theme	gaze	roam
league	file	strain	throne	fume

Spelling Strategy   Remember that a long vowel sound may be spelled vowel-consonant-**e** or with two vowels written together.

Write the word that is a synonym for each word below.
11. silent
13. stare
12. wander
14. topic

Write the word that rhymes with each word below.
15. pile
17. pain
16. hive
18. lone

Write the word that fits each meaning.
19. smoke, vapor, or gas
20. group of sports teams

11. _____
12. _____
13. _____
14. _____
15. _____
16. _____
17. _____
18. _____
19. _____
20. _____

Unit 3   More Vowel Spellings   pages 24–29

|ī| cycle
|ĕ| sweat

| pleasant | cycle | routine | rhythm | shove |
| ravine | myth | thread | sponge | deny |

Spelling Strategy   Keep in mind these less common spellings when you try to spell a new word with these vowel sounds:

|ē| → **ine** |ī| → **y** |ĕ| → **ea** |ĭ| → **y** |ŭ| → **o**-consonant-**e**

Write the word that fits each meaning.
21. thin cord   **23.** push roughly   **25.** something absorbent
22. to declare untrue   **24.** agreeable   **26.** ride a bike

Write the word that completes each sentence.
27. The waterfall spilled into a deep _____.
28. The school band learned a song with a jazzy _____.
29. A story that explains a natural occurrence is a _____.
30. Getting dressed, eating breakfast, and brushing your teeth are all part of your daily _____.

21. _____

22. _____

23. _____

24. _____

25. _____

26. _____

27. _____

28. _____

29. _____

30. _____

Unit 4   Spelling |ou|, |ōō|, |ô|, |oi| pages 30–35

| sought | annoy | crouch | naughty | squawk |
| clause | mound | groove | appoint | hoist |

|ou| sprout |ōō| bloom

Spelling Strategy

|ou| → **ou** |ōō| → **oo** |ô| → **au, aw, augh, ough** |oi| → **oi, oy**

Write the word that matches each definition. Circle the word with the |oi| sound.
31. stoop   **33.** disobedient
32. bother   **34.** looked for

Write six words by adding the missing letters. Circle the words with the |ô| sound.
35. gr_ _ ve   **38.** h _ _ st
36. app _ _ nt   **39.** squ _ _ k
37. m _ _ nd   **40.** cl _ _ se

31. _____

32. _____

33. _____

34. _____

35. _____

36. _____

37. _____

38. _____

39. _____

40. _____

earth

sword	chart	skirt	earth	snarl
pierce	mourn	starch	curb	earnest

Spelling Strategy   Remember that vowel + |r| sounds can have these patterns:

|ûr| → **ir, ur, ear** |är| → **ar** |ôr| → **or, our** |îr| → **ier**

Write the word that rhymes with each word below. Underline the letters that spell the vowel + |r| sounds in each word.

41. shirt

42. lord

43. part

44. parch

Write the word that belongs with each group of words.

45. street, gutter, _____

46. growl, roar, _____

47. ocean, sky, _____

48. grieve, cry, _____

49. sincere, serious, _____

50. stab, puncture, _____

41. _____

42. _____

43. _____

44. _____

45. _____

46. _____

47. _____

48. _____

49. _____

50. _____

intact	tepid	endeavor	refute	coax
absurd	turmoil	trampoline	turquoise	taut

Write the Challenge Word that completes each of the analogies below.

51. *Cold* is to *cool* as *hot* is to _____.

52. *Broken* is to *shattered* as *whole* is to _____.

53. *Reasonable* is to *logical* as *ridiculous* is to _____.

54. *Runner* is to *track* as *acrobat* is to _____.

55. *Loose* is to *slack* as *tight* is to _____.

56. *Red* is to *ruby* as *bluish-green* is to _____.

Write the Challenge Word that is a synonym for each word below.

57. persuade

58. confusion

59. attempt

60. disprove

51. _____

52. _____

53. _____

54. _____

55. _____

56. _____

57. _____

58. _____

59. _____

60. _____

Spelling-Meaning Strategy

Vowel Changes: Long to Short Vowel Sound

cycle
bicycle

You know that words, like people, can be related to each other. Look at the related words *cycle* and *bicycle*.

On Saturday morning Bernadette decided to **cycle** out to Cary Park. She called Terry and invited him to bring his **bicycle** and join her for a ride around the lake.

Think

• How are *cycle* and *bicycle* related in meaning?
• What vowel sound does *y* spell in each word?

Here are more related words that have the same spelling pattern even though the vowel sound is different, as in *cycle* and *bicycle*.

p**a**le	p**a**ge	m**i**nus
p**a**llid	p**a**ginate	m**i**nimum

Apply and Extend

Complete these activities on a separate sheet of paper.

1. Look up the words in the word box above in your Spelling Dictionary, and write their meanings. Then write a short paragraph, using one pair of words. Can you make the relationship between the words' meanings clear?

2. With a partner list as many words as you can that are related to *cycle, pale, page,* and *minus.* Then look in the section "Vowel Changes: Long to Short Vowel Sound," beginning on page 273 of your Spelling-Meaning Index. Add any other words that you find in these families to your list.

Summing Up

Words that are related in meaning are often related in spelling, even though one word has a long vowel sound and the other word has a short vowel sound.

from Grandpa's Miracle
by Eve Bunting

Cathy and her grandfather were special friends until he retired. What details help you understand why Cathy thinks her relationship with Grandpa has changed?

"Do you want to come to the park with me?" I asked Grandpa today. Our park is terrific; it has lots of space, and there's even a river that runs through it. That's where Grandpa taught me to skip rocks when I was little.

"I don't want to go to the park," Grandpa said, and he turned his head away.

So I went with my best friend, Laura, who lives in my building. We decided to go for a run along the river path.

As we jogged along at an easy pace, I thought about Grandpa and how he'd changed.

Laura stopped to tie her shoelace. I knew she really stopped to rest because she was huffing and puffing like a train. I decided to tell her about my problem.

"Grandpa's no fun at all these days," I told her. I wanted Laura to talk about him. I wanted her to help me understand why he was suddenly the way he was.

"Aw, he's not so bad," Laura said. What does Laura know—she's not even *related* to him.

Think and Discuss

1 What detail shows the relationship Cathy and Grandpa once had? What detail shows how Grandpa acts when Cathy asks him to go to the park?

2 How does the dialogue between Cathy and Grandpa help you understand Cathy's problem?

3 From whose point of view is the story told?

The Writing Process
Personal Narrative

What interesting experiences have you had? Write a personal narrative about one of them. Keep the guidelines in mind, and follow the Writing Process.

1 Prewriting
- Make a time line of your experiences: what happened when? Include words that describe how you felt (such as *curious* or *delighted*) at different times during the experience.

2 Draft
- Try several beginnings, such as an action, a surprising event, or a dialogue.

3 Revise
- Add details and dialogue that tell what you saw, heard, or felt.
- Use your Thesaurus to find exact words.
- Have a writing conference.

4 Proofread
- Did you spell each word correctly?
- Did you use correct end marks?
- Did you use commas correctly in compound sentences?

5 Publish
- Add a good title.
- Make a neat final copy of your story into a booklet for others to read.

Guidelines for Writing a Personal Narrative

✔ Tell the story from your point of view.
✔ Use a good beginning to capture your readers' attention.
✔ Use dialogue and details to help your readers see, hear, and feel your experience.

Composition Words

cliff
scrub
gaze
roam
pleasant
cycle
sought
whirl

Compound Words

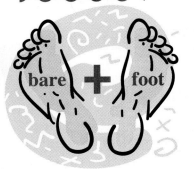

bare + foot

One Word

_____

_____

_____

_____

_____

_____

_____

_____

_____

_____

_____

_____

_____

_____

_____

_____

With a Hyphen

_____

_____

Two Words

_____

_____

Read and Say

READ the sentences.

SAY each bold word.

Basic

1. barefoot — We walked **barefoot** in the park.
2. sea gull — A **sea gull** flew over the boat.
3. driftwood — We found **driftwood** in the sand.
4. carefree — In the summer I feel happy and **carefree**.
5. somebody — Is **somebody** at the door?
6. nowhere — My book is **nowhere** to be found.
7. haircut — Dad got a **haircut** today.
8. runner-up — I was the **runner-up** in the essay contest.
9. teammate — My **teammate** is a good soccer player.
10. toothbrush — Don't forget your **toothbrush** and soap.
11. headache — Dan had a **headache** and a fever.
12. iceberg — The ship passed a huge **iceberg**.
13. fireproof — Our new roof is **fireproof**.
14. uproar — The crowd was in an **uproar** during the game.
15. whereas — I like plums, **whereas** my sister likes apples.
16. dead end — My street is a **dead end**.
17. forehead — She wears her hat low on her **forehead**.
18. grandchildren — They have six **grandchildren**.
19. old-fashioned — She likes **old-fashioned** clothes.
20. nevertheless — He is loud, but I like him **nevertheless**.

Think and Write

Each word is a compound word. A **compound word** is made up of two or more smaller words.

drift + **wood** = driftwood   **runner** + **up** = runner-up

sea + **gull** = sea gull

- What three ways can a compound word be written?

Now write each Basic Word under the heading that tells how it is written.

Review		Challenge	
	23. first aid		28. painstaking
21. wildlife	24. homemade	26. water-repellent	29. self-confident
22. weekend	25. baby-sit	27. ebb tide	30. crestfallen

Independent Practice

Spelling Strategy   A **compound word** is made up of two or more smaller words. Remember that a compound word may be written as one word, as a hyphenated word, or as separate words.

Word Analysis/Phonics   Complete the exercises with Basic Words.

1. Write the compound word made up of three smaller words.

2–4. Write the three words with the |k| sound.

Vocabulary: Definitions   Write the Basic Word that fits each definition.

5. top part of the face
6. a street with no exit
7. second-place winner
8. an ocean bird
9. not anywhere
10. of an earlier time
11. noisy confusion
12. without shoes or socks
13. made of materials that do not burn

Challenge Words   Write the Challenge Word that fits each clue. Use your Spelling Dictionary.

14. having assurance
15. like a good raincoat
16. extremely careful
17. synonym for *depressed*
18. ocean water between its high and low levels

Spelling-Meaning Connection

How can you remember that some compound words, such as *teammate* and *roommate,* have double consonants? Think of the two smaller words that are put together to form each compound word.

19–20. Write *teammate* and *roommate.* Underline the double consonants in each word.

Word Analysis

1. _____
2. _____
3. _____
4. _____

Vocabulary

5. _____
6. _____
7. _____
8. _____
9. _____
10. _____
11. _____
12. _____
13. _____

Challenge Words

14. _____
15. _____
16. _____
17. _____
18. _____

Spelling-Meaning

19. _____
20. _____

teammate
roommate

Stressed Syllables

1. _____
2. _____
3. _____
4. _____
5. _____
6. _____
7. _____
8. _____
9. _____
10. _____

Exchanging Word Parts

11. _____
12. _____
13. _____
14. _____
15. _____
16. _____
17. _____
18. _____
19. _____
20. _____
21. _____
22. _____
23. _____
24. _____
25. _____

Dictionary

Stressed Syllables A dictionary entry shows each entry word separated into syllables. In a word with two or more syllables, one syllable is pronounced with more **stress**, or emphasis. The dictionary pronunciation shows the stressed syllable in dark type and followed by an **accent mark** (′).

drift·wood |drîft′ wo͝od′|

Practice Look up each word below in your Spelling Dictionary. Write the word, and underline the stressed syllable.

1. rehearse	5. tragic	9. deny
2. naughty	6. lately	10. earnest
3. measure	7. meadow	
4. decline	8. ravine	

Review: Spelling Spree

Exchanging Word Parts Write the Basic or Review Word that has one of the parts in each compound word below.

11. woodchuck	16. nevermore	21. dead letter
12. icebox	17. waterproof	22. stepchildren
13. no one	18. first base	23. paintbrush
14. homeland	19. shortcut	24. inasmuch as
15. classmate	20. lifeboat	25. caretaker

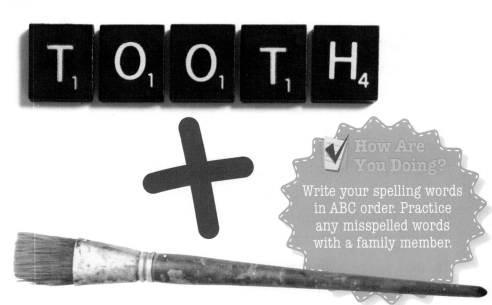

How Are You Doing?
Write your spelling words in ABC order. Practice any misspelled words with a family member.

Proofreading and Writing

Proofread for Spelling Use proofreading marks to correct ten misspelled Basic or Review Words in this diary entry.

carefree

Example: *I love these* ~~care-free~~ *summer days!*

July 18

I didn't have to babby-sit this weakend, so I went to the beach with my family. We walked bearfoot along the shore and passed an old-fashoned cottage. Then sombody said that one oddly shaped piece of driftwood looked like a see gull. In the afternoon we played volleyball on the sand. There was an up-roar when I fell down and hit my forhead. Dad gave me first aid by putting ice on the bump. Soon my headace passed, and later on I was first runner up in the paddleball contest.

Basic

1. barefoot
2. sea gull
3. driftwood
4. carefree
5. somebody
6. nowhere
7. haircut
8. runner-up
9. teammate
10. toothbrush
11. headache
12. iceberg
13. fireproof
14. uproar
15. whereas
16. dead end
17. forehead
18. grandchildren
19. old-fashioned
20. nevertheless

Review

21. wildlife
22. weekend
23. first aid
24. homemade
25. baby-sit

Challenge

26. water-repellent
27. ebb tide
28. painstaking
29. self-confident
30. crestfallen

Write to Compare and Contrast

Think of a beach and a city street on a hot summer day. What are the sights, sounds, and smells of each? Write two paragraphs comparing and contrasting the two places. Try to use five spelling words.

Proofreading Tip

Circle any word that you think you misspelled. Then look it up in a dictionary.

Proofreading Marks

¶ Indent
∧ Add
⊙ Add a period
 ⌐ Delete
≡ Capital letter
/ Small letter
∿ Reverse order

Expanding Vocabulary

Spelling Word Link
fireproof

Building Compound Words With a partner use the words listed here to build a compound word for each coil on the fire hose and each level of the fire escape. Each word you build must begin with the last half of the compound word above it. Two examples are shown on each chart. **Hint:** Some compound words have three parts.

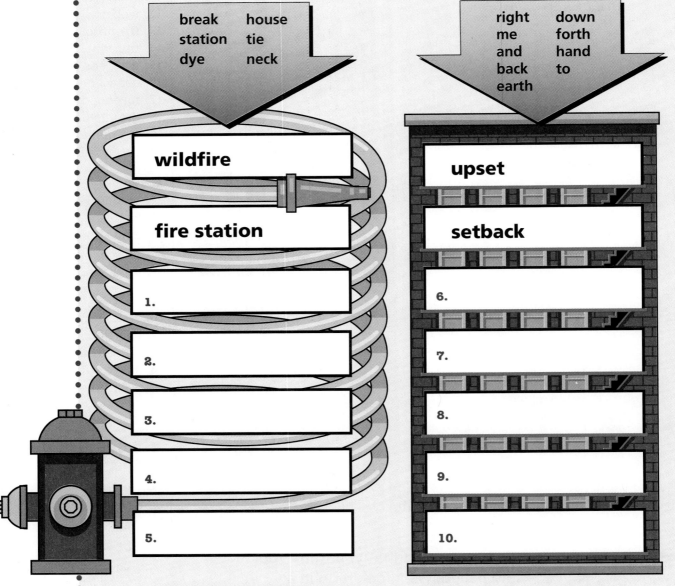

break	house
station	tie
dye	neck

right	down
me	forth
and	hand
back	to
earth	

wildfire

fire station

1.

2.

3.

4.

5.

upset

setback

6.

7.

8.

9.

10.

Show You Know! On your own write sentences for five of the compound words that you built. Use a separate sheet of paper.

52

Real-World Connection

Recreation: Beaches All the words in the box relate to beaches. Look up these words in your Spelling Dictionary. Then write the words to complete this trail guide.

Spelling Word Link

sea gull

sandbar
tern
kelp
pelican
conch
jetty
mussel
dune

Self-Guided Seaside Walk

Your walk starts on top of the windblown __(1)__ overlooking the ocean. From here you can see how the waves have shifted pebbles and dirt offshore to form a __(2)__. Walk out on the stone __(3)__, built to protect the harbor from rough waves. You may see a __(4)__ dive into the water and slip a fish into its pouch. A __(5)__ may fly by, flashing its forked tail. In the water you may see the seaweed called __(6)__, which feeds many marine animals. Look carefully for the spiral-shelled pink __(7)__ and the blue-shelled __(8)__.

1. _____
2. _____
3. _____
4. _____
5. _____
6. _____
7. _____
8. _____

Try This CHALLENGE

Yes or No? Write *yes* or *no* to answer each question.

9. Could you fly in a jetty?
10. Does a tern grow on the ocean floor?
11. Could you eat a mussel?
12. Would a conch make a comfortable seat?

9. _____
10. _____
11. _____
12. _____

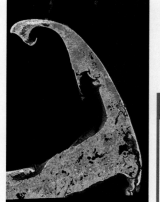

★★★ **Fact File**

Cape Cod, a peninsula on the coast of Massachusetts, is shaped like a curved arm. It was named Cape Cod for all the codfish caught in the ocean around it. Cape Cod is a popular vacation area.

Homophones

fur

fir

Homophones

_____

_____

_____

_____

_____

_____

_____

_____

_____

_____

_____

_____

_____

_____

_____

Read and Say

Basic

READ the sentences. **SAY** each bold word.

1. fir — They planted a **fir** tree.
2. fur — My dog has brown **fur**.
3. scent — That flower has a nice **scent**.
4. sent — My aunt **sent** me a package.
5. scene — Were you near the **scene** of the accident?
6. seen — I have **seen** this movie before.
7. vain — She is selfish and **vain**.
8. vein — The nurse took blood from a **vein** in my arm.
9. principal — She is **principal** violinist in the orchestra.
10. principle — What is one **principle** that you live by?
11. manor — The **manor** has a huge front lawn.
12. manner — His speaking **manner** is always polite.
13. who's — Please see **who's** at the door.
14. whose — Do you know **whose** coat this is?
15. tacks — Use **tacks** to put up the poster.
16. tax — How much **tax** did you pay on that?
17. hangar — The airplane is in the **hangar**.
18. hanger — Put your coat on a **hanger**.
19. died — My dog almost **died** when he was born.
20. dyed — She **dyed** her shirt green.

Think and Write

Each word is a homophone. **Homophones** are words that sound alike but have different spellings and meanings.

|vān| va**i**n   unsuccessful, fruitless
|vān| ve**i**n   a blood vessel

• How do the spellings differ in each homophone pair? What is the meaning of each homophone?

Now write the homophone pairs that make up the Basic Words.

Review	23. soar
21. berry	24. sore
22. bury	

Challenge	27. burrow
25. barren	28. burro
26. baron	29. borough

Independent Practice

Spelling Strategy

Homophones are words that sound alike but have different spellings and meanings. When you use a homophone, be sure to spell the word that has the meaning you want.

Having long recess periods is an important principle.

Context Sentences Write the Basic Word that completes each sentence.

1. The pilot parked the airplane in the _____.
2. Put your jacket on a _____ in the closet.
3. Jenny _____ three letters to me.
4. This fragrant perfume has a sweet _____.
5. "Be honest" is an important rule, or _____, to live by.
6. The head of a school is called a _____.

PRINCIPAL

Vocabulary: Word Clues Write the Basic Word that fits each clue.

7. an animal's coat
8. contraction for *who is*
9. opposite of *invisible*
10. a way of doing things
11. a type of evergreen tree
12. a wealthy landowner's house
13. opposite of *humble*

Challenge Words Write the Challenge Word that matches each definition. Use your Spelling Dictionary.

14. a small donkey
15. a nobleman
16. a self-governing town
17. without vegetation
18. a hole in the ground made by a small animal

Spelling-Meaning Connection

Scene comes from the Greek word *skene,* meaning "stage." The |k| sound is no longer pronounced. Because *scenic* and *scenery* are related in meaning to *scene,* they are also related in spelling.

scene
scenic
scenery

19–20. Write *scene* and *scenic.* Then underline the letters that are the same in both words.

Context Sentences

1. _____
2. _____
3. _____
4. _____
5. _____
6. _____

Vocabulary

7. _____
8. _____
9. _____
10. _____
11. _____
12. _____
13. _____

Challenge Words

14. _____
15. _____
16. _____
17. _____
18. _____

Spelling-Meaning

19. _____
20. _____

Homophones

1. _____
2. _____
3. _____
4. _____
5. _____
6. _____

Homophone Hints

7. _____
8. _____
9. _____
10. _____
11. _____
12. _____
13. _____
14. _____
15. _____
16. _____
17. _____
18. _____
19. _____
20. _____

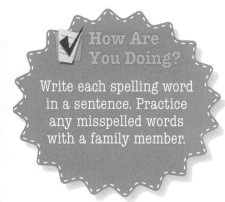

How Are You Doing?

Write each spelling word in a sentence. Practice any misspelled words with a family member.

Dictionary

Homophones A dictionary entry tells you whether a word has a homophone. The entry word and its homophone are listed at the end of the entry.

> **fir** |fûr| *n.* Any of several cone-bearing evergreen trees with rather flat needles. *These sound alike* **fir, fur.**

Practice Use your Spelling Dictionary to complete the exercises.

1. Look up *foul* and write its homophone.
2. Which word means "offensive to the taste or smell"?
3. Which word means "a bird that is raised for food"?
4. Look up *idle* and write its homophone.
5. Which word means "avoiding work; lazy"?
6. Which word means "a person or thing that is adored or greatly admired"?

Review: Spelling Spree

Homophone Hints Write a Basic or Review Word to fit each clue.

7. mailed a letter
8. painful
9. a small fruit
10. to rise or fly high
11. a blood vessel
12. past tense of *die*
13. money people must pay to support the government
14. small nails
15. a hook for clothing
16. conceited
17. changed the color of
18. another name for perfume
19. a home for airplanes
20. what dogs sometimes do with bones

Proofreading and Writing

Proofread for Spelling Use proofreading marks to correct ten Basic or Review Words in this essay.

Example: Yes, summer has ~~dyed~~ *died*, but I love winter too!

Winter Walks

A winter day in the forest is a beautiful seen. The fur trees are covered with snow, and a strong scent of pine fills the air. On my walks I have scene small animals and birds who sometimes have called to me in a scolding manor. Two blue jays wonder whose disturbing them before they soar away. A chipmunk with striped fir asks who's footsteps it hears as it guards its manner. They should not worry. My principle rule in the forest is "Leave nothing there and take nothing away." This principal helps keep the forest beautiful.

Write Homophone Riddles

If you mailed perfume to your mom, what would you have done? Sent scent! Write five riddles using spelling-word pairs. Then exchange papers with a partner and solve the riddles.

Proofreading Tip   **If you use a computer spell-checker, remember that it cannot tell whether you have used the correct homophone.**

Basic

1. fir
2. fur
3. scent
4. sent
5. scene
6. seen
7. vain
8. vein
9. principal
10. principle
11. manor
12. manner
13. who's
14. whose
15. tacks
16. tax
17. hangar
18. hanger
19. died
20. dyed

Review
21. berry
22. bury
23. soar
24. sore

Challenge
25. barren
26. baron
27. burrow
28. burro
29. borough

Proofreading Marks

¶ Indent
∧ Add
⊙ Add a period
 Delete
≡ Capital letter
/ Small letter
∽ Reverse order

Expanding Vocabulary

Spelling Word Link

homophone

insight
incite
excite
situation
sightsee
citation
foresight
campsite
hindsight
recite

Homophone Word Families Homophones have different spellings and meanings because they come from different sources. Each homophone also has its own family of words that are related in spelling and meaning.

Look up *site* in your Spelling Dictionary. Read the History box for *cite*, *sight*, and *site*. In each house below, write the homophone that matches the origin. Then find the words in the box that are related to each homophone. Write those words in the correct house.

Latin word meaning "place":

1.
2.
3.

Latin word meaning "to call":

4.
5.
6.
7.
8.

Old English word meaning "something seen":

9.
10.
11.
12.
13.

14.
15.
16.
17.
18.

Show You Know! Write a word from one of the word families above to complete each sentence.

14. Anya will _____ her poem on parents' night.
15. Thousands of tourists _____ in San Antonio each summer.
16. Kiran had the _____ to bring an umbrella.
17. We found a good _____ and pitched our tent.
18. The firefighter received a _____ for bravery.

Real-World Connection

Science: Trees All the words in the box relate to trees. Look up these words in your Spelling Dictionary. Then write the words to complete this encyclopedia entry.

Trees

Magnolia tree

Uses of Trees Trees have many uses. The pleasant-smelling wood of the __(1)__, an evergreen, is used to make chests. Beautiful furniture is made from __(2)__, a strong, reddish-brown wood. The blue berries of the __(3)__ flavor medicines, and tea is made from the root bark of the __(4)__. The lovely pink and white flowers of the __(5)__ add beauty to gardens, as does the __(6)__, first found in China. The __(7)__, with its many trunks, and the __(8)__, with its ball-like seeds, offer cool, leafy shade.

Try This CHALLENGE

Clue Match Write a word from the box to match each clue.

9. It frequently grows along streams.
10. Its bark, roots, and leaves have a spicy taste.
11. It has fan-shaped leaves.
12. One of these trees sometimes looks like a forest.

 Fact File

The redwood, an evergreen that grows along the Pacific Coast from California to southern Oregon, is among the world's tallest kinds of trees. It can reach a height of more than two hundred feet.

1. _____
2. _____
3. _____
4. _____
5. _____
6. _____
7. _____
8. _____

9. _____
10. _____
11. _____
12. _____

UNIT 9 Final |ər|

er

_____

_____

_____

_____

_____

_____

or

_____

_____

_____

_____

_____

_____

_____

ar

_____

_____

_____

_____

Another Spelling

_____

Read and Say

Basic

READ the sentences. **SAY** each bold word.

1. senator — We will elect a new **senator**.
2. director — She is the **director** of our play.
3. minister — Our new **minister** will preach this Sunday.
4. similar — You and I have **similar** ideas.
5. senior — My sister is in the **senior** class.
6. junior — My brother is the **junior** golf champ.
7. messenger — The **messenger** delivered a note.
8. superior — The best student has **superior** grades.
9. familiar — Is his face **familiar** to you?
10. acre — They own one **acre** of land.
11. calendar — Your birthday is circled on my **calendar**.
12. elevator — He took an **elevator** to the third floor.
13. inner — I live in the **inner** city.
14. minor — She got a **minor** cut when she fell.
15. barrier — The fence is a **barrier** to our dog.
16. grammar — Try to use correct **grammar**.
17. surrender — The defeated army will **surrender** today.
18. particular — I love that **particular** shade of blue.
19. youngster — That **youngster** is cute.
20. passenger — The **passenger** lost her ticket.

Think and Write

Each word ends with the schwa sound + *r*. The **schwa sound**, shown as |ə|, is a weak vowel sound often found in an unstressed syllable. Because the spelling of the |ə| sound is not clear, learn how this sound is spelled.

|ər| minist**er**, juni**or**, simil**ar**

• What three patterns can spell the final |ər| sounds? How are these sounds spelled in the Elephant Word?

Write each Basic Word under its spelling of the final |ər| sounds.

Review
21. mayor
22. popular
23. banner
24. regular
25. consider

Challenge
26. ambassador
27. chancellor
28. councilor
29. corridor
30. courier

60

Independent Practice

Spelling Strategy When you hear the final |ər| sounds in words of two or more syllables, think of the spelling patterns *er*, *or*, and *ar*.

Word Analysis/Phonics Complete the exercises with Basic Words.

1. Write the word with the |ŭ| sound spelled *ou*.
2. Write the word with the |ī| sound.
3–4. Write the two words with the |j| sound spelled *g*.
5–8. Write the four words with the |k| sound spelled *c*.

Vocabulary: Making Inferences Write the Basic Word that fits each clue.

9. A dam and a fort's wall are examples of this.
10. This is something you study in English class.
11. This is what one side does at the end of a war.
12. This can get you to the top floor of a tall building.
13. A student almost ready to graduate from high school is one.

Challenge Words Write the Challenge Word that completes each sentence. Use your Spelling Dictionary.

14. The senator's office is at the end of a long _____ .
15. A United States _____ works to create goodwill abroad.
16. The President sent the urgent message by _____ .
17. The townspeople voted to elect a new _____ .
18. Some European countries are run by a _____.

Spelling-Meaning Connection

How can you remember how to spell the final |ər| sounds in *similar*? Think of the |ăr| sounds in the related word *similarity*.

19-20. Write *similar*. Then write the related word that helps you remember how to spell the final |ər| sounds in *similar*.

Word Analysis
1. _____
2. _____
3. _____
4. _____
5. _____
6. _____
7. _____
8. _____

Vocabulary
9. _____
10. _____
11. _____
12. _____
13. _____

Challenge Words
14. _____
15. _____
16. _____
17. _____
18. _____

similar
similarity

Spelling-Meaning
19. _____
20. _____

Pronunciation Key

1. _____
2. _____
3. _____
4. _____
5. _____
6. _____

Contrast Clues

7. _____
8. _____
9. _____
10. _____
11. _____
12. _____
13. _____
14. _____
15. _____
16. _____
17. _____
18. _____
19. _____
20. _____
21. _____
22. _____
23. _____
24. _____
25. _____

Dictionary

Pronunciation Key   How can you find out what the symbols in a pronunciation mean? Use the **pronunciation key**. The pronunciation key gives an example word that has the sound shown by each symbol. For example, *pit* has the vowel sound shown by |ĭ|.

PRONUNCIATION	PART OF A PRONUNCIATION KEY
in·ner |ĭn′ ər|	ĭ pit ə ago, it**e**m, pen**c**il, at**o**m, circ**u**s

Practice   Write the word below that matches each pronunciation. Use the pronunciation key on page 283. Check your answers in your Spelling Dictionary.

leather   police   pass
pace   leisure   policy

1. |pŏl′ ĭ sē| 3. |lē′ zhər| 5. |păs|
2. |lĕth′ ər| 4. |păs| 6. |pə lēs′|

Review: Spelling Spree

Contrast Clues   The second part of each clue contrasts with the first part. Write a Basic or Review Word to fit each clue.

Example: not different, but _____ *similar*

7. not spelling, but _____
8. not an actor, but a _____
9. not outer, but _____
10. not inferior, but _____
11. not senior, but _____
12. not a priest, but a _____
13. not a driver, but a _____
14. not unknown, but _____
15. not a passageway, but a _____
16. not an escalator, but an _____
17. not fight, but _____
18. not disliked, but _____
19. not major, but _____
20. not a governor, but a _____
21. not junior, but _____
22. not unlike, but _____
23. not an old-timer, but a _____
24. not unusual, but _____
25. not general, but _____

How Are You Doing?

Write each spelling word as a partner reads it aloud. Did you misspell any words?

Proofreading and Writing

Proofread for Spelling Use proofreading marks to correct ten misspelled Basic or Review Words in this part of a letter.

Example: Maybe you can get a ~~simulas~~ *similar* job next summer!

GOOD CITIZEN

SENATE. . . . . No. 1809
HOUSE . . . . No. 3334
By Mr. Herren of Fall River,
Montigny J

Dear Lori,

   This has been a baner year! I won the Good Citizen Award. Now I'm the yongster in a group of pages at the Capitol. My reguler job is to be a mesenger for a senetor. The Senate is about to concider a bill to pay farmers for each acer of crops. This particuliar bill is popular in the Midwest. A similiar bill and some minor bills are on the calender too.

as Been Printed On   Paper.

Basic

1. senator
2. director
3. minister
4. similar
5. senior
6. junior
7. messenger
8. superior
9. familiar
10. acre
11. calendar
12. elevator
13. inner
14. minor
15. barrier
16. grammar
17. surrender
18. particular
19. youngster
20. passenger

Review

21. mayor
22. popular
23. banner
24. regular
25. consider

Challenge

26. ambassador
27. chancellor
28. councilor
29. corridor
30. courier

Write Slogans

Re-elect Our **Super SENATOR**

Make Giggles your regular toothpaste! Write several snappy slogans for an election campaign or an advertising campaign. Create them as bumper stickers or magazine ads if you like. Try to use five spelling words.

Proofreading Tip

Check for words in which an extra letter has accidentally been added.

Proofreading Marks

¶ Indent
∧ Add
⊙ Add a period
⌅ Delete
≡ Capital letter
/ Small letter
∿ Reverse order

Vocabulary Enrichment

Expanding Vocabulary

Spelling Word Link

minor

minimum
minus
minute
minuscule
mince

The Word Root *min* The spelling word *minor* and many other English words contain the word root *min*. A **word root** is a word part that has meaning but cannot stand alone, as a base word can. *Min* comes from Latin words meaning "small," "least," and "to lessen." Work with a partner to write what one person in each cartoon might be saying. Use the word on the cartoon in your sentence.

1. minus
2. minute
3. mince
4. minimum
5. minuscule

1. _____
2. _____
3. _____
4. _____
5. _____

Real-World Connection

Social Studies: Government All the words in the box relate to government. Look up these words in your Spelling Dictionary. Then write the words to complete this news bulletin.

Spelling Word Link

senator

republic
parliament
cabinet
monarchy
dictatorship
embassy
citizens
anarchy

Last Transaction Report   Fax 900 Series   Version: 01.05
Time 04:36   Remote Fax Number 1 555 234 5555   Duration 0:24:11   Diagnostic 403M4IRM

WIRE SERVICE BULLETIN

King Oscar of Arzat is about to step down, ending the days of his __(1)__. The staff at the United States __(2)__ in Arzat had wondered what would happen. The people who are __(3)__ of Arzat had to choose a new government quickly to avoid a confused state of __(4)__. No one wanted a prime minister with a lawmaking __(5)__ or the absolute authority of a __(6)__. Finally, all agreed that Arzat will become a __(7)__, governed by an elected president and the members of an appointed __(8)__.

Try This CHALLENGE

Yes or No? Write *yes* if the underlined word is used correctly. Write *no* if it is not.

9. The <u>cabinet</u> gives the President important advice.
10. A <u>republic</u> can be headed by a king.
11. A <u>senator</u> lives in an <u>embassy</u>.
12. A president can sail aboard a <u>dictatorship</u>.

★★★ **Fact File**

In 1945 the United Nations (UN) was formed to help keep world peace. Representatives from more than 150 nations meet at UN headquarters in New York City to help unite the governments of the world.

1. _____
2. _____
3. _____
4. _____
5. _____
6. _____
7. _____
8. _____

9. _____
10. _____
11. _____
12. _____

Final |ən|, |əl|, and |ər|

|ən| **weapon**

Final |n| or |ən| Sounds

_____

_____

_____

_____

_____

Final |l| or |əl| Sounds

_____

_____

_____

_____

_____

_____

_____

_____

_____

_____

Final |ər| Sounds

_____

_____

_____

_____

Read and Say

Basic	**READ** the sentences. **SAY** each bold word.
1. weapon	Did the robber have a **weapon**?
2. struggle	I had to **struggle** to open the jar.
3. frighten	Do not **frighten** the baby.
4. horror	We watched in **horror** as our team lost.
5. mental	She made a **mental** note of the address.
6. channel	Please change the television **channel**.
7. sample	Would you like to **sample** this bread?
8. moral	The story had a **moral**.
9. litter	Do not leave **litter** outside.
10. soldier	The **soldier** stood on guard.
11. kitchen	We ate in the **kitchen**.
12. gallon	I need a **gallon** of red paint.
13. stumble	Did you **stumble** over the rug?
14. linen	This dress is made of **linen**.
15. panel	The control **panel** on a plane is complex.
16. error	There is one **error** on your test.
17. rural	We live in a **rural** area.
18. quarrel	They had a **quarrel** about money.
19. bundle	I carried the **bundle** inside.
20. cancel	Dad had to **cancel** his meeting.

Think and Write

Each word ends with the schwa + |n|, schwa + |l|, or schwa + |r| sounds. (Some dictionaries show only the final consonant sound.)

|n| or |ən| weap**on**, fright**en** |ər| litt**er**, horr**or**
|l| or |əl| samp**le**, chann**el**, ment**al**

• What are two patterns for the final |n| or |ən| sounds? three patterns for the final |l| or |əl| sounds? two patterns for the final |ər| sounds?

Now write each Basic Word under its final sounds.

Review		Challenge	
	23. novel		28. agricultural
21. loyal	24. major	26. corporal	29. valor
22. matter	25. dozen	27. colonel	30. maneuver

Independent Practice

Spelling Strategy
Remember these spelling patterns for these final sounds:

final |n| or |ən| *on, en*   final |ər| *er, or*
final |l| or |əl| *le, el, al*

Word Analysis/Phonics Complete the exercises with Basic Words.

1–7. Write the seven words that have double consonants.

Vocabulary: Analogies Write a Basic Word to complete each of the following analogies.

8. *Voice* is to *physical* as *thought* is to _____.
9. *Teacher* is to *classroom* as *chef* is to _____.
10. *Hammer* is to *tool*
as *sword* is to _____.
11. *Wood* is to *oak* as
cloth is to _____.
12. *City* is to *country* as
urban is to _____.
13. *Navy* is to *sailor* as
army is to _____.

Challenge Words Write the Challenge Word that fits each clue. Use your Spelling Dictionary.

14. homophone for *kernel*
15. relating to farming
16. courage or bravery
17. the rank below sergeant
18. to make changes in course or position

Courage

moral
morality

Spelling-Meaning Connection

How can you remember how to spell the schwa sound in *moral*? Think of the |ă| sound in the related word *morality*.

19–20. Write *moral* and *morality*. Then underline the letter in *morality* that helps you remember how to spell the schwa sound in *moral*.

Word Analysis
1. _____
2. _____
3. _____
4. _____
5. _____
6. _____
7. _____

Vocabulary
8. _____
9. _____
10. _____
11. _____
12. _____
13. _____

Challenge Words
14. _____
15. _____
16. _____
17. _____
18. _____

Spelling-Meaning
19. _____
20. _____

The Third Word

1. _____
2. _____
3. _____
4. _____
5. _____
6. _____
7. _____
8. _____
9. _____
10. _____
11. _____
12. _____
13. _____
14. _____
15. _____

Puzzle Play

16. _____
17. _____
18. _____
19. _____
20. _____
21. _____
22. _____
23. _____
24. _____
25. _____

Review: Spelling Spree

The Third Word Write the Basic or Review Word that belongs with each group of words.

1. trash, garbage, _____
2. trustworthy, faithful, _____
3. important, significant, _____
4. strive, labor, _____
5. terror, fear, _____
6. argue, disagree, _____
7. startle, scare, _____
8. taste, try, _____
9. pint, quart, _____
10. mistake, fault, _____
11. poem, biography, _____
12. stagger, trip, _____
13. bedroom, den, _____
14. cotton, wool, _____
15. lesson, principle, _____

Puzzle Play Write a Basic or Review Word to fit each clue. Circle the letter that would appear in the box.

Example: a young cat __ __ __ __ __ ☐ kitte(n)

16. a waterway __ __ ☐ __ __ __ __
17. several things tied or wrapped together ☐ __ __ __ __ __
18. what everything is made of __ __ __ __ ☐ __
19. all in your head __ __ __ __ __ ☐
20. a member of an army __ __ __ __ ☐ __ __
21. something to fight with __ __ __ __ __ ☐
22. to call off or put an end to ☐ __ __ __ __ __
23. another word for twelve __ ☐ __ __ __
24. what an area in the country is __ __ __ __ __ ☐
25. one piece of a wooden wall __ __ ☐ __ __

Now write the circled letters in order.
They will spell a mystery person's name.
Mystery Name:

__ __ __   __ __ __ __ __ __ __

They call me Honest __ __ __ __!

Proofreading and Writing

Proofread: Spelling and Possessive Nouns Form the possessive of a singular noun by adding *'s*. Form the possessive of a plural noun ending with *s* by adding an apostrophe. Add *'s* to form the possessive of plural nouns that do not end with *s*.

SINGULAR POSSESSIVE NOUN:	Tess**'s** bike	a dog**'s** paw
PLURAL POSSESSIVE NOUN:	girl**s'** sizes	men**'s** hats

Use proofreading marks to correct four misspelled Basic or Review Words and two incorrect possessive nouns in this paragraph from a student's social studies report.

Example: The units commander gave the ~~solder~~ *soldier* an order.

> The Civil War started during Lincolns presidency. The North and the South were caught in a struggel over states rights. The moral debate over slavery was a matter of majer concern. The war caused family members to quarel and even to be loyel to opposite sides.

Write a Diary Entry

During the Civil War, family members often fought on opposing sides. Have you quarreled with a family member? Write a diary entry about it. Try to use five spelling words and at least two possessive nouns.

Check any possessive nouns in your writing to be sure that you wrote them correctly.

Proofreading Tip

Proofreading Marks

¶ Indent
∧ Add
⊙ Add a period
⌐ Delete
≡ Capital letter
/ Small letter
∿ Reverse order

Expanding Vocabulary

Spelling Word Link

channel
litter

1. _____
2. _____
3. _____
4. _____
5. _____

Multiple-Meaning Words Many words in English have several meanings. Look at this dictionary entry for *channel*.

chan·nel |chăn′ əl| *n.* **1.** A part of a harbor deep enough for ships. **2.** A broad strait. **3.** A passage for liquids. **4.** A way through which ideas may travel. **5.** A band of radio-wave frequencies for broadcasting.

Write the number of the meaning of *channel* that is used in each sentence.

1. We switched the <u>channel</u> to find a good program.
2. Huge ships dock in the deep <u>channel</u> of the harbor.
3. A newspaper is a good <u>channel</u> for new information.
4. Oil flowed through a <u>channel</u> and into the tank.
5. The English <u>Channel</u> separates France and England.

Work Together On a separate sheet of paper, write a sentence for each meaning of *litter.* Use your Spelling Dictionary. Then exchange papers with a partner, and tell which meaning fits each sentence.

Real-World Connection

Social Studies: The Civil War All the words in the box relate to the Civil War. Look up each word in your Spelling Dictionary. Then write the words to complete this paragraph from a social studies textbook.

The Civil War
Introduction

The Civil War began in 1861 when Southern states tried to __(1)__ from the Union and formed the __(2)__. Among other things, they wanted to keep the right to have slaves work their __(3)__. Many Northerners wanted to __(4)__ slavery. President Lincoln proclaimed the __(5)__ of the slaves in 1863, but the war lasted until 1865. Both sides were able to __(6)__ large armies. The North sent its navy to __(7)__ Southern ports. The South had skilled riders in its __(8)__ and brilliant generals, but it could not defeat the North.

Spelling Word Link

struggle

Confederacy
secede
recruit
blockade
abolish
emancipation
plantations
cavalry

1. _____
2. _____
3. _____
4. _____
5. _____
6. _____
7. _____
8. _____

Try This CHALLENGE

Yes or No? Write *yes* if the underlined word is used correctly. Write *no* if it is not.

9. The <u>cavalry</u> set sail in their warships.
10. Cotton was grown on many Southern <u>plantations</u>.
11. Not every new <u>recruit</u> had a uniform at first.
12. The soldiers tried hard to <u>secede</u> at winning the war.

9. _____
10. _____
11. _____
12. _____

Fact File

President Abraham Lincoln's Emancipation Proclamation declared slaves "forever free." In 1865 the Thirteenth Amendment to the United States Constitution officially abolished slavery.

VCCV and VCCCV Patterns

ten nis

V C C V

VCCV

Read and Say

Basic

READ the sentences. **SAY** each bold word.

1. lawyer — The **lawyer** talked to the judge.
2. dentist — The **dentist** looked at my teeth.
3. author — He is the **author** of that book.
4. system — Our town has a good school **system**.
5. custom — Shaking hands is a friendly **custom**.
6. method — Your study **method** works better than mine.
7. standard — Candy is below the **standard** for healthy food.
8. admit — I **admit** that I was wrong.
9. supply — Our **supply** of pencils is getting low.
10. whisper — May I **whisper** in the library?
11. tennis — Have you played **tennis** on a clay court?
12. instant — We became **instant** friends.
13. burden — My backpack is a heavy **burden** when it is full.
14. rescue — They had to **rescue** me from the surf.
15. banquet — We ate well at the **banquet**.
16. bullet — The rocket is shaped like a **bullet**.
17. surface — The **surface** of the table is dirty.
18. journey — When does your **journey** begin?
19. laundry — I took my clothes to the **laundry**.
20. campus — The school has a pretty **campus**.

Think and Write

Each two-syllable word has the VCCV or the VCCCV pattern. In each syllable look for familiar spelling patterns.

VC	CV	V	CCV	VCC	V	VC	CCV
sur | face		**au | thor**		**meth | od**		**in | stant**	

• Where is each word divided into syllables? Why are *method* and *author* not divided between the consonants?

Now write each Basic Word under its syllable pattern.

VCCCV

Review		Challenge	
	23. merchant		28. enhance
21. actor	24. employ	26. aspire	29. structure
22. surgeon	25. effort	27. intern	30. astute

Independent Practice

Spelling Strategy To spell a two-syllable word, divide the word into syllables. Look for spelling patterns you have learned, and spell the word by syllables.

Word Analysis/Phonics Complete the exercises with Basic Words.

1–3. Write the three words with the |ô| sound.

4–5. Write the two words that begin with the |k| sound.

6–8. Write the three words with double consonants.

Vocabulary: Context Sentences Write a Basic Word to fit each sentence.

9. Most actresses do not achieve _____ success.

10. Five astronauts prepared for a long _____ through space.

11. The doctor asked us to _____ because her patient was asleep.

12. The chef prepared delicious food for the _____.

13. A police officer climbed the tree to _____ the frightened child.

Challenge Words Write the Challenge Word that matches each definition. Use your Spelling Dictionary.

14. keen in judgment

15. to have great ambition

16. an arrangement of parts

17. to add to; make greater

18. a graduate undergoing supervised training

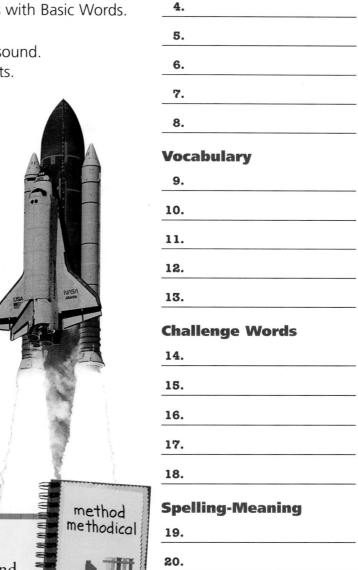

method
methodical

Word Analysis

1. _____
2. _____
3. _____
4. _____
5. _____
6. _____
7. _____
8. _____

Vocabulary

9. _____
10. _____
11. _____
12. _____
13. _____

Challenge Words

14. _____
15. _____
16. _____
17. _____
18. _____

Spelling-Meaning

19. _____
20. _____

Spelling-Meaning Connection

How can you remember how to spell the |ə| sound in *method?* Think of the |ŏ| sound in the related word *methodical.*

19–20. Write *method* and *methodical.* Underline the letter in *methodical* that reminds you how to spell the |ə| sound in *method.*

Using Clues

1. _____
2. _____
3. _____
4. _____
5. _____
6. _____
7. _____
8. _____
9. _____
10. _____
11. _____

Syllable Addition

12. _____
13. _____
14. _____
15. _____
16. _____
17. _____
18. _____
19. _____
20. _____
21. _____
22. _____
23. _____
24. _____
25. _____

Review: Spelling Spree

Using Clues Write the Basic or Review Word for each clue.

1. You should go to one of these when you want a lot to eat.
2. You might buy something at a store run by this person.
3. This person writes books.
4. A set of parts working together forms this.
5. This is a rule or model used to judge quality and value.
6. You would do this to a drowning person.
7. You need a net to play this.
8. This person would be able to defend you in court.
9. This word means "a way of doing something."
10. This person can fill a cavity in your tooth.
11. This word means "the outermost layer of an object."

Syllable Addition Combine the first syllable of the first word with the second syllable of the second word to write a Basic or Review Word.

Example: transport + confer *transfer*

12. adhere + permit
13. inside + constant
14. launder + sundry
15. suppose + apply
16. cuspid + bottom
17. surprise + sturgeon
18. effect + comfort
19. journal + chutney
20. whistle + supper
21. bully + mallet
22. empire + deploy
23. campaign + rumpus
24. active + doctor
25. burlap + garden

✓ **How Are You Doing?**

Write your spelling words in ABC order. Practice any misspelled words with a partner.

Proofreading and Writing

Proofread: Spelling and Appositives An **appositive** is a word or group of words that identify or explain the noun that they follow. Commas separate an appositive from the rest of the sentence.

Sarah Kirwin, Judy's mother, is also my professor.

Use proofreading marks to correct four misspelled Basic or Review Words and four missing commas in this book-jacket blurb.

Example: Li Wong a ~~tenis~~ *tennis* pro is the subject of this book.

Li Wong: World Tennis Champion

Li Wong and Tim Rosten a well-known auther cowrote this book. Wong a world champion discusses her tennis method and how she reached instent fame in a sport that demands a high standerd of performance and efort.

Basic

1. lawyer
2. dentist
3. author
4. system
5. custom
6. method
7. standard
8. admit
9. supply
10. whisper
11. tennis
12. instant
13. burden
14. rescue
15. banquet
16. bullet
17. surface
18. journey
19. laundry
20. campus

Review

21. actor
22. surgeon
23. merchant
24. employ
25. effort

Challenge

26. aspire
27. intern
28. enhance
29. structure
30. astute

Write a Personal Essay

What career would you choose if you had to make a choice today? Write a one-paragraph personal essay explaining why this career appeals to you. Try to use five spelling words and at least one appositive. Share your essay with a classmate.

Proofreading Tip

Read your paper from right to left so that you can focus on each word.

Proofreading Marks

¶ Indent
∧ Add
⊙ Add a period
ℐ Delete
≡ Capital letter
/ Small letter
∿ Reverse order

Expanding Vocabulary

Spelling Word Link
journey

expedition
tour
safari
cruise
trek
mission

Thesaurus: Exact Words for *journey* The spelling word *journey* has numerous **synonyms**, words with the same or similar meanings. Look up *journey* in your Thesaurus. Then write each synonym in the picture that suggests its meaning.

2. _____

1. _____

3. _____

journey

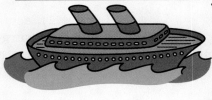

6. _____

4. _____

5. _____

7. _____

8. _____

9. _____

10. _____

11. _____

12. _____

Show You Know! Write a word from the box that best replaces *journey* in each item. Use your Thesaurus.

7. We went on a photographing <u>journey</u> to Africa.
8. The king sent his servant on an important <u>journey</u>.
9. On our <u>journey</u> we saw Italy, France, and Spain.
10. Our desert <u>journey</u> lasted three long months.
11. We loved the <u>journey</u> aboard the large ship.
12. The historian led a(n) <u>journey</u> to study old ruins.

Real-World Connection

Careers: Professions All the words in the box relate to professions. Look up these words in your Spelling Dictionary. Then write the words to complete this schedule.

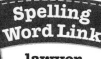

Spelling Word Link

lawyer

programmer
florist
architect
engineer
professor
pharmacist
dietician
broadcaster

Valley Middle School Career Day
Schedule of Events

9:00 A.M.: An __(1)__ will show designs for a new arena, and an __(2)__ will discuss how roads are built safely.

10:00 A.M.: A __(3)__ will talk about college courses, and a __(4)__ will explain how computers can help students with their homework.

1:00 P.M.: Two health professionals will speak. A __(5)__ will talk about nutrition, and a __(6)__ will discuss medicines.

2:00 P.M.: A radio __(7)__ will describe her show, and a __(8)__ will demonstrate how to arrange flowers.

Try This CHALLENGE

Write an Opinion Choose one of the professions in the word box. Write one paragraph about the pros of that profession and one paragraph about the cons. What do you think you would like or dislike about it? Be sure to proofread your paper. You might want to read your opinion aloud to see whether your classmates agree.

★★★ **Fact File**

Architect I. M. Pei is famous for using irregular geometric shapes in his designs for buildings. One example of his architecture is the East Wing of the National Gallery of Art in Washington, D.C.

1. _____
2. _____
3. _____
4. _____
5. _____
6. _____
7. _____
8. _____

12 Review: Units 7–11

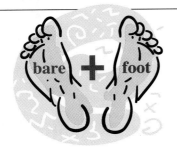

Unit 7   Compound Words   pages 48–53

carefree	sea gull	barefoot	teammate	runner-up
forehead	headache	whereas	grandchildren	nevertheless

Spelling Strategy   A compound word is made up of two or more smaller words. Remember that a compound word may be written as one word, as a hyphenated word, or as separate words.

Write the compound word that completes each sentence.
1. Ellen captured the football and passed it to a _____.
2. The water felt cold as we walked _____ across the creek.
3. The coach took off his cap to mop his perspiring _____.
4. We had worn our warmest clothes, but we were cold _____.
5. Because Lia finished the race second, she was the _____.

Write the compound word that includes each word below.
6. ache   7. sea   8. as   9. grand   10. care

1. _____
2. _____
3. _____
4. _____
5. _____
6. _____
7. _____
8. _____
9. _____
10. _____

Unit 8   Homophones   pages 54–59

principal	vain	scent	died	hangar
principle	vein	sent	dyed	hanger

Spelling Strategy   Homophones are words that sound alike but have different spellings and meanings. When you use a homophone, be sure to spell the word that has the meaning you want.

Write the word that matches each definition.
11. an odor   14. a basic truth
12. stopped living   15. part of the framework of a leaf
13. unsuccessful   16. an aircraft storage building

Write the word that belongs in each group.
17. colored, tinted, _____   19. closet, hook, _____
18. teacher, superintendent, _____   20. shipped, mailed, _____

11. _____
12. _____
13. _____
14. _____
15. _____
16. _____
17. _____
18. _____
19. _____
20. _____

Unit 9   Final |ər| pages 60–65

familiar	superior	messenger	similar	acre
surrender	grammar	calendar	elevator	barrier

Spelling Strategy   When you hear the final |ər| sounds in words of two or more syllables, think of the spelling patterns **er, or,** and **ar.**

Write the word that belongs in each group.

21. well-known, common, _____
22. square foot, square yard, _____
23. spelling, vocabulary, _____
24. better, finer, _____
25. yield, submit, _____
26. resembling, like, _____

Write the word that fits each clue.

27. A tall building needs one.
28. It stops someone or something from going forward.
29. One might bring good news.
30. You can record important dates on this.

21. _____
22. _____
23. _____
24. _____
25. _____
26. _____
27. _____
28. _____
29. _____
30. _____

|ən| **weapon**

Unit 10   Final |ən|, |əl|, and |ər| pages 66–71

struggle	mental	channel	frighten	soldier
kitchen	error	gallon	rural	bundle

Spelling Strategy

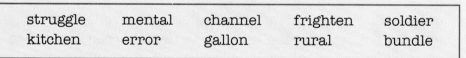

|n| or |ən| → **on, en** |l| or |əl| → **le, el, al** |ər| → **er, or**

Write the word that is a synonym for each word below.

31. mistake   32. battle   33. startle   34. passageway   35. package

Write the word that completes each analogy.

36. *Sleep* is to *bedroom* as *eat* is to _____.
37. *Airplane* is to *paratrooper* as *tank* is to _____.
38. *Butter* is to *pound* as *milk* is to _____.
39. *Body* is to *mind* as *physical* is to _____.
40. *Skyscraper* is to *urban* as *barn* is to _____.

31. _____
32. _____
33. _____
34. _____
35. _____
36. _____
37. _____
38. _____
39. _____
40. _____

ten nis

V C C V

Unit 11   VCCV and VCCCV Patterns   pages 72–77

admit	lawyer	method	supply	whisper
laundry	rescue	instant	tennis	journey

Spelling Strategy   To spell a two-syllable word, divide the word into syllables. Look for spelling patterns you have learned, and spell the word by syllables.

Write the word that fits each definition.

41. a way of doing something   **43.** to save from danger
42. to speak very softly   **44.** to confess as a fact

Write the word formed by adding a syllable to each syllable below. Circle the two words that end with the |ē| sound.

45. laun | _____   **48.** law | _____
46. ten | _____   **49.** in | _____
47. _____ | ply   **50.** _____ | ney

41. _____
42. _____
43. _____
44. _____
45. _____
46. _____
47. _____
48. _____
49. _____
50. _____

Challenge Words   Units 7–11   pages 48–77

ambassador	crestfallen	maneuver	baron	courier
agricultural	water-repellent	structure	barren	enhance

Write the word that matches each definition.

51. a wealthy, powerful businessman
52. resisting moisture
53. unable to bear fruit
54. dejected
55. to increase, as in value or beauty

Write the word that answers each question.

56. Who represents his or her government in another country?
57. Who carries important messages?
58. What is a general term for a building or a bridge?
59. What can a small car do easily?
60. What is a word that refers to growing crops or raising livestock?

51. _____
52. _____
53. _____
54. _____
55. _____
56. _____
57. _____
58. _____
59. _____
60. _____

Spelling-Meaning Strategy

Vowel Changes: Schwa to Short Vowel Sound

It is hard to spell the schwa sound. Thinking of a word related in meaning to the word you want to spell may help you remember the spelling of the schwa sound. Read this paragraph.

> My brother loves the **mental** challenge of brain teasers and secret codes. I find them very frustrating. His **mentality** and mine are very different.

mental
mentality

Think
- How are *mental* and *mentality* related in meaning?
- What vowel sound does the letter *a* spell in each word?

Here are more pairs of related words with the *al* spelling in which *a* spells the schwa sound in one word and the |ă| sound in the other.

| general | personal | individual |
| generality | personality | individuality |

Apply and Extend

Complete these activities on a separate sheet of paper.

1. Look up the words in the word box above in your Spelling Dictionary, and write their meanings. Then write a short paragraph, using one pair of words. Can you show how the meanings of the words are related?

2. With a partner list as many words as you can that are related to *mental*, *general*, *personal*, and *individual*. Then look in the section "Vowel Changes: Schwa to Short Vowel Sound," beginning on page 274 of your Spelling-Meaning Index. Add any other words that you find in these families to your list.

Summing Up

To remember the spelling of an unclear schwa sound in some words, think of the spelling of the short vowel sound in a related word.

Albert Einstein

Comparison and Contrast

based on

How Do They Find It?

by George Sullivan

Tornadoes and hurricanes cause destruction and death nearly every year. How do the winds of a tornado differ from those of a hurricane?

A tornado and a hurricane are similar in some ways. Both are dangerous storms that have strong winds. Both occur more often at certain times of year. Both destroy life and property.

In other ways, however, a tornado and a hurricane are very different. A hurricane, made up of spiraling rain clouds that swirl about a calm center, or eye, may be 500 miles wide. Its strongest winds can blow at about 100 miles an hour. A hurricane can blow for several days, the whole swirling mass moving along at a rate of about 15 to 30 miles an hour until it dies out. In contrast, an average tornado cuts a path a quarter of a mile wide and 16 miles long. Its death-dealing winds have been measured at up to 300 miles an hour. The forward speed of a tornado is about 40 miles an hour, but speeds of up to 70 miles an hour have often been recorded.

Think and Discuss

1. **Contrast** the winds of a tornado with those of a hurricane.

2. What is the **main idea** of each paragraph? Which sentence in each is the **topic sentence**?

3. What other **supporting details** serve to contrast hurricanes and tornadoes?

The Writing Process
Comparison and Contrast

Compare and contrast two similar subjects, such as two climates, sports, animals, or singing groups. Keep the guidelines in mind, and follow the Writing Process.

1 Prewriting
- Work with a partner. Tell your partner how your two subjects are alike. Ask your partner to tell how they are different. List the ideas.

2 Draft
- Write about how your subjects are alike in one paragraph. In another paragraph write about how they are different.

3 Revise
- Be sure that each paragraph has a topic sentence and that all the sentences support the main idea.
- Use your Thesaurus to find exact words.
- Have a writing conference.

4 Proofread
- Did you spell each word correctly?
- Did you write possessive nouns correctly?
- Did you use commas correctly with appositives?

5 Publish
- Add a good title.
- Make a poster, and attach a neat final copy of your paragraphs.

Guidelines for Comparing and Contrasting

✔ Begin each paragraph with a topic sentence that tells the main idea.
✔ Include supporting details that tell how your two subjects are alike and different.

Composition Words

whereas
nevertheless
rural
manner
standard
method
similar
particular

Deserts and Swamps

Deserts and swamps have some things in common. They are both unusual types of land with harsh conditions where humans do not often want to live. Dangerous animals inhabit deserts and swamps.

Deserts and swamps are also very different. Deserts are so dry that little can grow there, but swamps are watery and have lots of vegetation. The sun is hot in deserts because they are big open spaces, but swamps are shady and crowded.

Words with *-ed* or *-ing*

map ^p ed

Final Consonant Doubled

_____

_____

_____

_____

_____

_____

_____

No Change

_____

_____

_____

_____

_____

_____

_____

_____

_____

Read and Say

READ the sentences.

SAY each bold word.

Basic

1. mapped	We **mapped** out several hikes for the summer.
2. piloting	Who will be **piloting** the plane?
3. permitting	Mom is **permitting** me to stay up late tonight.
4. beginning	The **beginning** of this story is very funny!
5. bothered	Flies **bothered** the campers.
6. limited	We have **limited** space in this small classroom.
7. forgetting	I am always **forgetting** your phone number!
8. reasoning	Your **reasoning** helped to solve the problem.
9. preferred	I **preferred** the fish to the chicken.
10. equaled	The two numbers **equaled** thirty.
11. wondering	I was **wondering** whether it would rain.
12. slipped	He **slipped** on the wet floor.
13. listening	Are you **listening** to the radio?
14. fitting	Pajamas are not **fitting** dress for school.
15. pardoned	The prisoner was **pardoned** and released.
16. shoveling	She hates **shoveling** snow.
17. favored	Most people **favored** Ms. Chen for mayor.
18. knitting	I am **knitting** a sweater.
19. answered	He **answered** my question.
20. modeling	Are we **modeling** clay objects in art class?

Think and Write

Each word has *-ed* or *-ing* added to a base word.

map**ped**   fit**ting**   pilot**ing**   begin**ning**

• What happens when *-ing* or *-ed* is added to a one-syllable word ending with one vowel and one consonant? Is *pilot* changed? Is *begin* changed? Which of the two words has a stressed final syllable?

Write each Basic Word under the heading that tells how the word is changed when *-ed* or *-ing* is added.

Review	
21. ordered	23. spotted
22. planned	24. winning
	25. gathering

Challenge	
26. propelling	28. transmitted
27. equipped	29. recurring
	30. profited

Independent Practice

Spelling Strategy Remember that when a one-syllable word ends with one vowel and one consonant, the final consonant is usually doubled before *-ed* or *-ing* is added. When a two-syllable word ends with a stressed syllable, double the final consonant before adding *-ed* or *-ing*.

Word Analysis/Phonics Complete the exercises with Basic Words.

1–3. Write three words by adding a silent consonant to each group of letters below.

   1. lis_ening   **2.** _nitting   **3.** ans_ered

4–5. Write the word that rhymes with *ripped*. Then write another word with the same double consonant.

Vocabulary: Word Clues Write the Basic Word that fits each clue.

  6. synonym for *digging*
  7. opposite of *ending*
  8. posing for a photo
  9. synonym for *annoyed*
 10. forgave
 11. opposite of *forbidding*
 12. flying an airplane
 13. opposite of *remembering*

Challenge Words Write the Challenge Word that is a synonym for each word below. Use your Spelling Dictionary.

 14. supplied   **16.** benefited   **18.** sent
 15. moving   **17.** repeating

Spelling-Meaning Connection

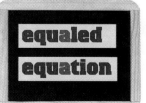

Equaled and *equation* are related in spelling and meaning even though they have different vowel sounds. Both words come from the Latin word *aequus,* meaning "even."

19–20. Write *equation*. Then write the Basic Word that is related in spelling and meaning to *equation*.

Word Analysis
1. _____
2. _____
3. _____
4. _____
5. _____

Vocabulary
6. _____
7. _____
8. _____
9. _____
10. _____
11. _____
12. _____
13. _____

Challenge Words
14. _____
15. _____
16. _____
17. _____
18. _____

Spelling-Meaning
19. _____
20. _____

Base Words

1. _____
2. _____
3. _____
4. _____
5. _____
6. _____
7. _____
8. _____
9. _____

Base Word Match

10. _____
11. _____
12. _____
13. _____
14. _____
15. _____
16. _____
17. _____
18. _____
19. _____
20. _____
21. _____
22. _____
23. _____
24. _____
25. _____

Dictionary

Base Words If a verb changes its spelling when *-ed* or *-ing* is added, the dictionary shows the correct spelling. To find the spellings of these other word forms, look up the base word.

> **pre·fer** |prĭ fûr′| *v.* pre·ferred, pre·fer·ring
>
> **pre·pare** |prĭ pâr′| *v.* pre·pared, pre·par·ing
>
> **re·ply** |rĭ plī′| *v.* re·plied, re·ply·ing

Practice Write the word formed by joining each base word and ending. Use your Spelling Dictionary.

1. rescue + ed
2. admit + ing
3. deny + ed
4. scrub + ed
5. struggle + ing
6. apply + ing
7. equip + ed
8. clarify + ing
9. shove + ing

Review: Spelling Spree

Base Word Match Write a Basic or Review Word that has the same base word as each word below.

10. beginner
11. forgetful
12. remodel
13. preferable
14. permitted
15. reorder
16. unequal
17. wonderment
18. listener
19. disfavor
20. gathered
21. spotless
22. unpardonable
23. knitter
24. shoveled
25. fitful

How Are You Doing?

Write each spelling word in a sentence. Practice any misspelled spelling words with a family member.

Proofreading and Writing

Proofread for Spelling Use proofreading marks to correct nine misspelled Basic or Review Words in this newspaper report.

Example: David Benson would have ~~prefered~~ *preferred* an easy flight.

Weekly Reporter News

Fitting End to Skillful FLIGHT

ORANGE—David Benson is a flier who isn't barthered by major problems. He has been pilotting a small plane for ten years, and he carefully maped yesterday's flight from Bangor, Maine, to Orange. At the beginning, everything went as planed. Then the plane sliped into a fog, and Benson's view was limitted. No one answerd his call for help—the radio was dead. Benson used a compass, resoning, and courage to fly into Orange. His troubled flight became a wining one when he was the one hundredth pilot to land at the new airport!

Proofreading Marks

¶ Indent
∧ Add
⊙ Add a period
˞ Delete
≡ Capital letter
/ Small letter
∿ Reverse order

Write a Description

Write a description of your neighborhood or town as it might look from the air. How do the streets, houses, hills, and other features look? Try to use five spelling words.

Proofreading Tip

Read your work slowly to make sure you have not left out any words.

Expanding Vocabulary

Idioms If someone "lets a secret slip," does it fall on the floor? The expression *to let slip* is an idiom. An **idiom** has a special meaning as a whole that is different from the meanings of its separate words.

Idiom: To let slip

Meaning: To say unintentionally

1. _____
2. _____
3. _____
4. _____
5. _____

Write the letter of the meaning of each idiom. Check your Spelling Dictionary for the main word in each phrase if you need help.

1. It <u>stands to reason</u> that flowers grow with lots of rain.
   a. makes sense   **b.** is amazing   **c.** is not true
2. I love acting so much that sometimes I <u>forget myself</u>.
   a. get lost   **b.** sleep   **c.** lose my fears
3. You studied so hard that it is <u>no wonder</u> you got all *A*'s.
   a. unlikely   **b.** not surprising   **c.** incredible
4. Mom is <u>in favor of</u> my dream of becoming a pilot.
   a. in support of   **b.** upset about   **c.** in charge of
5. Jan will always <u>bend over backward</u> to help a friend.
   a. refuse   **b.** do gymnastics   **c.** do her best

Work Together With a partner write two sentences of your own for each idiom. Use the idiom in the first sentence. Then rewrite the sentence, using words that express the meaning of the idiom. Write on a separate sheet of paper.

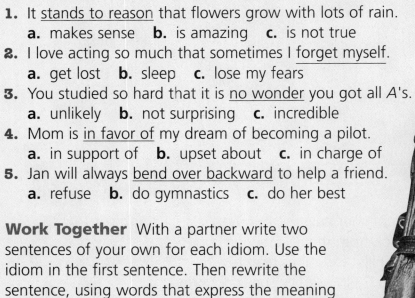

Real-World Connection

Careers: Air Navigation All the words in the box relate to air navigation. Look up these words in your Spelling Dictionary. Then write the words to complete this paragraph from a script for a television documentary on flight.

Spelling Word Link

piloting

navigate
altitude
destination
landmark
longitude
latitude
radar
bearing

SCRIPT

Voice-over: In order to ___(1)___ a flight, a pilot studies charts to determine the exact location of the flight's final ___(2)___. That point is measured in degrees of ___(3)___, or distance north or south of the equator, and ___(4)___, or distance east or west of the meridian at Greenwich, England. The pilot uses instruments to check the direction, or ___(5)___, of a ___(6)___, such as a lighthouse. To avoid flying too low, the pilot monitors the plane's ___(7)___. Finally, the pilot uses ___(8)___ to detect distant objects and to land the plane safely.

1. _____
2. _____
3. _____
4. _____
5. _____
6. _____
7. _____
8. _____

Try This CHALLENGE

Questions and Answers Write a word from the box to answer each question.

9. What is the Statue of Liberty?
10. Where do you arrive at the end of a flight?
11. What is measured in relation to sea level?
12. What measures distance north or south of the equator?

9. _____
10. _____
11. _____
12. _____

Fact File

In 1932 Amelia Earhart became the first woman to fly alone across the Atlantic Ocean. In 1937 Earhart vanished without a trace during an attempted solo flight around the world.

Endings and Suffixes

advanc ~~e~~ **ed**

Final _e_ Dropped

_____

_____

_____

_____

_____

No Spelling Change

_____

_____

_____

_____

_____

_____

_____

_____

_____

_____

Read and Say

READ the sentences.

SAY each bold word.

Basic

1. graceful	A **graceful** dancer never moves clumsily.
2. divided	Have you **divided** the pie into four pieces?
3. advanced	He moved up to the **advanced** tennis class.
4. privately	We planned the surprise party **privately**.
5. replacement	We need a **replacement** for our old oven.
6. excitement	The good news caused much **excitement**.
7. adorable	I love my **adorable** puppy!
8. teasing	Stop **teasing** me about my new haircut!
9. forgiveness	I made a mistake and asked for **forgiveness**.
10. mileage	Our car gets good **mileage** on long trips.
11. barely	With my sore foot, I can **barely** walk.
12. forceful	A **forceful** wind knocked down our big tree.
13. scarcely	Mom can **scarcely** read without her glasses.
14. blaming	I am not **blaming** you for being late.
15. entirely	My bike was **entirely** buried in snow.
16. usable	Is the torn bag still **usable**?
17. sincerely	She was **sincerely** sorry for her error.
18. amusement	The **amusement** park has two new rides.
19. lifeless	The colors in this old rug are **lifeless** and dull.
20. changeable	This red is **changeable** in different lights.

Think and Write

Each word ends with a suffix or an ending. A **suffix** adds meaning.

> divide + ed = divid**ed**   grace + ful = grace**ful**

• What happens to a base word ending with _e_ when the ending or the suffix begins with a vowel? with a consonant? How are the Elephant Words different?

Write each Basic Word under the heading that tells what happens to a base word when a suffix or ending is added.

Review   23. valuable
21. breathless 24. retirement
22. collapsed   25. government

Challenge   28. consecutively
26. coordinated 29. silhouetted
27. disciplined 30. refinement

Independent Practice

Spelling Strategy Remember that if a word ends with *e*, the *e* is usually dropped when a suffix or an ending beginning with a vowel is added. The *e* is usually not dropped when a suffix beginning with a consonant is added.

Word Analysis/Phonics Complete the exercises with Basic Words.

1–2. Write the two words with the |j| sound.

3–5. Write the three words with the |z| sound spelled *s*.

6–7. Write the two words that begin with the word part *re-* or *ex-*.

Vocabulary: Antonyms Write the Basic Word that is an **antonym**, or opposite, of each word.

8. clumsy
9. partly
10. weak
11. united
12. alive
13. dishonestly

Challenge Words Write the Challenge Word that matches each definition below. Use your Spelling Dictionary.

14. successively
15. improvement
16. working together efficiently
17. darkly outlined and filled in with a solid color
18. trained to behave in a controlled manner

Spelling-Meaning Connection

Can you see *adore* in *adorable* and *adoration*? These words are related in spelling and meaning. **Think of this:** I *adore* the *adorable* puppy.

adore
adorable
adoration

19–20. Write *adoration*. Then write the Basic Word that is related in spelling and meaning to *adoration*.

Word Analysis

1. _____
2. _____
3. _____
4. _____
5. _____
6. _____
7. _____

Vocabulary

8. _____
9. _____
10. _____
11. _____
12. _____
13. _____

Challenge Words

14. _____
15. _____
16. _____
17. _____
18. _____

Spelling-Meaning

19. _____
20. _____

Match Game

1. _____
2. _____
3. _____
4. _____
5. _____
6. _____
7. _____
8. _____
9. _____
10. _____
11. _____
12. _____
13. _____
14. _____

Questions

15. _____
16. _____
17. _____
18. _____
19. _____
20. _____
21. _____
22. _____
23. _____
24. _____
25. _____

Review: Spelling Spree

Match Game Write a Basic or Review Word by matching each base word with a suffix or an ending. Underline the words that drop the final e.

| less | ed | ing | ly | able | ment | ful |

1. breath   5. force   9. scarce   13. govern

2. collapse   6. use   10. change   14. value

3. replace   7. bare   11. blame

4. divide   8. life   12. entire

Questions Write a Basic or Review Word to answer each question.

15. What is something that entertains you?
16. What class comes after beginner and intermediate?
17. What is enjoyed by many people who are sixty-five or older?
18. How do you do something in secret?
19. What is the measure of distance traveled by a car?
20. What does a pest or a bully enjoy doing?
21. What can be granted to someone who apologizes?
22. How do you speak when you are truthful?
23. What do you feel before a long-awaited vacation?
24. How does a good dancer look on-stage?
25. What is a cute baby often called?

How Are You Doing?

Write each spelling word as a family member reads it aloud. Did you misspell any words?

Proofreading and Writing

Proofread: Spelling and Capitalization A **proper noun** names a specific person, place, or thing. A **proper adjective** is formed from a proper noun. Capitalize both kinds of words.

PROPER NOUNS: **W**illiam **S**hakespeare **C**anada
PROPER ADJECTIVES: **S**hakespearean **C**anadian

Use proofreading marks to correct four misspelled Basic or Review Words and two words that need capital letters in this ad.

Example: There is ~~barly~~ *barely* time to sign up for tony's class.

Develop valueable skills at the Rainbow school of Dance!

- Learn to be graceful.
- Enjoy the excitment of tap.
- Study european folk dancing.

Classes are devided into beginner, intermediate, and advansed groups.

Call 555-TAPS today!

Write an Ad

Write an ad for an event, a product, or a service. Try to use five spelling words and at least one proper noun or proper adjective.

GUITAR FOR SALE

Proofreading Tip

Be sure that you have capitalized any proper nouns or proper adjectives in your work.

Proofreading Marks

¶ Indent
∧ Add
⊙ Add a period
⌦ Delete
≡ Capital letter
/ Small letter
∽ Reverse order

Expanding Vocabulary

Building Words with Endings and Suffixes You can build new words by adding different suffixes and endings to the same base word. You can also build new words by adding more than one suffix or ending. What spelling change occurs when *-able* is added to *use* and when *-ly* is added to *usable*?

use + **able** = us**able** + **ly** = us**ably**

Fill in the chart below. Build as many words as you can by adding suffixes and endings to *excite* and *grace*. Use your Spelling Dictionary.

-less   -ness   -ful   -ly   -able   -ment   -ing

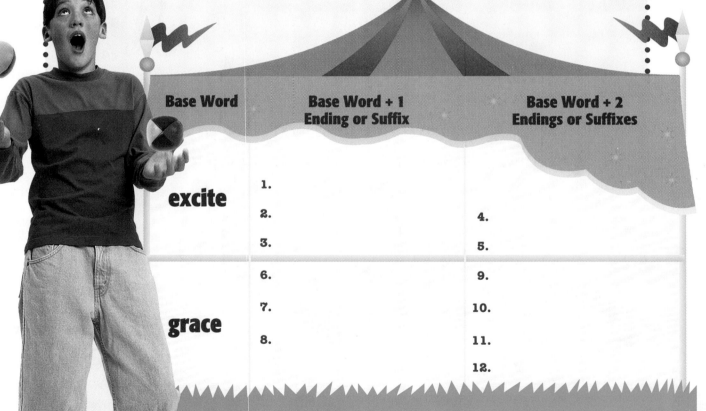

Base Word	Base Word + 1 Ending or Suffix	Base Word + 2 Endings or Suffixes
excite	1.	
	2.	4.
	3.	5.
grace	6.	9.
	7.	10.
	8.	11.
		12.

Show You Know! Write four sentences, using a word that you built from *excite* or *grace* in each. Write on another sheet of paper.

Real-World Connection

Performing Arts: Dance All the words in the box relate to dance. Look up these words in your Spelling Dictionary. Then write the words to complete this review.

Spelling Word Link

graceful

ballet
posture
leotard
jazz
recital
stamina
arch
limber

Marblehead Daily Record

Living Arts

Young Dancers Strut Their Stuff

The all-city dance __(1)__ on Saturday night was a treat for all who attended. One of the best numbers was performed to the swinging rhythms of __(2)__ by a dancer in a stretchy black __(3)__. His movements showed how flexible and __(4)__ he was. A young woman performed a dance from a __(5)__ almost entirely on her toes. How strong the __(6)__ of each foot must be! Other dances were equally good. All of the dancers had prepared well, concentrating on good __(7)__ and building the physical __(8)__ necessary for such a performance. The recital was a tribute to their hard work!

1. _____
2. _____
3. _____
4. _____
5. _____
6. _____
7. _____
8. _____

Try This CHALLENGE

Yes or No? Write *yes* if the underlined word is used correctly. Write *no* if it is not.

9. William's bad <u>posture</u> gives him backaches.
10. The scenery for the dance show was made of <u>limber</u>.
11. Dancers go to <u>recital</u> two or three times a day.
12. Rob has the <u>stamina</u> to run a ten-mile race.

9. _____
10. _____
11. _____
12. _____

Fact File

In the musical comedy *Oklahoma!*, lively dances help tell the story. They were choreographed, or arranged, by Agnes de Mille, whose ballets often were based on American themes.

The Prefix *in-*

immense
incomplete

in-

_____
_____
_____
_____
_____
_____
_____
_____
_____
_____
_____

im-

_____
_____
_____
_____
_____
_____

Read and Say

Basic

READ the sentences. **SAY** each bold word.

1. *impolite* — It is **impolite** to talk with your mouth full.
2. *informal* — I wore jeans to the **informal** party.
3. *include* — The gifts **include** a baseball and glove.
4. *involve* — Will this job **involve** a lot of work?
5. *individual* — Each **individual** here is on the soccer team.
6. *improper* — Talking with your mouth full is **improper**.
7. *inquire* — Did you **inquire** how to get the book?
8. *innocent* — Is he **innocent** of the crime?
9. *immediate* — Give me an **immediate** answer.
10. *immigrant* — Our new student is an **immigrant** from Asia.
11. *immovable* — That stone bench is **immovable**.
12. *indirect* — We are late because we took an **indirect** route.
13. *infection* — An ear **infection** can cause great pain.
14. *indent* — Please **indent** the first line of each paragraph.
15. *import* — We **import** millions of cars from Japan.
16. *incomplete* — Can you finish this **incomplete** story?
17. *instrument* — He plays the trumpet, a brass **instrument**.
18. *inclined* — I am **inclined** to believe you.
19. *immense* — This stone looks **immense** to an ant.
20. *inactive* — The animals are **inactive** in hot weather.

Think and Write

Each word begins with the prefix *in-*. A **prefix** is a word part added to the beginning of a base word or a word root to add meaning. A **word root** is a word part that has meaning but cannot stand alone.

PREFIX + BASE WORD
informal, **im**polite

PREFIX + WORD ROOT
involve, **im**mense

• Before which consonants is the prefix *in-* spelled *im*?

Now write each Basic Word under its spelling of the prefix *in-*.

Review
21. insist
22. impress
23. improve
24. insult
25. increase

Challenge
26. imply
27. infer
28. impartial
29. inflexible
30. inadequate

Independent Practice

Spelling Strategy The prefix *in-* is spelled *im* before a base word or a word root beginning with *m* or *p*. First, find the prefix, the base word or the word root, and any ending. Then spell the word by parts.

Word Analysis/Phonics Complete the exercises with Basic Words.

1. Write the word with the suffix *-able*.

2–7. Write the six words with the |k| sound spelled c.

Vocabulary: Analogies Write the Basic Word that completes each analogy.

8. *Talk* is to *speak* as *ask* is to _____.

9. *Many* is to *one* as *crowd* is to _____.

10. *Little* is to *small* as *huge* is to _____.

11. *True* is to *false* as *guilty* is to _____.

12. *Artist* is to *paintbrush* as *musician* is to _____.

13. *Respectful* is to *courteous* as *rude* is to _____.

Challenge Words Write the Challenge Word that fits each clue. Use your Spelling Dictionary.

14. opposite of *sufficient*

15. suggest without stating

16. opposite of *prejudiced*

17. synonym for *rigid*

18. to conclude from evidence

Spelling-Meaning Connection

How can you tell the difference between *immigrant* and *emigrant*? Think of the prefixes *in-* ("to") and *ex-* ("from") that are added to the base word *migrant*. Don't let the spelling changes fool you.

immigrant

emigrant

19–20. Write *emigrant*. Then write the Basic Word that has a different prefix but the same base word.

Word Analysis

1. _____
2. _____
3. _____
4. _____
5. _____
6. _____
7. _____

Vocabulary

8. _____
9. _____
10. _____
11. _____
12. _____
13. _____

Challenge Words

14. _____
15. _____
16. _____
17. _____
18. _____

Spelling-Meaning

19. _____
20. _____

Stress

1. _____
2. _____
3. _____
4. _____
5. _____
6. _____
7. _____
8. _____
9. _____

Syllable Scramble

10. _____
11. _____
12. _____
13. _____
14. _____
15. _____
16. _____
17. _____
18. _____
19. _____
20. _____
21. _____
22. _____
23. _____
24. _____
25. _____

Dictionary

Stress The syllables in a word are said with different levels of stress. ngest stress is called **primary stress**. A dictionary shows with primary stress in bold print and followed by a heavy accent mark. Syllables said slightly softer, or with **secondary stress**, are followed by a light accent mark.

> **in·di·vid·u·al** |ĭn′ də vĭj′ o͞o əl|

Practice Write the words below in syllables. Circle the syllable with the primary stress. Underline the syllable with the secondary stress. Use your Spelling Dictionary.

1. advertise
2. celebrate
3. criticize
4. cucumber
5. impolite
6. advocate
7. dedicate
8. destination
9. habitat

Review: Spelling Spree

Syllable Scramble Rearrange the syllables in each item to write a Basic or Review Word. There is one extra syllable in each item.

Example: tial par sen im   *impartial*

10. sist ry in
11. tim rect in di
12. clude ing in
13. ble mov ner a im
14. press mal im
15. im u grant mi
16. sult in or
17. ger dent in
18. port tion im
19. er prop im di
20. fec tion par in
21. te clined in
22. ac in ble tive
23. cent ex no in
24. may plete in com
25. mense un im

How Are You Doing?

List the spelling words that are hard for you. Practice them with a family member.

Proofreading and Writing

Proofread for Spelling Use proofreading marks to correct ten misspelled Basic or Review Words on this poster.

Example: Don't be ~~inactiv~~ *inactive* in a group discussion!

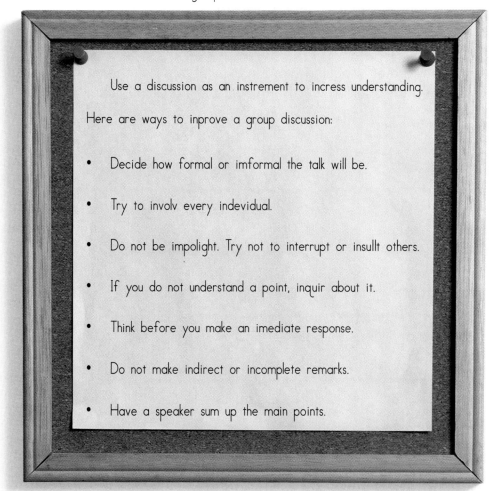

Use a discussion as an instrement to incress understanding.

Here are ways to inprove a group discussion:

- Decide how formal or imformal the talk will be.

- Try to involv every indevidual.

- Do not be impolight. Try not to interrupt or insullt others.

- If you do not understand a point, inquir about it.

- Think before you make an imediate response.

- Do not make indirect or incomplete remarks.

- Have a speaker sum up the main points.

Basic

1. impolite
2. informal
3. include
4. involve
5. individual
6. improper
7. inquire
8. innocent
9. immediate
10. immigrant
11. immovable
12. indirect
13. infection
14. indent
15. import
16. incomplete
17. instrument
18. inclined
19. immense
20. inactive

Review

21. insist
22. impress
23. improve
24. insult
25. increase

Challenge

26. imply
27. infer
28. impartial
29. inflexible
30. inadequate

Write a Discussion

Write an imaginary discussion among several famous people, living or dead. For example, Christopher Columbus could discuss exploration with some astronauts. Try to use five spelling words.

Proofreading Tip   **Check for letters that have been left out of words.**

Proofreading Marks

¶ Indent
∧ Add
⊙ Add a period
⌇ Delete
≡ Capital letter
/ Small letter
∽ Reverse order

Expanding Vocabulary

group
finished
tiny
straightforward
export
native
long-range

Antonyms **Antonyms** are words with opposite meanings. The lawyer tried to prove that the person on trial was **guilty**, but the jury found the defendant **innocent**.

Guilty means "responsible for a crime or wrongdoing." *Innocent* means "not guilty of a specific crime or fault."

Write an antonym for each spelling word in the arrows. Use the words in the box. Look up the spelling words in your Spelling Dictionary if you need help.

immigrant	1.
individual	2.
immediate	3.
import	4.
immense	5.
incomplete	6.
indirect	7.

Work Together Write sentences with a partner, using one pair of antonyms in each sentence. Write on another sheet of paper.

Example: Serving a meal from the left is <u>correct</u>, but taking the plate away from the left is <u>improper</u>.

Real-World Connection

Language Arts: Group Discussions All the words in the box relate to group discussions. Look up these words in your Spelling Dictionary. Then write the words to complete this paragraph from some club minutes, or notes from a meeting.

Spelling Word Link

informal

clarify
viewpoint
participate
contradict
agenda
advocate
differ
proposal

• Activity Club Minutes •

for April 4

Carmen, the club's president, opened the meeting by giving the members a written __(1)__ of things to discuss. One topic was a plan, or __(2)__, to clean the park. Carmen, an __(3)__ of community involvement, thought that the club should clean the park. Opposing members tried to __(4)__ her. Her idea of civic duty seemed to __(5)__ from theirs; they did not share her __(6)__. Once she was able to __(7)__ some vague details, however, they agreed to __(8)__ in the cleanup.

1. _____
2. _____
3. _____
4. _____
5. _____
6. _____
7. _____
8. _____

Try This CHALLENGE

Yes or No? Write *yes* or *no* to answer each question.

9. Does a secretary take agenda during a meeting?
10. Does an advocate support a proposal?
11. Does an inactive club member like to participate?
12. Do people who agree contradict one another?

9. _____
10. _____
11. _____
12. _____

 Fact File

To help people conduct orderly meetings, Henry M. Robert wrote a book called *Robert's Rules of Order*. The book provides a set of rules for discussion, based on the British Parliament's rules.

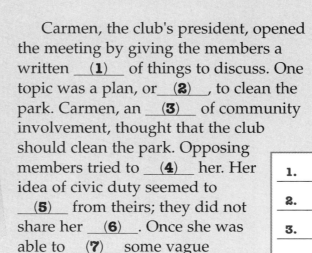

VCV Pattern

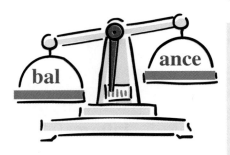

bal ance

Unstressed First Syllable

_____
_____
_____
_____
_____
_____
_____
_____

Unstressed Second Syllable

_____
_____
_____
_____
_____
_____
_____
_____

Read and Say

READ the sentences.
SAY each bold word.

Basic

1. balance   My bank account has a **balance** of two dollars.
2. item   Is this **item** on sale?
3. secure   We watched the fireworks from a **secure** place.
4. require   Plants **require** a lot of attention.
5. minus   Three **minus** two equals one.
6. release   Rangers will **release** the bear in the wilderness.
7. unite   Two countries **unite** to become one larger one.
8. panic   I felt **panic** when I got lost.
9. stupid   I felt **stupid** when I forgot my lunch.
10. vital   Water is **vital** to most living things.
11. recent   The **recent** news made us happy.
12. rebel   Don't **rebel** against our class rules.
13. beware   The sign says to **beware** of the dog.
14. relief   I felt **relief** when you arrived safely.
15. pirate   The **pirate** Captain Kidd robbed ships at sea.
16. deserve   You **deserve** thanks for your hard work.
17. adopt   We will **adopt** your idea for a game.
18. poison   Weed killer is a **poison**.
19. spirit   We sang with great **spirit**.
20. alert   Be **alert** for thin ice as you skate.

Think and Write

Each two-syllable word has the VCV pattern. Divide a VCV word into syllables before or after the consonant.

vc|v   **pan | ic** |păn′ ĭk| v|cv   **se | cure** |sĭ kyŏŏr′|

• Which syllable in each example is unstressed? Why should you pay attention to the unstressed syllables?

Now write each Basic Word under the heading that tells which syllable is unstressed. (List _rebel_ under the first heading.)

Review		Challenge	
23. remind		28. flourish	
21. credit	24. protect	26. delete	29. vigor
22. value	25. report	27. decade	30. crevice

Independent Practice

Spelling Strategy To find the syllables of a VCV word, divide the word before or after the consonant. Note carefully the spelling of the unstressed syllable. Spell the word by syllables.

Word Analysis/Phonics Complete the exercises with Basic Words.

1–2. Write the two words that begin with the |ə| sound.

3–5. Write the three words with the |ē| sound. Underline the letters that spell that sound.

6–7. Write the two words with the |z| sound spelled *s*.

Vocabulary: Antonyms Write the Basic Word that is an antonym for each word.

8. plus	**10.** unsafe	**12.** clever
9. unnecessary	**11.** calm	**13.** obey

Challenge Words Write the Challenge Word that completes each sentence. Use your Spelling Dictionary.

14. I got my own savings account nearly a _____ ago.

15. Mrs. Martin signed her name on the check with a _____.

16. Diane had to _____ an incorrect entry in her bankbook.

17. The energetic workers finished their tasks with _____.

18. The spider disappeared into a _____ in the stone wall.

Spelling-Meaning Connection

Did you know that *unite* and *unity* both come from the Latin word *unis,* meaning "one"? These words are related in spelling and meaning, even though they have different vowel sounds.

19–20. Write *unity*. Then write the Basic Word that is related in spelling and meaning to *unity*.

Word Analysis

1. _____
2. _____
3. _____
4. _____
5. _____
6. _____
7. _____

Vocabulary

8. _____
9. _____
10. _____
11. _____
12. _____
13. _____

Challenge Words

14. _____
15. _____
16. _____
17. _____
18. _____

Spelling-Meaning

19. _____
20. _____

Word Magic

1. _____
2. _____
3. _____
4. _____
5. _____
6. _____
7. _____
8. _____

Word Maze

9. _____
10. _____
11. _____
12. _____
13. _____
14. _____
15. _____
16. _____
17. _____
18. _____
19. _____
20. _____
21. _____
22. _____
23. _____
24. _____
25. _____

Review: Spelling Spree

Word Magic Write a Basic or Review Word to fit each clue.

1. Change the beginning of *preserve* to write a word meaning "to have a right to."
2. Add a consonant to *vial* to write a synonym for *necessary*.
3. Change a vowel in *mines* to write a word for a math sign.
4. Replace two consonants in *assert* with a single consonant to write a word meaning "watchful."
5. Add a vowel to *unit* to write a word meaning "to join."
6. Change a consonant in *revel* to write a synonym for *resist*.
7. Add a vowel to *vale* to write a word meaning "worth."
8. Add a consonant to *irate* to write a word for an outlaw.

Word Maze 9–25. Begin at the arrow and follow the Word Maze to find seventeen Basic or Review Words. Write the words in order.

START

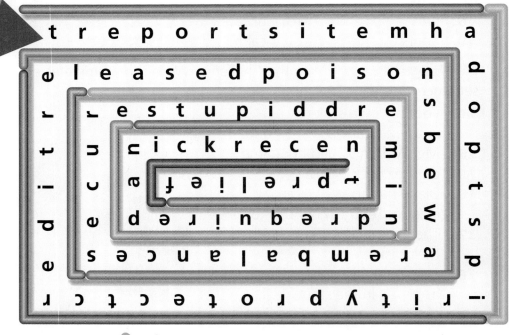

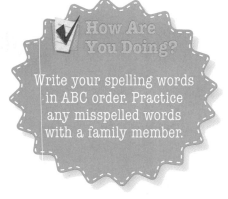

How Are You Doing?

Write your spelling words in ABC order. Practice any misspelled words with a family member.

Proofreading and Writing

Proofread: Spelling and Forms of *good* and *bad* To compare two or more people, places, or things, use the following forms of *good* and *bad*:

	good	**bad**
COMPARING TWO:	better	worse
COMPARING MORE THAN TWO:	best	worst

Use proofreading marks to correct four misspelled Basic or Review Words and two incorrect forms of *good* or *bad* in this magazine article.

Example: The ~~recint~~ *recent* interest rates are ~~good~~ *better* here than at my bank.

Our Readers Ask

Cash or Credit?

In some ways, credet cards are better than money. Many stores do not requier cash when you buy an item if you have a card. Yet cards can be worst than money because a fee is charged if you have an unpaid balence on your bill. Be allert, and pay your bill on time. That is the better policy of all.

KIDBANK
75 9981 3304 7651
/96   08/31/99
TER S. FINLEY
95
KIDCARD

Write a Persuasive Paragraph

Should people keep their money in a bank or not? State your opinion in a paragraph, and support your argument. Try to use five spelling words and at least one comparison using a form of *good* or *bad*.

Proofreading Tip

Be sure that you have used the correct form of *good* or *bad* when you compare two or more things.

Proofreading Marks

¶   Indent
∧   Add
⊙   Add a period
ℒ   Delete
≡   Capital letter
/   Small letter
∿   Reverse order

Expanding Vocabulary

require
lively
control
decline
changeable

Thesaurus: Finding Synonyms What synonym can replace *secure* in this sentence?

Please **secure** the gate when you leave.

acquire

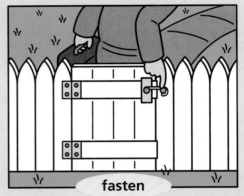

fasten

Your Thesaurus gives two synonyms for *secure*: *acquire* and *fasten*. The definitions and example sentences in the entry show that *fasten* is a good synonym to replace *secure*.

Look up each underlined word in your Thesaurus. Write a synonym that can replace that word in each sentence.

1.
2.
3.
4.
5.
6.
7.
8.
9.
10.

1. The law does <u>require</u> school to be open at least 180 days each year.
2. The fans gave a <u>lively</u> yell when their team won.
3. Traffic lights <u>control</u> the flow of cars and people.
4. Risa will always <u>decline</u> offers to dance in public.
5. It is hard to know how to dress in <u>changeable</u> weather.
6. When we have guests, my parents <u>require</u> that I help.
7. I sometimes feel grumpy, but on most days I wake up feeling <u>lively</u>.
8. You must <u>control</u> your desire to eat sweets before dinner.
9. Did Mom absolutely <u>decline</u> your request for extra money?
10. The volcano is so <u>changeable</u> that it can erupt at any time.

Work Together With a partner write one sentence for each word in the box. Use a synonym that you have not used yet for each word. Use your Thesaurus. Write on a separate sheet of paper.

Vocabulary Enrichment

Real-World Connection

Life Skills: Banking All the words in the box relate to banking. Look up these words in your Spelling Dictionary. Then write the words to complete the first paragraph shown below.

Spelling Word Link

balance

checkbook
interest
investment
dividend
mortgage
endorse
teller
transfer

Section 3 Banks and Banking

Banking at a branch office can be very convenient. There you can deposit your paycheck. Just __(1)__ it on the back and hand it to a __(2)__. Then record the transaction in your __(3)__. You can also __(4)__ money from your checking account to your savings account, where your dollars will earn greater __(5)__. If you want to buy a house, you can apply for a home __(6)__. Finally, you can learn the __(7)__, or share of profit, being earned on the bank's __(8)__ in various stocks.

Banking by computer is also convenient. It is discussed in the next section.

1. _____
2. _____
3. _____
4. _____
5. _____
6. _____
7. _____
8. _____

Try This CHALLENGE

Write an Ad Create a poster that will attract customers to a new bank. What services does the bank offer? Try to use some words from the box. Decorate and hang your poster if you like.

★★★ Fact File

The United States Department of the Treasury is in charge of making money. It runs the Bureau of the Mint, which makes coins, and the Bureau of Engraving and Printing, which makes paper money.

Unstressed Syllables

success

Two Syllables

_____
_____
_____
_____
_____
_____
_____
_____

Three Syllables

_____
_____
_____
_____
_____
_____
_____
_____
_____

Read and Say

Basic

READ the sentences. **SAY** each bold word.

1. company	That **company** makes computer games.
2. success	The **success** of our play thrilled us.
3. position	Please move the chair to a different **position**.
4. problem	Can you solve the math **problem**?
5. policy	My mother has a strict bedtime **policy**.
6. difficult	She played a **difficult** song easily.
7. document	That **document** is ten pages long.
8. quality	That dress cloth is of fine **quality**.
9. surprise	Was the party a **surprise** for the teacher?
10. physical	I am in good **physical** shape from exercising.
11. crisis	The house fire caused a financial **crisis**.
12. awake	The baby is sleeping but will **awake** soon.
13. example	This vase is an **example** of her work.
14. ignore	Try to **ignore** his teasing.
15. accept	Please **accept** this gift.
16. parallel	She drew **parallel** lines across the chart.
17. admiral	The **admiral** led the fleet into the harbor.
18. desire	I **desire** always to be your friend.
19. garage	Is the car in the **garage**?
20. ambulance	The **ambulance** had a loud siren.

Think and Write

Each word has two or three syllables. Look for familiar patterns in each syllable. Note how to spell all unstressed syllables. Spell the words by syllables.

prob | lem |prŏb′ ləm| **po | si | tion** |pə zĭsh′ ən|

• Is the |ə| sound usually in a stressed or an unstressed syllable? Why should you remember how to spell any unstressed syllables?

Now write each Basic Word under the number of its syllables.

Review	23. president	**Challenge**	28. morale
21. industry	24. absent	26. efficient	29. ethical
22. partner	25. attention	27. punctual	30. potential

Independent Practice

Spelling Strategy   To spell a two-syllable or three-syllable word, divide the word into syllables. Look for familiar spelling patterns. Note the spelling of any unstressed syllables, and spell the word by syllables.

Word Analysis/Phonics   Complete the exercises with Basic Words.

1–4.   Write the four words with double consonants.

5–7.   Write the three words with these sounds.

   5.   the |kw| sounds   **6.**   the |sh| sound   **7.**   the |ôr| sounds

Vocabulary: Making Inferences
Write the word that fits each clue.

   8.   an unexpected gift
   9.   a passport, for example
   10.   where someone might store a lawn mower
   11.   a sample answer
   12.   a sailor's boss
   13.   what you do when the alarm clock rings

Challenge Words   Write the Challenge Word that matches each definition. Use your Spelling Dictionary.

   14.   capacity for further growth or progress
   15.   acting effectively, with little waste or effort
   16.   conforming to accepted standards of right behavior
   17.   acting or arriving on time
   18.   the state of a person's or a group's spirits

Spelling-Meaning Connection

Did you know that *physical* is related to *physician*? Both words contain the Greek word part *phys*, meaning "nature." Words that contain the same word part are related in spelling and meaning.

19–20.   Write *physician*. Then write the Basic Word that has the same Greek word part as *physician*.

physical
physician
Rx

Word Analysis

1. _____
2. _____
3. _____
4. _____
5. _____
6. _____
7. _____

Vocabulary

8. _____
9. _____
10. _____
11. _____
12. _____
13. _____

Challenge Words

14. _____
15. _____
16. _____
17. _____
18. _____

Spelling-Meaning

19. _____
20. _____

Base Words

1. _____
2. _____
3. _____
4. _____
5. _____
6. _____
7. _____
8. _____
9. _____

Syllable Spot

10. _____
11. _____
12. _____
13. _____
14. _____
15. _____
16. _____
17. _____
18. _____
19. _____
20. _____
21. _____
22. _____
23. _____
24. _____
25. _____

Dictionary

Base Words If you look up the past tense of an irregular verb, the dictionary will direct you to its base word.

a•woke |ə wōk′| *v.* Past tense of **awake**.

To find the definition of *awoke*, you must look up its base word, *awake*.

Practice Write the base word of each irregular past tense verb below. Use your Spelling Dictionary.

1. sought	**4.** strove	**7.** bore
2. stung	**5.** sunk	**8.** forgot
3. sent	**6.** caught	**9.** sprang

Review: Spelling Spree

Syllable Spot Write the Basic or Review Word that has one of the syllables in each word below.

Example: fancy *policy*

10. attitude	**14.** doctor	**18.** ignite	**22.** succotash
11. delight	**15.** surgeon	**19.** impart	**23.** parasol
12. concept	**16.** physician	**20.** abound	**24.** difference
13. admit	**17.** probable	**21.** compete	**25.** crier

How Are You Doing?

Write each spelling word in a sentence. Practice any misspelled spelling words with a partner.

Proofreading and Writing

Proofread for Spelling Use proofreading marks to correct nine misspelled Basic or Review Words in this memo.

Example: Did Kiwi find liver ~~dificult~~ *difficult* to swallow?

From: Vice President
Subject: Product Quality

MEMO: TO ALL EMPLOYEES

Our presedent, Ray Carson, was rushed by ambulence to Oak Hospital yesterday after eating some of Bow-Wow's new freeze-dried liver. He was stricken near his garge. Kiwi, his pet Pomeranian, was nearby.

"I was showing Kiwi how good our liver is," Mr. Carson reported, "but he wouldn't touch it. Our polisy has been to use Kiwi as an exsample of our customers. I guess we will have to re-evaluate the qualty of this product if we want to keep our top postion in the industrie."

Mr. Carson is recovering well, but he will be apsent from work for several days.

Write a Consumer Letter

Write a brief letter to the manager of a business, such as a restaurant or a clothing store. What do you like about his or her services or products? Try to use five spelling words.

Mary Green
302 Morning Lane
My Town, State 90008

Manager
Buffy's Bags & Togs
22 Busy Blvd.
My Town, State 90009

Proofreading Tip

Check that your *a*'s are written clearly so that they do not look like *o*'s or *u*'s.

Basic

1. company
2. success
3. position
4. problem
5. policy
6. difficult
7. document
8. quality
9. surprise
10. physical
11. crisis
12. awake
13. example
14. ignore
15. accept
16. parallel
17. admiral
18. desire
19. garage
20. ambulance

Review

21. industry
22. partner
23. president
24. absent
25. attention

Challenge

26. efficient
27. punctual
28. morale
29. ethical
30. potential

Proofreading Marks

¶ Indent
∧ Add
⊙ Add a period
ℐ Delete
≡ Capital letter
/ Small letter
∿ Reverse order

Vocabulary Enrichment

Expanding Vocabulary

inconvenient
complicated
puzzling
stubborn
strenuous

Thesaurus: Exact Words for *difficult* Why is *inconvenient* a better word to use than *difficult* in this example?

    It was **difficult** for Ed to call Mary.

    It was **inconvenient** for Ed to call Mary.

Inconvenient is better because it is more exact; it gives a reason for Ed's difficulty in calling Mary.

Find the entry for *difficult* in your Thesaurus. Then write the best synonym to replace *difficult* in each sentence.

1.
2.
3.
4.
5.

1. The high school textbook is too <u>difficult</u> for a sixth grader to understand.
2. Sue had plans for Friday night, so it was <u>difficult</u> for her to meet her aunt at the airport.
3. The <u>difficult</u> cat refused to eat its food.
4. Carrying the piano up four flights of stairs was <u>difficult</u>.
5. Figuring out the ending to a mystery can be <u>difficult</u>.

Show You Know! Write captions for these pictures. Use a different synonym for *difficult* in each one. Write on a separate sheet of paper.

Vocabulary Enrichment

Real-World Connection

Business: Business Management All the words in the box relate to business management. Look up each word in your Spelling Dictionary. Then write the words to complete this announcement.

Spelling Word Link

company

management
executive
personnel
corporation
supervise
memo
salary
motivate

Sweet Talk
FROM THE PRESIDENT

Pat Sweet, president and chief __(1)__ of the Cornish Company, called a meeting of all supervisors, or __(2)__, to discuss the company's future. Cornish, once a small company, has grown into a large __(3)__ where managers have to __(4)__ the work of many employees. At the meeting Sweet announced that all employees will receive an increase in __(5)__ as a reward for their good work. She hopes the raise will __(6)__ them to excel further. Sweet has written a __(7)__ to all company __(8)__ about the raise.

1. _____
2. _____
3. _____
4. _____
5. _____
6. _____
7. _____
8. _____

Try This
CHALLENGE

Yes or No? Write *yes* if the underlined word is used correctly. Write *no* if it is not.

9. The workers <u>supervise</u> their boss.
10. The workers learn how to <u>motivate</u> the computers.
11. The <u>salary</u> for this job is two hundred dollars a week.
12. The <u>memo</u> described the company's plan to relocate.

9. _____
10. _____
11. _____
12. _____

★ Fact File

In some countries the government decides what people produce and sell. The United States, however, has a free enterprise system, which means that people can start a business of their choice.

18 Review: Units 13–17

map ^ped

Unit 13   Words with *-ed* or *-ing*   pages 84–89

bothered	permitting	preferred	reasoning	mapped
modeling	pardoned	listening	slipped	fitting

Spelling Strategy

slip + ed = slip**ped**   model + ing = model**ing**

permit + ing = permit**ting**

Write the word formed by joining each base word and ending.

1. permit + ing   **4.** pardon + ed
2. reason + ing   **5.** map + ed
3. prefer + ed   **6.** slip + ed

Write the word that completes each sentence.

7. A potter was _____ the clay into a lovely vase.
8. Paul did not hear the answer because he was not _____.
9. Although we were _____ by insects, the picnic was fun.
10. Dad had some difficulty _____ our luggage into the car.

Unit 14   Endings and Suffixes   pages 90–95

graceful	teasing	excitement	divided	mileage
entirely	lifeless	amusement	usable	changeable

Spelling Strategy   Remember that if a word ends with **e**, the **e** is usually dropped when a suffix or an ending beginning with a vowel is added. The **e** is usually not dropped when a suffix beginning with a consonant is added.

Combine each word with the ending or suffix. Write the new word correctly.

11. tease + ing   **13.** excite + ment   **15.** use + able
12. mile + age   **14.** grace + ful

Write the word that is a synonym for each word below.

16. separated   **18.** entertainment   **20.** completely
17. dull   **19.** variable

advanc _e ed

1. _____
2. _____
3. _____
4. _____
5. _____
6. _____
7. _____
8. _____
9. _____
10. _____

11. _____
12. _____
13. _____
14. _____
15. _____
16. _____
17. _____
18. _____
19. _____
20. _____

**immense
incomplete**

Unit 15   The Prefix *in-*   pages 96–101

| immediate | impolite | individual | inquire | innocent |
| inclined | immense | immovable | import | instrument |

Spelling Strategy   The prefix **in-** is spelled **im** before a base word or a word root beginning with **m** or **p**. First, find the prefix, the base word or the word root, and any ending. Then spell the word by parts.

Write a word by adding the prefix *in-* to each base word or word root below. Be sure to spell the prefix correctly.

21. _____ | mediate
22. _____ | clined
23. _____ | strument
24. _____ | port
25. _____ | dividual

Write the word that is an antonym for each word below.

26. courteous
27. tiny
28. reply
29. guilty
30. portable

21. _____
22. _____
23. _____
24. _____
25. _____
26. _____
27. _____
28. _____
29. _____
30. _____

Unit 16   VCV Pattern   pages 102–107

| release | require | panic | balance | unite |
| spirit | recent | rebel | relief | pirate |

Spelling Strategy   To find the syllables of a VCV word, divide the word before or after the consonant. Note carefully the spelling of the unstressed syllable. Spell the word by syllables.

Write the word that completes each analogy.

31. *Want* is to *desire* as *need* is to _____.
32. *Separate* is to *combine* as *divide* is to _____.
33. *Bank* is to *robber* as *ship* is to _____.
34. *Agree* is to *differ* as *obey* is to _____.

Write the word that matches each definition.

35. to set free
36. to keep equal
37. sudden terror
38. a lively mood
39. just before now
40. ease from pain

31. _____
32. _____
33. _____
34. _____
35. _____
36. _____
37. _____
38. _____
39. _____
40. _____

Unit 17   Unstressed Syllables   pages 108–113

success	problem	company	difficult	policy
awake	accept	crisis	ambulance	example

41. _____

42. _____

43. _____

44. _____

45. _____

46. _____

47. _____

48. _____

49. _____

50. _____

Spelling Strategy   To spell a two-syllable or three-syllable word, divide the word into syllables. Look for familiar spelling patterns. Note the spelling of any unstressed syllables, and spell the word by syllables.

Write each word by adding an unstressed syllable.
41. dif | _____ | cult   43. _____ | cept   45. _____ | cess
42. cri | _____   44. exam | _____   46. pol | _____ | cy

Write the word that completes each sentence.
47. My parents invite _____ to dinner every Sunday.
48. I speak loudly to my uncle because of his hearing _____.
49. The neighbors' loud music kept Mica _____ all night.
50. The injured man was taken to the hospital in an _____.

Challenge Words   Units 13–17   pages 84–113

propelling	flourish	crevice	consecutively	potential
inflexible	profited	efficient	silhouetted	impartial

51. _____

52. _____

53. _____

54. _____

55. _____

56. _____

57. _____

58. _____

59. _____

60. _____

Write the word that answers each question.
51. Which word is an antonym for *changeable*?
52. Which word is a synonym for *fair*?
53. Which word is an antonym for *wither*?
54. Which word is a synonym for *possible*?
55. Which word is an antonym for *randomly*?

Write the word that belongs with each group of words below.
56. pushing, throwing, _____
57. crack, opening, _____
58. capable, productive, _____
59. outlined, profiled, _____
60. gained, benefited, _____

Spelling-Meaning Strategy

The Greek Word Part *poli*

police
policy

Did you know that *metropolitan* and *policy* are related in meaning? Each word has the Greek word part *poli*, meaning "city" or "government." A Greek word part affects the meaning of each word that contains it. *Policy* used to mean "the practice of government." Now it means "a way of management." *Metropolitan* refers to things in and around a major city. Knowing the meaning of *poli* can help you spell and understand other words with the same word part.

Here are more words that have the word part *poli*.

police	**poli**tician	cosmo**poli**tan
metro**poli**s	**poli**tics	megalo**poli**s

Think

• Look up each word in the word box above in your Spelling Dictionary. How does the word part *poli* affect the meaning of each word?

Apply and Extend

Complete these activities on a separate sheet of paper.

1. Write six sentences. Use one word from the word box above in each sentence. Can you make the words' meanings clear?

2. With a partner list as many other words as you can that include the word part *poli*. Then look in the section "Word Parts," beginning on page 276 of your Spelling-Meaning Index. Add any other words that you find with this word part to your list.

Summing Up

The Greek word part *poli* means "government" or "city." Words with the same Greek word part are often related in spelling and meaning. Knowing the meaning of *poli* can help you understand and spell the words in that family.

from The Mural

by Emilia Durán

Why is Mercedes unhappy about the results of the contest?

The class party was almost over when Mercedes saw Mr. Alva standing in the door. He was holding a large portfolio. Here it was, the moment she had been waiting for all those weeks, ever since she had entered the art contest. The winner would paint a mural on the side of Mr. Alva's store, overlooking the little park. The mural would symbolize the neighborhood's Chicano heritage, and all the students in the school had been invited to submit ideas for its design. Mr. Alva had brought the winning picture to show the class.

Mercedes held her breath. "Please," she thought, "please let it be mine—I've never wanted anything so much!" She could hardly sit quietly through Mr. Alva's long introduction, but finally she heard him say, ". . . in fact, it was impossible for us to choose between two such excellent entries. The contest is a tie between two members of this class—Mercedes and Inez Gálvez. We want them to paint the mural together."

"Oh, no," Mercedes thought. "Not a tie. That's almost worse than not winning at all!" She looked at Inez's picture and wondered, "What did they see in that?"

Think and Discuss

1 Why is Mercedes unhappy about Mr. Alva's decision? What **problem** is created?

2 How might the story **plot** solve this problem?

3 What is the **setting** for this part of the story?

4 What do you learn about the main **character**, Mercedes?

The Writing Process
Story

What might happen to interesting characters in different settings? Write a story about one idea. Keep the guidelines in mind. Follow the Writing Process.

1 Prewriting
- Ask *What if . . . ?* to help you think of plot ideas.
- Make a story map.

2 Draft
- Use dialogue that fits each character's personality.

3 Revise
- Add details to describe the characters, settings, and actions.
- Use your Thesaurus to find exact words.
- Have a writing conference.

4 Proofread
- Did you spell each word correctly?
- Did you capitalize proper nouns and proper adjectives?
- Did you use the correct forms of *good* and *bad*?

5 Publish
- Make a neat final copy, and add a good title.
- Make a book jacket. Share your story.

Guidelines for Writing a Story

✓ The plot focuses on a problem, builds to a turning point, and concludes with a fitting resolution.
✓ Choose characters and settings that fit the story.
✓ Use details and dialogue to bring the story to life.

Composition Words

problem
surprise
teasing
excitement
listening
wondering
immense
relief

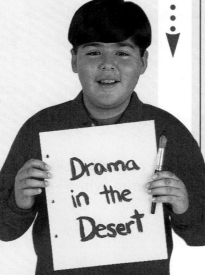

Drama in the Desert

Adding *-ion* or *-ation*

No Spelling Change

_____

_____

_____

_____

_____

Final *e* Dropped

_____

_____

_____

_____

_____

_____

_____

_____

_____

_____

_____

Read and Say

Basic

READ the sentences.
SAY each bold word.

1. construct	They will **construct** a new house.
2. construction	The school is under **construction**.
3. connect	You can **connect** those two puzzle pieces.
4. connection	There is a **connection** between old friends.
5. combine	I will **combine** the milk and the flour.
6. combination	This paste is a **combination** of flour and water.
7. cooperate	Let's **cooperate** on this project.
8. cooperation	Your **cooperation** helped the team win.
9. attract	That sign will **attract** his attention.
10. attraction	The next **attraction** at the theater is a play.
11. admire	I **admire** your handwriting.
12. admiration	Actors love the **admiration** of the crowd.
13. situate	Try to **situate** yourself at the front of the room.
14. situation	When our ship sank, the **situation** was grave.
15. examine	Please **examine** my work for mistakes.
16. examination	His doctor gave him an **examination**.
17. contribute	I will **contribute** money to the fund.
18. contribution	Your food **contribution** was helpful.
19. explore	We want to **explore** the cave.
20. exploration	In our cave **exploration,** we found a gem.

Think and Write

Each pair of words includes a verb and a noun. The noun is formed by adding the suffix *-ion* or *-ation* to the end of the verb.

connect, connect**ion**   situate, situat**ion**   admire, admir**ation**

• What spelling changes take place when *-ion* or *-ation* is added to a verb that ends with *e*?

Now write each Basic Word under the heading that shows the spelling change when *-ion* or *-ation* is added.

Review
21. inspect   23. locate
22. inspection 24. location

Challenge
25. excavate   27. insulate
26. excavation 28. insulation

Independent Practice

Spelling Strategy

The suffix *-ion* or *-ation* can change verbs into nouns. If the verb ends with *e*, drop the *e* before adding *-ion* or *-ation*.

Word Analysis/Phonics Complete the exercises with Basic Words.

1–2. Write the pair of words that includes the base word *operate*.
3–6. Write the two pairs of words that begin with the prefix *ex-*.
7–8. Write one pair of words with a double consonant.

Vocabulary: Synonyms Write the Basic Word that is a synonym for each word.

9. give
10. build
11. locate
12. mixture
13. donation
14. approval

Challenge Words Write the Challenge Word that completes each sentence. Use your Spelling Dictionary.

15. The cabin will be warmer this winter if we _____ it.
16. The buried objects were revealed after the _____.
17. Archaeologists will try to _____ the ruins of the lost city.
18. Most homes built today have over six inches of _____ in their walls.

Spelling-Meaning Connection

Attract contains the word root *tract,* meaning "pull." Knowing the root *tract* can also help you spell and understand the related words *attraction* and *tractor*.

19–20. Write *attraction* and *tractor*. Underline the word root in each word.

attraction

attract

tractor

Word Analysis
1. _____
2. _____
3. _____
4. _____
5. _____
6. _____
7. _____

8. _____

Vocabulary
9. _____
10. _____
11. _____
12. _____
13. _____
14. _____

Challenge Words
15. _____
16. _____
17. _____
18. _____

Spelling-Meaning
19. _____
20. _____

Parts of Speech

1. _____
2. _____
3. _____
4. _____
5. _____
6. _____

Alphabet Puzzler

7. _____
8. _____
9. _____
10. _____
11. _____
12. _____
13. _____
14. _____
15. _____
16. _____
17. _____
18. _____
19. _____
20. _____
21. _____
22. _____

Dictionary

Parts of Speech Many words can be used as more than one part of speech. The abbreviations for the parts of speech are given before the definitions to which they apply.

n. = noun   *v.* = verb   *adj.* = adjective

Practice Write *noun*, *verb*, or *adjective* to tell how each underlined word is used. Use your Spelling Dictionary.

1. The politician gave a <u>prompt</u> reply to the question.
2. This reminder will <u>prompt</u> people to vote.
3. Furniture <u>polish</u> will hide these scratches.
4. Please <u>polish</u> the silverware.
5. After three days of <u>foul</u> weather, the sunshine returned.
6. In basketball, running with the ball is a <u>foul</u>.

Review: Spelling Spree

Alphabet Puzzler Write these Basic and Review Words in alphabetical order. Circle the letters that are underlined.

7. cooperation
8. admire
9. examine
10. cooperate
11. combine
12. attraction
13. connect
14. locate
15. explore
16. construction
17. situation
18. inspection
19. situate
20. combination
21. contribute
22. inspect

When the words are in alphabetical order, the circled letters will name three things used in construction. Write the words.

Mystery Words: __ __ __ __ __   __ __ __ __ __ __ __   __ __ __ __ __ __

How Are You Doing?

Write each spelling word as a family member reads it aloud. Did you misspell any words?

Proofreading and Writing

Proofread for Spelling Use proofreading marks to correct eight misspelled Basic or Review Words in this paragraph from a biographical dictionary.

Example: Many people ~~admir~~ *admire* the work of Frank Lloyd Wright.

Wright, Frank Lloyd

Many people admire Frank Lloyd Wright, an architect who made a significant contribusion to modern design. Wright saw a close conection between a building and its loction. His explortion of this idea led him to construckt one of his houses over a waterfall. Wright also had an addmiration for ancient structures. An examanation of his buildings shows a combination of Mayan, Incan, and Japanese influences. His ideas still atract and inspire architects today.

Basic
1. construct
2. construction
3. connect
4. connection
5. combine
6. combination
7. cooperate
8. cooperation
9. attract
10. attraction
11. admire
12. admiration
13. situate
14. situation
15. examine
16. examination
17. contribute
18. contribution
19. explore
20. exploration

Review
21. inspect
22. inspection
23. locate
24. location

Challenge
25. excavate
26. excavation
27. insulate
28. insulation

Write Instructions

Write a paragraph that explains how to construct something, such as a game board, a diorama, or another object. Give detailed steps. Try to use five spelling words.

Proofreading Tip

Read your paper aloud to a classmate. Sometimes you notice mistakes more easily when you hear them.

Proofreading Marks

¶ Indent
∧ Add
⊙ Add a period
⌇ Delete
≡ Capital letter
/ Small letter
∿ Reverse order

Expanding Vocabulary

Meanings for *examination* The word *examination* has several meanings. Look at this dictionary entry.

> **ex·am·i·na·tion** |ĭg zăm′ ə nā′ shən| *n.*
> **1.** Investigation; analysis. **2.** A set of written or oral questions or exercises designed to test knowledge or skills. **3.** An inspection of part or all of the body, as by a physician. **4.** A formal questioning.

Using the entry above, write *1, 2, 3,* or *4* to show which meaning of *examination* is used in each sentence.

1. The lawyer began her <u>examination</u> of the witness.
2. The dental <u>examination</u> showed that Amy had no tooth decay.
3. Close <u>examination</u> revealed that the pearls were fake.
4. Rob received a high grade on the history <u>examination</u>.
5. Do you have an eye <u>examination</u> every year?
6. Bring a tap-water sample to the lab for <u>examination</u>.

1. _____
2. _____
3. _____
4. _____
5. _____
6. _____

Work Together Look up the word *air* in your Spelling Dictionary. On your own and on a separate sheet of paper, write four sentences about the picture, using a different meaning for *air* in each. Then trade papers with a partner, and write which meaning of *air* is used in each of your partner's sentences.

7–10.

Real-World Connection

Industrial Arts: Construction All the words in the box relate to construction. Look up these words in your Spelling Dictionary. Then write the words to complete this summary of a television documentary.

Spelling Word Link

construction

carpentry
foundation
beam
concrete
plumbing
bulldozer
interior
exterior

Documentary: The House That Jack Is Building

Week 1: Workers use a __(1)__ to dig a hole in the ground. Then they pour __(2)__, a mixture of sand, pebbles, and cement, into the hole to make a __(3)__ that will support the building.

Week 2: Viewers see the __(4)__ involved in putting up the wooden frame. A long wooden __(5)__ is put in place to support the ceiling.

Week 3: When the __(6)__, or outside, is complete, workers put up walls and lay floors.

Week 4: Workers install wires for electricity and pipes for __(7)__ and then finish the inside, or __(8)__.

1. _____
2. _____
3. _____
4. _____
5. _____
6. _____
7. _____
8. _____

Try This CHALLENGE

Yes or No? Write *yes* or *no* to answer each question.

9. Is the kitchen in the interior of a house?
10. Are the pipes under the sink part of the plumbing?
11. Does a foundation go on top of a building?
12. Does carpentry involve fixing the plumbing?

9. _____
10. _____
11. _____
12. _____

Fact File

The pyramids of Egypt were built more than four thousand years ago without the use of modern tools. The Egyptians hauled two-ton limestone blocks up huge ramps to build these royal tombs.

More Words with *-ion*

graduate
graduation

Read and Say

Basic

1.	instruct	She will **instruct** us in math.
2.	instruction	Have you had any music **instruction**?
3.	graduate	Our class will **graduate** soon.
4.	graduation	My brother's **graduation** is today.
5.	confuse	This problem may **confuse** you.
6.	confusion	Your answer clears up my **confusion**.
7.	conclude	How does the movie **conclude**?
8.	conclusion	The **conclusion** of the story surprised me.
9.	oppose	They **oppose** our views.
10.	opposition	The two teams are in **opposition**.
11.	explode	I heard the firecracker **explode**.
12.	explosion	The **explosion** shook the ground.
13.	affect	Does the cold **affect** you?
14.	affection	I have a lot of **affection** for my cat.
15.	suggest	What do you **suggest** we do?
16.	suggestion	My **suggestion** is that we hike.
17.	discuss	They like to **discuss** books.
18.	discussion	Who will lead the **discussion**?
19.	except	Mom may **except** me from doing chores today.
20.	exception	This is an **exception** to the rule.

No Spelling Change

_____

_____

_____

_____

_____

_____

_____

_____

Final *e* Dropped

_____

_____

_____

_____

Other Spelling Change

_____

_____

_____

_____

_____

Think and Write

Each pair of words is made up of a verb and a noun. The noun is formed by adding the suffix *-ion* to the end of the verb.

VERBS:	instruct	confus**e**	oppos**e**	conclud**e**
NOUNS:	instruct**ion**	confus**ion**	oppos**ition**	conclus**ion**

• How do the spellings of the verbs change when *-ion* is added?

Write each pair of Basic Words under the heading that tells how the spelling is changed when *-ion* is added to the verb.

Review
21. correct   23. express
22. correction 24. expression

Challenge
25. substitute 27. exclude
26. substitution 28. exclusion

Independent Practice

Spelling Strategy The suffix *-ion* can change verbs to nouns. The suffix *-ion* is added to many words without a spelling change. In some words the final *e* is dropped or another spelling change occurs when *-ion* is added. Remember the spellings of these words.

Word Analysis/Phonics Complete the exercises with Basic Words.

1–2. Write the word pair with the |ō| sound in both words.

3–4. Write the word pair in which the |ō| sound in the verb changes to the |ə| sound in the noun.

5–6. Write the word pair with the |j| sound spelled *d*.

Vocabulary: Definitions Write the Basic Word that matches each verb definition. Then write the noun form of the verb.

7–8. to influence

9–10. to mistake for something else

11–12. to speak together about

13–14. to bring or come to an end

Challenge Words Write the Challenge Word that fits each definition. Use your Spelling Dictionary.

15. to replace

16. to leave out

17. the act of leaving out

18. the act of replacing

Spelling-Meaning Connection

How can you remember that the |sh| sound in *instruction, graduation, suggestion, affection,* and *exception* is spelled with a *t*? Think of the *t* at the end of the related words *instruct, graduate, suggest, affect,* and *except*.

19–20. Write *instruct* and *instruction*. Underline the letter in *instruct* that helps you spell the |sh| sound in *instruction*.

Word Analysis

1. _____
2. _____
3. _____
4. _____
5. _____
6. _____

Vocabulary

7. _____
8. _____
9. _____
10. _____
11. _____
12. _____
13. _____
14. _____

Challenge Words

15. _____
16. _____
17. _____
18. _____

Spelling-Meaning

19. _____
20. _____

Using Clues

1. _____
2. _____
3. _____
4. _____
5. _____
6. _____
7. _____
8. _____
9. _____
10. _____
11. _____
12. _____

Questions

13. _____
14. _____
15. _____
16. _____
17. _____
18. _____
19. _____
20. _____
21. _____
22. _____
23. _____
24. _____

Review: Spelling Spree

Using Clues Write a Basic or Review Word that fits each clue.

Example: This *ion* is a test.   *examination*

1. This *ion* teaches.
2. This *ion* blows up.
3. This *ion* is a talk.
4. This *ion* is the end.
5. This *ion* is mixed up.
6. This *ion* does not obey the rules.
7. This *ion* is an idea.
8. This *ion* rights a wrong.
9. This *ion* involves a diploma.
10. This *ion* is a tender feeling.
11. This *ion* is against something.
12. This *ion* is a phrase.

Questions Write a Basic or Review Word to answer each question.

13. What do endings do?
14. What can too many unfamiliar things do?
15. What do teachers do?
16. What do proofreaders do?
17. What do high school seniors do?
18. What do people who reveal what they feel do?
19. What do advisors do?
20. What do people who have a conversation do?
21. What does a stick of dynamite do?
22. What do people who want to influence something try to do?
23. What do people who omit or exclude something do?
24. What do people who disagree with something do?

I thought "It's raining cats and dogs" was only a saying.

How Are You Doing?

List the spelling words that are hard for you. Practice them with a family member.

Proofreading and Writing

Proofread: Spelling and Interjections An **interjection** is a word that shows feeling. It is usually followed by an exclamation point. If an interjection begins a sentence, set it off with a comma.

Hooray**!** Tomorrow is a holiday!
Oh**,** I can hardly wait!

Use proofreading marks to correct four misspelled words and two missing punctuation marks in this conversation.

Example: Hey!Can you clear up this ~~confussion~~? *confusion*

Wow This spelling instruckion is difficult. How can I remember the corect spelling?

Oh did this lesson confuse you? Let's discuss it. Here's a sugestion! Write the rule, and then write the word that is an exception.

Write a Conversation

Good morning, class!

Should computers replace teachers in the future? What might be some of the problems or advantages? With a partner write a conversation between two people whose opinions differ. Try to use five spelling words and at least one interjection.

Proofreading Tip   Be sure to punctuate correctly any interjections that you use.

Basic

1. instruct
2. instruction
3. graduate
4. graduation
5. confuse
6. confusion
7. conclude
8. conclusion
9. oppose
10. opposition
11. explode
12. explosion
13. affect
14. affection
15. suggest
16. suggestion
17. discuss
18. discussion
19. except
20. exception

Review

21. correct
22. correction
23. express
24. expression

Challenge

25. substitute
26. substitution
27. exclude
28. exclusion

Proofreading Marks

¶   Indent
∧   Add
⊙   Add a period
✄   Delete
≡   Capital letter
/   Small letter
∾   Reverse order

Expanding Vocabulary

Spelling Word Link

affect

affect
effect

Easily Confused Words The words *affect* and *effect* are often confused. Read their most common meanings:

affect To influence: *Music can affect your mood.*
effect A result: *The advertising had a good effect.*

Notice that *affect* is most commonly used as a verb, whereas *effect* is most commonly used as a noun.

Write *affect* or *effect* to complete each sentence.

1. A good teacher can _____ you for the rest of your life.
2. The high test scores had an immediate _____ on the class's mood.
3. How will losing the race _____ you?
4. Dr. Lopez studied the cause and _____ of the illness.
5. One _____ of exercise is a stronger heart.
6. New ideas can _____ your point of view.

1. _____
2. _____
3. _____
4. _____
5. _____
6. _____

Show You Know! Write two sentences about the pictures below. Use *affect* in one sentence and *effect* in the other. Write on a separate sheet of paper.

Vocabulary Enrichment

Real-World Connection

Careers: Teaching All the words in the box relate to teaching. Look up these words in your Spelling Dictionary. Then write the words to complete this part of a business letter.

Dear Governor Washington:

I would like to nominate Ms. Eling Chan as Teacher of the Year. She teaches sixth grade in our __(1)__ school. She became a member of the school's __(2)__ last year. Ms. Chan wants her students to receive a good __(3)__ . She wants us to be ready for __(4)__ school. Every week she gives a __(5)__ to test us on the material that we have read in the __(6)__ . She posts helpful hints on the __(7)__ , and she is always ready to help us work on a complicated math problem or other difficult __(8)__ . She would make a very good model for other teachers.

Please consider my suggestion.

Spelling Word Link

instruction

education
elementary
secondary
assignment
faculty
quiz
textbook
bulletin board

1. _____
2. _____
3. _____
4. _____
5. _____
6. _____
7. _____
8. _____

Try This CHALLENGE

Yes or No? Write *yes* if the underlined word or words are used correctly. Write *no* if they are not.

9. We stared at the <u>bulletin board</u> that we saw along the highway.
10. Ellen is a third grader at the local <u>elementary</u> school.
11. The math <u>textbook</u> was filled with equations.
12. All the students at the school are <u>faculty</u> members.

9. _____
10. _____
11. _____
12. _____

Fact File

Anne Sullivan was a loving and devoted teacher. Using the sense of touch, she taught Helen Keller how to read, write, and speak. Keller had been stricken blind, deaf, and mute at the age of two.

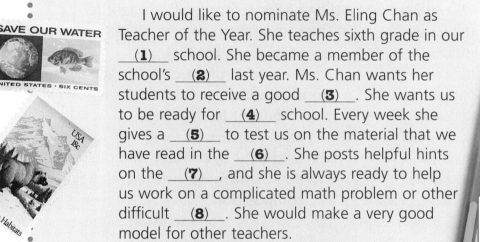

The Prefix *con-*

con-

_____
_____
_____
_____
_____
_____
_____
_____
_____
_____
_____

com-

_____
_____
_____
_____
_____
_____

Read and Say

Basic

READ the sentences. **SAY** each bold word.

1. consumer — A good **consumer** shops carefully.
2. control — Try to **control** your temper.
3. constitution — A **constitution** states a country's basic laws.
4. comment — Will you **comment** on the book?
5. confront — The teams will **confront** each other today.
6. compete — When will the runners **compete**?
7. conference — I had a **conference** with my teacher.
8. computer — The **computer** saves time for mathematicians.
9. conflict — Our ideas are in **conflict**.
10. commotion — There was a **commotion** when the bell rang.
11. conquer — I must **conquer** my fear of spiders.
12. content — She is **content** to stay home.
13. concert — The band **concert** is tonight.
14. contact — My hand came in **contact** with the hot iron.
15. confirm — Can you **confirm** the news about Mike?
16. composition — The **composition** of that music took a year.
17. conversation — What was your **conversation** with Dad about?
18. community — We live in a small **community**.
19. contest — Who won the spelling **contest**?
20. complicate — Being late will **complicate** our plans.

Think and Write

Each word has the prefix *con-*, meaning "together" or "with." Sometimes *con-* is spelled *com.*

    con + trol = **con**trol   con + ment = **com**ment
    con + front = **con**front   con + pete = **com**pete

- Before which consonants is the prefix *con-* spelled *com*?

Now write each Basic Word under its spelling of the prefix *con-*.

Review		Challenge	
	23. concern		28. commission
21. compare	24. complex	26. consequence	29. compensate
22. contain	25. convince	27. comprehensive	30. compliance

Independent Practice

Spelling Strategy The prefix *con-* is often spelled *com* before the consonant *m* or *p*. Find the prefix, the base word or the word root, and any ending. Spell the word by parts.

Word Analysis/Phonics Complete the exercises with Basic Words.

1–3. Write the noun form of each verb below.

1. confer   **2.** converse   **3.** compose

4–8. Write five words by adding the prefix *con-* or *com-* to each base word or word root.

4. _____ + firm   **7.** _____ + ment
5. _____ + test   **8.** _____ + tact
6. _____ + motion

Vocabulary: Classifying Write the Basic Word that belongs with each group of words.

9. government, laws, _____
10. recital, performance, _____
11. neighborhood, district, _____
12. keyboard, printer, _____
13. merchant, product, _____

Challenge Words Write the Challenge Word that matches each definition. Use your Spelling Dictionary.

14. obedience
15. thorough
16. an effect or result
17. to make up for
18. the act of doing something

Word Analysis

1. _____
2. _____
3. _____
4. _____
5. _____
6. _____
7. _____
8. _____

Vocabulary

9. _____
10. _____
11. _____
12. _____
13. _____

Challenge Words

14. _____
15. _____
16. _____
17. _____
18. _____

Spelling-Meaning

19. _____
20. _____

Spelling-Meaning Connection

How can you remember to spell the schwa sound in *compete* with an *o*? Think of the |ŏ| sound in the related word *competition*.

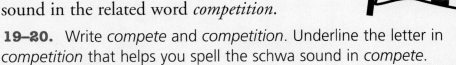

compete
competition

19–20. Write *compete* and *competition*. Underline the letter in *competition* that helps you spell the schwa sound in *compete*.

Homographs

1. _____
2. _____
3. _____
4. _____

Changing Prefixes

5. _____
6. _____
7. _____
8. _____
9. _____
10. _____
11. _____
12. _____
13. _____
14. _____
15. _____
16. _____
17. _____
18. _____

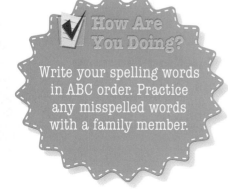

How Are You Doing?

Write your spelling words in ABC order. Practice any misspelled words with a family member.

Dictionary

Homographs   Some words have two dictionary entries.

> **con·tent**¹ |kŏn′ tĕnt′| *n.* The amount of a substance contained in something: *Cream has a high fat content.*
> **con·tent**² |kən tĕnt′| *adj.* Happy with what one has: *I am content with my life as it is. —v.* To make content or satisfied.

*Content*¹ and *content*² are homographs. **Homographs** are words with the same spelling but different meanings. Notice that the two words are also pronounced differently.

THE CONTENT OF THIS SWEATER IS 100% WOOL.

I'M CONTENT MAKING SWEATERS ALL DAY.

Practice   Write *1* or *2* to show which entry for *content* is used in each sentence.

1. Matthew was not <u>content</u> to be second best.
2. Ocean water has a high salt <u>content</u>.
3. Simple pleasures are enough to <u>content</u> her.
4. What is the wool <u>content</u> of this sweater?

Review: Spelling Spree

Changing Prefixes   Change the underlined prefix in each word to write a Basic or Review Word.

Example: <u>in</u>ference   *conference*

5. <u>re</u>tain
6. <u>im</u>munity
7. <u>in</u>flict
8. <u>dis</u>puter
9. <u>ex</u>tent
10. <u>in</u>stitution
11. <u>pro</u>test
12. <u>in</u>firm
13. <u>re</u>position
14. <u>de</u>motion
15. <u>in</u>tact
16. <u>fore</u>front
17. <u>dis</u>cern
18. <u>im</u>plicate

Proofreading and Writing

Proofread for Spelling Use proofreading marks to correct eleven misspelled Basic or Review Words in this announcement.

Example: Bad spending habits can ~~complecate~~ *complicate* your budget!

Special Announcement!

A confrence about consoomer awareness will be held on Friday. Work in consert with other members of the community. Help conker the complecks problems of shopping wisely. Learn how to compair prices and to controll what you spend! Find out how businesses compeat for your dollar. Time is planned for convesation with the speakers, who will be interested in any concern or coment. Try to convience your friends to come too!

Basic
1. consumer
2. control
3. constitution
4. comment
5. confront
6. compete
7. conference
8. computer
9. conflict
10. commotion
11. conquer
12. content
13. concert
14. contact
15. confirm
16. composition
17. conversation
18. community
19. contest
20. complicate

Review
21. compare
22. contain
23. concern
24. complex
25. convince

Challenge
26. consequence
27. comprehensive
28. commission
29. compensate
30. compliance

Write a Business Letter

Have you ever bought a product that did not work properly or that could be made to work better? Write a letter to the manufacturer explaining what is wrong with the product or how it might be improved. Try to use five spelling words.

Proofreading Tip **Check that your *i*'s and e's are written clearly so that readers are not confused.**

Proofreading Marks

¶ Indent
∧ Add
⊙ Add a period
ꝰ Delete
≡ Capital letter
/ Small letter
∽ Reverse order

Expanding Vocabulary

Spelling Word Link

conference

consultation
interview
dialogue
chat
argument

1. _____
2. _____
3. _____
4. _____
5. _____

Thesaurus: Exact Words for *conversation* Why is *conference* a better word to use in this sentence than *conversation*?

The senators held a **conference** to discuss product safety.

Conference is better because it means "a meeting to discuss a particular subject." A conversation is an informal talk.

Write the word from the box that best replaces *conversation* in each sentence. Look up the entry for *conversation* in your Thesaurus if you need help.

1. I had a <u>conversation</u> with Dr. Li about my sprain.
2. A loud <u>conversation</u> arose over the umpire's call.
3. When Jay and I met, we had a friendly <u>conversation</u>.
4. The two actors entertained us with witty <u>conversation</u>.
5. The reporter questioned me during our <u>conversation</u>.

Show You Know! Write three sentences about the pictures. Use an exact word for *conversation* in each sentence. Write on a separate sheet of paper.

6. 7. 8.

Real-World Connection

Life Skills: Consumer Awareness All the words in the box relate to consumer awareness. Look up these words in your Spelling Dictionary. Then write the words to complete this ad.

Spelling Word Link

consumer

warranty
refund
budget
coupon
wholesale
retail
fraud
complaint

Do you have a __(1)__ about faulty merchandise? Have you been the victim of advertising __(2)__? Don't let it happen again! Penny Pinchers Discount Store offers a guarantee, or __(3)__, for everything we sell. If you return an item, we will __(4)__ your money. Are you short of cash? We buy in quantity so that we can sell to you at __(5)__ prices. Don't pay more at a __(6)__ store. We will accept any money-saving __(7)__. Why worry about your monthly __(8)__? Shop at Penny Pinchers today!

Try This CHALLENGE

Yes or No? Write *yes* if the underlined word is used correctly. Write *no* if it is not.

9. My new radio has a ninety-day <u>warranty</u> against defects.
10. John made the <u>wholesale</u> by himself.
11. Eva returned the broken radio and got a <u>refund</u>.
12. Sonia keeps to a <u>budget</u> so that she can save money.

1. _____
2. _____
3. _____
4. _____
5. _____
6. _____
7. _____
8. _____

9. _____
10. _____
11. _____
12. _____

★★★ Fact File

A government agency called the Consumer Product Safety Commission works to prevent the sale of unsafe products. Goods investigated by the commission include toys, baby clothes, and appliances.

Read and Say

Advert ise

Final |īz| Sounds

_____

_____

_____

_____

_____

_____

Final |ĭv| Sounds

_____

_____

_____

_____

Final |ĭj| Sounds

_____

_____

_____

_____

_____

_____

READ the sentences. **SAY** each bold word.

Basic

1. advertise
2. attractive
3. image
4. recognize
5. descriptive
6. usage
7. criticize
8. realize
9. percentage
10. college
11. positive
12. exercise
13. organize
14. courage
15. storage
16. civilize
17. protective
18. advantage
19. modernize
20. sausage

Did you **advertise** the play?
She is an **attractive** woman.
The dog barks at its **image** in the mirror.
He did not **recognize** me in the dark.
Her poems are very **descriptive**.
We can save our forests through careful **usage**.
Did they **criticize** your work?
I did not **realize** how late it was.
What **percentage** of the class plays basketball?
He wants to go to **college** after high school.
I am **positive** that I left my coat here.
Playing soccer is good **exercise**.
We should **organize** our books.
The soldier received a medal for his **courage**.
She put her winter coat in **storage**.
The teacher tried to **civilize** the wild students.
Please wear **protective** clothing in the rain.
The runner's strength was her best **advantage**.
We will **modernize** our house.
Do you eat **sausage** for breakfast?

Think and Write

Each word ends with the final |īz|, |ĭv|, or |ĭj| sounds.

|īz| advert**ise**, recogn**ize** |ĭv| attract**ive** |ĭj| im**age**

• What are two spelling patterns for the final |īz| sounds? What is one spelling pattern for the final |ĭv| sounds? for the final |ĭj| sounds? How is the Elephant Word different?

Now write each Basic Word under its final sounds.

Review
21. message
22. televise
23. language
24. creative
25. sensitive

Challenge
26. merchandise
27. aggressive
28. visualize
29. alternative
30. beverage

Independent Practice

Spelling Strategy When you hear the final |īz|, |ĭv|, or |ĭj| sounds, think of these patterns:

final |īz| *ize, ise*   final |ĭv| *ive*   final |ĭj| *age*

Word Analysis/Phonics Complete the exercises with Basic Words.

1. Write the word with the word root *tract,* meaning "to pull."
2–5. Write the words that have these base words.
    2. use   **3.** percent   **4.** store   **5.** civil

Vocabulary: Word Clues Write the Basic Word that fits each clue.

6. synonym for *bravery*
7. to announce a product
8. to bring up-to-date
9. strengthens your muscles
10. synonym for *benefit*
11. may be a pizza topping
12. to know or understand
13. a place for learning

Challenge Words Write the Challenge Word that completes each sentence. Use your Spelling Dictionary.

14. The ad described the food so clearly that I could _____ it.
15. This ad is for a new _____ made from several juices.
16. A salesperson sells a company's _____ .
17. A newspaper ad is a good _____ to a radio ad.
18. A store that runs many ads has an _____ marketing plan.

Spelling-Meaning Connection

How can you remember to spell the |s| sound in *criticize* with *c*? Think of the related words *critic* and *critical*. The sound of the *c* changes, but the spelling remains the same.

19–20. Write *critic* and *criticize*. Underline the letter in *critic* that helps you spell the |s| sound in *criticize*.

Daily Review

critic

criticize

critical

Word Analysis
1. _____
2. _____
3. _____
4. _____
5. _____

Vocabulary
6. _____
7. _____
8. _____
9. _____
10. _____
11. _____
12. _____
13. _____

Challenge Words
14. _____
15. _____
16. _____
17. _____
18. _____

Spelling-Meaning
19. _____
20. _____

Meaning Match

1. _____
2. _____
3. _____
4. _____
5. _____
6. _____

Syllable Scramble

7. _____
8. _____
9. _____
10. _____
11. _____
12. _____
13. _____
14. _____
15. _____
16. _____
17. _____
18. _____
19. _____
20. _____
21. _____
22. _____
23. _____
24. _____
25. _____

Review: Spelling Spree

Meaning Match Each item below contains a meaning for a base word followed by an ending. Add the base word to the underlined ending to write a Basic or Review Word.

Example: someone who breaks into a house + <u>ize</u>   *burglarize*

1. polite and courteous + <u>ize</u>
2. having to do with the present time + <u>ize</u>
3. to keep from harm + <u>ive</u>
4. a person who writes reviews + <u>ize</u>
5. one part in a hundred + <u>age</u>
6. to pull toward oneself + <u>ive</u>

Syllable Scramble Rearrange the syllables to write a Basic or Review Word. There is one extra syllable in each item.

Example: chan cer dise mer   *merchandise*

7. age ege im
8. vise e or tel
9. ad er tage van
10. tar lege col
11. er til cise ex
12. si sen ber tive
13. men age stor
14. ad age tise ver
15. sage per sau
16. a pen tive cre
17. ive age us
18. og rec age nize
19. gor guage lan
20. tive de vish scrip
21. tain age cour
22. tive re i pos
23. gan ize di or
24. ize re al age
25. sage more mes

mer   chan   dise   cer

How Are You Doing?
Write each spelling word in a sentence. Practice any misspelled spelling words with a partner.

Proofreading and Writing

Proofread: Spelling and Commas in a Series Use commas to separate a series of three or more items.

Artists, musicians, and writers work in advertising. Use proofreading marks to correct four misspelled words and four missing commas in this ad.

Example: It pays to ~~advertyze~~ *advertise* with clear simple and direct ads.

Create a new imaje with a modern mesage!

ADVANTAGE Sportswear

Wear clothes that look classy

sassy and fun.

Wear clothes that make you feel

atractive creative and possitive.

ADVANTAGE
SPORTSWEAR

They're the only clothes you'll ever want.

Write an Ad

Write a magazine ad for an unusual new product; create a product if you like. What are the product's selling points? Try to use five spelling words and at least one series of three or more items.

NEW Amazatron

Proofreading Tip

Check to see that you used commas correctly with items in a series.

Basic

1. advertise
2. attractive
3. image
4. recognize
5. descriptive
6. usage
7. criticize
8. realize
9. percentage
10. college
11. positive
12. exercise
13. organize
14. courage
15. storage
16. civilize
17. protective
18. advantage
19. modernize
20. sausage

Review

21. message
22. televise
23. language
24. creative
25. sensitive

Challenge

26. merchandise
27. aggressive
28. visualize
29. alternative
30. beverage

Proofreading Marks

¶ Indent
∧ Add
⊙ Add a period
◡ Delete
≡ Capital letter
/ Small letter
∿ Reverse order

Expanding Vocabulary

Spelling Word Link

description

The Word Root *scribe* or *script* The word root *scribe* or *script* comes from the Latin word *scribere*, meaning "to write." In English, verbs use the *scribe* form of *scribere*, and nouns use the *script* form. Many other words in English with common roots follow this pattern.

The ad **describes** the car. The **description** is accurate.

Complete the chart below with the appropriate form of the word shown. Use your Spelling Dictionary if you need help.

Verb: scribe	Noun: script
describe	description
inscribe	1.
2.	subscription
prescribe	3.

Work Together With a partner write two sentences for each picture below, using word pairs from the chart. Use the verb form of the word in one sentence and the noun form in the other. Write on a separate sheet of paper.

4–5.   6–7.   8–9.

Real-World Connection

Business: Advertising All the words in the box relate to advertising. Look up these words in your Spelling Dictionary. Then write the words to complete this news release.

News Item
For Immediate Release

AD VENTURES

Ad Ventures, a local ad agency, is organizing a __(1)__ to promote a new __(2)__ of jeans. The agency's copywriters have come up with a catchy __(3)__, and its art department has designed an attractive __(4)__. The ad will be so __(5)__ that it will be impossible to forget these jeans. The ad agency will use several different __(6)__, including television, radio, and __(7)__ displays on highways, to promote this product. People will be able to buy the jeans in stores and through a mail-order __(8)__.

Spelling Word Link
advertise

brand
slogan
campaign
media
logo
catalog
billboard
memorable

1. _____
2. _____
3. _____
4. _____
5. _____
6. _____
7. _____
8. _____

Try This CHALLENGE

Yes or No? Write *yes* if the underlined word is used correctly. Write *no* if it is not.

9. The campaign to advertise the store was successful.
10. The company's logo appears on its products.
11. The catalog lists every dress the company makes.
12. The teacher wrote our assignment on the billboard.

9. _____
10. _____
11. _____
12. _____

Fact File

When an advertiser puts together a TV commercial, an artist designs a storyboard. The storyboard is a series of pictures illustrating the script. It gives directions for filming the commercial.

Suffixes: *-ent, -ant; -able, -ible*

-ent

_____

_____

_____

-ant

_____

_____

_____

_____

-able

_____

_____

_____

_____

_____

_____

_____

-ible

_____

_____

_____

Read and Say

Basic

READ the sentences. **SAY** each bold word.

1. brilliant — Her **brilliant** idea produced a great invention.
2. excellent — His **excellent** drawing won a prize.
3. enjoyable — The book was **enjoyable** to read.
4. evident — Her happiness is **evident** from her smile.
5. visible — The house is just **visible** through the fog.
6. lovable — He has a **lovable** cat.
7. passable — Is that snowy road still **passable**?
8. ignorant — She is **ignorant** of current events.
9. impossible — Skating is nearly **impossible** on rough ice.
10. noticeable — His small error was not **noticeable**.
11. workable — Your plan to row to Africa is not **workable**.
12. fragrant — Roses are **fragrant** flowers.
13. client — The lawyer wrote a letter to her **client**.
14. washable — Is this fabric **washable**?
15. gallant — We read about a **gallant** knight.
16. agent — I bought the tickets from an **agent**.
17. hesitant — The shy child was **hesitant** to speak.
18. capable — My doctor is experienced and **capable**.
19. considerable — The gold ring had **considerable** value.
20. responsible — Who is **responsible** for the accident?

Think and Write

Each word ends with *-ent, -ant, -able,* or *-ible*. Because the spelling of the schwa sound is not clear, you must remember the spelling pattern for each suffix.

|ənt| evid**ent**, brilli**ant** |ə bəl| pass**able**, vis**ible**

• What are two spelling patterns for |ənt|? for |ə bəl|? How is |ə bəl| spelled when it follows a word root that ends with *s*?

Now write each Basic Word under its suffix.

Review
21. terrible
22. different
23. remarkable
24. constant
25. student

Challenge
26. improbable
27. irresistible
28. predominant
29. magnificent
30. apparent

Independent Practice

Spelling Strategy The suffixes *-ent*, *-ant*, *-able*, and *-ible* are sometimes added to base words or word roots. You must remember the spelling pattern for the suffix in each word.

Word Analysis/Phonics Complete the exercise with Basic Words.

1–8. Write the words that have these base words.

1. ignore	**4.** notice	**7.** work
2. pass	**5.** excel	**8.** love
3. enjoy	**6.** consider	

Vocabulary: Analogies Write the Basic Word that completes each analogy.

9. *Food* is to *flavorful* as *flower* is to _____.

10. *Doctor* is to *patient* as *lawyer* is to _____.

11. *Timid* is to *cowardly* as *brave* is to _____.

12. *Self-assured* is to *confident* as *uncertain* is to _____.

13. *Dull* is to *dim* as *dazzling* is to _____.

Challenge Words Write the Challenge Word that fits each clue. Use your Spelling Dictionary.

14. synonym for *splendid*
15. easily understood or seen
16. synonym for *unlikely*
17. impossible to say no to
18. greater in strength or importance

Spelling-Meaning Connection

Evident contains the word root *vid*, meaning "see." Knowing the root *vid* can also help you spell and understand the related words *video* and *provide*.

19–20. Write *video*. Then write the Basic Word that has the same word root as *video*.

Word Analysis
1. _____
2. _____
3. _____
4. _____
5. _____
6. _____
7. _____
8. _____

Vocabulary
9. _____
10. _____
11. _____
12. _____
13. _____

Challenge Words
14. _____
15. _____
16. _____
17. _____
18. _____

Spelling-Meaning
19. _____
20. _____

evident
video
provide

Adding Suffixes

1. _____
2. _____
3. _____
4. _____
5. _____
6. _____
7. _____
8. _____
9. _____
10. _____
11. _____
12. _____
13. _____

Puzzle Play

14. _____
15. _____
16. _____
17. _____
18. _____
19. _____
20. _____
21. _____
22. _____
23. _____
24. _____
25. _____

Review: Spelling Spree

Adding Suffixes Write a Basic or Review Word by adding the correct suffix to the word part in each phrase below.

1. a terr_____ storm
2. a work_____ plan
3. a brilli_____ color
4. a pass_____ road
5. a differ_____ idea
6. a gall_____ knight
7. an evid_____ solution
8. a vis_____ change
9. an enjoy_____ vacation
10. a notice_____ stain
11. a remark_____ feat
12. an excell_____ meal
13. a skilled and cap_____ worker

Puzzle Play Write a Basic or Review Word to fit each clue. Circle the letter that would appear in the box.

Example: The film was very _ _ _ _ _ _ _ _ ☐. *enjoyabl(e)*

14. This cannot be done. It is simply _ ☐ _ _ _ _ _ _ _ _.
15. Do your chores on time. Be _ _ _ _ ☐ _ _ _ _ _ _.
16. Mom brought home a cute and _ _ ☐ _ _ _ _ puppy.
17. The lawyer handled a case for her _ _ ☐ _ _ _.
18. The actor hired a publicity _ _ ☐ _ _.
19. The toddler's first steps were slow and _ _ ☐ _ _ _ _ _.
20. The woodpecker's _ _ _ _ _ ☐ _ _ tapping annoyed me.
21. Dad was _ _ _ _ ☐ _ _ _ of the surprise party plans.
22. This sweater will clean easily because it is _ _ _ _ _ _ _ ☐.
23. I gave my aunt a bouquet of ☐ _ _ _ _ _ _ _ roses.
24. Next year I will be a seventh grade _ _ ☐ _ _ _ _.
25. The fire caused _ _ ☐ _ _ _ _ _ _ _ _ _ damage.

Now write the circled letters in order. They will spell a sentence about movies.

Mystery Words: _ _ _ _ _ _ _ _ _ _ _ _.

How Are You Doing?

Write each word as a partner reads it aloud. Did you misspell any words?

Proofreading and Writing

Proofread: Spelling and Commas Use commas to set off the name of a person who is directly spoken to.

Did you enjoy the movie, Anton? Yes, Sasha, I did.

Use proofreading marks to correct five misspelled Basic or Review words and three missing commas in this television script.

Example: Miki this movie was really ~~enjoyible?~~ *enjoyable*

SCRIPT

ANTON: Sasha didn't you think that Ken Troy's

acting was brillant in his last movie?

SASHA: Yes, Anton his performance was exellent.

MIKI: How can you say that Sasha? Troy was

terrable. His acting wasn't even pasable.

ANTON: Isn't it remarkable how people can have

such diffrent views of the same movie?

Write a Script

Write another script for Anton, Sasha, and Miki. Have them discuss part of a book or a movie that you like. Try to use five spelling words and at least one comma in direct address.

The Anton, Sasha, and Miki Show

Proofreading Tip **Check that you have used commas in direct address correctly.**

Proofreading Marks

¶ Indent
∧ Add
⊙ Add a period
↶ Delete
≡ Capital letter
/ Small letter
∩ Reverse order

Expanding Vocabulary

unreliable
boring
impractical
cowardly
informed

Antonyms When you try something new, are you usually hesitant or confident? *Hesitant* means "doubtful or uncertain," and *confident* means "sure of oneself." These words are antonyms because they have opposite meanings.

hesitant   confident

1. _____
2. _____
3. _____
4. _____
5. _____

Write a word from the box that is an antonym for each underlined spelling word. Look up the spelling words in your Spelling Dictionary for clues.

1. If you read the newspaper, you will be _____, not <u>ignorant</u>.
2. In this tale the hero is <u>gallant</u>, whereas the villain is _____.
3. This idea is <u>workable</u>, whereas that one seems _____.
4. When Jan delivers newspapers, she must be responsible, not _____.
5. LaToya thought the television show was <u>enjoyable</u>, but Jamal thought it was very _____.

Work Together Many entries in your Thesaurus include antonyms. With a partner use your Thesaurus to find the antonyms for each entry word below. Then write three sentences, using one of the words and one of its antonyms in each. Write on a separate sheet of paper.

problem   let   brief

Real-World Connection

Language Arts: Movie Reviews All the words in the box relate to movie reviews. Look up these words in your Spelling Dictionary. Then write the words to complete this newspaper article.

Spelling Word Link

excellent

critic
rating
opinion
evaluate
rave
recommend
sequel
summary

★★★★ Must see!

★★★ Worth seeing

★★ Only okay

★ Why bother?

Arts and Entertainment
Introducing Estelle Howe

Today's paper carries its first review by Estelle Howe, our new film __(1)__. Howe always tries to __(2)__ movies objectively. When she loves a movie, she gives it a __(3)__ review. Yet she is not at all shy about stating her __(4)__, even if it is negative. Read her review of *Return of the Terrible Titans*, the __(5)__ to *The Terrible Titans*. She begins with a __(6)__ of the plot, but she does not give away the end. Although she thinks the movie is flawed, she does __(7)__ seeing it for the special effects. Howe gives the film a two-star __(8)__.

1. _____
2. _____
3. _____
4. _____
5. _____
6. _____
7. _____
8. _____

Try This CHALLENGE

Write Guidelines Many students write movie reviews for their school newspapers or for electronic bulletin boards. Write several numbered guidelines explaining to students how they should write their reviews. Try to use some words from the box on this page.

 Fact File

The Academy of Motion Picture Arts and Sciences presents the Academy Awards, or Oscars, for outstanding film achievements. First awarded in 1929, the Oscars are gold-plated statues.

Popcorn

24 Review: Units 19–23

Unit 19　　Adding *-ion* or *-ation*　　pages 120–125

combine	cooperate	connect	situate	admire
combination	cooperation	connection	situation	admiration

Spelling Strategy　　The suffix **-ion** or **-ation** can change verbs into nouns. If the verb ends with **e**, drop the **e** before adding **-ion** or **-ation**.

Write a word pair to complete each sentence.

1–2. The operator finally was able to _____ the call, but all the static caused a bad _____.

3–4. To _____ a house on the edge of a cliff might create an unsafe _____.

5–6. When you _____ yellow and blue, the _____ makes green.

7–8. Please _____, as we need everyone's _____ to succeed.

9–10. Although I somewhat _____ Renoir's paintings, Picasso's art has my complete _____.

1. _____
2. _____
3. _____
4. _____
5. _____
6. _____
7. _____
8. _____
9. _____
10. _____

Unit 20　　More Words with *-ion*　　pages 126–131

confuse	oppose	conclude	discuss	explode
confusion	opposition	conclusion	discussion	explosion

Spelling Strategy　　The suffix **-ion** can change verbs to nouns. The suffix **-ion** is added to many words without a spelling change. In some words the final **e** is dropped or another spelling change occurs when **-ion** is added. Remember the spellings of these words.

Write the noun that fits each clue.

11. conversation
12. the end of the play
13. resistance
14. a feeling of being mixed up
15. what happens when a bomb goes off

Write the verb that belongs with each group of words.

16. fight, resist, _____
17. baffle, puzzle, _____
18. burst, erupt, _____
19. speak, converse, _____
20. end, halt, _____

11. _____
12. _____
13. _____
14. _____
15. _____
16. _____
17. _____
18. _____
19. _____
20. _____

Unit 21   The Prefix *con-*   pages 132–137

comment	conference	commotion	conflict	computer
contact	complicate	conversation	conquer	community

Spelling Strategy   The prefix **con-** is often spelled **com** before the consonant **m** or **p**. Find the prefix, the base word or the word root, and any ending. Spell the word by parts.

Write a word by adding *con-* or *com-* to each word part.

21. _____ I ment   **24.** _____ I puter
22. _____ I tact   **25.** _____ I versation
23. _____ I flict   **26.** _____ I motion

Write the word that completes each analogy.

27. *Talk* is to *discussion* as *meeting* is to _____.
28. *Easy* is to *hard* as *simplify* is to _____.
29. *Lose* is to *surrender* as *win* is to _____.
30. *Member* is to *club* as *citizen* is to _____.

21. _____
22. _____
23. _____
24. _____
25. _____
26. _____
27. _____
28. _____
29. _____
30. _____

Unit 22   Final |īz|, |ĭv|, and |ĭj| pages 138–143

percentage	realize	advertise	attractive	college
positive	storage	civilize	exercise	sausage

Spelling Strategy

final |īz| → **ize** or **ise**   final |ĭv| → **ive**   final |ĭj| → **age**

Write the word that completes each sentence.

31. Most businesses _____ in order to attract customers.
32. Walking briskly is a safe and healthy form of _____.
33. Last night I put my summer clothes away for winter _____.
34. What _____ of the population voted in this election?
35. I did not _____ how late it was!

Write the word that fits each clue.

36. certain   **39.** kind of meat
37. to educate   **40.** after high school
38. appealing

31. _____
32. _____
33. _____
34. _____
35. _____
36. _____
37. _____
38. _____
39. _____
40. _____

brilliant	impossible	enjoyable	excellent	visible
washable	fragrant	hesitant	responsible	client

Spelling Strategy   The suffixes **-ent**, **-ant**, **-able**, and **-ible** are sometimes added to base words or word roots. You must remember the spelling pattern for the suffix in each word.

Write the word that is an antonym for each word below.

41. odorless   **44.** bold

42. undependable   **45.** likely

43. unseen   **46.** pale

Write the word that answers each question.

47. What kind of cloth is not harmed by soap and water?

48. What kind of homework deserves an *A*?

49. How might you describe an activity that you like to do?

50. Whom does a lawyer represent?

Challenge Words   Units 19–23   pages 120–149

consequence	alternative	substitute	excavate
merchandise	irresistible	substitution	excavation
comprehensive	predominant		

Write the word that is a synonym for the underlined word.

51. Jacki's research report was very detailed and <u>thorough</u>.

52. How long will it take to <u>uncover</u> the ancient <u>village</u>?

53. When I saw the lake, I had an <u>overwhelming</u> desire to swim.

54. Red is the <u>main</u> color used in this painting.

55. We did not want to leave Arkansas, but we had no <u>choice</u>.

Write the word that matches each definition.

56. result of an action

57. the act of digging out

58. to use in place of another

59. goods that are bought or sold

60. something that is used as a replacement

41. _____

42. _____

43. _____

44. _____

45. _____

46. _____

47. _____

48. _____

49. _____

50. _____

51. _____

52. _____

53. _____

54. _____

55. _____

56. _____

57. _____

58. _____

59. _____

60. _____

Spelling-Meaning Strategy

The Latin Word Root *vis*

Did you know that *visible* and *vision* are related in meaning? Each word has the Latin word root *vis,* meaning "see." A Latin word root affects the meaning of each word that contains it. *Visible* means "capable of being seen." *Vision* refers to the sense of sight. Knowing the meaning of *vis* can help you spell and understand other words with the same word root.

Here are more words with the word root *vis.*

visit	**vis**or	**vis**ta
re**vis**e	ad**vis**e	**vis**ualize

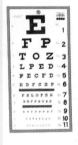

**visible
vision**

Think

- Look up each word in the word box above in your Spelling Dictionary. How does the word root affect the meaning of each word?

Apply and Extend

Complete these activities on a separate sheet of paper.

1. Write six sentences. Use one word from the word box above in each sentence. Can you write sentences that make the words' meanings clear?

2. With a partner list as many other words as you can that include the word root *vis.* Then look in the section "Word Parts," beginning on page 276 of your Spelling-Meaning Index. Add any other words that you find with this word root to your list.

Summing Up

The Latin word root *vis* means "see." Words that come from the same word root are often related in both spelling and meaning. Knowing the meaning of the word root can help you understand and spell the words in that family.

UNIT
24

Description

from Kon-Tiki
by Thor Heyerdahl

The author of this passage once met a whale shark face to face. What other animals does he compare the shark to?

The head was broad and flat like a frog's, with two small eyes right at the sides and a toadlike jaw that was four or five feet wide and had long fringes drooping from the corners of the mouth. Behind the head was an enormous body ending in a long thin tail with a pointed tail fin that stood straight up and showed that this sea monster was not any kind of whale. The body looked brownish under the water, but both head and body were thickly covered with small white spots.

The monster came quietly, lazily swimming after us. It grinned like a bulldog and lashed gently with its tail. The large round dorsal fin projected clear of the water, and sometimes the tail fin as well, and the water flowed about the broad back as though washing around a submerged reef. In front of the broad jaws swam a whole crowd of pilot fish in fan formation, and large remora fish and other parasites sat firmly attached to the huge body and traveled with it through the water, so that the whole thing looked like a curious zoological collection crowded round something that resembled a floating deep-water reef.

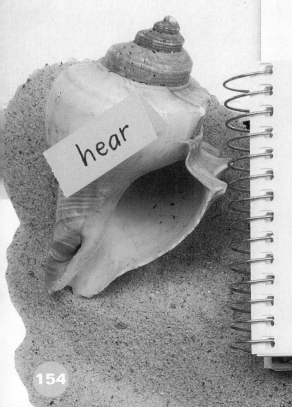

Think and Discuss

1 What similes, or comparisons using *like* or *as*, does the author use to describe the whale shark?

2 Is this description organized by moving from specific details to a general picture—or is it the reverse?

3 What exact words does the author use?

The Writing Process
Description

Write a word picture to help someone see, hear, smell, taste, or feel a special object or a place—or describe a person you know. Use the guidelines, and follow the Writing Process.

1 Prewriting
- In a web, list words that describe how your topic looks, feels, sounds, smells, or tastes.

2 Draft
- Write several similes describing your topic. Try beginning your description with one of them.

3 Revise
- Organize your details in a different order. Is it better?
- Use your Thesaurus to find exact words.
- Have a writing conference.

4 Proofread
- Did you spell each word correctly?
- Did you use capital letters and punctuation marks correctly?

5 Publish
- Make a neat final copy, and add a good title.
- Make a booklet to share your description.

···· **Guidelines for Writing a Description**

✓ Open with an interesting topic sentence.
✓ Use details to create a clear picture.
✓ Use sense words, exact words, and comparisons.
✓ Put the details in an easy-to-follow order.

Composition Words

conclusion
admire
content
attractive
image
recognize
fragrant
brilliant

Smell

|sh| **glacier**

sh

_____
_____
_____
_____
_____

ti

_____
_____
_____
_____
_____
_____
_____

ci

_____
_____
_____
_____

ss

_____
_____
_____

Read and Say

Basic

READ the sentences. **SAY** each bold word.

1. glacier — The **glacier** looked like a river of snow.
2. motion — The child likes the **motion** of the swing.
3. pressure — The **pressure** will flatten the leaf.
4. direction — I went in the wrong **direction**.
5. caution — Use **caution** as you climb the steps.
6. partial — This **partial** list is missing five names.
7. ancient — This **ancient** bone belonged to a dinosaur.
8. polish — Did you **polish** the car with wax?
9. station — The train pulled into the **station**.
10. shallow — We can wade in this **shallow** water.
11. official — What are the **official** rules?
12. edition — I read a new **edition** of this book.
13. musician — The **musician** plays the drums.
14. mention — Did she **mention** her sister in her letter?
15. mission — The spy went on a secret **mission**.
16. portion — He ate a large **portion** of salad.
17. session — I missed the first **session** of the class.
18. selfish — John is **selfish** and will not lend his books.
19. establish — We will **establish** a tennis team.
20. cushion — This chair needs a new **cushion**.

Think and Write

Each word has the |sh| sound. The |sh| sound is usually spelled with two letters.

|sh| poli**sh**, mo**ti**on   offi**ci**al, mi**ss**ion

• What are four spelling patterns for the |sh| sound?

Now write each Basic Word under its spelling of the |sh| sound.

Review
21. vanish
22. action
23. condition
24. migration
25. confession

Challenge
26. expedition
27. diminish
28. recession
29. beneficial
30. technician

Independent Practice

Spelling Strategy When you hear the |sh| sound, think of the patterns *sh*, *ti*, *ci*, and *ss*.

Word Analysis/Phonics Complete the exercises with Basic Words.

1. Write the word with the |ô| sound spelled *au*.
2. Write the word that ends with the |ō| sound spelled *ow*.
3. Write the word that begins with the |ə| sound spelled *o*.
4–5. Write two words that begin with the |ĭ| sound spelled *e*.
6–7. Write the two words that end with the |ər| sounds. Underline the letters that spell the |ər| sounds.

Vocabulary: Synonyms Write the Basic Word that is a synonym for each word below.

8. old
9. movement
10. pillow
11. task
12. shine
13. meeting

Challenge Words Write the Challenge Word that fits each definition. Use your Spelling Dictionary.

14. become less
15. advantageous
16. trip made by a group with a purpose
17. the act of withdrawing or going back
18. a person who is skilled in certain scientific techniques

An international team crosses Antarctica by dogsled, July 1989 to March 1990.

Spelling-Meaning Connection

How can you remember that the |sh| sound is spelled with a *t* in *partial?* Think of the related word *part*, in which the *t* is pronounced.

part
partial

19–20. Write *part* and *partial*. Underline the letter in *part* that helps you remember the spelling of |sh| in *partial*.

Word Analysis

1. _____
2. _____
3. _____
4. _____
5. _____
6. _____
7. _____

Vocabulary

8. _____
9. _____
10. _____
11. _____
12. _____
13. _____

Challenge Words

14. _____
15. _____
16. _____
17. _____
18. _____

Spelling-Meaning

19. _____
20. _____

Word Histories

1. _____

2. _____

3. _____

4. _____

5. _____

Comparisons

6. _____

7. _____

8. _____

9. _____

10. _____

11. _____

12. _____

13. _____

14. _____

15. _____

16. _____

17. _____

18. _____

19. _____

20. _____

How Are You Doing?

List the spelling words that are hard for you. Practice them with a partner.

Dictionary

Word Histories As you know, a word history gives the origin of a word and shows how its spelling and meaning have changed.

> **History**
>
> **Cushion** comes from the Latin word *coxa,* meaning "hip." From *coxa,* Romans formed the word *coxinus,* meaning "hip rest."

Practice Read the word history for each word below in your Spelling Dictionary. Then answer the questions.

cancel   pace   crisis   poison   principle

1. Which word comes from a Latin word meaning "lattice"?
2. What does the word *crisis* mean?
3. What language does *pace* come from?
4. What Old French word means "a first or basic truth"?
5. Which word is from the Middle English word *poysoun*?

Review: Spelling Spree

Comparisons Write the Basic or Review Word that best completes each comparison.

Example: as _____ as night *dark*

6. as seasonal as animal _____
7. as soothing as the _____ of a rocking chair
8. as _____ as a greedy dog
9. as exciting as a secret _____
10. as _____ as an Egyptian pyramid
11. as flashy as a photo _____
12. as rare as a book's first _____
13. as _____ as a birth certificate
14. as noisy as a train _____
15. as _____ as a puddle
16. as soft as a _____
17. as revealing as a _____
18. as talented as a _____
19. as icy as a _____
20. as shiny as _____

Proofreading and Writing

Proofread for Spelling Use proofreading marks to correct ten misspelled Basic or Review Words in this paragraph.

Example: The ice here is still in ~~moshun~~! *motion*

Glacier National Park

In 1910 the U.S. Congress decided to astablish Glacier National Park in Montana. The park's beautiful condision is evident from every dirrection, as even a parcial glimpse of the area reveals. Many visitors mension that they like the Lewis Overthrust, a porshion of the park where a ridge was created by underground prassure. The government has exercised great causion in protecting the park's wildlife and has taken actin so that the animals will not vannish from the area.

Basic

1. glacier
2. motion
3. pressure
4. direction
5. caution
6. partial
7. ancient
8. polish
9. station
10. shallow
11. official
12. edition
13. musician
14. mention
15. mission
16. portion
17. session
18. selfish
19. establish
20. cushion

Review

21. vanish
22. action
23. condition
24. migration
25. confession

Challenge

26. expedition
27. diminish
28. recession
29. beneficial
30. technician

Write a List

Many parks post rules to protect visitors and to preserve the land and animals. Write a list of rules for visiting a local or national park. Try to use five spelling words.

Proofreading Tip

Make sure that you have not capitalized any words needlessly.

Proofreading Marks

¶ Indent
∧ Add
⊙ Add a period
⌐ Delete
≡ Capital letter
/ Small letter
∩ Reverse order

Vocabulary Enrichment

Expanding Vocabulary

Spelling Word Link

mission

missile
missionary
commission
dismiss
submission

The Word Root *miss* A *mission* is an assignment that a person is sent to carry out. A *missive* is a message. Each word includes the word root *miss,* a word part that has meaning but cannot stand alone.

ROOT	MEANING	WORDS
miss	to send, to let go	**miss**ion, **miss**ive

Use the words in the box to complete the web below. Write the word that matches each definition. Use your Spelling Dictionary.

something offered for consideration
2.

to direct or allow to leave
1.

miss

person sent out to do religious or charitable work
3.

group authorized to perform certain duties
5.

object or weapon launched at a target
4.

1. _____
2. _____
3. _____
4. _____
5. _____

Show You Know! Write the word from the box that completes each sentence. Use your Spelling Dictionary.

1. A special _____ conducted a study of the nation's schools.
2. The relief group sent a _____ to help flood victims.
3. Ella wants the magazine to print her poetry _____.
4. The engineer designed a _____ for the space program.
5. Mr. Ponti decided to _____ his students early.

Real-World Connection

Spelling Word Link

glacier

erode
arctic
continental
mass
fjord
crevasse
debris
cirque

Science: Glaciers All the words in the box relate to glaciers. Look up these words in your Spelling Dictionary. Then write the words to complete this paragraph.

Glaciers

A glacier is a __(1)__ of ice, found in __(2)__ regions, that moves slowly over land. It leaves behind rock __(3)__ that can weigh hundreds of tons. All types of glaciers are able to wear away, or __(4)__, the land. Thick sheets of ice that cover huge amounts of land are called __(5)__ glaciers. The valley glacier is long and narrow and may form a __(6)__, a narrow inlet from the sea. Near its top is a __(7)__, a bowl-shaped hollow. As it flows over rough terrain, a glacier may crack, creating a __(8)__.

1. _____
2. _____
3. _____
4. _____
5. _____
6. _____
7. _____
8. _____

Try This CHALLENGE

Yes or No? Write *yes* if the underlined word is used correctly. Write *no* if it is not.

9. A warm <u>arctic</u> wind blew over the city.
10. The ocean can <u>erode</u> the land.
11. A huge <u>mass</u> of rock blocked the entrance to the cave.
12. After the hurricane, <u>debris</u> covered the streets.

9. _____
10. _____
11. _____
12. _____

Fact File

Norway, a northern European country, was once covered by glaciers. Their movement carved deep valleys in the land. When the glaciers melted, seawater filled the valleys and formed fjords.

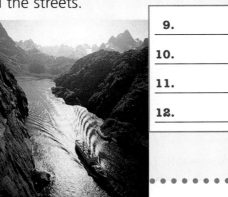

Plurals

half   staff
halves   **staff**s

-s **Added**

_____

_____

_____

_____

_____

_____

_____

_____

-es **Added**

_____

_____

_____

_____

f **Changed to** *v*, *-es* **Added**

_____

_____

_____

_____

_____

Read and Say

Basic

READ the sentences. **SAY** each bold word.

1. *pianos* — The musicians played the **pianos**.
2. *cellos* — The **cellos** had a deep sound.
3. *solos* — I sang two **solos**.
4. *altos* — The **altos** do not sing the highest notes.
5. *sopranos* — The **sopranos** sing high notes.
6. *staffs* — The **staffs** of both schools will meet.
7. *stereos* — We listened to music on our **stereos**.
8. *potatoes* — Dad peeled and cooked the **potatoes**.
9. *halves* — Give the apple **halves** to the two girls.
10. *chiefs* — The **chiefs** are the leaders of their tribes.
11. *echoes* — Our shouts made **echoes** in the canyon.
12. *calves* — Many cows have two **calves**.
13. *studios* — The art show was held in four **studios**.
14. *shelves* — Put these books on the **shelves**.
15. *ratios* — What are the **ratios** of students to teachers?
16. *volcanoes* — Melted rock flowed out of the **volcanoes**.
17. *loaves* — He bought three **loaves** of bread.
18. *wolves* — The big dogs look like **wolves**.
19. *heroes* — The men were **heroes** for saving the child.
20. *scarves* — These **scarves** will keep our necks warm.

Think and Write

Each word is the plural form of a noun ending with *f* or *o*.

sta**ff**	chie**f**	hal**f**	ster**eo**	pi**ano**	pota**to**
sta**ffs**	chie**fs**	hal**ves**	ster**eos**	pi**anos**	pota**toes**

• How do you form the plural of a noun ending with *ff*? with a single *f*? with a vowel followed by *o*? with a consonant followed by *o*?

Now write each Basic Word under the heading that tells how its plural is formed.

Review
21. abilities
22. countries
23. duties
24. enemies
25. lilies

Challenge
26. piccolos
27. maestros
28. tuxedos
29. vetoes
30. mementos

Independent Practice

Spelling Strategy Remember these patterns to form the plurals of nouns ending with *f* or *o*:
- nouns ending with *ff*: add *-s*
- nouns ending with *f*: add *-s* or change *f* to *v* and add *-es*
- nouns ending with a vowel + *o*: add *-s*
- nouns ending with a consonant + *o*: add *-s* or *-es*.

Word Analysis/Phonics Complete the exercises with Basic Words.

1. Write the word that has the |ō| sound spelled *oa*.
2. Write the word that has the |f| sound spelled *ff*.
3. Write the word that has the |k| sound spelled *ch*.
4–5. Write the two words that have a silent *l*.

Vocabulary: Making Inferences Write the Basic Word that fits each clue.

6. used for playing tapes
7. 1:2 and 7:4
8. tasty baked or mashed
9. where artists work
10. have black and white keys
11. look like dogs
12. used to hold books
13. worn on cold days

Challenge Words Write the Challenge Word that matches each definition. Use your Spelling Dictionary.

14. masters in an art, especially in music
15. small flutes
16. formal suits for men
17. rejections
18. reminders of the past

Spelling-Meaning Connection

Cello is unusual because *c* spells the |ch| sound. Because *cellist* is related in meaning to *cello*, it has the same spelling for the |ch| sound. **Think of this:** The *cellist* played the *cello* beautifully.

cello
cellist

19–20. Write *cellist* and the Basic Word related to *cellist*.

Word Analysis

1. _____
2. _____
3. _____
4. _____
5. _____

Vocabulary

6. _____
7. _____
8. _____
9. _____
10. _____
11. _____
12. _____
13. _____

Challenge Words

14. _____
15. _____
16. _____
17. _____
18. _____

Spelling-Meaning

19. _____
20. _____

Silly Titles

1. _____
2. _____
3. _____
4. _____
5. _____
6. _____
7. _____
8. _____
9. _____
10. _____
11. _____
12. _____
13. _____
14. _____
15. _____

Jobs Match

16. _____
17. _____
18. _____
19. _____
20. _____
21. _____
22. _____
23. _____
24. _____
25. _____

Review: Spelling Spree

Silly Titles Write a Basic or Review Word to complete each book title. Remember to use capital letters.

1. *Mittens, Hats, and _____* by Win D. Wether
2. *How to Avoid Chores and _____* by Dewey Haveto
3. *Keyboards on _____* by Babe E. Grand
4. *My Voice _____ When I Yell* by Inna Kanyon
5. *Dividing Whole Pies into Two _____* by E. Quill Pieces
6. *Cities, States, and _____* by Reed N. Atlas
7. *Make Friends, Not _____* by Lotta Love
8. *Famous Heroines and _____* by Noble Deeds
9. *I'd Rather Sing _____ than Duets* by Opra Singer
10. *Writing Musical Notes on Lined _____* by Melody Maker
11. *In Charge: Fire and Police _____* by Ima Dee Fender
12. *Listen to the Wild _____* by Howell Atnite
13. *Using Your Skills and _____* by Manuel Laber
14. *Singers, Part I: The High-Voiced _____* by I. Sing Hi
15. *Singers, Part II: The Low-Voiced _____* by Harmon Izer

Jobs Match Write the Basic or Review Words that name some things these workers make, use, or deal with on the job.

16. florists
17. artists
18. carpenters
19. cellists
20. earth scientists
21. bread bakers
22. dairy farmers
23. mathematicians
24. vegetable gardeners
25. audio equipment makers

Do I have flour on my face?

✔ How Are You Doing?

Write your spelling words in ABC order. Practice any misspelled words with a family member.

Proofreading and Writing

Proofread: Spelling and Abbreviations Most abbreviations begin with a capital letter and end with a period. (See also page 247.)

Rd. (Road)　　**Mt.** (Mount)　　**P.O.** (Post Office)　　**IA** (Iowa)

Use proofreading marks to correct five misspelled Basic or Review Words and three incorrect abbreviations in this flyer.

Example: 46 ~~Centrel~~ *Central* St., Irving, ~~TEX~~ *TX* 75060

Concerts in Mnt. Vernon Park

June 1: Concerto for chellos and pianoes

July 8: Folk songs from Latin countrys

Aug. 10: Opera soloes for altos and soppranos

Music for All, P.o. Box 10, Pasadena, CAL 91103

Write an Ad

Write an ad announcing the opening of a new business, such as a music store or a restaurant. Be sure to include the address. Try to use five spelling words. You may want to illustrate your ad.

GRAND OPENING

Proofreading Tip

Check that you wrote all abbreviations correctly.

Proofreading Marks

¶ Indent
∧ Add
⊙ Add a period
⤴ Delete
≡ Capital letter
/ Small letter
∿ Reverse order

Vocabulary Enrichment

Expanding Vocabulary

Spelling Word Link

heroes

atlas
jovial
titanic
herculean
odyssey
martial
panic

Words from Myths Some English words come from the names of characters in Greek and Roman mythology.

History

An **atlas** is a book of maps. Its name comes from Atlas, the Greek god who held the world on his shoulders.

Write the word from the box that matches each character.

Character	Word	Meaning
Atlas, the Greek god who held the world on his shoulders	atlas	a book of maps
Mars, the Roman god of war	1.	warlike
Hercules, a hero of super-human strength	2.	very strong
Odysseus, a king who traveled ten years	3.	a long journey
Titan, one of a family of twelve giants	4.	of great size or importance
Pan, a god who caused fear in crowds	5.	sudden terror
Jove, the supreme Roman god, source of all happiness	6.	full of good cheer

Work Together With a partner write a sentence for each word you wrote on the chart. Write on a separate sheet of paper.

Real-World Connection

Performing Arts: Music Each word in the box relates to music. Look up these words in your Spelling Dictionary. Then write the words to complete this ad.

Spelling Word Link

cellos

violin
cymbals
bassoon
oboe
clarinet
guitar
trombone
tambourine

Harmony School of Music

Learn to play a new instrument at the Harmony School of Music. We can teach you how to strum a folk __(1)__ or how to draw a bow across a __(2)__. If you want to play a single-reed woodwind instrument, try the __(3)__. Perhaps you prefer the double-reed woodwinds, such as the booming __(4)__ or its high-pitched cousin, the __(5)__. You may like using the slide on the __(6)__ or jingling the disks on a __(7)__. You can even clang two __(8)__ together at the Harmony School of Music!

Try This CHALLENGE

Questions and Answers Write a word from the box to answer each question.

9. What plays brassy notes in a marching band?
10. What makes a loud crash?
11. What do you sometimes play with a pick?
12. Which woodwind makes the lowest sound?

1. _____
2. _____
3. _____
4. _____
5. _____
6. _____
7. _____
8. _____

9. _____
10. _____
11. _____
12. _____

Fact File

Ragtime, one of the first forms of jazz to gain wide popularity, has a steady beat in the bass notes set off by catchy, offbeat rhythms in the high notes. Scott Joplin wrote the most famous "rags."

Prefixes: *dis-, ex-, inter-*

ex haust

dis-

_____
_____
_____
_____
_____
_____
_____

ex-

_____
_____
_____
_____
_____
_____
_____
_____

inter-

_____
_____
_____

Read and Say

Basic

READ the sentences.
SAY each bold word.

1. disease	The doctor treated the **disease**.
2. experiment	I want to **experiment** with this paint.
3. discovery	The **discovery** of oil changed our lives.
4. disable	Did the accident **disable** the car?
5. international	The border with Canada is **international**.
6. dishonest	A liar is a **dishonest** person.
7. export	We **export** wheat to other countries.
8. experience	Ronda has no cooking **experience**.
9. interrupt	Please do not **interrupt** the speakers.
10. extreme	The lake froze in the **extreme** cold.
11. exhaust	The long hike may **exhaust** you.
12. distress	The bad news caused her much **distress**.
13. expand	Air will make the balloon **expand**.
14. extent	What is the **extent** of the damage?
15. disturb	Loud noises **disturb** the baby.
16. interfere	Do not **interfere** with his work.
17. disguise	That costume is a great **disguise**!
18. discourage	Do not let little problems **discourage** you.
19. expensive	He paid too much for that **expensive** hat.
20. interview	Mia was early for her job **interview**.

Think and Write

Each word is made up of the prefix *dis-, ex-,* or *inter-* and a base word or a word root. A base word can stand alone; a word root cannot.

PREFIX + BASE WORD: **dis**able

PREFIX + WORD ROOT: **ex**port   **inter**rupt

• What three prefixes do you see? Which Basic Words have a prefix with a base word? Which have a prefix with a word root?

Now write each Basic Word under its prefix.

Review
21. disaster
22. disagree
23. explain
24. district
25. excuse

Challenge
26. disinfectant
27. expertise
28. intervene
29. exposure
30. interdependent

Independent Practice

Spelling Strategy *Dis-*, *ex-*, and *inter-* are prefixes. To spell a word with a prefix, find the prefix, the base word or the word root, and any ending. Spell the word by parts.

Word Analysis/Phonics Complete the exercises with Basic Words.

1. Write the word that has the |sh| sound spelled with a *t*.
2. Write the word that has the |g| sound spelled *gu*.
3–5. Write three words that contain the base words below.
    3. able
    4. view
    5. cover

Vocabulary: Word Clues Write the Basic Word that fits each clue.

6. antonym for *cheap*
7. synonym for *test*
8. untruthful
9. antonym for *mild*
10. synonym for *enlarge*
11. fumes from a car
12. antonym for *encourage*
13. break in on a conversation

Challenge Words Write the Challenge Word that completes each sentence. Use your Spelling Dictionary.

14. Hospital workers clean with a strong _____ to kill germs.
15. Cliff caught a cold after his _____ to a sick friend.
16. Dentists use their _____ to treat decayed teeth.
17. A good diet and exercise are _____ factors in keeping fit.
18. Our teacher had to _____ to stop the argument.

Spelling-Meaning Connection

Export contains the word root *port*, meaning "to carry." The word *export* means "to carry to another country." Knowing the word root *port* can help you to spell and understand the related words *import* and *portable*.

export
import
portable

19–20. Write *import*. Then write the Basic Word that has the same word root.

Word Analysis
1. _____
2. _____
3. _____
4. _____
5. _____

Vocabulary
6. _____
7. _____
8. _____
9. _____
10. _____
11. _____
12. _____
13. _____

Challenge Words
14. _____
15. _____
16. _____
17. _____
18. _____

Spelling-Meaning
19. _____
20. _____

Prefixes and Suffixes

1. _____

_____

2. _____

_____

3. _____

_____

Alphabetizing

4. _____

5. _____

6. _____

7. _____

8. _____

9. _____

10. _____

11. _____

12. _____

13. _____

14. _____

15. _____

16. _____

17. _____

18. _____

19. _____

20. _____

Dictionary

Prefixes and Suffixes Dictionaries list prefixes and suffixes alphabetically as entries. For some words you must look up the base word and the prefix or the suffix separately. Then you can figure out their combined meaning.

> **ex-** A prefix meaning "out, out of": **exit**.

Practice Use your Spelling Dictionary to look up the base word and the underlined prefix or suffix in each word below. Then write the meaning of each word.

1. involve<u>ment</u>   **2.** excus<u>able</u>   **3.** <u>inter</u>league

Review: Spelling Spree

Alphabetizing Write the Basic or Review Word that fits alphabetically between the two words in each group.

4. exit, _____, expect
5. explode, _____, express
6. expire, _____, explode
7. exert, _____, exotic
8. extinct, _____, eye
9. exclude, _____, exempt
10. interval, _____, into
11. disgrace, _____, dish
12. interpret, _____, intersect
13. experienced, _____, expert
14. distort, _____, distribute
15. intern, _____, interpret
16. expensively, _____, explain
17. distrustful, _____, disuse
18. disappoint, _____, discard
19. distributor, _____, distrust
20. interest, _____, interior

How Are You Doing?

Write each spelling word in a sentence. Practice any misspelled spelling words with a family member.

Proofreading and Writing

Proofread for Spelling Use proofreading marks to correct eight misspelled Basic or Review Words in this text for a home page on the Internet.

Example: Can you ~~explan~~ *explain* the role of the FDA?

The U.S. Food and Drug Administration (FDA) tries to protect the public against harmful or disonest food and drug practices. The FDA works to discourige food tampering and other illegal activities that could cause desease or disabel people. It prosecutes violators to the full exstent of the law. The FDA also regulates researchers who want to experiment with a new medical drug descovery. Some people may disagre with the role of the FDA, but it has stopped the sale of dangerous and unjustly expencive medicines.

Write a Public Service Message

Write a thirty-second radio or television message about a public health issue, such as disease prevention or proper health care. Try to use five spelling words. "Broadcast" your message to some classmates.

Proofreading Tip

Be sure to write your *d*'s clearly so that they do not look like *cl*.

Proofreading Marks

¶ Indent
∧ Add
⊙ Add a period
⤷ Delete
≡ Capital letter
/ Small letter
∿ Reverse order

Expanding Vocabulary

Spelling Word Link

interrupt

abrupt
disrupt
erupt
corrupt

Building Words with *rupt* The spelling word *interrupt* is made up of the prefix *inter-* and the word root *rupt*. The meaning of *interrupt* is taken from the meaning of its parts.

inter + rupt = inter**rupt**
("between") ("to break") ("to break into a
conversation or action")

You can make other words by using different prefixes with *rupt*.

Write a word from the box to match the meaning next to each picture. Use your Spelling Dictionary. Then write a caption for each picture, using the new word.

1. To become violently active _____

_____
_____

2. Unexpectedly sudden _____

_____
_____

3. To throw into disorder _____

_____
_____

4. To taint; infect; spoil _____

_____
_____

Vocabulary Enrichment

Unit 27 BONUS

Real-World Connection

Health: Public Health All the words in the box relate to public health. Look up these words in your Spelling Dictionary. Then write the words to complete this paragraph.

Spelling Word Link

disease

virus
immunize
research
contagious
agency
epidemic
isolation
hazard

QUARANTINE

QUARANTINE
...hall leave
C.D.C.
Control

The Centers for Disease Control (CDC), an __(1)__ of the United States Public Health Service, works to control any __(2)__ disease that could become a widespread __(3)__. The CDC urges doctors to __(4)__ children against diseases such as measles. It may suggest temporary __(5)__ for some patients to keep the disease from spreading. The CDC also sponsors __(6)__ to discover which __(7)__ may cause a certain disease. The CDC tries to stop any conditions that could create a health __(8)__.

1. _____
2. _____
3. _____
4. _____
5. _____
6. _____
7. _____
8. _____

Try This CHALLENGE

Yes or No? Write *yes* if the underlined word is used correctly. Write *no* if it is not.

9. Stay away from me if your illness is <u>contagious</u>.
10. Betsy had an <u>epidemic</u> headache last night.
11. Alan was kept in <u>isolation</u> when he had chicken pox.
12. Eating fatty, salty foods can be a health <u>hazard</u>.

9. _____
10. _____
11. _____
12. _____

★★★ Fact File

In the 1850s Louis Pasteur discovered that many diseases were caused by bacteria. He invented pasteurization, a process that kills germs with heat. Today, much of the food we eat is pasteurized.

173

Suffixes: -ance, -ence, -ate

performance

-ance

_____

_____

_____

_____

_____

-ence

_____

_____

_____

_____

_____

_____

_____

-ate

_____

_____

_____

_____

_____

_____

Read and Say

Basic

READ the sentences.
SAY each bold word.

1. performance	His **performance** in the play was perfect.
2. audience	The **audience** loved the program.
3. appearance	Her messy **appearance** was unusual.
4. entrance	This door is the **entrance** to the building.
5. silence	The speaker tried to **silence** the crowd.
6. appreciate	I **appreciate** your concern for my health.
7. desperate	The thirsty child was **desperate** for water.
8. sentence	This **sentence** needs a period.
9. celebrate	We will **celebrate** with a party.
10. absence	Was your **absence** due to illness?
11. fortunate	I was **fortunate** to find my lost wallet.
12. violence	The **violence** of the storm scared us.
13. allowance	I spent my **allowance** for this week.
14. instance	What excuse will he use in this **instance**?
15. associate	I **associate** picnics with ants.
16. difference	The **difference** in our ages is two years.
17. separate	My sister and I rode in **separate** cars.
18. influence	Amy is a good **influence** on me.
19. importance	Farmers know the **importance** of rain.
20. considerate	Frank is **considerate** of my feelings.

Think and Write

Each word ends with a suffix. The suffixes *-ance* and *-ence* are pronounced the same. The suffix *-ate* may be pronounced two ways.

|əns| or |ns| import**ance**, sil**ence** |ĭt| desper**ate** |āt| appreci**ate**

• What two patterns spell the final |əns| and |ns| sounds? What pattern can spell the final |ĭt| and |āt| sounds?

Now write each Basic Word under its suffix.

Review	23. distance	**Challenge**	28. illuminate
21. imitate	24. educate	26. exaggerate	29. elaborate
22. decorate	25. science	27. resemblance	30. significance

Independent Practice

Spelling Strategy When you hear the final |əns|
and |ns| sounds, think of the patterns *ance* and *ence*.
When you hear the final |ĭt| or |āt| sounds, think of the
pattern *ate*.

Word Analysis/Phonics Complete the exercises with Basic Words.

1–2. Write the two words that have the |ī| sound.

3–7. Write the five words that have double consonants.

Vocabulary: Analogies Write a Basic Word to complete
each analogy.

8. *Leave* is to *exit* as *arrive* is to _____.

9. *Sad* is to *happy* as *mourn* is to _____.

10. *Jealous* is to *envious* as *lucky* is to _____.

11. *Letter* is to *word* as *word* is to _____.

12. *Comfort* is to *comfortable*
as *despair* is to _____.

13. *Together* is to *apart* as
join is to _____.

Challenge Words Write the Challenge
Word that fits each clue. Use your
Spelling Dictionary.

14. An heirloom has this.

15. tell a "tall tale"

16. synonym for *likeness*

17. provide with light

18. what you would call a detailed costume

Spelling-Meaning Connection

Absence is the noun form of *absent*.
Remembering how the *t* changes to *ce* in this
pair of words can help you predict the
spelling change in other words with the same
pattern, such as *silent* and *silence*.

absent
absence

19–20. Write *absent*. Then write the Basic Word that is related
to *absent* in spelling and meaning.

Word Analysis

1. _____
2. _____
3. _____
4. _____
5. _____
6. _____
7. _____

Vocabulary

8. _____
9. _____
10. _____
11. _____
12. _____
13. _____

Challenge Words

14. _____
15. _____
16. _____
17. _____
18. _____

Spelling-Meaning

19. _____
20. _____

Adding Suffixes

1. _____
2. _____
3. _____
4. _____
5. _____
6. _____
7. _____
8. _____
9. _____
10. _____
11. _____
12. _____
13. _____
14. _____
15. _____

Puzzle Play

16. _____
17. _____
18. _____
19. _____
20. _____
21. _____
22. _____
23. _____
24. _____
25. _____

Review: Spelling Spree

Adding Suffixes Write the Basic or Review Word that has each base word below. The spelling of a base word may change.

1. consider
2. allow
3. absent
4. appear
5. distant
6. fortune
7. differ
8. important
9. despair
10. silent
11. perform
12. violent
13. decor
14. instant
15. enter

Puzzle Play Write a Basic or Review Word to fit each clue. Circle each letter that would appear in the box.

Example: significance _ _ ☐ _ _ _ _ _ _ _   *importance*

16. connect in one's mind _ ☐ _ _ _ _ _ _
17. to have an effect on someone _ _ _ _ _ _ _ ☐ _
18. a complete thought _ _ _ _ _ _ _ ☐
19. hand-clappers _ _ _ _ _ ☐ _ _
20. to develop the mind ☐ _ _ _ _ _ _
21. not part of a group ☐ _ _ _ _ _ _ _
22. talk and act like someone else _ _ _ _ ☐ _ _
23. to recognize the value of _ _ _ _ _ ☐ _ _ _ _
24. what you do on your birthday _ _ _ _ _ _ _ ☐ _
25. biology, for example ☐ _ _ _ _ _ _

Now write the circled letters in order. They will spell two theater-related words.

Mystery Words: _ _ _ _ _ _ _   _ _ _ _

How Are You Doing?

Write each spelling word as a partner reads it aloud. Did you misspell any words?

176

Proofreading and Writing

Proofread: Spelling and Business Letters Capitalize and punctuate the greeting and closing of a business letter correctly.

GREETING: **D**ear Sir or Madam**:**

CLOSING: **S**incerely**,**

Use proofreading marks to correct five misspelled Basic or Review Words, three mistakes in capitalization, and two mistakes in punctuation in this partial business letter.

Example: yours ~~truely~~ *truly*

Dear sir or madam,

I was in the audience during a recent

performance of Us. During intermission I saw a

help-wanted sign for a design assosiate posted near the

enterance to the theater. I decerate sets and would greatly

appricate an interview for this job.

sincerely yours;

Abigail Cary

Abigail Cary

Write a Business Letter

Who is your favorite actor? Write a business letter to the actor, telling what you like best about his or her work. Try to use five spelling words.

Check that you used correct capitalization and punctuation in the greeting and the closing of your business letter.

Proofreading Tip

Proofreading Marks

¶   Indent
∧   Add
⊙   Add a period
  Delete
≡   Capital letter
/   Small letter
∿   Reverse order

Expanding Vocabulary

Spelling Word Link

audience

audio
auditory
audition
audible
auditorium

The Word Root *aud* The word root *aud* comes from the Latin word *audire,* meaning "to hear."

The **aud**ience laughed when they heard the joke.

Match a word in the box with each definition on the cassettes. Write the word below its definition. Use your Spelling Dictionary.

Capable of being heard

1. _____

To give a trial performance

5. _____

Large room or building for a big audience

2. _____

aud

Of or for the reproduction or broadcasting of sound

4. _____

Of hearing or the organ of hearing

3. _____

Work Together With a partner write a sentence to answer each question. Use the words in the box. Use a separate sheet of paper.

6. If you are asked to speak louder, what is wrong with your voice?
7. Where might you listen to a speaker?
8. If you want a part in the school play, what must you do?
9. If you purchase loudspeakers, what kind of equipment are you buying?
10. What type of organ is the ear?

Real-World Connection

Performing Arts: Theater All the words in the box relate to the theater. Look up these words in your Spelling Dictionary. Then write the words to complete this middle school course description.

Drama Department Courses

Students who take theater classes study how to act in a hilarious __(1)__, in a suspenseful, romantic __(2)__, and in a sad __(3)__. Each student is the star in one scene and the star's __(4)__ in another. Students learn how to act in group scenes as well as how to deliver a __(5)__ alone on stage. They study __(6)__ so that they can communicate without speaking and learn to __(7)__ so that they can act without a script. They master how to handle a __(8)__, such as a broom.

Spelling Word Link

performance

comedy
tragedy
melodrama
pantomime
improvise
monologue
prop
understudy

1. _____
2. _____
3. _____
4. _____
5. _____
6. _____
7. _____
8. _____

Try This CHALLENGE

Questions and Answers Write a word from the box to answer each question.

9. What do actors do if they forget their lines?
10. A performer using an invisible hat is doing what?
11. What might a stagehand call a toaster?
12. Who would replace the star of a play if she were sick?

9. _____
10. _____
11. _____
12. _____

Fact File

Thespis, a Greek dramatist and actor who lived in the sixth century B.C., is credited with creating the type of drama called tragedy. The word *thespian*, meaning "actor," comes from his name.

Prefixes: *per-, pre-, pro-*

per-

_____

_____

_____

_____

pre-

_____

_____

_____

_____

_____

_____

pro-

_____

_____

_____

_____

_____

_____

_____

Read and Say

READ the sentences. **SAY** each bold word.

Basic

1.	preview	We saw a **preview** of the movie.
2.	prehistoric	These fossils are **prehistoric**.
3.	prohibit	The rules **prohibit** running in school.
4.	permanent	Is this ink **permanent** or washable?
5.	permission	I have **permission** to stay up late.
6.	proceed	Please **proceed** with the story.
7.	project	We worked hard on our art **project**.
8.	profession	Will she choose the dental **profession**?
9.	progress	Did you make **progress** in your work?
10.	predict	I **predict** that you will win the contest.
11.	prepare	Please **prepare** dinner for us.
12.	promise	I **promise** to wash the dishes.
13.	prepaid	The lunches on the trip are **prepaid**.
14.	persuade	Did he **persuade** his friends to help?
15.	product	This **product** makes skin feel soft.
16.	persist	Must you **persist** in teasing your brother?
17.	perfume	That **perfume** smells like roses.
18.	prospect	She has the **prospect** of going to the fair.
19.	previous	We read this book in a **previous** class.
20.	process	What is the **process** for making cheese?

Think and Write

Each word begins with a prefix. Note the prefix, the base word or the word root, and any ending to help you spell the words.

permission   preview   proceed

• What three prefixes do you see?

Now write each Basic Word under its prefix.

Review	23. permit	**Challenge**	28. preservation
21. program	24. perhaps	26. procure	29. perspective
22. preserve	25. providing	27. perception	30. precipitation

Independent Practice

Spelling Strategy Many words begin with the prefix *per-*, *pre-*, or *pro-*. Find the prefix, the base word or the word root, and any ending. Spell the word by parts.

Word Analysis/Phonics Complete the exercises with Basic Words.

1–2. Write the two words that have the |s| sound spelled *c*.

3–4. Write the two words that have the |sh| sound spelled *ss*.

5–7. Write the three words that have these base words.

5. view **6.** history **7.** pay

Vocabulary: Synonyms Write the Basic Word that is a synonym for each word below.

8. lasting **10.** convince **12.** earlier
9. improvement **11.** continue **13.** forbid

Challenge Words Write the Challenge Word that completes each sentence. Use your Spelling Dictionary.

14. The museum is showing a film about the _____ of wildlife.

15. Eduardo volunteered to _____ tickets for the next show.

16. I brought my umbrella with me because of the heavy _____.

17. Ellen often wins at tennis because she has good depth _____.

18. Jean learned how to show size and _____ in her drawings.

Spelling-Meaning Connection

Predict includes the word root *dict*, meaning "to tell." The word *predict* means "to tell before." Knowing the word root *dict* can help you spell and understand the related words *dictate* and *dictionary*.

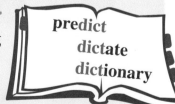

predict
dictate
dictionary

19–20. Write *dictate*. Then write the Basic Word that has the same word root.

Word Analysis

1. _____
2. _____
3. _____
4. _____
5. _____
6. _____
7. _____

Vocabulary

8. _____
9. _____
10. _____
11. _____
12. _____
13. _____

Challenge Words

14. _____
15. _____
16. _____
17. _____
18. _____

Spelling-Meaning

19. _____
20. _____

Word Root Hunt

1. _____
2. _____
3. _____
4. _____
5. _____
6. _____
7. _____
8. _____
9. _____
10. _____
11. _____
12. _____
13. _____
14. _____
15. _____
16. _____

Word Dinosaur

17. _____
18. _____
19. _____
20. _____
21. _____
22. _____
23. _____
24. _____
25. _____

Review: Spelling Spree

Word Root Hunt Write the Basic or Review Word that has the same root as each word below.

Example: compare *prepare*

1. resist
2. confession
3. remit
4. inhibit
5. diagram
6. dissuade
7. exceed
8. reserve
9. access
10. obvious
11. admission
12. regress
13. contradict
14. inspect
15. deduct
16. reject

Word Dinosaur 17–25. Begin at the arrow and follow the letters to find nine Basic or Review Words. Write the words in order. Don't let the other words fool you.

How Are You Doing?

List the spelling words that are hard for you. Practice them with a partner.

Proofreading and Writing

Proofread: Spelling and Commas in Headings Use a comma between the names of the city and the state and between the day and the year in a letter heading.

Waterbury, CT 06701   March 2, 1999

Use proofreading marks to correct five misspelled Basic or Review Words and three missing or incorrect commas in this friendly letter.

Example: ~~Febuary~~ *February* 5, 1999

21 Guild Drive

Lowell MA, 01852

April 26 1999

Dear Aunt Celeste,

My class's project on prehistorec tools is the main progam at the Lee Museum this month. Wednesday is the preveiw. Can I perswade you to come with us? I promis you will not be bored.

Love,

Katrina

Basic

1. preview
2. prehistoric
3. prohibit
4. permanent
5. permission
6. proceed
7. project
8. profession
9. progress
10. predict
11. prepare
12. promise
13. prepaid
14. persuade
15. product
16. persist
17. perfume
18. prospect
19. previous
20. process

Review

21. program
22. preserve
23. permit
24. perhaps
25. providing

Challenge

26. procure
27. perception
28. preservation
29. perspective
30. precipitation

Write a Letter

Write a friendly letter that Katrina's aunt might have written in response. Use your own address in the heading. Try to use five spelling words.

MUSEUM PASS

Check that you used commas correctly in your letter heading.

Proofreading Tip

Proofreading Marks

¶ Indent
∧ Add
⊙ Add a period
ϟ Delete
≡ Capital letter
/ Small letter
∽ Reverse order

Expanding Vocabulary

Easily Confused Words *Proceed* and *precede* look and sound similar, but the different prefixes affect their meanings. *Pre-* means "before." *Pro-* means "forward."

precede |prĭ sēd'| *v.* To go before: *Breakfast precedes supper.*

proceed |prə sēd'| *v.* To go forward: *A car proceeded down the road.*

1. _____

2. _____

3. _____

4. _____

5. _____

6. _____

Write *precede* or *proceed* to complete each sentence.

1. The guide will _____ us into the display area.
2. Follow the yellow line to _____ through the display.
3. Now we will _____ to a show about prehistoric birds.
4. If we are late, many people will _____ us in line.
5. A few opening words will _____ the lecture.
6. After the talk we will _____ to the gift shop.

Show You Know! Write a sentence for each picture. Use *proceed* in one and *precede* in the other. Write on a separate sheet of paper.

Real-World Connection

Science: Museums All the words in the box relate to museums. Look up these words in your Spelling Dictionary. Then write the words to complete this journal entry.

Spelling Word Link

prehistoric

museum
exhibit
dinosaur
specimen
skeleton
interactive
diorama
planetarium

Today our class visited the science __(1)__. We saw the bony __(2)__ of a one hundred million-year-old __(3)__. There was also a real fossil __(4)__, as well as plastic models. I could have spent hours at the permanent computer __(5)__, where I used an __(6)__ video program to learn about electricity. The wildlife wing has a __(7)__ showing jungle animals in their natural environment. What I liked best, though, was the tour of the solar system that was part of the show in the __(8)__.

1. _____
2. _____
3. _____
4. _____
5. _____
6. _____
7. _____
8. _____

Try This CHALLENGE

Write a Proposal What makes a museum exhibit exciting? Write a proposal for a dinosaur exhibit that will captivate museum-goers. Try to use some words from the box. Draw a floor plan to go with your proposal if you like.

⭐⭐ **Fact File**

Science museums often display dinosaur skeletons on metal frames. Because scientists rarely find entire skeletons, they replace missing bones with pieces made of plaster, fiberglass, or plastic.

30 Review: Units 25–29

|sh| **glacier**

ancient	caution	glacier	pressure	polish
portion	cushion	edition	musician	mission

Spelling Strategy   When you hear the |sh| sound, think of the patterns **sh**, **ti**, **ci**, and **ss**.

Write the word that matches each definition.

1. very old
2. an assignment that a group of persons is sent to carry out
3. a pillow used to sit, lie, or rest on
4. a part of a larger thing
5. a large mass of slowly moving ice
6. to warn against possible trouble or danger

Write a word by adding the letters that make the |sh| sound.

7. pre _ _ ure   9. poli _ _
8. musi _ _ an   10. edi _ _ on

1. _____
2. _____
3. _____
4. _____
5. _____
6. _____
7. _____
8. _____
9. _____
10. _____

half   staff
halves   staffs

cellos	staffs	stereos	chiefs	halves
volcanoes	echoes	calves	shelves	ratios

Spelling Strategy

ff → **ffs**   f → **fs** or **ves**
vowel + o → **os**   consonant + o → **os** or **oes**

Write the word that belongs in each group.

11. puppies, colts, _____   14. quarters, thirds, _____
12. rulers, leaders, _____   15. workers, employees, _____
13. violins, guitars, _____   16. records, speakers, _____

Write the word that fits each clue.

17. You can put your books on these.
18. Hot, melted rock can flow out of these.
19. They show relationships between numbers.
20. They repeat what you say.

11. _____
12. _____
13. _____
14. _____
15. _____
16. _____
17. _____
18. _____
19. _____
20. _____

Unit 27   Prefixes: *dis-*, *ex-*, *inter-*   pages 168–173

experiment	disease	experience	interrupt	extreme
interfere	interview	discourage	expensive	disguise

ex haust

Spelling Strategy   **Dis-**, **ex-**, and **inter-** are prefixes. To spell a word with a prefix, find the prefix, the base word or the word root, and any ending. Spell the word by parts.

Write a word by adding *dis-*, *ex-*, or *inter-* to each word part.

21. _____ | periment   **24.** _____ | ease
22. _____ | courage   **25.** _____ | perience
23. _____ | treme   **26.** _____ | view

Write the word that answers each question.
27. Which word is an antonym for *reveal*?
28. Which word is a synonym for *meddle*?
29. Which word is an antonym for *continue*?
30. Which word is a synonym for *costly*?

21. _____
22. _____
23. _____
24. _____
25. _____
26. _____
27. _____
28. _____
29. _____
30. _____

Unit 28   Suffixes: *-ance*, *-ence*, *-ate*   pages 174–179

audience	desperate	entrance	appreciate	appearance
separate	influence	associate	importance	difference

performance

Spelling Strategy

final |əns| or |ns| → **ance**, **ence**   final |ĭt| or |āt| → **ate**

Write the word that completes each sentence.
31. I did not let the opinions of my friends _____ my choice.
32. Pablo Picasso is a name we _____ with modern art.
33. I do not need any help, but I _____ your offer.
34. After the hot, dusty hike, Sandy was _____ for water.

Write the word that fits each clue.
35. what a doorway is   **38.** people watching a movie
36. how you look   **39.** an unlikeness
37. what walls do   **40.** what something you value has

31. _____
32. _____
33. _____
34. _____
35. _____
36. _____
37. _____
38. _____
39. _____
40. _____

prehistoric

Unit 29   Prefixes: *per-, pre-, pro-*   pages 180–185

permanent	prohibit	predict	permission	preview
prospect	persuade	process	previous	persist

Spelling Strategy   Many words begin with the prefix **per-**, **pre-**, or **pro-**. Find the prefix, the base word or the word root, and any ending. Spell the word by parts.

Write a word by changing the underlined prefix.

41. <u>re</u>spect   **44.** <u>inter</u>view
42. <u>in</u>sist   **45.** <u>ex</u>cess
43. <u>trans</u>mission   **46.** <u>de</u>vious

Write the word that completes each analogy.

47. *Movable* is to *fixed* as *temporary* is to _____.
48. *Amuse* is to *entertain* as *convince* is to _____.
49. *Begin* is to *quit* as *allow* is to _____.
50. *Realize* is to *know* as *foretell* is to _____.

41. _____
42. _____
43. _____
44. _____
45. _____
46. _____
47. _____
48. _____
49. _____
50. _____

Challenge Words   Units 25–29   pages 156–185

expedition disinfectant vetoes   resemblance interdependent
beneficial   perspective   piccolos significance   precipitation

Write the word that answers each question.

51. Which word is an antonym for *approvals*?
52. Which word is a synonym for *view*?
53. Which word is an antonym for *harmful*?
54. Which word is a synonym for *importance*?
55. Which word is an antonym for *difference*?
56. Which word is an antonym for *independent*?

Write the word that belongs in each group.

57. rain, snow, _____
58. clarinets, flutes, _____
59. trip, journey, _____
60. cleanser, antiseptic, _____

51. _____
52. _____
53. _____
54. _____
55. _____
56. _____
57. _____
58. _____
59. _____
60. _____

Spelling-Meaning Strategy

Consonant Changes: *t* to *ce*

The spelling of many adjectives that end with *-ent* or *-ant* changes to form the related noun. Read the paragraph.

Ralph bought a **different** brand of peanut butter, which he thought tasted much better than his usual brand. Colleen could not tell the **difference** between the two.

Think

- How are *different* and *difference* related in meaning?
- How are they different in spelling?

Here are other pairs of related words that have the same spelling change as *different* and *difference*.

permanen**t**	distan**t**	prominen**t**
permanen**ce**	distan**ce**	prominen**ce**

differen**t**
differen**ce**

Apply and Extend

Complete these activities on a separate sheet of paper.

1. Look up the words in the word box above in your Spelling Dictionary, and write their meanings. Then write a short paragraph, using one pair of words.

2. With a partner look at the Basic Words in Unit 23. Using words from that word list, write as many word pairs as you can that have the same spelling change as the pairs in the word box. Then look in the section "Consonant Changes: *t* to *ce*," beginning on page 273 of your Spelling-Meaning Index. Add any other pairs with that spelling pattern that you find.

Summing Up

Knowing the spelling change in one pair of words can help you predict the change in similar pairs of words with the same spelling pattern.

Persuasive Letter

In "The Gorillagram," by E. M. Hunnicutt, two girls raise money using gorilla costumes. Mai read that story, and then she wrote this letter. What does she want Mr. Lopez to do?

43 College Street
Arlington, MA 02174
April 7, 1999

Mr. George Lopez
Vintage Costumes
2305 Main Street
Arlington, MA 02174

Dear Mr. Lopez:

As you know, Valley Middle School is renting costumes from you for its annual musical. Would you be willing to lend us, at no extra charge, two gorilla suits as well? We want to use them in the lobby during intermission; two "gorillas" will perform a skit and collect donations for additional band instruments. You will be helping young musicians, since Valley lends instruments to students who can't buy them. This year there are 110 students in the band and the orchestra. Thirty of them are using school instruments.

I promise that we will take good care of these additional costumes. Valley Middle School has been renting costumes from you for many years, and we have always returned them in perfect condition.

Sincerely,
Mai Lin
Mai Lin

Think and Discuss

1. What does Mai want to persuade the company to do?

2. What reason does Mai use? What fact does she give to support it?

3. What objection does Mai answer?

4. Explain the six parts of a business letter. See page 253 for a model.

The Writing Process
Persuasive Letter

What would you like to persuade someone to do? Write a business letter to that person. Use the Guidelines for Persuading, and follow the Writing Process.

1 Prewriting
- In a chart, list the reasons and supporting facts and examples that might persuade your audience.
- Debate your argument with a partner. What objections came up?

2 Draft
- Follow each reason with its support.

3 Revise
- Put your reasons in the order that is most convincing.
- Use your Thesaurus to find exact words.
- Have a writing conference. Is your listener convinced?

4 Proofread
- Did you spell each word correctly?
- Did you use capital letters and punctuation marks correctly?

5 Publish
- Mail a neat final copy of your letter.

Guidelines for Persuading

✓ Introduce the problem or goal.
✓ State your goal clearly.
✓ Support strong reasons with facts or examples. Answer objections.
✓ Conclude by encouraging an action.

Composition Words

official
discovery
experience
interview
celebrate
importance
persuade
promise

Words with *ie* or *ei*

diesel   freight

i Comes Before e

_____

_____

_____

_____

_____

_____

_____

_____

_____

ei Follows c

_____

_____

_____

ei Spells |ā|

_____

_____

_____

_____

Other Spelling Patterns

_____

_____

_____

Read and Say

Basic

READ the sentences. **SAY** each bold word.

1. freight — Is lumber the only **freight** on that ship?
2. receipt — I got a **receipt** when I paid for the bike.
3. yield — Cars should **yield** to people on foot.
4. review — The newspaper has a **review** of that movie.
5. belief — I share your **belief** in his honesty.
6. eighty — Her grandfather is **eighty** years old.
7. brief — The judge gave a **brief** speech to the jury.
8. ceiling — The room has tall windows and a high **ceiling**.
9. neither — He likes **neither** dogs nor cats.
10. foreign — This display shows different **foreign** coins.
11. shield — The knight carried a **shield**.
12. diesel — Most large trucks run on **diesel** fuel.
13. reign — The old king had a long and peaceful **reign**.
14. fiery — The sunset was a **fiery** red.
15. conceit — Do his **conceit** and boastfulness bother you?
16. veil — A **veil** covered the bride's face.
17. grief — The loss of his dog caused him **grief**.
18. relieve — I hope the good news will **relieve** her worry.
19. seize — Why did you **seize** the ball from him?
20. leisure — I spend my **leisure** time shooting baskets.

Think and Write

Each word has the *ie* or *ei* vowel pair. Most of the words follow this rule: "Use *i* before *e* except after *c* or in words with the |ā| sound, as in *weigh*." Memorize the spellings of words that do not follow this rule.

y**ie**ld   rec**ei**pt   fr**ei**ght

• Which Basic Words follow the rule for using *ie* or *ei*? How are the Elephant Words different?

Now write each Basic Word under its spelling pattern.

Review		
	23. niece	
21. piece	24. pier	
22. thief	25. mischief	

Challenge		
	28. wield	
26. retrieve	29. eerie	
27. deceit	30. hygiene	

Independent Practice

![Spelling Strategy icon] **Spelling Strategy**   Use *i* before *e* except after *c* or in words with the |ā| sound, as in *weigh*. You must memorize exceptions to this generalization.

Word Analysis/Phonics   Complete the exercises with Basic Words.

1. Write the word that ends with the |zhər| sounds.
2. Write the word that is a homophone for *sees*.
3. Write the word that rhymes with *either*.
4. Write the word in which *c* spells both the |k| and the |s| sounds.

5–8. Write the four words that have a silent *g*.

Vocabulary: Classifying   Write the Basic Word that belongs with each group of words.

9. hat, scarf, _____
10. steam, electric, _____
11. floor, walls, _____
12. hot, glowing, _____
13. armor, helmet, _____

Challenge Words   Write the Challenge Word that fits each clue. Use your Spelling Dictionary.

14. antonym for *honesty*
15. synonym for *handle*
16. what a dog might do
17. good health practices
18. synonym for *weird*

Spelling-Meaning Connection

How can you remember that *receipt* has a silent *p*? Think of the related word *reception*, in which the *p* is pronounced.

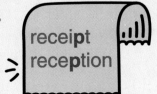

receipt
reception

19–20. Write *receipt* and *reception*. In both words underline the letter that is pronounced in one word and silent in the other.

Word Analysis

1. _____
2. _____
3. _____
4. _____
5. _____
6. _____
7. _____
8. _____

Vocabulary

9. _____
10. _____
11. _____
12. _____
13. _____

Challenge Words

14. _____
15. _____
16. _____
17. _____
18. _____

Spelling-Meaning

19. _____
20. _____

Clues

1. _____
2. _____
3. _____
4. _____
5. _____
6. _____
7. _____
8. _____
9. _____
10. _____
11. _____
12. _____
13. _____

Code Breaker

14. _____
15. _____
16. _____
17. _____
18. _____
19. _____
20. _____
21. _____
22. _____
23. _____
24. _____
25. _____

Review: Spelling Spree

Clues Write a Basic or Review Word for each clue.

1. You need to stand on a ladder to paint this.
2. A knight in armor might carry this.
3. You might listen to music during this time.
4. You could tie your boat to this.
5. Monarchs do this.
6. A stubborn person will never do this.
7. The death of a favorite pet would make you feel this.
8. You should do this before a test.
9. A person who is too proud feels this.
10. Little children are always getting into this.
11. Brides often wear one.
12. You should get this answer when you multiply 8 by 10.
13. A train might carry this instead of passengers.

Code Breaker Some Basic and Review Words have been written in code. Use the code below to figure out each word. Then write the words correctly.

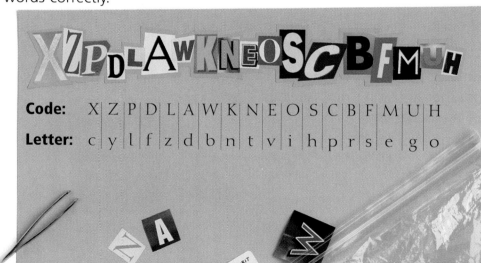

Code:	X	Z	P	D	L	A	W	K	N	E	O	S	C	B	F	M	U	H
Letter:	c	y	l	f	z	d	b	n	t	v	i	h	p	r	s	e	g	o

Example: XMOPOKU *ceiling*

14. KOMXM
15. DOMBZ
16. WBOMD
17. FMOLM
18. NSOMD
19. COMXM
20. AOMFMP
21. BMPOMEM
22. KMONSMB
23. WMPOMD
24. BMXMOCN
25. DHBMOUK

How Are You Doing?

Write your spelling words in ABC order. Practice any misspelled words with a partner.

Proofreading and Writing

Proofread: Spelling and Quotations Capitalize the first word of a quotation. Place the end punctuation inside the quotation marks.

"The new imports will arrive next week," said Eva.

Use proofreading marks to correct six misspelled Basic or Review Words, a missing capital letter, and two punctuation errors in this news article.

Example: "our inquiry will ~~yeild~~ *yield* answers", said Captain Ene.

Ship Burns in Port

NEW YORK A merchant ship carrying frieght from foreign ports burned at its peir last night, turning the sky a firey red. Two fire boats and five fire engines were at the scene.

"there were one hundred eaghty cars on board," said Sy Ene, the ship's captain. "Sadly, niether the forward nor the aft cargo was saved." He turned to the fire chief. "Do you know yet what caused this fire"? he asked.

"We will review each piece of evidence", said the chief, "but it's my beleaf that leaking diesel fuel may have been the cause."

Basic

1. freight
2. receipt
3. yield
4. review
5. belief
6. eighty
7. brief
8. ceiling
9. neither
10. foreign
11. shield
12. diesel
13. reign
14. fiery
15. conceit
16. veil
17. grief
18. relieve
19. seize
20. leisure

Review

21. piece
22. thief
23. niece
24. pier
25. mischief

Challenge

26. retrieve
27. deceit
28. wield
29. eerie
30. hygiene

Write a Conversation

Write a brief conversation between two fire fighters battling the blaze on the merchant ship. Try to use five spelling words and at least two quotations.

Proofreading Tip

Check that you have used capitalization and punctuation in quotations correctly.

Proofreading Marks

¶ Indent
∧ Add
⊙ Add a period
⌐ Delete
≡ Capital letter
/ Small letter
∿ Reverse order

Expanding Vocabulary

maverick
guppy
pants
praline
saxophone
mesmerize
cardigan
sideburns

Words from Names The diesel engine is named after its inventor, Rudolph Diesel. The names of some other people, such as those listed below, have also become English words.

Franz Mesmer, Austrian physician who introduced hypnotism as a cure for certain illnesses

R. J. Lechmere Guppy, discoverer of a small type of fish

Samuel Maverick, rancher whose unbranded cattle often did not stay with the herd

Maréchal Duplessis-Praslin, French army officer whose chef developed a confection of nut kernels and sugar

Adolphe Sax, instrument-maker who perfected a curved, conical wind instrument

Pantaleone, masked character in Italian comedy often shown wearing a tight-fitting combination of trousers and leggings

The Seventh Earl of Cardigan, British general who wore sweaters that buttoned down the front

Everett Burnside, Civil War general who wore short side whiskers and shaved his chin

Write a word from the box that completes each sentence. Use the clues above and your Spelling Dictionary.

1. Daryl plays the _____ in a jazz band.
2. We will each have ice cream and a _____ for dessert.
3. I prefer a _____ to a pullover sweater.
4. Gary is a _____ who doesn't like to follow the crowd.
5. Some men grow their _____ down their cheeks.
6. I want to have at least one _____ in my aquarium.
7. Please wear long _____ and a jacket and tie.
8. The clown will _____ the children with his antics.

1. _____
2. _____
3. _____
4. _____
5. _____
6. _____
7. _____
8. _____

Work Together With a partner write a sentence for each word in the box. Write on another sheet of paper.

Real-World Connection

Social Studies: World Trade All the words in the box relate to world trade. Look up these words in your Spelling Dictionary. Then write the words to complete this paragraph.

TARIFF

Trade, or __(1)__, began thousands of years ago. Early traders usually did not use money; they would __(2)__ goods. Later, as countries developed their own __(3)__, governments placed a tax called a __(4)__ on foreign goods to make them more costly and less competitive with their __(5)__ products. Sometimes a company was able to have sole control, or a __(6)__, over one __(7)__ so that it could charge higher prices. Then some people would try to __(8)__ cheaper goods into the country.

Spelling Word Link

freight

commerce
domestic
resources
tariff
monopoly
commodity
barter
smuggle

1. _____
2. _____
3. _____
4. _____
5. _____
6. _____
7. _____
8. _____

Try This CHALLENGE

Yes or No? Write *yes* if the underlined word is used correctly. Write *no* if it is not.

9. That waiter deserves a <u>tariff</u> for being helpful.
10. The farmer was able to <u>barter</u> fruits for fish.
11. The thief tried to <u>smuggle</u> the furs into the country.
12. Oil is a valuable <u>commodity</u> for a country to have.

9. _____
10. _____
11. _____
12. _____

⭐⭐⭐ **Fact File**

A country's money pictures people and things that are important to the country. In Guatemala, for example, the basic unit of currency is the quetzal, named after the national bird. Similarly, the United States once had a coin called an eagle, worth about ten dollars.

The Prefix *ad-*

account
addition

ad- Spelled ad

_____

_____

_____

_____

ad- Spelled ac

_____

_____

_____

_____

_____

_____

ad- Spelled ap

_____

_____

_____

_____

ad- Spelled as

_____

_____

_____

_____

ad- Spelled af

_____

Read and Say

READ the sentences. **SAY** each bold word.

Basic

1. account	I wrote an **account** of my trip to Alaska.
2. addition	Is my **addition** right on this math problem?
3. accurate	Your math answers are all **accurate**.
4. approve	My dad does not **approve** of my table manners.
5. advice	I took your **advice** and wore a jacket.
6. assist	May I **assist** you with that heavy box?
7. affair	Dinner is a formal **affair** at my house.
8. advise	I **advise** you to visit the dentist regularly.
9. applaud	Did the audience **applaud** the actors?
10. assure	I can **assure** you that it won't rain today.
11. assume	I **assume** that you will walk to school with me.
12. adjust	You need to **adjust** that crooked picture.
13. appeal	After the flood there was an **appeal** for help.
14. accuse	Did the police **accuse** him of a crime?
15. assign	Our teacher did not **assign** homework today.
16. accomplish	Did you **accomplish** your goal?
17. approach	Your **approach** to this problem is helpful.
18. according	You must play **according** to the rules.
19. acquire	Did you **acquire** that book recently?
20. assemble	My sister and I will **assemble** the bike.

Think and Write

Each word begins with the prefix *ad-*. Sometimes the spelling of *ad-* changes to match the first letter, or the sound of the first letter, of the base word or word root.

advise   **ac**count   **ac**quire   **ap**prove   **as**sist   **af**fair

• What are five spellings for the prefix *ad-*? Before which consonants does the spelling of *ad-* change?

Now write each Basic Word under its spelling of the prefix *ad-*.

Review	23. adventure	**Challenge**	28. accumulate
21. address	24. adore	26. approximate	29. affiliated
22. accident	25. arrive	27. appropriate	30. applicant

Independent Practice

Spelling Strategy Remember that the prefix *ad-* can be spelled *ac, ap, as,* or *af* to match the first consonant or consonant sound of the base word or the word root.

Word Analysis/Phonics Complete the exercises with Basic Words.

1. Write the word that has the |o͞o| sound spelled with an *o*.

2–3. Write the two words with the |sh| sound spelled with *ti* or *ss*.

4–5. Write the words that have these letters.

    4. a silent *g*   **5.** a silent *d*

Vocabulary: Definitions Write the Basic Word that fits each definition.

  6. to put together
  7. to clap hands
  8. to achieve or complete
  9. a financial record
10. an urgent request
11. to help

12. to offer guidance
13. to blame someone

Challenge Words Write the Challenge Word that completes each sentence. Use your Spelling Dictionary.

14. Our accounting club is _____ with a national group.

15. Beth is an _____ for the job of club treasurer.

16. Our teacher told us the _____ amount of money we have.

17. We decided to try to _____ seventy-five dollars by May.

18. Then we discussed _____ ways to spend the money.

Spelling-Meaning Connection

Knowing that the prefix *ad-* changes its spelling before certain consonants can help you remember to double the consonants in most words with this prefix, such as *assume* and *approach*.

assume
approach

19–20. Write *assume* and *approach*. Underline the prefix and the following consonant in each word.

Word Analysis

1. _____
2. _____
3. _____
4. _____
5. _____

Vocabulary

6. _____
7. _____
8. _____
9. _____
10. _____
11. _____
12. _____
13. _____

Challenge Words

14. _____
15. _____
16. _____
17. _____
18. _____

Spelling-Meaning

19. _____
20. _____

Idioms

1. _____

2. _____

3. _____

4. _____

5. _____

Changing Prefixes

6. _____

7. _____

8. _____

9. _____

10. _____

11. _____

12. _____

13. _____

14. _____

15. _____

16. _____

17. _____

18. _____

19. _____

20. _____

Dictionary

Idioms To find an idiom in the dictionary, look under the entry for the main word in the idiom.

> **ac·count** |ə kount′| _n._ A written or spoken description of events: _The explorers gave an exciting account of their adventures._ ◊**Idiom call to account.** To demand an explanation from: _He was called to account for being late so often._

Practice Write the letter of the meaning that matches each underlined idiom below. Use your Spelling Dictionary.

a. under no conditions
b. make good use of it
c. because of
d. for that reason
e. consider

1. We were delayed <u>on account of</u> the storm.
2. Arturo is honest and was elected <u>on that account</u>.
3. <u>On no account</u> should you behave rudely.
4. We must <u>take into account</u> what Cindy says.
5. If the day is rainy, turn it to <u>good account</u>.

You will be called to account for this!

On no account am I going out there now!

Review: Spelling Spree

Changing Prefixes Change the prefix in each word to write a Basic or Review Word.

Example: recording _according_

6. resume
7. discount
8. consign
9. excuse
10. repeal

11. dissemble
12. condition
13. incident
14. disprove
15. unfair

16. consist
17. unjust
18. reproach
19. unsure
20. revise

Proofreading and Writing

Proofread for Spelling Use proofreading marks to correct eleven misspelled Basic or Review Words in this memo.

Example: Soon we can ~~asist~~ *assist* you with your travel plans!

Finn & Co. Boat Builders
Future Plans

Do you addore travel and aventure? If so, we have some good news! Our company is about to aquire a travel agency. However, we may have to adress budget problems and ajust our expenses before we can afford the purchase, acording to our money managers. They have a new approach toward saving that will help us acomplish this goal. Yet they assure us that the cutbacks will not affect our salaries. The managers' predictions are usually acurate. Our bosses applaudd their good advise and hope to arive at a solution soon.

Write an Essay

Suppose that your school is offering one hundred dollars to the student who would spend that money most wisely. Write an essay explaining how you would spend the money and why. Try to use five spelling words.

Proofreading Tip

Check for words that should have double consonants.

Proofreading Marks

¶ Indent
∧ Add
⊙ Add a period
⊰ Delete
≡ Capital letter
／ Small letter
∽ Reverse order

Expanding Vocabulary

Spelling Word Link

advice
advise

Easily Confused Words Note how the noun *advice* and the verb *advise* differ in pronunciation and meaning.

ad•vice |ăd vīs′| *n.* An opinion about how to solve a problem: *Your advice helped me.*
ad•vise |ăd vīz′| *v.* **ad•vised, ad•vis•ing.** To give advice: *I advise you to go.*

1. _____
2. _____
3. _____
4. _____
5. _____

Write *advice* or *advise* to complete each sentence below.

1. Mom's banker gave her some _____ about savings accounts.
2. Please _____ us on the best route to take.
3. I would _____ you to wear your jacket.
4. I am sorry I did not follow your wise _____.
5. Your teacher can _____ you about your project.

Show You Know! Write two sentences about the picture below. Use *advice* in one sentence and *advise* in the other. Write on another sheet of paper.

So, what do you think of my first landscape? Should I add anything else?

Real-World Connection

Math: Accounting All the words in the box relate to accounting. Look up these words in your Spelling Dictionary. Then write the words to complete this paragraph about a career.

Spelling Word Link

account

asset
liability
accountant
creditor
invoice
revenue
audit
depreciate

Accountant

Every business tracks its finances in order to make plans for the future. A person called an __(1)__ records the income, or __(2)__. When the company owes money to a __(3)__, it receives an __(4)__ for the amount due. Any valuable property that the company owns is considered an __(5)__ that could be sold to pay a debt, or __(6)__. The accountant also must track the value of equipment, which will __(7)__ as it gets older. To examine the finances more closely, an outside expert may conduct an __(8)__ of the accountant's books.

1. _____
2. _____
3. _____
4. _____
5. _____
6. _____
7. _____
8. _____

Try This CHALLENGE

Yes or No? Write *yes* if the underlined word is used correctly. Write *no* if it is not.

9. Dad paid the amount shown on the <u>invoice</u>.
10. We really <u>depreciate</u> all that you have done.
11. Did you read the critic's <u>revenue</u> of that movie?
12. A tax accountant may <u>audit</u> a company's records.

9. _____
10. _____
11. _____
12. _____

Fact File

In 1862 the United States government formed the Office of Internal Revenue to collect taxes that would help pay for the Civil War. Today taxes paid to the Internal Revenue Service fund most government activities.

Endings: -ic, -ture, -ous

Read and Say

patriotic signature

Basic

READ the sentences. **SAY** each bold word.

1.	signature	Write your **signature** at the end of the letter.
2.	patriotic	The band played a **patriotic** song in the parade.
3.	democratic	This country has a **democratic** government.
4.	serious	She is a **serious** and hard-working person.
5.	nervous	Were you **nervous** before the test?
6.	terrific	The volcano erupted with a **terrific** explosion.
7.	gigantic	California has many **gigantic** redwood trees.
8.	generous	They are **generous** with their time.
9.	scientific	He made a **scientific** study of ants.
10.	temperature	Is the **temperature** under ten degrees today?
11.	tragic	That was a **tragic** accident.
12.	curious	The **curious** puppies explored the yard.
13.	jealous	I was **jealous** when he won the prize.
14.	torture	The last mile of the race was **torture** to me.
15.	furious	Mother gets **furious** when I am late for dinner.
16.	departure	What time is our **departure** for the field trip?
17.	dramatic	This book has a **dramatic** ending.
18.	fantastic	He writes fairy tales and other **fantastic** stories.
19.	numerous	She has **numerous** friends all over the world.
20.	specific	Do you want a **specific** number of nails?

Final |ĭk| Sounds

_____

_____

_____

_____

_____

_____

_____

Final |chər| Sounds

_____

_____

_____

_____

Final |əs| Sounds

_____

_____

_____

_____

_____

_____

_____

Think and Write

Each word has a final unstressed syllable with the |ĭk|, |chər|, or |əs| sounds. Pay careful attention to the spellings of these sounds in these words.

|ĭk| gigant**ic** |chər| signa**ture** |əs| nerv**ous**

What are spelling patterns for the final unstressed |ĭk|, |chər|, and |əs| sounds?

Now write each Basic Word under its final sounds.

Review	23. culture	**Challenge**	28. chronic
21. future	24. dangerous	26. unanimous	29. strategic
22. feature	25. romantic	27. symbolic	30. stature

Independent Practice

Spelling Strategy   Remember the spelling patterns for these final sounds:

final |ĭk| *ic*   final |chər| *ture*   final |əs| *ous*

Word Analysis/Phonics Complete the exercises with Basic Words.

1. Write the word that has the |ĕ| sound spelled *ea*.
2. Write the word that has a silent *c*.
3–5. Write the words that contain these base words.
   3. fury
   4. drama
   5. fantasy

Vocabulary: Antonyms Write the Basic Word that is an antonym for each word below.

6. calm
7. vague
8. arrival
9. stingy
10. tiny
11. silly
12. few
13. comic

Challenge Words Write the Challenge Word that fits each definition. Use your Spelling Dictionary.

14. height
15. having a plan of action
16. sharing the same opinion
17. lasting for a long time
18. representative of something else

Spelling-Meaning Connection

To help you remember that the |ə| sound in *democracy* is spelled *a*, think of the |ă| sound in the related word *democratic*.

19–20. Write *democracy* and *democratic*. Underline the letter in *democratic* that helps you spell the |ə| sound in *democracy*.

Word Analysis
1. _____
2. _____
3. _____
4. _____
5. _____

Vocabulary
6. _____
7. _____
8. _____
9. _____
10. _____
11. _____
12. _____
13. _____

Challenge Words
14. _____
15. _____
16. _____
17. _____
18. _____

Spelling-Meaning
19. _____
20. _____

205

Using Clues

1. _____

2. _____

3. _____

4. _____

5. _____

6. _____

7. _____

8. _____

9. _____

10. _____

11. _____

12. _____

13. _____

Puzzle Play

14. _____

15. _____

16. _____

17. _____

18. _____

19. _____

20. _____

21. _____

22. _____

23. _____

24. _____

25. _____

Review: Spelling Spree

Using Clues Write a Basic or Review Word to fit each clue.

1. This *ic* is huge.
2. This *ic* is definite.
3. This *ic* is imagined.
4. This *ous* is envious.
5. This *ous* is jittery.
6. This *ous* does not laugh.
7. This *ous* is angry.
8. This *ous* is eager to learn.
9. This *ure* is a time to come.
10. This *ure* is a characteristic.
11. This *ure* is a name.
12. This *ure* is painful.
13. This *ure* is a measure of heat or cold.

Puzzle Play Write a Basic or Review Word to fit each clue. Circle the letter that would appear in the box.

14. many _ ☐ _ _ _ _ _ _
15. risky or unsafe _ _ ☐ _ _ _ _ _ _
16. bringing great misfortune or sadness _ _ _ _ ☐ _
17. artistic and intellectual activity _ _ _ ☐ _ _ _
18. the act of going away _ ☐ _ _ _ _ _ _ _
19. theatrical ☐ _ _ _ _ _ _ _
20. having a factual basis ☐ _ _ _ _ _ _ _ _
21. feeling love for one's country _ _ ☐ _ _ _ _ _ _
22. full of the spirit of love or adventure _ _ _ ☐ _ _ _ _
23. upholding equal rights for all _ _ _ _ _ _ _ ☐ _ _
24. very great or intense _ ☐ _ _ _ _ _ _
25. unselfish _ _ _ _ _ _ _ ☐

Now write the circled letters in order. They spell two mystery words that relate to the Declaration of Independence.

Mystery Words: _ _ _ _ _ _   _ _ _ _ _ _ _

How Are You Doing?

Write each spelling word as a family member reads it aloud. Did you misspell any words?

Proofreading and Writing

Proofread: Spelling and Titles Titles of books, magazines, newspapers, and movies are underlined. Titles of short stories, articles, songs, book chapters, and most poems are enclosed in quotation marks. Capitalize the first, last, and all important words.

A chapter called "**T**he **F**reedom **F**ighters" is in the book <u>**G**reat **A**mericans</u>.

Use proofreading marks to correct five misspelled words, three missing capital letters, and two errors in punctuating titles in this reading list.

Example: Read the article A Historic Signiture.

1. The poem <u>A democratic Man</u> is a tribute to Thomas Jefferson, a generious, patreotic American, and his vision of the furture.

2. The book ben Franklin's Numerorous inventions describes the products of this man's courious, scientific mind.

Basic
1. signature
2. patriotic
3. democratic
4. serious
5. nervous
6. terrific
7. gigantic
8. generous
9. scientific
10. temperature
11. tragic
12. curious
13. jealous
14. torture
15. furious
16. departure
17. dramatic
18. fantastic
19. numerous
20. specific

Review
21. future
22. feature
23. culture
24. dangerous
25. romantic

Challenge
26. unanimous
27. symbolic
28. chronic
29. strategic
30. stature

Write a List

Write a list of four books that you would recommend to other students. Include a sentence for each that tells something about the book. Try to use five spelling words.

Proofreading Tip **Check that you have capitalized and punctuated titles correctly.**

Proofreading Marks
¶ Indent
∧ Add
⊙ Add a period
⤸ Delete
≡ Capital letter
/ Small letter
∿ Reverse order

Expanding Vocabulary

Spelling Word Link

fantastic

thrilling
enchanting
exquisite
sumptuous
inspiring

Thesaurus: Exact Words for *fantastic* The word *fantastic* is often used informally to mean "outstanding, superb." You can use other words, however, that are more precise than *fantastic*. In the box are some examples.

Look up the entry for *fantastic* in your Thesaurus. Then write the word from the box that can replace *fantastic* in each sentence below.

1. His <u>fantastic</u> story charmed us.
2. The royal cook was preparing a <u>fantastic</u> meal.
3. The steep slope made a <u>fantastic</u> ski trail.
4. Her <u>fantastic</u> speech filled us with emotion and hope.
5. The colors in the tapestry were <u>fantastic</u>.

Show You Know! Write a sentence for the speech balloon in each picture. Use a different word for *fantastic* in each sentence.

1. _____
2. _____
3. _____
4. _____
5. _____

6. _____
7. _____
8. _____

Real-World Connection

Social Studies: Declaration of Independence All the words in the box relate to the Declaration of Independence. Look up these words in your Spelling Dictionary. Then write the words to complete this part of a letter.

Spelling Word Link

patriotic

pursuit
assent
tyrant
obstructed
abuses
inhabitants
imposed
acknowledged

July 1776

Dear Cousin John,

You asked me to tell you the latest news about our conflict with England. We drafted a Declaration of Independence! Most of the __(1)__ of the American colonies can no longer tolerate the __(2)__ of the British __(3)__, King George III. The Declaration states that the king has __(4)__ unfair taxes, has refused to give his __(5)__ to fair laws, and has __(6)__ our attempts at self-government. This document also states that people have the right to life, liberty, and the __(7)__ of happiness. In it we have also __(8)__ that the colonists are free from all allegiance to Britain. We have made a new nation!

With kind regards,

Joshua

1. _____
2. _____
3. _____
4. _____
5. _____
6. _____
7. _____
8. _____

Try This CHALLENGE

Yes or No? Write *yes* if the underlined word is used correctly. Write *no* if it is not.

9. The building was <u>obstructed</u> of concrete and glass.
10. Maura and Tia <u>imposed</u> for a photograph.
11. Mr. Rivera <u>acknowledged</u> that he made a mistake.
12. My sister is in <u>pursuit</u> of a good education.

9. _____
10. _____
11. _____
12. _____

★★★ **Fact File**

Thomas Jefferson was the author of the Declaration of Independence. A brilliant leader, he later became the third President of the United States and the founder of the Democratic Party.

de-

_____
_____
_____
_____
_____
_____
_____
_____
_____
_____

ob-

_____
_____
_____
_____

oc-

_____
_____

Read and Say

Basic

READ the sentences. **SAY** each bold word.

1.	debate	We held a **debate** about year-round school.
2.	decision	The judge reached a **decision** in the case.
3.	defense	The **defense** of our rights is important.
4.	defeat	This is our first **defeat** of the baseball season.
5.	occasion	My birthday is an important **occasion**!
6.	obvious	His musical talent is **obvious** when he sings.
7.	describe	Can you **describe** your new jacket?
8.	occupy	Four people **occupy** that house.
9.	observe	Did you **observe** the birds building their nest?
10.	demand	Your **demand** for more money is unreasonable.
11.	determine	Please help us **determine** which answer is right.
12.	oblige	Jack cleaned out the garage to **oblige** you.
13.	occur	Where did the accident **occur**?
14.	dedicate	We **dedicate** an hour each day to band practice.
15.	decay	The garbage will **decay** after a while.
16.	demonstrate	Will you **demonstrate** your invention?
17.	decrease	Cars **decrease** in value as they get older.
18.	decline	Did he **decline** to join us, or will he come along?
19.	obtain	Where can I **obtain** tickets to the show?
20.	detour	The road took a **detour,** but we arrived on time.

Think and Write

Each word begins with the prefix *de-* or *ob-*. Notice that the prefix *ob-* is sometimes spelled *oc*.

debate	**ob**serve
decision	**oc**cupy

• Before what letter is the prefix *ob-* spelled *oc*?

Now write each Basic Word under the spelling of its prefix.

Review
21. detail
22. object
23. destroy
24. detective
25. deposit

Challenge
26. obscure
27. deliberate
28. obstacle
29. obstinate
30. deficient

Independent Practice

 **Spelling Strategy** *De-* and *ob-* are prefixes. *Ob-* is spelled *oc* before *c*. To spell a word with a prefix, find the prefix, the base word or word root, and any ending. Spell the word by parts.

Word Analysis/Phonics Complete the exercises with Basic Words.

1. Write the word that has the |ē| sound spelled *i*.
2. Write the word that has the |s| sound spelled *c*.
3–6. Write the word from which each word below is made.

    3. determination   **5.** dedication
    4. obligation   **6.** description

Vocabulary: Making Inferences Write the Basic Word that fits each clue.

7. A loser experiences this.
8. Onlookers do this.
9. A birthday is one.
10. Toothpaste fights this.
11. This lengthens a journey.
12. The military controls this.
13. You do this to show how a product works.

Challenge Words Write the Challenge Word that is a synonym for each word below. Use your Spelling Dictionary.

14. intentional   **17.** stubborn
15. inadequate   **18.** hindrance
16. vague

Spelling-Meaning Connection

occupy
occupation
occupant

The prefix *ob-* is spelled *oc* in *occupy* to match the first letter of the word root. Knowing this will help you remember that *occupy* and the related words *occupation* and *occupant* are spelled with two *c*'s.

19–20. Write *occupy* and *occupation*. Then underline the double consonant in each word.

Word Analysis

1. _____
2. _____
3. _____
4. _____
5. _____
6. _____

Vocabulary

7. _____
8. _____
9. _____
10. _____
11. _____
12. _____
13. _____

Challenge Words

14. _____
15. _____
16. _____
17. _____
18. _____

Spelling-Meaning

19. _____
20. _____

Run-on Entries

1. _____

2. _____

3. _____

4. _____

5. _____

6. _____

7. _____

Contrast Clues

8. _____

9. _____

10. _____

11. _____

12. _____

13. _____

14. _____

15. _____

16. _____

17. _____

18. _____

19. _____

20. _____

21. _____

22. _____

Dictionary

Run-on Entries Run-on entries are words made by adding a suffix to an entry word. They are listed in dark type at the end of the entry. The words *obviously* and *obviousness,* for example, are run-on entries for *obvious.*

> **ob·vi·ous** |ŏb′ vē əs| *adj.* Easily perceived or understood; evident. **—ob′ vi·ous·ly** *adv.*
> **—ob′ vi·ous·ness** *n.*

Practice Look up the words listed below in your Spelling Dictionary. Then write the run-on entries.

1. observe
2. defense
3. capable
4. expand
5. visible
6. considerable
7. familiar

Review: Spelling Spree

Contrast Clues The second part of each clue contrasts with the first part. Write a Basic or Review Word to fit each clue.

8. not hidden, but _____
9. not to vacate, but to _____
10. not a request, but a _____
11. not to ignore, but to _____
12. not to agree, but to _____
13. not a victory, but a _____
14. not to accept, but to _____
15. not a direct way, but a _____
16. not to flourish, but to _____
17. not to create, but to _____
18. not a main idea, but a _____
19. not a person, but an _____
20. not to increase, but to _____
21. not a criminal, but a _____
22. not a withdrawal, but a _____

How Are You Doing?

List the spelling words that are hard for you. Practice them with a family member.

Proofreading and Writing

Proofread for Spelling Use proofreading marks to correct ten misspelled Basic or Review Words in this news article.

Example: Each candidate hopes to ~~defeet~~ *defeat* the other.

★ Candidates Debate Issues ★

The presidential debate was an exciting occassion. Both candidates wanted to oblidge the voters. The Republican vowed to optain better tax benefits. The Democrat tried to demonstrait that the way to a better economy was obvious and began to discribe the changes that needed to occer. Both candidates promised to dedacate themselves to a strong national defence. Commentators could not determin the winner of the debate. The voters make that decission.

Basic

1. debate
2. decision
3. defense
4. defeat
5. occasion
6. obvious
7. describe
8. occupy
9. observe
10. demand
11. determine
12. oblige
13. occur
14. dedicate
15. decay
16. demonstrate
17. decrease
18. decline
19. obtain
20. detour

Review
21. detail
22. object
23. destroy
24. detective
25. deposit

Challenge
26. obscure
27. deliberate
28. obstacle
29. obstinate
30. deficient

Write Debate Questions

1. Should school be open year round ?
2.

Write five questions that two candidates might debate. The candidates could be running for president of the country or of your class. Try to use five spelling words.

Proofreading Tip

Remember that a computer spell-checker will not find a word that is misspelled as another word.

Proofreading Marks

¶ Indent
∧ Add
⊙ Add a period
ᵧ Delete
≡ Capital letter
/ Small letter
∿ Reverse order

Vocabulary Enrichment

Expanding Vocabulary

scrawny
slender
scent
odor
thrifty
cheap
scheme
strategy
snicker
guffaw

Thesaurus: Connotations The feelings and associations that a word has in addition to its dictionary meanings are called its connotations.

Word	Meaning	Connotations
look	"to use the eyes to see; perceive by sight"	neutral
gaze	"to look intently"	positive; suggests wonder or admiration
stare	"to look steadily and directly"	negative; can suggest rudeness

Fill in the chart below. For each "neutral" word, write the words from the box that have the same meaning but positive or negative connotations. Find the neutral words in your Thesaurus if you need help.

Positive	Neutral	Negative
gaze	look	stare
1.	laugh	6.
2.	frugal	7.
3.	plan	8.
4.	smell	9.
5.	thin	10.

Work Together With a partner write a sentence using each word that you added to the chart. Be sure that your sentences make use of the positive or negative connotations of each word. Write on another sheet of paper.

Vocabulary Enrichment

Unit 34 BONUS

Real-World Connection

Language Arts: Debate All the words in the box relate to debating. Look up these words in your Spelling Dictionary. Then write the words to complete this journal entry.

Our class held a debate on this **(1)** : All bike riders should wear helmets. Everyone in the class had an opinion; no one was **(2)** . Our teacher acted as **(3)** , presiding over the debate. Marcia Kirk represented those in favor of, or **(4)** , helmets. On the other side was Doug Fale, her **(5)** , who represented the anti-helmet, or **(6)** , side of the debate. Each speaker presented his or her point of view in a clear, **(7)** manner and responded to the other side's arguments with a strong **(8)** . Tomorrow we'll present our debate to the other sixth-grade class.

Spelling Word Link

debate

rebuttal
pro
con
neutral
opponent
moderator
resolution
logical

1. _____
2. _____
3. _____
4. _____
5. _____
6. _____
7. _____
8. _____

Write Guidelines What are the most persuasive techniques for student debaters to use? With a partner write some tips that will help students debate effectively. Try to use words from the box. Be sure to proofread your paper.

 Fact File

One famous series of debates was held between Abraham Lincoln and Stephen Douglas when they were running for the United States Senate in 1858. The main topic of the seven formal debates was slavery.

unbelievable invention

Basic Words

Read and Say

Basic

READ the sentences.
SAY each bold word.

1. development — Sunshine stimulates plant **development**.
2. information — This book contains important **information**.
3. preparation — Will our bike trip take much **preparation**?
4. improvement — Your skills show **improvement**.
5. invention — Is this tool a new **invention**?
6. advancement — The **advancement** of a glacier is slow.
7. accidentally — I **accidentally** broke that vase.
8. unkindness — Ignoring someone is a type of **unkindness**.
9. concentration — Threading a needle takes **concentration**.
10. unskillful — My drawings are still **unskillful**.
11. respectful — Be **respectful** and kind to others.
12. prevention — The **prevention** of tooth decay is important.
13. regardless — I exercise **regardless** of the weather.
14. repetition — I learned this song through **repetition**.
15. disgraceful — The run-down park was a **disgraceful** sight.
16. unbelievable — Your excuse is **unbelievable**.
17. disagreement — Our chess game ended in a **disagreement**.
18. imprisonment — The criminal received a long **imprisonment**.
19. encouragement — Your **encouragement** helps me study more.
20. intermission — We left the play at **intermission**.

Think and Write

Each word is made up of a prefix, a base word or a word root, and a suffix. Finding these parts can help you spell the words more easily.

unbeliev**able**   **in**vent**ion**
advance**ment**   **con**centr**ation**

• What is the prefix, the base word or the word root, and the suffix in each word on the list?

Write each Basic Word. Underline its prefix and circle its suffix.

Review	23. reaction
21. enjoyment	24. comfortable
22. delightful	25. conviction

Challenge	28. distinction
26. precision	29. intolerable
27. reputation	30. inevitable

Independent Practice

Many words are made up of a prefix, a base word or a word root, and a suffix. Find these parts in a word, and then spell the word by the parts.

Word Analysis/Phonics Complete the exercises with Basic Words.

1–4. Write the four words that have the |k| sound spelled *c*.

5–8. Write four words by adding a prefix and a suffix to each base word below.

    5. ___ grace ___   **7.** ___ skill ___

    6. ___ kind ___   **8.** ___ prove ___

Vocabulary: Context Sentences
Write the Basic Word that completes each sentence.

9. We ordered food in _____ for the author's luncheon.

10. The author gave us a lot of _____ about book publishing.

11. Many facts are incorrect, so this new biography is _____.

12. Getting a promotion is a noteworthy _____.

13. Between Act I and Act II of the play, there was an _____.

Challenge Words Write the Challenge Word that matches each definition. Use your Spelling Dictionary.

14. not capable of being avoided   **15.** a difference or unlikeness

16. public recognition   **17.** unbearable

18. the condition of being accurate

invent
invention

Spelling-Meaning Connection

How can you remember that the |sh| sound in *invention* is spelled with a *t*? Think of the related word *invent*, in which the *t* is pronounced.

19–20. Write *invent* and *invention*. Then underline the letter in *invent* that helps you spell the |sh| sound in *invention*.

Word Analysis

1. _____
2. _____
3. _____
4. _____
5. _____
6. _____
7. _____
8. _____

Vocabulary

9. _____
10. _____
11. _____
12. _____
13. _____

Challenge Words

14. _____
15. _____
16. _____
17. _____
18. _____

Spelling-Meaning

19. _____
20. _____

The Third Word

1. _____
2. _____
3. _____
4. _____
5. _____
6. _____
7. _____
8. _____
9. _____
10. _____
11. _____

Syllable Scramble

12. _____
13. _____
14. _____
15. _____
16. _____
17. _____
18. _____
19. _____
20. _____
21. _____
22. _____
23. _____
24. _____
25. _____

Review: Spelling Spree

The Third Word Write a Basic or Review Word that belongs with each group of words.

1. praise, support, _____
2. thoughtlessness, harshness, _____
3. mistakenly, unthinkingly, _____
4. response, reflex, _____
5. opinion, belief, _____
6. clumsy, incompetent, _____
7. polite, courteous, _____
8. creation, discovery, _____
9. captivity, confinement, _____
10. unconvincing, unimaginable, _____
11. quarrel, fight, _____

Syllable Scramble Rearrange the syllables in each item to write a Basic or Review Word. There is one extra syllable in each item.

12. less im gard re
13. op ment vel un de
14. ter mis un sion in
15. joy ment en dis
16. e ti rep tion ed
17. tion un ven pre
18. ble a ment fort com
19. re ment prove im
20. im tion in for ma
21. ment ad in vance
22. tion tra con dem cen
23. tion ac ra prep a
24. dis ful de grace
25. ful im light de

How Are You Doing?

Write your spelling words in ABC order. Practice any misspelled words with a partner.

Proofreading and Writing

Proofread: Spelling and Using *I* and *me* *I* is used as a subject. *Me* is used as an object. When using *I* or *me* with nouns or other pronouns, name yourself last.

Susan and **I** edited the book.   Jesse helped **her** and **me**.

Use proofreading marks to correct four misspelled words and three mistakes in using *I* and *me* in this memo.

Example: The author joined ~~I~~ *him* and ~~him~~ *me* at ~~intermision.~~ *intermission.*

Memorandum

To: Jim Evans   **From:** Peggy Tout

Re: How to Have Fun

   Maura Zim's new book, How to Have Fun, is delightfull and full of informaton. Its ideas for projects, games, and outings will give readers many hours of injoyment. The section on costume parties is unbeliveable. Can I and you meet today? Maura Zim and me are meeting tomorrow.

Write a Personal Story

Write a personal story about a time when you and another person had fun. Try to use five spelling words, and use *I* and *me* with a noun or another pronoun at least once.

Proofreading Tip

Be sure that you have used *I* and *me* correctly.

Proofreading Marks

¶ Indent
∧ Add
⊙ Add a period
⌿ Delete
≡ Capital letter
/ Small letter
∿ Reverse order

Expanding Vocabulary

Building Words with Prefixes and Suffixes You can build new words by adding either a prefix or a suffix to a base word or a word root, but how many can you build by adding both?

BASE WORD/WORD ROOT	PREFIX	SUFFIX	PREFIX AND SUFFIX
form	**in**form	form**ation**	**in**form**ation**
vent	**pre**vent		**pre**vent**ion**
vent	**in**vent		**in**vent**ion**

Look at the diagram. Add both prefixes and suffixes to the word roots *form* and *vent* to build fifteen new words. Do not repeat the example words given above. Use your Spelling Dictionary.

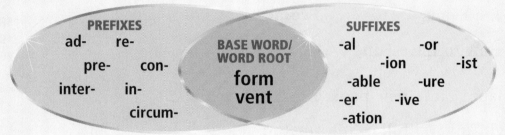

PREFIXES
ad- re-
pre- con-
inter- in-
circum-

BASE WORD/ WORD ROOT
form
vent

SUFFIXES
-al -or
-ion -ist
-able -ure
-er -ive
-ation

form	*vent*
1.	8.
2.	9.
3.	10.
4.	11.
5.	12.
6.	13.
7.	14.
	15.

Work Together With a partner write five sentences, using any five of the words you built with *form* and *vent*. Write on another sheet of paper.

Real-World Connection

Careers: Publishing All the words in the box relate to publishing. Look up these words in your Spelling Dictionary. Then write the words to complete this paragraph.

Spelling Word Link

information

publisher
manuscript
revise
proofread
italics
compositor
galleys
copyright

How a Book Is Published

The author completes writing the __(1)__ for a book. The author sends it to the editor, who will __(2)__ the writing so that it is clearer. A designer designs the pages and the book's cover. The edited work is set into type by a __(3)__, who will use various styles of type, including the slanted letters called __(4)__. The typeset __(5)__ are returned to the editor to be __(6)__ for errors. The __(7)__, the company that has produced the book, releases the book and distributes it to stores. The company holds the __(8)__, or legal rights to the book.

Try This
CHALLENGE

Yes or No? Write *yes* if the underlined word is used correctly. Write *no* if it is not.

9. Tom put <u>italics</u> around the title of his paper.
10. The <u>galleys</u> were marked with spelling corrections.
11. Look for missing commas as you <u>proofread</u>.
12. An author is also known as a <u>compositor</u>.

1. _____
2. _____
3. _____
4. _____
5. _____
6. _____
7. _____
8. _____

9. _____
10. _____
11. _____
12. _____

★★★ Fact File

In the 1400s Johann Gutenberg created the first printing press that could make copies of a book quickly. Because of this invention, books became less expensive and available to more people.

36 Review: Units 31–35

diesel   freight

Unit 31   Words with *ie* or *ei*   pages 192–197

receipt	freight	yield	foreign	neither
fiery	conceit	veil	seize	leisure

Spelling Strategy   Use **i** before **e** except after **c** or in words with the |ā| sound, as in **weigh**. You must memorize exceptions to this generalization.

Write the word that completes each analogy.
1. *Or* is to *nor* as *either* is to _____.
2. *Cold* is to *icy* as *hot* is to _____.
3. *Drop* is to *release* as *grab* is to _____.
4. *Modest* is to *humble* as *pride* is to _____.

Write the word that fits each clue.
5. Some trains carry it.
6. It is a time to relax.
7. It might hide a face.
8. It is from another country.
9. It proves that you paid.
10. You do this when you give in.

account
addition

Unit 32   The Prefix *ad-*   pages 198–203

advice	approve	assist	affair	accurate
assemble	accomplish	acquire	adjust	approach

Spelling Strategy   The prefix **ad-** can be spelled **ac**, **af**, **ap**, or **as** to match the first consonant or consonant sound of the base word or the word root.

Write a spelling word by changing the underlined prefix in each word.
11. <u>im</u>prove   12. <u>re</u>semble   13. <u>in</u>sist   14. <u>un</u>just

Write the word that belongs with each group of words below.
15. finish, complete, _____
16. occurrence, event, _____
17. opinion, guidance, _____
18. correct, exact, _____
19. method, way, _____
20. get, gain, _____

1. _____
2. _____
3. _____
4. _____
5. _____
6. _____
7. _____
8. _____
9. _____
10. _____
11. _____
12. _____
13. _____
14. _____
15. _____
16. _____
17. _____
18. _____
19. _____
20. _____

Unit 33   Endings: *-ic, -ture, -ous*   pages 204–209

generous	temperature	terrific	nervous	scientific
curious	departure	jealous	specific	torture

John Hancock

patriotic signature

Spelling Strategy

final |ĭk| → **ic**
final |chər| → **ture**
final |əs| → **ous**

Write the word that is a synonym for each word below.
21. exact   **22.** envious   **23.** uneasy   **24.** splendid   **25.** pain

Write the word that completes each sentence.
26. Hana's many donations to charity show how _____ she is.
27. By sunset the _____ had dropped below the freezing point.
28. Our guest said good-bye and made a hasty _____.
29. The chemist worked on a _____ experiment.
30. My niece asks many questions, as she is very _____.

21. _____
22. _____
23. _____
24. _____
25. _____
26. _____
27. _____
28. _____
29. _____
30. _____

Unit 34   Prefixes: *de-, ob-*   pages 210–215

occupy	decision	defense	occasion	obvious
obtain	dedicate	occur	determine	detour

de bate

Spelling Strategy   **De-** and **ob-** are prefixes. **Ob-** is spelled **oc** before **c**. To spell a word with a prefix, find the prefix, the base word or word root, and any ending. Spell the word by parts.

Write the word that completes each analogy.
31. *Watch* is to *observe* as *happen* is to _____.
32. *Protect* is to *protection* as *defend* as to _____.
33. *Promise* is to *vow* as *devote* is to _____.
34. *Winter* is to *season* as *birthday* is to _____.

Write a spelling word by adding a prefix to each word part.
35. _____ I termine   **37.** _____ I tour   **39.** _____ I vious
36. _____ I tain   **38.** _____ I cupy   **40.** _____ I cision

31. _____
32. _____
33. _____
34. _____
35. _____
36. _____
37. _____
38. _____
39. _____
40. _____

unbelievable invention

Unit 35   Word Parts   pages 216–221

accidentally	unkindness	concentration	improvement
development	regardless	encouragement	disgraceful
unbelievable	prevention		

41. _____

42. _____

43. _____

44. _____

45. _____

46. _____

47. _____

48. _____

49. _____

50. _____

Spelling Strategy   Many words are made up of a prefix, a base word or a word root, and a suffix. Find these parts in a word, and then spell the word by the parts.

Write a spelling word by adding a suffix to each word below.

41. regard   **43.** concentrate   **45.** encourage

42. develop   **44.** unkind   **46.** prevent

Write the word that answers each question.

47. Which word describes a story that sounds untrue?

48. Which word names a change that makes something better?

49. Which word means the opposite of *purposely*?

50. Which word describes shameful behavior?

Challenge Words   Units 31–35   pages 192–221

deceit	unanimous	accumulate	strategic	approximate
retrieve	obstinate	deliberate	distinction	intolerable

51. _____

52. _____

53. _____

54. _____

55. _____

56. _____

57. _____

58. _____

59. _____

60. _____

Write the word that is an antonym for each word below.

51. bearable

52. lose

53. exact

54. accidental

55. honesty

Write the word that completes each sentence.

56. Tani hoped that six inches of snow would _____ overnight.

57. Chess players plan _____ moves to try to win the game.

58. We begged Dad to change his mind, but he remained _____.

59. The twins are so alike I can't make a _____ between them.

60. Because Jay was the only one to oppose the plan, the vote was not _____.

Spelling-Meaning Strategy

occur
op**pose**

Absorbed Prefixes

You know that the words *observe* and *occur* both have the same prefix. Each of these words has a Latin root, and each begins with the prefix *ob-* meaning "toward," "in front of," or "against." However, in *occur* the spelling of the prefix has changed to match the initial consonant sound of the word root. The prefix *ob-* has been absorbed into the word.

Here are other words that begin with the Latin prefix *ob-*. In each word the prefix has been absorbed.

offer	**opp**ose	**occ**urrence
offend	**opp**osite	**opp**ortunity

Think
- How did the spelling of the prefix *ob-* change in each word?
- Before which consonants does the spelling of *ob-* change?

Apply and Extend

Complete these activities on a separate sheet of paper.

1. Look up each word in the word box above in the Spelling Dictionary. Write six sentences, using one word from the word box in each sentence.

2. The prefix *in-*, meaning "without" or "not," may be spelled *il*, *im*, or *ir* when it is absorbed. With a partner list as many words as you can in which the prefix *in-* has been absorbed. Then look in the section "Absorbed Prefixes," beginning on page 275 of your Spelling-Meaning Index. Add any other words with this absorbed prefix to your list.

Summing Up

Knowing that the prefixes *ob-* and *in-* change spelling when absorbed into base words or word roots that begin with certain consonants can help you remember the double consonants in those words.

from

Digging the Past

by Bruce Porell

Archaeologists look at the past. What do they study to learn how people once lived?

The objects that archaeologists study are called artifacts. They are the pots we cook in and the dishes we eat from. Artifacts are the chairs and tables in your living room, the rubber ball in your bedroom, the toothbrush in the rack over your bathroom sink, and the chicken bones you threw away after supper last night. They are everywhere. They are our tools, toys, decorations, furniture, clothes, and weapons, and even the buildings we live and work in. Look around you. You are wearing artifacts, and you are surrounded by them.

Very old artifacts have often been changed by nature's forces, but some materials stand up better than others. Cloth, paper, and wood can be destroyed by water, fire, and insects. They can be impossible to recognize after only a few years. Metals such as iron, bronze, and copper can rust or corrode, if they are in damp places. Pots and stone tools are the artifacts most often found, because they last the longest. Modern plastics may last as long as pottery and stone. Some of these new materials will be around for ten thousand years before breaking down and returning to the soil.

granite

basalt

Think and Discuss

1 What kinds of artifacts do archaeologists study?

2 What facts did you learn about different materials? Does the author include any opinions in this passage?

3 What is the topic sentence in each paragraph?

The Writing Process
Research Report

What topic would you like to learn about? Choose one to research, and write a short report. Use the guidelines, and follow the Writing Process.

1 Prewriting
- Write five questions to answer about your topic.
- Take notes to answer the questions.
- Organize your notes into an outline.

2 Draft
- Follow your outline. State each main idea in a topic sentence.

3 Revise
- Move sentences or paragraphs that are out of order.
- Use your Thesaurus to find exact words.
- Have a writing conference.

4 Proofread
- Did you spell each word correctly?
- Did you use capital letters and punctuation marks correctly?

5 Publish
- Make a neat final copy, and add a title.
- Present your report to some classmates.

Guidelines for Writing a Research Report

✓ Write topic sentences that state the main ideas.
✓ Support each main idea with facts and details.
✓ Arrange paragraphs in an order that makes sense.
✓ Include an introduction and a conclusion.

Composition Words

review
accurate
according
specific
curious
observe
development
invention

Student's Handbook

Extra Practice and Review Cycle 1

Unit 1 — Short Vowels — pages 12–17

depth	plunge	film	switch	length
cliff	scrub	stung	pitch	else

craft |ă|

Spelling Strategy   Remember that a short vowel sound is usually spelled **a, e, i, o,** or **u** and is followed by a consonant sound. A short vowel sound spelled by one vowel and followed by a consonant sound is the **short vowel pattern**.

Write the word that completes each sentence.
1. As we left the theater, we talked about the _____.
2. The batter swung, but the _____ was too low.
3. The hiker was unable to climb the steep _____.
4. Monica swam the entire _____ of the pool underwater.

Write the word that matches each definition.
5. to clean by rubbing
6. a distance downward
7. wounded with a sharp point
8. other; different
9. to exchange
10. to dive into swiftly

1. _____
2. _____
3. _____
4. _____
5. _____
6. _____
7. _____
8. _____
9. _____
10. _____

Unit 2 — Long Vowels — pages 18–23

quote	pace	preach	trait	sleeve
brake	grease	frame	soak	toast

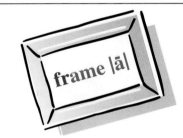

frame |ā|

Spelling Strategy   Remember that a long vowel sound may be spelled vowel-consonant-**e** or with two vowels written together.

Write the word that is a synonym for each word below.
11. feature   12. step   13. oil   14. rim   15. drench

Write the word that matches each definition.
16. to teach and urge others to accept or follow
17. a device for slowing or stopping motion
18. to repeat a statement by someone
19. sliced bread, heated and browned
20. the part of a garment that covers the arm

11. _____
12. _____
13. _____
14. _____
15. _____
16. _____
17. _____
18. _____
19. _____
20. _____

|ī| cycle
|ĕ| sweat

Unit 3 — More Vowel Spellings — pages 24–29

sweat	rely	cleanse	reply	meant
rhyme	meadow	threat	apply	leather

Spelling Strategy   Keep in mind these less common spellings when you try to spell a new word with these vowel sounds:

|ē| → **ine** |ī| → **y** |ĕ| → **ea** |ĭ| → **y** |ŭ| → **o**-consonant-**e**

Write the word that matches each definition.

21. to say or give an answer   **24.** a possible danger
22. to make clean or pure   **25.** grassy ground
23. to trust confidently   **26.** intended to say

Write the word that completes each sentence.

27. The pair of shoes was made of soft, brown _____.
28. After the long run, our T-shirts were soaked with _____.
29. In this poem, two words _____ with *pace*.
30. For a summer job, you will have to _____ at the office.

21. _____
22. _____
23. _____
24. _____
25. _____
26. _____
27. _____
28. _____
29. _____
30. _____

Unit 4 — Spelling |ou|, |o͞o|, |ô|, and |oi| — pages 30–35

|ou| sprout |o͞o| bloom

bloom	sprout	droop	vault	avoid
gloom	noun	foul	trout	roost

Spelling Strategy

|ou| → **ou** |ô| → **au, aw, augh, ough**
|o͞o| → **oo** |oi| → **oi, oy**

Write the word that belongs with each group of words.

31. sadness, depression, _____   **34.** verb, adjective, _____
32. jump, leap, _____   **35.** catfish, bass, _____
33. unpleasant, offensive, _____

Write a word by adding the missing letters. Circle the word with the |oi| sound.

36. bl _ _ m   **38.** spr _ _ t   **40.** dr _ _ p
37. r _ _ st   **39.** av _ _ d

31. _____
32. _____
33. _____
34. _____
35. _____
36. _____
37. _____
38. _____
39. _____
40. _____

Cycle 1

Unit 5   Spelling Vowel + |r| Sounds   pages 36–41

fierce	thorn	court	urge	yarn
whirl	purse	scorn	rehearse	birch

|ûr|

earth

Spelling Strategy   Vowel + |r| sounds can have these patterns:

|ûr| → **ir, ur, ear** |är| → **ar** |ôr| → **or, our** |îr| → **ier**

Write the word that is a synonym for each word below.
Underline the letters that spell the vowel + |r| sounds.

41. spin   **43.** encourage   **45.** reject
42. practice   **44.** wild   **46.** pocketbook

Write the word that completes each sentence.

47. I want to play tennis, but the _____ is too wet.
48. Ingrid cut her finger on the _____.
49. My favorite kind of tree is the _____.
50. Mary bought enough _____ to knit three sweaters.

Challenge Words   Units 1–5   pages 12–41

habitat	forfeit	deft	dynamic	emphasize
oxygen	magnetic	realm	sparse	microphone
pertain	heirloom	adjoin	bountiful	circumstances

Write the word that matches each definition.

51. plentiful   **54.** not dense   **56.** to accent
52. belong to   **55.** give up   **57.** to lie side by side
53. dwelling

Write the word that completes each sentence.

58. A witness was asked to describe the _____ of the accident.
59. Everyone heard the speaker because she used a _____.
60. The king was loved by those who lived within his _____.
61. We watched the _____ hands of the concert pianist.
62. A scuba diver carries a tank filled with _____.
63. Donna's _____ personality inspired us to work harder.
64. His science report was about the earth's _____ poles.
65. My great-grandmother's silver teapot is an _____.

41. _____
42. _____
43. _____
44. _____
45. _____
46. _____
47. _____
48. _____
49. _____
50. _____
51. _____
52. _____
53. _____
54. _____
55. _____
56. _____
57. _____
58. _____
59. _____
60. _____
61. _____
62. _____
63. _____
64. _____
65. _____

Unit 7   Compound Words   pages 48–53

driftwood	somebody	nowhere	toothbrush	haircut
fireproof	dead end	uproar	old-fashioned	iceberg

1. _____

2. _____

3. _____

4. _____

5. _____

6. _____

7. _____

8. _____

9. _____

10. _____

Spelling Strategy   A **compound word** is made up of two or more smaller words. Remember that a compound word may be written as one word, as a hyphenated word, or as separate words.

Write the compound word that includes each word below.

1. end   3. drift   5. some
2. ice   4. no   6. roar

Write the word that fits each clue.

7. helps prevent cavities
8. safe from burning matches
9. can be just a trim
10. out of style

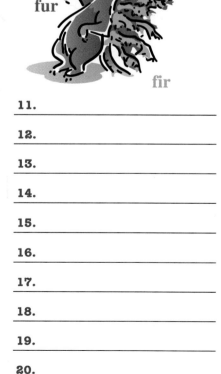

Unit 8   Homophones   pages 54–59

fir	scene	manor	who's	tacks
fur	seen	manner	whose	tax

11. _____

12. _____

13. _____

14. _____

15. _____

16. _____

17. _____

18. _____

19. _____

20. _____

Spelling Strategy   **Homophones** are words that sound alike but have different spellings and meanings. When you use a homophone, be sure to spell the word that has the meaning you want.

Write the word that matches each definition.

11. viewed
12. a lord's estate
13. a style of behavior
14. a cone-bearing tree
15. a view
16. an animal's thick, soft hair

Write the word that completes each sentence.

17. I wonder _____ going to win the election.
18. Attach the sign to the bulletin board with _____.
19. A _____ on gasoline helped to pay for road repairs.
20. Does anyone know _____ car is parked in the driveway?

Cycle 2

Unit 9   Final |ər| pages 60–65

senator	director	minister	senior	junior
minor	youngster	particular	inner	passenger

Spelling Strategy   When you hear the final |ər| sounds in words of two or more syllables, think of the spelling patterns **er, or,** and **ar.**

Write the word that fits each clue.

21. This is the school year before senior year.
22. A two-year-old child is this.
23. This person is elected to his or her job.
24. This could be someone riding on a bus.

Write the word that matches each definition.

25. older or oldest
26. farther inside
27. a church pastor
28. smaller in amount or size
29. one who manages something
30. about a single thing

21. _____
22. _____
23. _____
24. _____
25. _____
26. _____
27. _____
28. _____
29. _____
30. _____

Unit 10   Final |ən|, |əl|, and |ər| pages 66–71

weapon	horror	sample	moral	litter
stumble	quarrel	panel	cancel	linen

| |ən| weapon |

Spelling Strategy

|n| or |ən| → **on, en** |l| or |əl| → **le, el, al** |ər| → **er, or**

Write the word that is a synonym for each word below.

31. falter   **33.** rubbish   **35.** dread
32. example   **34.** argue

Write the word that answers each question.

36. What is something a soldier might carry?
37. What do you do when you call off a date?
38. What might a tablecloth be made out of?
39. What do you call a flat, wooden board?
40. What do you call the lesson taught in a fable?

31. _____
32. _____
33. _____
34. _____
35. _____
36. _____
37. _____
38. _____
39. _____
40. _____

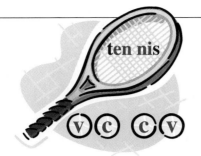

ten nis

V C C V

Unit 11   VCCV and VCCCV Patterns   pages 72–77

dentist	author	system	custom	standard
burden	banquet	bullet	surface	campus

Spelling Strategy   To spell a two-syllable word, divide the word into syllables. Look for spelling patterns you have learned, and spell the word by syllables.

Write the word that completes each analogy.

41. *Symphony* is to *composer* as *novel* is to _____.

42. *Small* is to *large* as *snack* is to _____.

43. *Unload* is to *lighten* as *overload* is to _____.

44. *Medicine* is to *doctor* as *dentistry* is to _____.

Add a syllable to each syllable below. Write the word.

45. cam | ___   **47.** sys | ___   **49.** stan | ___

46. cus | ___   **48.** sur | ___   **50.** bul | ___

Challenge Words   Units 7–11   pages 48–77

valor	burro	intern	astute	councilor
ebb tide	burrow	corridor	aspire	painstaking
corporal	borough	chancellor	colonel	self-confident

Write the word that is a synonym for each word below.

51. careful   **54.** self-assured   **56.** desire

52. donkey   **55.** hallway   **57.** tunnel

53. fearlessness

Write the word that fits each description.

58. It has three syllables. The last syllable has an *a* in it.

59. It has two syllables. It is a compound word.

60. It has three syllables. It has only one *o*.

61. It has two syllables. Two consonants are not pronounced.

62. It has two syllables. Two of its consonants are *t*'s.

63. It has three syllables. Two of its four vowels are *o*'s.

64. It has two syllables, but it looks as if it has three.

65. It has two syllables. The second and last letters match.

41. _____
42. _____
43. _____
44. _____
45. _____
46. _____
47. _____
48. _____
49. _____
50. _____
51. _____
52. _____
53. _____
54. _____
55. _____
56. _____
57. _____
58. _____
59. _____
60. _____
61. _____
62. _____
63. _____
64. _____
65. _____

Unit 13   Words with *-ed* or *-ing*   pages 84–89

piloting	beginning	limited	forgetting	equaled
wondering	favored	knitting	answered	shoveling

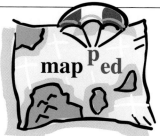

map ^ped

Spelling Strategy

pilot + ing = pilot**ing**   permit+ ing = permit**ting**
   fit + ing = fit**ting**

Write the word formed by joining each base word and ending.

1. begin + ing   3. forget + ing   5. knit + ing
2. shovel + ing   4. answer + ed   6. favor + ed

Write the word that completes each sentence.

7. When Jon was an hour late, we began _____ what happened.
8. The advanced class was _____ to those with experience.
9. The captain who was _____ the flight greeted the crew.
10. The loser _____ the winner in grace but not in speed.

1. _____
2. _____
3. _____
4. _____
5. _____
6. _____
7. _____
8. _____
9. _____
10. _____

Unit 14   Endings and Suffixes   pages 90–95

advanced	privately	replacement	adorable	forgiveness
forceful	scarcely	blaming	barely	sincerely

advanc ̷ **ed**
   e

Spelling Strategy   Remember that if a word ends with **e**, the **e** is usually dropped when a suffix or an ending beginning with a vowel is added. The **e** is usually not dropped when a suffix beginning with a consonant is added.

Write the word that is a synonym for each word below.

11. accusing   13. secretly   15. powerful
12. lovable   14. honestly   16. substitution

Write the word that fits each clue.

17. a word that means "to pardon" + *ness*
18. a word that means "without clothing" + *ly*
19. a word that means "not enough" + *ly*
20. a word that means "to move forward" + *ed*

11. _____
12. _____
13. _____
14. _____
15. _____
16. _____
17. _____
18. _____
19. _____
20. _____

immense
incomplete

21. _____
22. _____
23. _____
24. _____
25. _____
26. _____
27. _____
28. _____
29. _____
30. _____

Unit 15 — The Prefix *in-* — pages 96–101

| informal | include | improper | involve | immigrant |
| indirect | infection | inactive | indent | incomplete |

Spelling Strategy The prefix **in-** is spelled **im** before a base word or a word root beginning with **m** or **p**. Find the prefix, the base word or the word root, and any ending. Then spell the word by parts.

Write a word by adding the prefix *in-* to each base word or word root below. Be sure to spell the prefix correctly.

21. ___ | dent
22. ___ | proper
23. ___ | fection
24. ___ | migrant
25. ___ | volve

Write the word that is a synonym for each word below.

26. roundabout
27. contain
28. unofficial
29. unfinished
30. idle

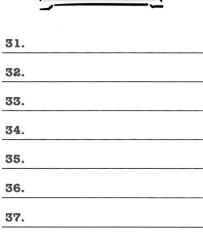

bal ance

31. _____
32. _____
33. _____
34. _____
35. _____
36. _____
37. _____
38. _____
39. _____
40. _____

Unit 16 — VCV Pattern — pages 102–107

| item | secure | minus | stupid | vital |
| beware | deserve | adopt | poison | alert |

Spelling Strategy To find the syllables of a VCV word, divide the word before or after the consonant. Note carefully the spelling of the unstressed syllable. Spell the word by syllables.

Write the word that completes each sentence.

31. Eating wild berries can be as deadly as swallowing _____.
32. Sam made a list of every _____ that he needed to buy.
33. Dad warned me to _____ of cars when I cross the street.
34. Your stories are so clever that they _____ to win a prize.

Write the word that is an antonym for each word below.

35. unimportant
36. unaware
37. plus
38. unfasten
39. reject
40. intelligent

Unit 17   Unstressed Syllables   pages 108–113

position	document	quality	surprise	physical
ignore	parallel	desire	admiral	garage

Spelling Strategy   To spell a two-syllable or three-syllable word, divide the word into syllables. Look for familiar spelling patterns. Note the spelling of any unstressed syllables, and spell the word by syllables.

Write each word by adding an unstressed syllable.

41. physi | ___   **43.** ___ | prise   **45.** docu | ___

42. ___ | sition   **44.** ___ | sire   **46.** ___ | rage

Write the word that completes each sentence.

47. Decisions about naval defense may be made by an _____.

48. The streets that border the river run _____ to each other.

49. Mr. Myers complimented Nita on the high _____ of her work.

50. My little brother feels left out when I _____ him.

Challenge Words   Units 13–17   pages 84–113

imply	vigor	infer	recurring	coordinated
equipped	morale	decade	refinement	transmitted
punctual	delete	ethical	inadequate	disciplined

Write a word by combining the first syllable of the first word with the last syllable of the second word.

51. decorate + lemonade   **53.** inquire + refer

52. debate + athlete   **54.** immune + reply

Write the word that is a synonym or an antonym for each word below.

55. weakness   **61.** enough

56. spirits   **62.** late

57. uncontrolled   **63.** reappearing

58. moral   **64.** elegance

59. furnished   **65.** harmonized

60. received

41. _____
42. _____
43. _____
44. _____
45. _____
46. _____
47. _____
48. _____
49. _____
50. _____
51. _____
52. _____
53. _____
54. _____
55. _____
56. _____
57. _____
58. _____
59. _____
60. _____
61. _____
62. _____
63. _____
64. _____
65. _____

Extra Practice and Review

Unit 19   Adding *-ion* or *-ation*   pages 120–125

construct	attract	examine	contribute	explore
construction	attraction	examination	contribution	exploration

1. _____

2. _____

3. _____

4. _____

5. _____

6. _____

7. _____

8. _____

9. _____

10. _____

Spelling Strategy   The suffix **-ion** or **-ation** can change verbs into nouns. If the verb ends with **e,** drop the **e** before adding **-ion** or **-ation**.

Write the word that completes each sentence.

1. You need certain materials for the _____ of a building.
2. The pioneer drew a map during his _____ of the wilderness.
3. An international food stand was the main _____ at the fair.
4. A microscope lets you _____ a single thread in detail.

Write the word that matches each definition.

5. a test   7. to supply   9. something given
6. to build   8. to try out   10. to draw to itself

Unit 20   More Words with *-ion*   pages 126–131

instruct	graduate	affect	suggest	except
instruction	graduation	affection	suggestion	exception

11. _____

12. _____

13. _____

14. _____

15. _____

16. _____

17. _____

18. _____

19. _____

20. _____

Spelling Strategy   The suffix **-ion** can change verbs to nouns. The suffix **-ion** is added to many words without a spelling change. In some words the final **e** is dropped or another spelling change occurs when **-ion** is added. Remember the spellings of these words.

Write the word that fits each clue.

11. a feeling for a best friend   14. an offer of an idea
12. a cap-and-gown ceremony   15. receive a diploma
13. does not follow the rule   16. another word for education

Write the verb that belongs with each group of words.

17. exclude, omit, _____   19. change, influence, _____
18. imply, bring up, _____   20. explain, teach, _____

Unit 21   The Prefix *con-*   pages 132–137

| consumer | control | constitution | confront | compete |
| content | concert | confirm | composition | contest |

Spelling Strategy   The prefix **con-** is often spelled **com** before the consonant **m** or **p**. Find the prefix, the base word or the word root, and any ending. Spell the word by parts.

Write a word by adding the prefix *con-* or *com-* to each base word or word root.

21. ___ | stitution   23. ___ | position   25. ___ | sumer
22. ___ | pete   24. ___ | trol   26. ___ | front

Write the word that completes each analogy.

27. *Unhappy* is to *glad* as *dissatisfied* is to _____.
28. *No* is to *yes* as *deny* is to _____.
29. *Actor* is to *play* as *musician* is to _____.
30. *Baseball* is to *game* as *spelling bee* is to _____.

Unit 22   Final |īz|, |ĭv|, and |ĭj| pages 138–143

| image | recognize | descriptive | usage | criticize |
| protective | modernize | organize | courage | advantage |

Spelling Strategy

final |īz| → **ize** or **ise**   final |ĭv| → **ive**   final |ĭj| → **age**

Write the word that completes each sentence.

31. The lake reflected an _____ of the sky.
32. To prevent injury, the hockey player wears a _____ mask.
33. Replacing typewriters with computers will _____ an office.
34. Did the reviewer _____ the movie for being too long?

Write the word that fits each clue.

35. fearlessness   38. full of details
36. antonym for *difficulty*   39. remember a person's face
37. arrange neatly   40. the act of using something

21.
22.
23.
24.
25.
26.
27.
28.
29.
30.
31.
32.
33.
34.
35.
36.
37.
38.
39.
40.

239

brilliant

evident	lovable	passable	ignorant	noticeable
agent	considerable	workable	capable	gallant

Spelling Strategy   The suffixes **-ent, -ant, -able,** and **-ible** are sometimes added to base words or word roots. You must remember the spelling pattern for the suffix in each word.

Write the word that is an antonym for each word below.

41. blocked   **43.** small   **45.** educated

42. cowardly   **44.** unskilled

Combine the words below with the suffixes given. Write the new words correctly.

46. love + able   **47.** notice + able

Write the word that is a synonym for each word below.

48. practical   **49.** clear   **50.** representative

Challenge Words   Units 19–23   pages 120–149

exclude	beverage	magnificent	exclusion	aggressive
insulate	improbable	compensate	visualize	
apparent	compliance	commission	insulation	

Write the word that is an antonym for each word below.

51. inclusion   **53.** ordinary   **55.** disobedience

52. timid   **54.** hidden   **56.** likely

Write a word to replace the underlined word or phrase in each sentence below.

57. Did the mayor place an order for those roads to be built?

58. When packing for a trip, omit the unnecessary items.

59. A bird's feathers prevent the loss of heat from its body.

60. Did the thrill of success make up for all your hard work?

61. I want a drink, such as milk or juice, with my meal.

62. I lined the ceiling with material to prevent heat loss.

63. The portrait helped us to form a mental image of the man.

41. _____
42. _____
43. _____
44. _____
45. _____
46. _____
47. _____
48. _____
49. _____
50. _____
51. _____
52. _____
53. _____
54. _____
55. _____
56. _____
57. _____
58. _____
59. _____
60. _____
61. _____
62. _____
63. _____

Cycle 5

Unit 25   Spelling |sh| pages 156–161

motion	direction	partial	station	shallow
official	mention	session	selfish	establish

|sh| glacier

Spelling Strategy   When you hear the |sh| sound, think of the patterns **sh, ti, ci,** and **ss.**

Write the word that matches each definition.

1. showing lack of regard for others
2. management, supervision, or guidance
3. measuring little from the bottom to the top
4. the act of changing position
5. to speak or write about briefly
6. a place for taking on and letting off passengers

Write a word by adding the letters that make the |sh| sound.

7. par _ _ al   **8.** offi _ _ al   **9.** se _ _ ion   **10.** establi _ _

Unit 26   Plurals   pages 162–167

pianos	solos	altos	sopranos	potatoes
wolves	loaves	studios	heroes	scarves

half   staff
halves   staffs

Spelling Strategy

ff → **ffs**   vowel + **o** → **os**
f → **fs** or **ves**   consonant + **o** → **os** or **oes**

Write the word that belongs in each group.

11. carrots, radishes, _____
12. hats, gloves, _____
13. muffins, rolls, _____
14. lions, bears, _____
15. trios, duets, _____
16. guitars, drums, _____

Write the word that fits each clue.

17. You admire them.
18. They sing high.
19. Artists work in these.
20. They sing low.

1. _____
2. _____
3. _____
4. _____
5. _____
6. _____
7. _____
8. _____
9. _____
10. _____
11. _____
12. _____
13. _____
14. _____
15. _____
16. _____
17. _____
18. _____
19. _____
20. _____

ex haust

Unit 27 Prefixes: *dis-*, *ex-*, *inter-*   pages 168–173

discovery	disable	international	dishonest	export
disturb	extent	distress	exhaust	expand

Spelling Strategy **Dis-**, **ex-**, and **inter-** are prefixes. To spell a word with a prefix, find the prefix, the base word or the word root, and any ending. Spell the word by parts.

Write a word by adding a prefix to each word part.

21. ___ | haust   **23.** ___ | covery   **25.** ___ | national
22. ___ | port   **24.** ___ | tent   **26.** ___ | able

Write the word that answers each question.

27. Which word is an antonym for *truthful*?
28. Which word is a synonym for *suffering*?
29. Which word is an antonym for *shrink*?
30. Which word is a synonym for *bother*?

21. _____
22. _____
23. _____
24. _____
25. _____
26. _____
27. _____
28. _____
29. _____
30.

Unit 28 Suffixes: *-ance*, *-ence*, *-ate*   pages 174–179

performance	silence	sentence	celebrate	absence
considerate	allowance	instance	violence	fortunate

performance

Spelling Strategy

final |əns| or |ns| → **ance, ence**   final |ĭt| or |āt| → **ate**

Write the word that completes each sentence.

31. Lisa's illness was the reason for her _____ from class.
32. It is _____ for a dinner guest to help clear the table.
33. This year there has been one _____ of a skating injury.
34. The movie was silly, but the actors gave a fine _____.

Write the word that fits each clue.

35. Winners feel this way.   **38.** It states a complete thought.
36. Noise breaks it.   **39.** You can save it or spend it.
37. It can cause damage.   **40.** You do this on holidays.

31. _____
32. _____
33. _____
34. _____
35. _____
36. _____
37. _____
38. _____
39. _____
40. _____

Unit 29 Prefixes: *per-, pre-, pro-* pages 180–185

prehistoric	proceed	project	profession	progress
prepare	prepaid	promise	product	perfume

Spelling Strategy Many words begin with the prefix **per-**, **pre-**, or **pro-**. Find the prefix, the base word or the word root, and any ending. Spell the word by parts.

Write a word by changing the underlined prefix.

41. <u>con</u>gress   43. <u>con</u>duct   45. <u>in</u>ject
42. <u>com</u>pare   44. <u>pre</u>mise   46. <u>un</u>paid

Write the word that completes each analogy.

47. *Confess* is to *confession* as *profess* is to _____.
48. *Whale* is to *modern* as *dinosaur* is to _____.
49. *Appearance* is to *clothing* as *scent* is to _____.
50. *Stop* is to *stay* as *go* is to _____.

Challenge Words Units 25–29 pages 156–185

diminish	tuxedos	elaborate	mementos	exposure
technician	procure	illuminate	perception	maestros
exaggerate	expertise	intervene	recession	preservation

Write a word by adding the missing syllables.

51. ___ | per | ___   55. ___ | min | ___
52. ___ | men | ___   56. ___ | ces | ___
53. ___ | e | ___   57. ___ | ni | ___
54. ___ | po | ___   58. ___ | ter | ___

Write the word that fits each clue.

59. A lamp, a flashlight, and a torch all do this.
60. You do this if you say, "We had to wait in line for ages!"
61. Some conduct symphony orchestras.
62. Two of its synonyms are *obtain* and *acquire*.
63. This is something that is very detailed.
64. A wildlife refuge is concerned with this.
65. This is an awareness through a sense, such as sight.

41. _____
42. _____
43. _____
44. _____
45. _____
46. _____
47. _____
48. _____
49. _____
50. _____
51. _____
52. _____
53. _____
54. _____
55. _____
56. _____
57. _____
58. _____
59. _____
60. _____
61. _____
62. _____
63. _____
64. _____
65. _____

diesel freight

Unit 31   Words with *ie* or *ei*   pages 192–197

| review | eighty | brief | belief | ceiling |
| reign | shield | grief | relieve | diesel |

Spelling Strategy   Use **i** before **e** except after **c** or in words with the |ā| sound, as in **weigh**. You must memorize exceptions to this generalization.

Write the word that completes each analogy.

1. *Twenty* is to *forty* as *forty* is to _____.
2. *Below* is to *above* as *floor* is to _____.
3. *Thirst* is to *quench* as *pain* is to _____.
4. *Vain* is to *vein* as *rain* is to _____.

Write the word that fits each clue.

5. a sad feeling
6. a train's engine
7. an antonym for *long*
8. a critic's opinion
9. used for protection
10. a synonym for *trust*

1. _____
2. _____
3. _____
4. _____
5. _____
6. _____
7. _____
8. _____
9. _____
10. _____

account
addition

Unit 32   The Prefix *ad-*   pages 198–203

| account | addition | advise | assure | applaud |
| according | accuse | assume | assign | appeal |

Spelling Strategy   The prefix **ad-** can be spelled **ac, af, ap,** or **as** to match the first consonant or consonant sound of the base word or the word root.

Write a word by adding a prefix to each word part.

11. ___ | count   13. ___ | cording   15. ___ | sure
12. ___ | sign   14. ___ | dition   16. ___ | vise

Write the word that matches each definition.

17. to blame for wrongdoing
18. to take for granted; suppose
19. an urgent or earnest request
20. to express praise or approval by clapping

11. _____
12. _____
13. _____
14. _____
15. _____
16. _____
17. _____
18. _____
19. _____
20. _____

Unit 33   Endings: *-ic, -ture, -ous*   pages 204–209

signature	patriotic	democratic	serious	gigantic
tragic	dramatic	fantastic	furious	numerous

John Hancock

patriotic signature

Spelling Strategy

final |ĭk| → **ic**   final |chər| → **ture**   final |əs| → **ous**

Write the word that is a synonym for each word below.

21. raging   **24.** enormous
22. dreadful   **25.** grave
23. weird   **26.** striking

Write the word that completes each sentence.

27. People who love their country are _____.
28. That sweater is available in _____ colors.
29. The United States is a _____ country.
30. Print your name and then write your _____.

21. _____
22. _____
23. _____
24. _____
25. _____
26. _____
27. _____
28. _____
29. _____
30. _____

Unit 34   Prefixes: *de-, ob-*   pages 210–215

debate	defeat	describe	observe	demand
demonstrate	decay	oblige	decrease	decline

de bate

Spelling Strategy

De- and **ob-** are prefixes. **Ob-** is spelled **oc** before **c**. To spell a word with a prefix, find the prefix, the base word or word root, and any ending. Spell the word by parts.

Write the word that completes each analogy.

31. *Expand* is to *increase* as *shrink* is to _____.
32. *Win* is to *lose* as *victory* is to _____.
33. *Noun* is to *name* as *adjective* is to _____.
34. *Tell* is to *show* as *explain* is to _____.

Write a word by adding a prefix to each word part below.

35. ___ | cay   **37.** ___ | mand   **39.** ___ | cline
36. ___ | lige   **38.** ___ | serve   **40.** ___ | bate

31. _____
32. _____
33. _____
34. _____
35. _____
36. _____
37. _____
38. _____
39. _____
40. _____

unbelievable invention

Unit 35   Word Parts   pages 216–221

invention	information	preparation	advancement
unskillful	respectful	imprisonment	intermission
disagreement	repetition		

Spelling Strategy   Many words are made up of a prefix, a base word or a word root, and a suffix. Find these parts in a word, and then spell the word by the parts.

Write a word by adding a prefix or a suffix to each word.

41. agreement   **43.** imprison   **45.** advance

42. prepare   **44.** skillful   **46.** invent

Write the word that answers each question.

47. How do you feel toward those you admire?

48. What often comes between the acts of a play?

49. What is a synonym for *data*?

50. What helps you memorize the multiplication tables?

Challenge Words   Units 31–35   pages 192–221

wield	eerie	hygiene	appropriate	affiliated
applicant	symbolic	chronic	stature	obscure
obstacle	deficient	precision	reputation	inevitable

Write a word that is a synonym for each word below.

51. barrier   **53.** insufficient   **55.** size   **57.** esteem

52. exactness   **54.** representative   **56.** suitable

Write the word that fits each clue.

58. This person wants a job.

59. You can do this with a sword.

60. This describes something you cannot prevent.

61. This word is an antonym for *clear*.

62. A dark alley might be described this way.

63. This type of disease lasts for a long time.

64. Students sometimes enroll in this health class.

65. This word means "associated" or "joined."

41.
42.
43.
44.
45.
46.
47.
48.
49.
50.
51.
52.
53.
54.
55.
56.
57.
58.
59.
60.
61.
62.
63.
64.
65.

Writer's Resources

Capitalization and Punctuation Guide

Abbreviations

Abbreviations are shortened forms of words. Most abbreviations begin with a capital letter and end with a period.

Titles

Mr. *(Mister)* Mr. Juan Albano   Sr. *(Senior)* John Helt, Sr.
Mrs. *(Mistress)* Mrs. Frances Wong   Jr. *(Junior)* John Helt, Jr.
Ms. Susan Clark   Dr. *(Doctor)* Dr. Janice Dodd

Note: *Miss* is not an abbreviation and does not end with a period.

Words used in addresses

St. *(Street)*   Dr. *(Drive)*   Pkwy. *(Parkway)*
Rd. *(Road)*   Rte. *(Route)*   Mt. *(Mount or Mountain)*
Ave. *(Avenue)*   Apt. *(Apartment)* Expy. *(Expressway)*

Words used in business

Co. *(Company)*   Corp. *(Corporation)*   Inc. *(Incorporated)*

Other abbreviations

Some abbreviations are written in all capital letters, with a letter standing for each important word.

P.D. *(Police Department)*   P.O. *(Post Office)*
J.P. *(Justice of the Peace)*   R.N. *(Registered Nurse)*

Some abbreviations do not have capital letters or periods.

mph *(miles per hour)*   hp *(horsepower)*   km *(kilometer)*

Abbreviations of government agencies or national organizations usually do not have periods.

NPR *(National Public Radio)*   FBI *(Federal Bureau of Investigation)*

The United States Postal Service uses two capital letters and no period in each of its state abbreviations.

AL *(Alabama)*   DE *(Delaware)*   IA *(Iowa)*
AK *(Alaska)*   FL *(Florida)*   KS *(Kansas)*
AZ *(Arizona)*   GA *(Georgia)*   KY *(Kentucky)*
AR *(Arkansas)*   HI *(Hawaii)*   LA *(Louisiana)*
CA *(California)*   ID *(Idaho)*   ME *(Maine)*
CO *(Colorado)*   IL *(Illinois)*   MD *(Maryland)*
CT *(Connecticut)*   IN *(Indiana)*   MA *(Massachusetts)*

(continued)

Other abbreviations (continued)	MI (Michigan)	NY (New York)	TN (Tennessee)
	MN (Minnesota)	NC (North Carolina)	TX (Texas)
	MS (Mississippi)	ND (North Dakota)	UT (Utah)
	MO (Missouri)	OH (Ohio)	VT (Vermont)
	MT (Montana)	OK (Oklahoma)	VA (Virginia)
	NE (Nebraska)	OR (Oregon)	WA (Washington)
	NV (Nevada)	PA (Pennsylvania)	WV (West Virginia)
	NH (New Hampshire)	RI (Rhode Island)	WI (Wisconsin)
	NJ (New Jersey)	SC (South Carolina)	WY (Wyoming)
	NM (New Mexico)	SD (South Dakota)	

Titles

Underlining

Titles of books, newspapers, and movies are underlined.

Oliver Twist (book)   Springfield Herald (newspaper)
Cricket (magazine)   The Black Stallion (movie)

Quotation marks

Titles of short stories, articles, songs, book chapters, and most poems are enclosed in quotation marks.

"The Necklace" (short story)   "Home on the Range" (song)
"Three Days in the Sahara" (article) "Wind Song" (poem)

Quotations

Quotation marks with commas and periods

Quotation marks are used to set off a speaker's exact words. The first word of a quotation begins with a capital letter. Punctuation belongs inside the closing quotation marks. Commas separate a quotation from the rest of the sentence.

"Where," asked the visitor, "is the post office?"
"Please put away your books now," said Mr. Emory.
Mary said, "Let's eat lunch."

Capitalization

Rules for capitalization

Capitalize the first word of every sentence.

What an unusual color the roses are!

Capitalize the pronoun I.

What should I do next?

Capitalize every important word in the names of particular people, places, or things (proper nouns).

Emily G. Hesse   District of Columbia   Lincoln Memorial

Capitalize titles or abbreviations used with a person's name.

Governor Bradford   Senator Smith   Dr. Lin

Capitalize proper adjectives.

We ate at a Chinese restaurant.   She is French.

Capitalize the names of months and days.

My birthday is not on the last Monday in March.

Capitalize the names of buildings and companies.

The Empire State Building   The Bell Company

Capitalize the names of holidays.

Flag Day   Thanksgiving   Fourth of July

Capitalize the first and last words and all important words in the titles of books, newspapers, movies, and songs.

From Earth to the Moon   "The Rainbow Connection"
The New York Times   "Growing Up in the South"

Capitalize the first word in the greeting and the closing of a letter.

Dear Marcia,   Yours truly,

Rules for capitalization (*continued*)	**Capitalize the first word of each main topic and subtopic in an outline.**
	
	1. <u>T</u>ypes of libraries
	    A. <u>L</u>arge public library
	    B. <u>B</u>ookmobile

Punctuation

End marks	**There are three end marks. A period (.) ends a declarative or imperative sentence. A question mark (?) follows an interrogative sentence. An exclamation point (!) follows an exclamatory sentence.** The scissors are on my desk<u>.</u> (*declarative*) Look up the spelling of that word<u>.</u> (*imperative*) How is the word spelled<u>?</u> (*interrogative*) This is your best poem so far<u>!</u> (*exclamatory*)
Apostrophe	**To form the possessive of a singular noun, add an apostrophe and s.** sister<u>'s</u> family<u>'s</u> Tess<u>'s</u> Jim Dodge<u>'s</u>
	For a plural noun that ends in s, add an apostrophe only. sisters<u>'</u> families<u>'</u> Smiths<u>'</u> Evanses<u>'</u>
	For a plural noun that does not end in s, add an apostrophe and s. women<u>'s</u> mice<u>'s</u> children<u>'s</u>
	Use an apostrophe in contractions in place of the dropped letters. isn<u>'</u>t (*is not*) wasn<u>'</u>t (*was not*) I<u>'</u>m (*I am*) can<u>'</u>t (*cannot*) we<u>'</u>re (*we are*) they<u>'</u>ve (*they have*) won<u>'</u>t (*will not*) it<u>'</u>s (*it is*) they<u>'</u>ll (*they will*)
Colon	**Use a colon after the greeting in a business letter.** Dear Mrs. Trimby<u>:</u> Dear Realty Homes<u>:</u>

Comma	**A comma tells the reader to pause between words. Use commas to separate words in a series. Use a comma before the conjunction that connects the items.**
	We bought apples, peaches, and grapes.
	Use a comma to separate the simple sentences in a compound sentence.
	Some students were at lunch, but others were studying.
	Use commas to set off an appositive in most cases.
	Vermont, the Green Mountain State, has lovely scenery.
	Use commas after introductory words such as *yes, no, oh,* and *well*.
	Well, it's just too cold out. No, it isn't six yet.
	Use a comma to set off a noun in direct address.
	Jean, help me fix this tire. How was your trip, Grandpa?
	Use a comma to separate the month and day from the year. Use a comma to separate the year from the rest of the sentence.
	My sister was born on April 9, 1980, in Detroit. July 4, 1776, is the birthday of our nation.
	Use a comma between the names of a city and a state.
	Chicago, Illinois Miami, Florida
	Use a comma after the greeting in a friendly letter.
	Dear Deena, Dear Uncle Rudolph,
	Use a comma after the closing in a letter.
	Your nephew, Sincerely yours,
	Use a comma after an interjection that begins a sentence.
	Hey, I got the tickets.
Exclamation point	**Use an exclamation point after an interjection that stands alone.**
	Wow! Did you see that?

Letter Models

Friendly Letter

Use correct letter format, capitalization, and punctuation in a friendly letter. A friendly letter has **five** parts.

1 The **heading** contains your complete address and the date.

2 The **greeting** usually includes the word *Dear* and the name of the person to whom you are writing.

3 The **body** is the main part of the letter. It includes all the information that you want to tell your reader.

4 The **closing** says "good-bye." Use closings such as *Your friend* or *Love*.

5 The **signature** is your first name. Sign it under the closing.

Study this model.

RF D1
Woodsville, NH 03785
October 20, 1998 **Heading**

Dear Stacy, **Greeting**

Body

How do you like having a pen pal from New Hampshire? I think it'll be fun to have a friend from Georgia!

I'm sure we do many of the same things, but we probably do different things, too. Today I stacked firewood for the winter. How do you prepare for winter? Write soon and tell me!!

Closing → Your new friend,
William

Signature

Letter Models

Business Letter

Use correct letter format, capitalization, and punctuation in a business letter. A business letter has **six** parts.

1. The **heading** is the same as in a friendly letter.
2. The **inside address** includes the name and address of the person or business that will receive the letter.
3. The **greeting** follows the inside address. If you do not know whom to address, use *Dear Sir or Madam* or the company's name. Use a colon (:) after the greeting.
4. The **body** is your message. Be direct and polite.
5. The **closing** is formal. Use *Yours truly*, for example.
6. The **signature** is your full name. Write it under the closing. Print or type your name under your signature.

Study this model.

Heading
23 Mirador Street
Santa Rosa, CA 95405
May 20, 1998

Inside address
Wide World of Hobbies
318 Market Street
San Francisco, CA 94102

Dear Wide World of Hobbies: **Greeting**

Body
I purchased Kit #321, the Space Shuttle Model, at your store. While working on this model, I discovered that a piece was missing.

I circled the missing piece on the enclosed diagram. Can you send it to me? Thank you.

Sincerely, **Closing**
Signature Ronald Chin
Ronald Chin

Using the Thesaurus

Why Use a Thesaurus?

A **thesaurus** is a reference that can help you make your writing clearer and more interesting. Use it to find a word to replace an overused word or to find an exact word to say what you mean.

How to Use This Thesaurus

This thesaurus includes main entries for words you often use. The **main entry words** appear in blue and are in alphabetical order. The main entry for *bad* is shown below. Each main entry includes

- the **part of speech,** a **definition,** and a **sample sentence** for the main entry word;

- several **subentry words** that could be used in place of the main entry word, with a definition and a sample sentence for each one;

- **antonyms,** or opposites, for the main entry word.

For example   **How would you decide which subentry to use to replace *bad* in this sentence?**

*The rotten eggs had a **bad** odor.*

1 Find each subentry word given for *bad.* They are *awful, foul, inferior,* and *naughty.*

2 Read the definition and the sample sentence for each subentry. Decide which subentry fits the meaning of the sentence most closely.

*The rotten eggs had a **foul** odor.*

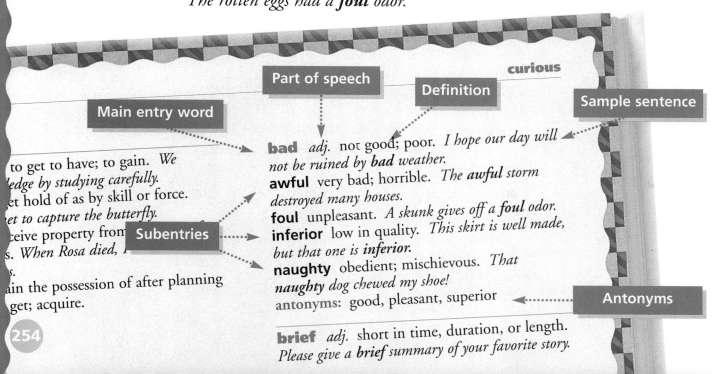

Part of speech

Definition

curious

Main entry word

Sample sentence

to get to have; to gain. *We*
ledge by studying carefully.
et hold of as by skill or force.
et to capture the butterfly.
ceive property from
s. *When Rosa died,*
s.

Subentries

ain the possession of after planning
get; acquire.

bad *adj.* not good; poor. *I hope our day will*
*not be ruined by **bad** weather.*
awful very bad; horrible. *The **awful** storm*
destroyed many houses.
foul unpleasant. *A skunk gives off a **foul** odor.*
inferior low in quality. *This skirt is well made,*
*but that one is **inferior**.*
naughty obedient; mischievous. *That*
***naughty** dog chewed my shoe!*
antonyms: good, pleasant, superior

Antonyms

brief *adj.* short in time, duration, or length.
*Please give a **brief** summary of your favorite story.*

254

Using the Thesaurus Index

The Thesaurus Index will help you find a word in this Thesaurus. The Thesaurus Index lists **all** of the main entry words, the subentries, and any antonyms included in the Thesaurus. The words in the Thesaurus Index are in alphabetical order.

When you look in the Thesaurus Index, you will see that words are shown in three ways.

Main entry words are shown in blue. For example, the word *bad* is a main entry.

Antonyms are shown in regular print. For example, *ban* is an antonym.

Subentries are shown in dark print. For example, *brilliant* is a subentry.

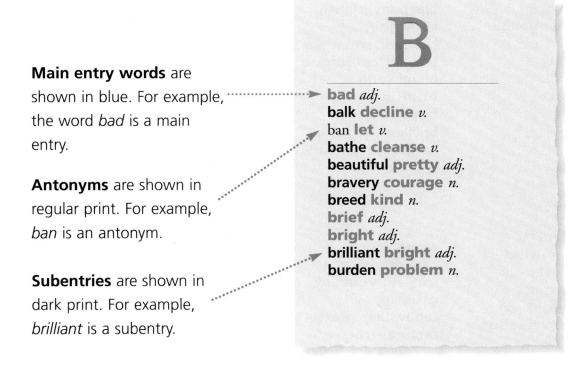

B

bad *adj.*
balk decline *v.*
ban let *v.*
bathe cleanse *v.*
beautiful pretty *adj.*
bravery courage *n.*
breed kind *n.*
brief *adj.*
bright *adj.*
brilliant bright *adj.*
burden problem *n.*

Practice Look up each word below in the Thesaurus Index. Write the main entry word for each word.

1. change **2.** accurate **3.** homely **4.** scrub **5.** reply

Use the Thesaurus to choose a more exact word to replace each underlined word. Rewrite each sentence, using the new word.

6. One day Erin could not <u>find</u> her hamster anywhere.
7. She asked her brother to <u>help</u> her search for Fuzzy.
8. Mom scolded Erin for not paying <u>strict</u> attention to her pet.
9. Then Erin found Fuzzy in an <u>unusual</u> place — her slipper!
10. "That's a clever <u>method</u> for keeping warm," thought Erin.

Thesaurus Index

A

abridged **brief** *adj.*
absolute **strict** *adj.*
abundant **numerous** *adj.*
accept **decline** *v.*
accurate **right** *adj.*
acquire *v.*
acquire **secure** *v.*
adaptable **changeable** *adj.*
adjust **change** *v.*
admire **respect** *v.*
advance **go** *v.*
advancement *n.*
advise **help** *v.*
agree **decline** *v.*
alarm **frighten** *v.*
alert **lively** *adj.*
amaze **surprise** *v.*
ancient **old** *adj.*
answer **ask** *v.*
answer **problem** *n.*
anxious **nervous** *adj.*
appealing **pretty** *adj.*
appreciate **respect** *v.*
appropriate **right** *adj.*
argument **conversation** *n.*
aroma **smell** *n.*
assemble **make** *v.*
assist **help** *v.*
ask *v.*
assume **think** *v.*
astonish **surprise** *v.*
assure **frighten** *v.*
attention **concentration** *n.*
attractive **pretty** *adj.*
attribute **quality** *n.*
author *n.*
authorize **let** *v.*
awful **bad** *adj.*
awful **fantastic** *adj.*

B

bad *adj.*
balk **decline** *v.*
ban **let** *v.*
bathe **cleanse** *v.*
bawl **laugh** *v.*
beautiful **pretty** *adj.*
blueprint **plan** *n.*
bony **thin** *adj.*
bouquet **smell** *n.*
bravery **courage** *n.*
breed **kind** *n.*
brief *adj.*
bright *adj.*
brilliant **bright** *adj.*
burden **problem** *n.*

C

cackle **laugh** *v.*
calm **frighten** *v.*
calm **nervous** *adj.*
capable *adj.*
captivating **pretty** *adj.*
capture **acquire** *v.*
cautiousness **courage** *n.*
change *v.*
changeable *adj.*
characteristic **quality** *n.*
charming **delightful** *adj.*
charming **pretty** *adj.*
chat **conversation** *n.*
cheap **frugal** *adj.*
chipper **lively** *adj.*
chortle **laugh** *v.*
chuckle **laugh** *v.*
civilize **change** *v.*
clamor **silence** *n.*
cleanse *v.*
comely **pretty** *adj.*
comfort **frighten** *v.*
command **control** *v.*
common **unusual** *adj.*
complicated **difficult** *adj.*

compromising **strict** *adj.*
conceal **find** *v.*
concentration *n.*
concise **brief** *adj.*
conference **conversation** *n.*
consent **decline** *v.*
consent **let** *v.*
consider **think** *v.*
constant **changeable** *adj.*
construct **make** *v.*
consultation **conversation** *n.*
contaminate **cleanse** *v.*
contemplate **look** *v.*
contemporary **old** *adj.*
contribute **help** *v.*
control *v.*
conversation *n.*
convert **persuade** *v.*
convince **persuade** *v.*
cooperate **help** *v.*
courage *n.*
course **method** *n.*
cowardice **courage** *n.*
crave **wish** *v.*
crisis **problem** *n.*
cruise **journey** *n.*
cry **laugh** *v.*
curb **control** *v.*
curious **unusual** *adj.*

D

data **information** *n.*
decline *v.*
decrease **grow** *v.*
dedicated **earnest** *adj.*
defeat **surrender** *v.*
delightful *adj.*
demand **require** *v.*
demanding **strict** *adj.*
demonstrate **show** *v.*
denigrate **respect** *v.*
density **concentration** *n.*
deny **decline** *v.*
depart **go** *v.*
dependable **responsible** *adj.*
design **plan** *n.*

desire **wish** *v.*
destroy **make** *v.*
determine **think** *v.*
determined earnest *adj.*
devalue **respect** *v.*
develop grow *v.*
dialogue conversation *n.*
difficult *adj.*
difficulty problem *n.*
dim **bright** *adj.*
dirty **cleanse** *v.*
disapprove **respect** *v.*
disassemble **make** *v.*
discharge **control** *v.*
discover find *v.*
disgraceful *adj.*
dishonorable disgraceful *adj.*
display show *v.*
disturb frighten *v.*
dramatic strong *adj.*
dramatist author *v.*
dry-clean cleanse *v.*
dull **bright** *adj.*
dull **lively** *adj.*
dust cleanse *v.*

E

earnest *adj.*
easy **difficult** *adj.*
economical **frugal** *adj.*
edgy nervous *adj.*
educated **ignorant** *adj.*
efficient capable *adj.*
enchanting fantastic *adj.*
engaging pretty *adj.*
enjoyable delightful *adj.*
enlarge grow *v.*
erroneous **right** *adj.*
exact strict *adj.*
exacting strict *adj.*
examine ask *v.*
examine search *v.*
exceptional unusual *adj.*
exhibit show *v.*
expand grow *v.*
expedition journey *n.*

explore *v.*
exquisite fantastic *adj.*
extended **brief** *adj.*
extravagant **frugal** *adj.*
extreme numerous *adj.*

F

faint **bright** *adj.*
fair pretty *adj.*
faithful strict *adj.*
fall *v.*
familiar **unusual** *adj.*
fantastic *adj.*
fasten secure *v.*
fat **thin** *adj.*
fear **courage** *n.*
feeble **strong** *adj.*
few **numerous** *adj.*
find *v.*
flexible changeable *adj.*
flexible **strict** *adj.*
foolhardiness courage *n.*
forbid **let** *v.*
forceful strong *adj.*
forfeit **acquire** *v.*
forgo **acquire** *v.*
fortitude courage *n.*
foul **bad** *adj.*
fragrance smell *n.*
frighten *v.*
frivolous **earnest** *adj.*
frugal *adj.*
full strict *adj.*

G

gallantry courage *n.*
gaze look *v.*
generous **frugal** *adj.*
giggle laugh *v.*
glamorous pretty *adj.*
glance look *v.*
go *v.*
good **bad** *adj.*

good-looking pretty *adj.*
gorgeous pretty *adj.*
grow *v.*
guffaw laugh *v.*

H

heedfulness **courage** *n.*
help *v.*
heroism courage *n.*
hide **find** *v.*
hinder **help** *v.*
homely **pretty** *adj.*
horrible **fantastic** *adj.*
hubbub **silence** *n.*
hush silence *n.*

I

ignorant *adj.*
ignore **look** *v.*
impede **help** *v.*
imperfect **strict** *adj.*
imprecise **strict** *adj.*
improvement advancement *n.*
incapable **capable** *adj.*
incompetent **capable** *adj.*
incomplete **strict** *adj.*
inconvenient difficult *adj.*
incorrect **right** *adj.*
inferior bad *adj.*
inflexible strict *adj.*
information *n.*
inherit acquire *v.*
innocent ignorant *adj.*
inquire ask *v.*
insist require *v.*
inspiring fantastic *adj.*
intelligent **ignorant** *adj.*
interview conversation *n.*
investigate explore *v.*
irresponsible **responsible** *adj.*

Thesaurus Index

J

journalist **author** *n.*
journey *n.*

K

keep **change** *v.*
kind *n.*

L

laugh *v.*
launder cleanse *v.*
lax **strict** *adj.*
lean **thin** *adj.*
lengthy **brief** *adj.*
lenient **strict** *adj.*
let *v.*
liberal **strict** *adj.*
lifeless **lively** *adj.*
lively *adj.*
locate find *v.*
long **brief** *adj.*
look *v.*
lose **acquire** *v.*
lose **find** *v.*
lovely pretty *adj.*

M

make *v.*
manner kind *n.*
manner method *n.*
manufacture make *v.*
meager **numerous** *adj.*
mediocre **fantastic** *adj.*
meekness **courage** *n.*
method *n.*
mettle courage *n.*
miserly **frugal** *adj.*
miss **find** *v.*

miss **look** *v.*
mission journey *n.*
modern **old** *adj.*
modernize change *v.*
mop cleanse *v.*
moral right *adj.*

N

naughty bad *adj.*
necessitate require *v.*
nervous *adj.*
new **old** *adj.*
news information *n.*
novelist author *n.*
numerous *adj.*

O

oblige **decline** *v.*
observe look *v.*
obtain acquire *v.*
obvious **difficult** *adj.*
odor smell *n.*
old *adj.*
old-fashioned old *adj.*
oppose **help** *v.*
overlook **look** *v.*
overpower **surrender** *v.*

P

panic frighten *v.*
partial **strict** *adj.*
pattern method *n.*
peculiarity quality *n.*
perfect strict *adj.*
perform show *v.*
permanent **changeable** *adj.*
permit let *v.*
persist **surrender** *v.*
persuade *v.*
placid **nervous** *adj.*
plan *n.*

plan **method** *n.*
pleasant **bad** *adj.*
plunge fall *v.*
poet author *n.*
policy method *n.*
polish cleanse *v.*
pollute **cleanse** *v.*
portly **thin** *adj.*
powerless **strong** *adj.*
practice method *n.*
precise right *adj.*
precise strict *adj.*
prehistoric old *adj.*
prepare make *v.*
preserve **change** *v.*
pretty *adj.*
prevent **let** *v.*
probe explore *v.*
problem *n.*
procedure method *n.*
proceed go *v.*
process method *n.*
prodigal **frugal** *adj.*
progress go *v.*
progress advancement *n.*
prohibit **let** *v.*
protest decline *v.*
prudence **courage** *n.*
puzzling difficult *adj.*

Q

quality *n.*
qualified capable *adj.*
question ask *v.*

R

rashness courage *n.*
ravishing pretty *adj.*
reaction *n.*
recklessness courage *n.*
reek smell *n.*
reflex reaction *n.*
refuse decline *v.*

regulate **control** *v.*
relaxed **nervous** *adj.*
release **control** *v.*
reliable responsible *adj.*
relieve **control** *v.*
relieve **frighten** *v.*
remain **go** *v.*
reply **ask** *v.*
require *v.*
resolution **problem** *n.*
respect *v.*
respond **ask** *v.*
response reaction *n.*
responsible *adj.*
restrain control *v.*
retain **change** *v.*
reticence silence *n.*
right *adj.*
rigid strict *adj.*
rigorous strict *adj.*
rinse cleanse *v.*
routine method *n.*
routine **unusual** *adj.*
ruin make *v.*

S

safari journey *n.*
scant **numerous** *adj.*
scanty brief *adj.*
scent smell *n.*
scheme method *n.,*
 plan *n.*
scour cleanse *v.*
scrape cleanse *v.*
scrawny thin *adj.*
scrub cleanse *v.*
search *v.*
secure *v.*
secure acquire *v.*
seek search *v.*
serious earnest *adj.*
several numerous *adj.*
severe strict *adj.*
shameful disgraceful *adj.*

shining bright *adj.*
show *v.*
shrink **grow** *v.*
simple **difficult** *adj.*
silence *n.*
skinny thin *adj.*
slender thin *adj.*
slim thin *adj.*
slow **lively** *adj.*
smell *n.*
snicker laugh *v.*
snigger laugh *v.*
soak cleanse *v.*
sob **laugh** *v.*
soil **cleanse** *v.*
solid responsible *adj.*
solution **problem** *n.*
spare thin *adj.*
sparing frugal *adj.*
spendthrift frugal *adj.*
spirit courage *n.*
spirited lively *adj.*
sponge cleanse *v.*
spot **cleanse** *v.*
spot find *v.*
sprout grow *v.*
stable **changeable** *adj.*
stain **cleanse** *v.*
startle frighten *v.*
stay **go** *v.*
steadfast earnest *adj.*
stench smell *n.*
stern strict *adj.*
stingy frugal *adj.*
stink smell *n.*
stop **go** *v.*
stout thin *adj.*
strain kind *n.*
strategy plan *n.*
strenuous difficult *adj.*
strict *adj.*
strong *adj.*
struggle problem *n.*
stubborn difficult *adj.*
stumble fall *v.*
stunning pretty *adj.*

stupid ignorant *adj.*
submit surrender *v.*
succumb surrender *v.*
sumptuous fantastic *adj.*
superior **bad** *adj.*
surprise *v.*
surrender *v.*
switch change *v.*
system method *n.*

T

tarnish **cleanse** *v.*
technique method *n.*
thin *adj.*
think *v.*
thrifty frugal *adj.*
thrilling fantastic *adj.*
titter laugh *v.*
total strict *adj.*
tour journey *n.*
trait quality *n.*
tranquillity silence *n.*
trek journey *n.*
trustworthy responsible *adj.*
tumble fall *v.*

U

ugly **pretty** *adj.*
unattractive **pretty** *adj.*
uncommitted **earnest** *adj.*
unconventional unusual
 adj.
undependable **responsible**
 adj.
unearth find *v.*
uneducated ignorant *adj.*
uninformed ignorant *adj.*
unreliable **responsible** *adj.*
unstable changeable *adj.*
unusual *adj.*
unyielding strict *adj.*
uproar **silence** *n.*

Thesaurus Index

V

valor courage *n.*
variable changeable *adj.*
variety kind *n.*

W

wail **laugh** *v.*
weak **strong** *adj.*
weep **laugh** *v.*
wither **grow** *v.*
wise **ignorant** *adj.*
wish *v.*
wrong **right** *adj.*

Y

yield surrender *v.*

Thesaurus

A

acquire *v.* to get to have; to gain. *We acquire knowledge by studying carefully.*
capture to get hold of as by skill or force. *They used a net to capture the butterfly.*
inherit to receive property from someone after he or she dies. *When Rosa died, I inherited her family pictures.*
obtain to gain the possession of after planning or endeavor; get; acquire. *After years of schooling, John obtained a medical degree.*
secure to gain possession of. *Mary secured a loan to pay for her car.*
antonyms: forfeit, forgo, lose

advancement *n.* development. *Galileo contributed greatly to the advancement of science.*
improvement a change or advancement that makes something better. *Rick's grades showed improvement last term.*
progress steady improvement, as in a civilization or individual. *There has been tremendous progress in the field of computers over the past twenty years.*

ask *v.* to raise a question. *Meg asked, "What time does the play begin?"*
examine to question to obtain information or facts. *The lawyer examined the witness to find out when the crime took place.*
inquire to ask in order to find out. *I inquired about the date of the party.*
question to seek information from. *Burt's employer questioned him about his future plans.*
antonyms: answer *v.*, reply *v.*, respond

author *n.* a person who writes a book, story, article, and so on. *E. B. White is the author of* Charlotte's Web.
dramatist a person who writes plays. *Which dramatist wrote our class play?*

journalist a person who writes for a newspaper. *My mother is a journalist who writes articles about politics for the* Kansas City Star.
novelist a person who writes book-length fiction. *Robert Louis Stevenson was a Scottish novelist who wrote* Treasure Island *and many other exciting books.*
poet a person who writes poems. *The poet Robert Frost wrote "The Road Not Taken," my favorite poem.*

B

bad *adj.* not good; poor. *I hope our day will not be ruined by bad weather.*
awful very bad; horrible. *The awful storm destroyed many houses.*
foul unpleasant. *A skunk gives off a foul odor.*
inferior low in quality. *This skirt is well made, but that one is inferior.*
naughty obedient; mischievous. *That naughty dog chewed my shoe!*
antonyms: good, pleasant, superior

brief *adj.* short in time, duration, or length. *Please give a brief summary of your favorite story.*
abridged reduced in length. *The magazine printed an abridged version of the long story.*
concise expressing much in a few words; brief and clear. *Write concise directions so that your readers will understand them easily.*
scanty too small or brief. *His scanty description of the scene didn't allow readers to picture it in their minds.*
antonyms: extended, lengthy, long

bright *adj.* giving off or filled with light. *The stadium looks bright under the big spotlights.*
brilliant shining brightly; glittering. *The brilliant stars twinkled in the dark sky.*

shining giving off or reflecting light; glowing. *The **shining** floor had just been waxed.*
antonyms: dim *adj.*, dull *adj.*, faint, *adj.*

C

capable *adj.* able; skilled; competent. *Is Ernie **capable** of repairing a bike?*
efficient working without wasting time, materials, or energy. *Because Al is an **efficient** worker, he was promoted.*
qualified suited for a particular purpose, position, or task. *Peggy practiced the skills she needed to become a **qualified** lifeguard.*
antonyms: incapable, incompetent

change *v.* to make or become different. *Add onions to **change** the flavor of the pizza.*
adjust to change, set, or regulate in order to achieve a desired result. *I **adjusted** the television picture to make the wavy lines disappear.*
civilize to refine by training. *A good school can **civilize** young minds.*
modernize to make modern; alter or bring up-to-date so as to meet current needs. *They **modernized** the old farmhouse by adding a new kitchen.*
switch to shift, transfer, or change. *Suddenly our talk **switched** from a friendly chat to a disagreement.*
antonyms: keep, preserve *v.*, retain

changeable *adj.* capable of changing. *If you plan an outside function, be prepared for **changeable** weather.*
adaptable able to change or be adjusted so as to fit in with new or different situations. *The cat was so **adaptable** that it could sleep happily in a drawer.*
flexible capable of or responsive to change; adaptable. *The rules must be **flexible** enough to work in all situations.*

unstable having a strong tendency to change. *The country was so **unstable** that the government changed twice in one year.*
variable subject to change. *Variable weather threatened our baseball game and canceled our picnic.*
antonyms: constant, permanent, stable *adj.*

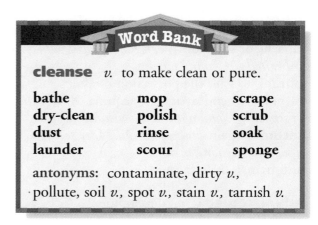

Word Bank

cleanse *v.* to make clean or pure.

bathe	mop	scrape
dry-clean	polish	scrub
dust	rinse	soak
launder	scour	sponge

antonyms: contaminate, dirty *v.*, pollute, soil *v.*, spot *v.*, stain *v.*, tarnish *v.*

concentration *n.* close, undivided attention. *The loud car horn made the golfer lose his **concentration**.*
attention concentration of the mental powers upon something or someone. *Pay close **attention** to the directions on the test.*
density the condition of being dense; thickness of consistency. *The density of the forest did not allow new plants to grow easily.*

control *v.* to exercise influence or authority over. *Who **controls** and guides the workers in this factory?*
command to direct with authority; give orders to. *The general **commanded** the soldiers to march.*
curb to check, restrain, or control. *She must **curb** her habit of bossing other people around.*
regulate to control the flow or rate of something. *A faucet **regulates** the flow of hot and cold water.*
restrain to hold back by physical force. *I wish you'd **restrain** your dog with a leash.*
antonyms: discharge *v.*, release *v.*, relieve

conversation *n.* an informal talk in which people exchange thoughts and feelings. *Use the telephone for a **conversation** with a faraway friend.*

argument a quarrel or dispute. *They had a loud **argument** over who would pay for the tickets.*

chat a relaxed, friendly conversation. *Sue had a long **chat** with her cousin Ken.*

conference a meeting to discuss a particular subject. *I had a **conference** with my teacher to discuss my report.*

consultation a conference at which advice is given or views are exchanged. *After a **consultation** with Dr. Wong, I knew the cause of my backache.*

dialogue the words spoken between actors in a play. *The actors playing Big Red and Little Bo practiced their **dialogue**.*

interview a conversation between a reporter and another person for the purpose of obtaining facts and statements. *The reporter based his story on his **interview** with Dan.*

Shades of Meaning

courage *n.* the quality of mind or spirit that enables one to face danger or hardship with confidence, resolution, and firm control of oneself.

1. noble courage:

gallantry	heroism	valor

2. ability to face danger with reason and confidence:

bravery	mettle
fortitude	spirit

3. foolish courage; unreasonable boldness:

foolhardiness	rashness	recklessness

antonyms: **1-2.** cowardice, fear *n.*, meekness **3.** cautiousness, prudence, heedfulness

---

D

decline *v.* to refuse to accept or do. *I'm sorry, but I must **decline** your invitation for dinner tonight.*

balk to refuse; shrink back. *Ken **balked** in horror when I asked him to wear a chicken costume to the party.*

deny to refuse to grant; withhold. *The guard **denied** us permission to photograph the paintings.*

protest to express strong objections to something. *The children **protested** when they were told it was bedtime.*

refuse to say no; to decline to do something. *Michael **refused** to join me for dinner.*

antonyms: accept, agree, consent *v.*, oblige

---

delightful *adj.* giving delight; very pleasant. *We enjoyed a **delightful** picnic near the river.*

charming delightful; attractive; very pleasing. *Michele painted a **charming** picture for her mother.*

enjoyable giving enjoyment; pleasant; agreeable. *Ricardo had an **enjoyable** visit with his grandparents.*

---

difficult *adj.* hard to do, accomplish, or perform. *Please help me solve this **difficult** math problem.*

complicated not easy to understand, deal with, or make one's way through. *His directions were too **complicated** for us to follow.*

inconvenient causing difficulty, trouble, or discomfort. *Can we talk now, or is this an **inconvenient** time for you?*

puzzling confusing; perplexing. *The police worked hard to solve the **puzzling** case of the missing keys.*

strenuous requiring great effort, energy, or exertion. *Running a mile is a **strenuous** activity.*

stubborn unreasonable; uncooperative.
*The **stubborn** boy refused to help us.*
antonyms: easy, obvious, simple

---

disgraceful *adj.* worthy of or causing shame, dishonor, or disfavor. *Dad punished Sid for his **disgraceful** behavior.*
dishonorable causing or deserving loss of respect or station. *The soldier was dismissed from the army because of his **dishonorable** conduct.*
shameful bringing or deserving shame; disgraceful. *Todd regretted his **shameful** remark, and promised not to be rude again.*

earnest *adj.* serious and determined in purpose. *It is my **earnest** wish to be a poet.*
dedicated committed fully to something, such as a course of action. *Alexander was **dedicated** to learning as much as he could about classical music.*
determined firm; showing determination. *I am **determined** to learn how to ski.*
serious not joking or speaking casually; in earnest. *Bill is **serious** when he says he wants to be a pilot.*
steadfast fixed in place or opinion; firm. *Amy is **steadfast** in her refusal to give up her dreams.*
antonyms: frivolous, uncommitted

---

explore *v.* to conduct a systematic search. *The cat **explored** every corner of the house.*
investigate to research carefully. *Who will **investigate** the disappearance of the jewels?*
probe to search deeply. *An investigator **probed** Rick's past for clues.*

fall *v.* to come down suddenly from a standing position. *Hal tripped and **fell**.*
plunge to dive swiftly and with force. *Tina **plunged** into the waves.*
stumble to trip and almost fall. *Ted hurt his toe when he **stumbled** on the path.*
tumble to fall with a rolling motion. *Apples **tumbled** from the crate.*

---

fantastic *adj.* remarkable; outstanding; superb. *We enjoyed the **fantastic** beauty of the sunset.*
enchanting bewitching; charming. *I will never forget the **enchanting** legend about this old forest.*
exquisite of special beauty or elegance. *She wore an **exquisite** gown of blue silk.*
inspiring filling one with emotion, pride, or awe. *The **inspiring** poem filled Al with the courage to face his problem.*
sumptuous of a size or splendor suggesting great expense. *Everyone was amazed by the **sumptuous** dinner that was provided at the wedding reception.*
thrilling causing a great deal of joy, fear, or excitement. *I couldn't sleep after finishing that **thrilling** story.*
antonyms: awful, horrible, mediocre

---

find *v.* to come upon or become aware of something after a search or by accident or chance. *Roy helped me to **find** my lost keys.*
discover to be the first to find, learn of, or observe. *Christopher Columbus **discovered** America in 1492.*
locate to find by searching or asking. *Jim **located** information at the library for his report.*
spot to recognize or locate. *Mary **spotted** John at the movies.*
unearth to dig up from, or as if from, the earth. *The police **unearthed** some clues that helped solve the crime.*
antonyms: conceal, hide, lose, miss

frighten *v.* to make or become suddenly afraid. *The large, growling dog frightened me.*

alarm to fill with sudden fear. *The cat's appearance alarmed the birds.*

disturb to trouble emotionally or mentally. *The strange noise disturbed and worried me.*

panic to cause sudden, overwhelming terror. *Allen's disappearance panicked Mom.*

startle to fill with sudden surprise; shock. *The loud bang startled me, and I jumped from my chair.*

antonyms: assure, calm *v.,* comfort *v.,* relieve

Shades of Meaning

frugal *adj.* Practicing or marked by economy, as in the expenditure of money or the use of material resources.

1. exercising care in the use of resources such as money:

economical   sparing   thrifty

2. giving or spending (money) reluctantly:

cheap   miserly   stingy

antonyms: **1.** generous, extravagant
2. spendthrift, prodigal

G

go *v.* to move to or from a place. *Let's get a group of our friends together and go to the park after school.*

advance to move forward, onward, or ahead. *When it's your turn, advance one space.*

depart to go away; leave. *The train will depart from the station soon.*

proceed to go forward or onward, especially after an interruption. *We proceeded on our way after stopping at the diner for lunch.*

progress to move along; advance; proceed. *Turtles progress very slowly.*

antonyms: remain, stay, stop *v.*

---

grow *v.* to become larger. *Your puppy will grow to be a big dog.*

develop to grow or cause to grow. *Soon the tadpole will develop legs and turn into a frog.*

enlarge to become larger. *The snapshot was enlarged to make a poster.*

expand to increase in one or more physical dimensions, as length or volume. *With air, the balloon expanded.*

sprout to begin to grow; produce or appear as a bud, shoot, or new growth. *New leaves sprouted from the branches.*

antonyms: decrease, shrink, wither

H

help *v.* to give support or aid. *Amy helped Bob repair his bike.*

advise to give advice to or offer advice; recommend. *Jim advised Carol to be careful on the icy sidewalk.*

assist to help; aid. *You can assist Mrs. Fox by chopping her firewood.*

contribute to aid in bringing about. *A good breakfast contributes to good health.*

cooperate to work or act with another or others for a common purpose. *If we all cooperate, the job will be easy and will take less time to complete.*

antonyms: hinder, impede, oppose

I

ignorant *adj.* without education or knowledge. *Humans are intelligent, but dogs are ignorant.*

innocent not experienced or worldly; naive. *The innocent child was not aware of the dangers she faced.*

stupid not sensible; unintelligent. *Going outside on a cold day without a coat is stupid.*

uneducated lacking in schooling. *Don't be uneducated; stay in school.*

uninformed lacking in information or knowledge. *If you feel uninformed on a subject, ask questions.*

antonyms: educated, intelligent, wise

information *n.* facts about a certain event or subject. *You will find the information you need in the encyclopedia.*

data information, especially when it is to be analyzed or used as the basis for a decision. *We collected data for our report.*

news information about one or more recent or current events. *We heard the news about the election on a radio broadcast.*

J

journey *n.* a trip, especially one over a great distance. *Mel took a journey to Ireland.*

cruise a sea voyage for pleasure. *Our cruise to the island was relaxing.*

expedition a group trip made with a definite purpose. *The explorers were on an expedition to find the river's source.*

mission an assignment that a person or group of persons is sent to carry out. *Dad was sent on an important mission to Rome.*

safari a hunting trip or journey of exploration. *George went on a safari to take pictures of lions.*

tour a trip during which many places are visited. *The family took a tour of Michigan, Wisconsin, and Illinois.*

trek a long and difficult journey. *The trek up the mountain took an entire week.*

K

kind *n.* a group of similar things; a type. *What kind of bread would you like?*

breed a particular type of animal. *What breed of dog makes the best pet?*

manner kind; sort. *What manner of clothes should we wear to the party?*

strain a group or type having similar characteristics. *Parsnips and carrots belong to the same strain of plants.*

variety a kind, sort, or form. *Rosa grows many varieties of flowers.*

L

Shades of Meaning

laugh *v.* To make sounds and facial movements to express certain emotions, especially happiness, amusement, scorn, or nervousness.

1. to laugh with amusement, happiness, or satisfaction:
  chortle   chuckle   guffaw

2. to laugh in a nervous or silly way:
  giggle   titter

3. to laugh in an unpleasant or scornful way:
  cackle   snicker   snigger

antonyms: bawl, cry *v.*, sob *v.*, wail, weep

let *v.* to grant permission to. *Please let me help you wash the dishes.*

authorize to grant power to. *Betsy's boss authorized her to buy a new computer.*

consent to give permission; agree. *Mother consented to our getting a new pet.*
permit to give consent to; allow. *Will you permit me to wait with you?*
antonyms: ban *v.*, forbid, prevent, prohibit

lively *adj.* full of life, energy, or activity. *The lively pony pranced and trotted across the field.*
alert mentally quick; perceptive; intelligent. *Jen is alert and clever.*
chipper active; cheerful. *I was sad, but now I'm feeling chipper again.*
spirited full of or marked by life, vigor, or enthusiasm. *We gave a spirited cheer when the kitten was rescued from the tree.*
antonyms: dull, lifeless, slow

look *v.* to focus one's eyes or attention on. *Look at the gorgeous sunset!*
contemplate to look at thoughtfully. *Mimi contemplated the stack of old letters.*
gaze to look intently, as with wonder or curiosity; stare. *We sat on the porch and gazed at the view all morning.*
glance to look briefly or quickly. *The reporter glanced at the newspaper's headline.*
observe to perceive, notice, or watch attentively. *I observed a robin in my yard.*
antonyms: ignore, miss *v.*, overlook

M

make *v.* to bring into being. *Carlos made me a beautiful birthday card.*
assemble to perform the assembly of; put together. *Help me assemble the puzzle.*
construct to build; erect. *Todd helped me construct a bookcase.*
manufacture to make, usually with machines. *We use machines to manufacture pins.*
prepare to put together and make from various ingredients. *Let's prepare pizza!*
antonyms: destroy, disassemble, ruin

Word Bank

method *n.* a regular or deliberate way of doing something.

course	policy	routine
manner	practice	scheme
pattern	procedure	system
plan	process	technique

N

nervous *adj.* having nerves easily affected; high-strung; jittery. *The nervous actor was afraid he would forget his lines.*
anxious fearful or worried about something uncertain. *Waiting for test results makes me anxious.*
edgy tense. *Before the exam, Sue was edgy.*
antonyms: calm *adj.*, placid, relaxed

numerous *adj.* existing or occurring in large numbers; many. *The people at the sale were too numerous to count.*
abundant existing in great supply; very plentiful. *We have abundant supplies for the trip.*
extreme very great or intense. *An extreme amount of noise burst from the room.*
several many. *The bus was so crowded that several people had to stand.*
antonyms: few, meager, scant

old *adj.* in existence for a long time; made or known long ago. *Her old dolls are rare.*
ancient very old; aged. *The ancient fort was built a thousand years ago.*

old-fashioned belonging to or typical of an earlier time and no longer in style. *My aunt owns an old-fashioned gown.*

prehistoric belonging to the time before history or events were recorded in writing. *The dinosaur is a prehistoric animal.*
antonyms: contemporary, modern, new

P

persuade *v.* to cause (someone) to do or believe something by arguing, pleading, or reasoning. *Stanley persuaded me to sing.*

convert to persuade (someone) to adopt a certain religion or belief. *Bill converted me from an eater of meat to a vegetarian.*

convince to cause someone to believe. *Peg convinced me to read this book.*

Shades of Meaning

plan *n.* a program or method thought out ahead of time for the accomplishment of a goal.

1. a carefully coordinated plan using many resources:
   strategy

2. a carefully worked-out plan:
   blueprint   **design**

3. an impractical or unrealistic plan:
   scheme

Shades of Meaning

pretty *adj.* pleasing to the eye.

1. somewhat pretty:
   appealing   **attractive**   **fair**

2. quite pretty:
   charming   **engaging**
   comely   **lovely**

3. extremely pretty:
   beautiful   **gorgeous**
   captivating   **ravishing**
   glamorous   **stunning**

antonyms: homely, ugly, unattractive

problem *n.* a question or situation that presents uncertainty, confusion, or difficulty. *Help me solve this problem.*

burden something endured or assumed as a duty or responsibility, often with difficulty. *Living with a messy pet can become a terrible burden.*

crisis an unstable condition in political, international, or economic affairs; a time of danger. *Smoke and smog could cause an air pollution crisis.*

difficulty a source of trouble or worry. *I have difficulty reading anything without my glasses.*

struggle strenuous effort or striving. *It was a struggle to lift the big box.*
antonyms: answer, resolution, solution

Q

quality *n.* a personal trait, especially a character trait. *Honesty and fairness are among Jim's good qualities.*

attribute a distinctive feature. *Karen's athletic attributes include speed and grace.*

characteristic a feature or quality in a person or thing. *Clean air is a characteristic of our city that we must preserve.*

peculiarity a strange or odd characteristic. *I find Al's interest in snakes interesting, but some people find it a peculiarity.*

trait a distinctive feature or characteristic. *Curiosity was a major character trait of Goldilocks.*

R

reaction *n.* an action, feeling, or attitude aroused by something. *John's positive reaction to the news showed on his smiling face.*

reflex an involuntary response to a stimulus. *Blinking your eyes is a reflex.*

response an answer or reply. *Margaret's response to my criticism was encouraging.*

require *v.* to need; demand; call for. *Skiing requires good balance.*

demand to need or require. *The preparation for the event demanded our complete attention to many details.*

insist to be firm in one's demand; to require assertively. *She insisted that I help her wash the dishes.*

necessitate to make necessary or unavoidable. *Icy roads necessitate caution on the part of drivers.*

respect *v.* to have or show honor or esteem for. *I respect Maria for working so hard.*

admire to have a high opinion of; feel respect for. *We admire the courage and leadership qualities of Martin Luther King, Jr.*

appreciate to recognize the worth, quality, importance, etc., of; value highly. *Because Gus appreciates music, I like to play the piano for him.*

antonyms: denigrate, devalue, disapprove

responsible *adj.* dependable; reliable; trustworthy. *Parents are always happy to find responsible baby-sitters.*

dependable steady; able to be relied upon. *A dependable employee arrives at the job on time and works hard.*

reliable capable of being relied upon. *Use a reliable watch to time the race.*

solid upstanding and dependable. *A solid student, June works hard on her homework assignments.*

trustworthy dependable; reliable. *I tell my secrets only to my most trustworthy friend.*

antonyms: irresponsible, undependable, unreliable.

right *adj.* correct, suitable, fitting, or proper. *Telling the truth is the right thing to do.*

accurate free from errors or mistakes; correct. *Jane's accurate summary of the accident helped the police officer write a detailed report.*

appropriate suitable or fitting for a particular situation. *An evening gown is not appropriate clothing for a football game.*

moral being or acting in accord with standards of what is good and just; right. *Being a moral person, John refused to tell a lie.*

precise exact; without error. *Measure the precise amount of flour and add it to the batter carefully.*

antonyms: erroneous, incorrect, wrong

S

search *v.* to look thoroughly and carefully. *The explorers searched for a cave in the rocks.*

examine to investigate (someone or something) in detail; observe carefully. *They examined every paper in the file before writing their report.*

seek to try to find or get. *The police are seeking a witness to the crime.*

Thesaurus

secure *v.* to make firm or tight. *We will secure the door with a new lock.*
acquire to get to have; gain; obtain. *She acquired a lamp at the yard sale and then resold it to an antique dealer.*
fasten to make fast or secure. *Always fasten your seatbelt in the car.*

show *v.* to cause or allow to be seen or viewed. *Please show me the rabbit that you bought at the fair.*
demonstrate to describe or explain by experiment or reasoning. *My piano teacher demonstrated how to play the song.*
display to hold up to view or put on view. *Josh displayed his stamp collection at the sixth-grade hobby show.*
exhibit to present for the public to view. *Kathy will exhibit her photographs at a local gallery.*
perform to present or enact (a musical work, dramatic role, or feat) before an audience. *The eighth-grade class will perform its play, "Leaving for Vacation," for the entire school next Thursday afternoon.*

silence *n.* the absence of sound; stillness. *We were calmed by the silence of the beautiful forest.*
hush a silence or stillness; quiet. *A hush settled throughout the theater as the audience waited for the play to begin.*
reticence a hesitation to speak; a tendency to remain silent. *We tried to solve the child's reticence by asking him questions.*
tranquillity peacefulness; calm silence. *The tranquillity of a long, quiet walk made him feel happy once again.*
antonyms: clamor, hubbub, uproar

Shades of Meaning

smell *n.* The quality that permits something to be perceived by the sense of smell.

1. a pleasing smell:

aroma	fragrance
bouquet	scent

2. an unpleasant smell:

odor	stench
reek	stink

Shades of Meaning

strict *adj.*

1. demanding or imposing an exacting discipline:

demanding	severe	unyielding
exacting	stern	

2. conforming completely to established rules:

exact	precise	rigorous
inflexible	rigid	

3. complete:

absolute	full	total
faithful	perfect	

antonyms: 1. compromising, lenient, liberal. **2.** flexible, imprecise, lax. **3.** imperfect, incomplete, partial

strong *adj.* having much power, energy, or force. *The strong weightlifter could lift two hundred pounds.*
dramatic striking in appearance or effect; stirring. *The dramatic rescue of the injured dog moved us to tears.*
forceful full of force; strong; powerful. *The forceful wind blew down several trees.*
antonyms: feeble, powerless, weak

surprise *v.* to cause to feel mild astonishment, as by being unexpected. *The sudden thunder surprised the picnickers.*
amaze to fill with surprise or wonder. *The juggler amazed us with his performance.*
astonish to surprise greatly. *The discovery of the new comet astonished the scientists.*

surrender *v.* to give oneself up, as to a pursuer or enemy. *After a long chase, the criminal surrendered to the police.*
submit to render oneself to the will or authority of another. *When they ran out of supplies, the soldiers were forced to submit to their enemies.*
succumb to submit to something overpowering or overwhelming. *The rabbit succumbed to its enemy, the hawk.*
yield to give up; surrender. *The angry man refused to yield to the unreasonable wishes of the real estate developer.*
antonyms: defeat *v.*, overpower, persist

T

Shades of Meaning

thin *adj.* lean or slender form or build.

1. pleasingly thin:
   slender   **slim**

2. thin with good muscle tone:
   lean   **spare**

3. unattractively thin:
   bony   **scrawny**   **skinny**

antonyms: fat *adj.*, portly, stout, obese

---

think *v.* to exercise the power of reason. *When did people begin to think that the world is round?*

assume to take for granted; suppose. *When it began to rain, we assumed that the ball game was cancelled.*
consider to regard as; to think of in a certain way. *I consider you my best friend.*
determine to fix, settle, or decide. *After some discussion, we determined that the dance would be held in the gym.*

U

unusual *adj.* not usual, common, or ordinary. *A rainbow is an unusual sight.*
curious interesting because unusual or extraordinary. *It is a curious fact that sharks move even when they sleep.*
exceptional unusual; extraordinary. *Because he was deaf, Beethoven was a particularly exceptional composer.*
unconventional unusual, different. *They had an unconventional wedding on a boat.*
antonyms: common, familiar, routine *adj.*

W

wish *v.* to want; hope for. *What sights do you wish to see in the city?*
crave to long for intensely. *The thirsty runners craved water.*
desire to wish or long for; want; crave. *Jan desired a trip to Europe.*

Spelling-Meaning Index

This Spelling-Meaning Index contains words related in spelling and meaning. The Index has four sections: Consonant Changes, Vowel Changes, Absorbed Prefixes, and Word Parts. The first two sections contain related word pairs and other words in the same word families. The last two sections contain a list of absorbed prefixes, Latin word roots and Greek word parts, and words that contain these word parts. The words in each section of this Index are in alphabetical order.

Consonant Changes

The letters in dark print show that the spelling stays the same even though the sound changes.

Consonant Changes:
Silent to Sounded

Sometimes you can remember how to spell a word with a silent consonant by thinking of a related word in which the letter is pronounced.

bomb-bombard

bombarded, bombarder, bombardier, bombarding, bombardment, bombards, bombed, bomber, bombing, bombs

receipt-reception

receipts, receptacle, receptionist, receptions, receptive

Consonant Changes:
The Sound of *c*

The |k| sound spelled c may change to the |s| sound in some words. Thinking of a related word can help you remember that the |s| sound is spelled c.

critic-criticize

critical, critically, criticism, criticized, criticizer, criticizes, criticizing, critics, uncritical

practical-practice

impractical, impracticality, impractically, practicality, practically, practiced, practices, practicing, unpracticed

Consonant Changes:
The Sound of *t*

The sound of a final *t* may change to the |sh| or the |ch| sound when an ending or a suffix is added. Thinking of a related word can help you remember those sounds are spelled *t*.

affect-affection

affected, affecting, affectionate, affectionately, affective, affects, disaffected, unaffected

except-exception

excepted, excepting, exceptional, exceptionally, exceptions, excepts, unexceptional, unexceptionally

graduate-graduation

graduated, graduates, graduating, graduations, postgraduate, undergraduate

instruct-instruction

instructed, instructing, instructional, instructions, instructive, instructor, instructorship, instructs, uninstructive

invent-invention

invented, inventing, inventions, inventive, inventively, inventiveness, inventor, invents

part-partial

parted, partially, particle, parting, partition, partly, parts

regulate-regulation

regulated, regulates, regulating, regulations, regulator, regulatory, unregulated

suggest-suggestion

suggested, suggestible, suggesting, suggestions, suggestive, suggests

Consonant Changes:

t to *ce*

Knowing the spelling change in one adjective-noun word pair in which a final *t* changes to *ce* can help you predict the spelling change in other word pairs with the same spelling pattern.

absent-absence
affluent-affluence
assistant-assistance
attendant-attendance
brilliant-brilliance
competent-competence
confident-confidence
correspondent-correspondence
defiant-defiance
dependent-dependence
different-difference
distant-distance
elegant-elegance
evident-evidence
excellent-excellence
extravagant-extravagance

fragrant-fragrance
ignorant-ignorance
important-importance
innocent-innocence
insistent-insistence
intelligent-intelligence
magnificent-magnificence
patient-patience
permanent-permanence
persistent-persistence
predominant-predominance
prominent-prominence
radiant-radiance
relevant-relevance
reluctant-reluctance
significant-significance
silent-silence

Vowel Changes

The letters in dark print show that the spelling stays the same even though the sound changes.

Vowel Changes:

Long to Short Vowel Sound

Words that are related in meaning are often related in spelling, even though one word has a long vowel sound and the other word has a short vowel sound.

clean-cleanse

cleanable, cleaned, cleaner, cleanest, cleaning, cleanliness, cleanly, cleanness, cleans, cleansed, cleanser, cleanses, cleansing, unclean, uncleanable

cycle-bicycle

bicycled, bicycles, bicycling, bicyclist, cycled, cycler, cycles, cyclical, cycling, cyclist, recycle, tricycle, unicycle, unicyclist

Spelling-Meaning Index

dream-dreamt
dreamed, dreamer, dreamily, dreaminess, dreaming, dreamless, dreamlike, dreams, dreamy

mean-meant
meaning, meaningful, meaningless, means, unmeant

minus-minimum
minimal, minimize, minimums, minuscule

mute-mutter
muted, mutely, muteness, mutes, muting, muttered, muttering, mutters

page-paginate
paged, pages, paginated, paginates, paginating, pagination, paging

pale-pallid
paled, paleness, paler, pales, palest, paling, pallor

sole-solitary
solely, solitarily, solitariness, solitude, solo, soloist

unite-unity
reunite, unit, united, uniting

Vowel Changes:
Schwa to Long Vowel Sound
You can remember how to spell the schwa sound in some words by thinking of a related word with a long vowel sound spelled the same way.

equaled-equation
equal, equaling, equality, equalize, equals, equate, equations, equator, inequality, unequal

proposition-propose
proposal, proposed, proposes, proposing, propositions

Vowel Changes:
Schwa to Short Vowel Sound
You can remember how to spell the schwa sound in some words by thinking of a related word with a short vowel sound spelled the same way.

compete-competition
competed, competes, competing, competitions, competitive, competitively, competitiveness, competitor

democracy-democratic
democracies, democrat, democratically, democratization, democratize, undemocratic

formal-formality
form, formalism, formalist, formalities, formalize, formally, format, formula, informal, informality, informally

general-generality
generalist, generalities, generalization, generalize, generally, generalness

individual-individuality
individualism, individualist, individualistic, individualities, individualize, individually, individuals

medal-medallion
medalist, medallions, medals

mental-mentality
mentalities, mentally

metal-metallic
metallically, metallography, metallurgy, metals

method-methodical
methodic, methodically, methodicalness, methods

moral-morality
immoral, morale, moralism, moralist, moralistic, moralities, moralize, morally, morals

personal-personality
impersonal, interpersonal, person, personalism, personalities, personalize, personally

reside-resident
resided, residence, residency, residential, residentially, resides, residing

similar-similarity
dissimilar, dissimilarity, similarities, similarly

total-totality
totaled, totaling, totalitarian, totalities, totally, totals

Absorbed Prefixes

Some prefixes change their spellings to match the first letter or sound of the word roots or base words to which they are attached. Knowing this can help you remember to double the consonant in some words with these prefixes. The letters in dark print highlight the prefix.

ad- "to" or "toward"

accept	**af**flict
accident	**ap**peal
accomplish	**ap**plaud
accord	**ap**plicant
according	**ap**ply
account	**ap**proach
accumulate	**ap**propriate
accurate	**ap**prove
accuse	**ap**proximate
affair	**as**semble
affect	**as**sign
affiliate	**as**sist
affiliated	**as**sume
affirm	**as**sure

in- "in"; "to"; "without"; "not"

illegal	**im**moral
illegible	**im**mortal
illiterate	**im**movable
illusion	**im**mune
illustrate	**ir**rational
immaculate	**ir**replaceable
immature	**ir**resistible
immediate	**ir**responsible
immense	**ir**rigate
immigrant	**ir**ritate
immigrate	

ob- "toward"; "in front of"; "against"

occasion	**of**fice
occupant	**of**ficial
occupation	**op**ponent
occupy	**op**portune
occur	**op**portunity
occurrence	**op**pose
offend	**op**posite
offer	**op**press

Spelling-Meaning Index

Word Parts

Words with the same Latin word root or the same Greek word part are related in spelling and meaning. Knowing the meaning of a word part can help you understand and spell the words in that family. The letters in dark print highlight the word part.

Latin Word Roots

aud, "to hear"

audible	**aud**it
audience	**aud**ition
audio	**aud**itorium
audio-visual	**aud**itory

cit(e), "to call"

citation	in**cite**
cite	re**cite**
ex**cite**	

dict, "to tell"

contra**dict**	**dict**ionary
dictate	pre**dict**
dictator	vale**dict**orian
diction	ver**dict**

form, "form; shape"

con**form**	in**form**al
de**form**	in**form**ant
de**form**ity	in**form**ation
form	in**form**er
formal	re**form**
format	re**form**ation
formation	trans**form**
formula	trans**form**ation
formulate	uni**form**
in**form**	

ject, "to throw"

ad**ject**ive	pro**ject**
de**ject**	pro**ject**or
in**ject**	re**ject**
inter**ject**	sub**ject**
ob**ject**	sub**ject**ive
ob**ject**ive	

loc, "place"

al**loc**ate	**loc**ate
dis**loc**ate	**loc**ation
local	**loc**omotion
locale	**loc**omotive
locality	re**loc**ate

min, "small"

di**min**ish	**min**or
mince	**min**us
minimal	**min**uscule
minimalize	**min**ute
minimize	**min**utia
minimum	

miss or **mit,** "to send; let go" or "throw"

com**miss**ion	ad**mit**
dis**miss**	com**mit**
missile	com**mit**tee
mission	per**mit**
missionary	sub**mit**
missive	trans**mit**
sub**miss**ion	

ped, "foot"

centi**ped**e	**ped**estrian
milli**ped**e	**ped**igree
pedal	**ped**ometer
pedestal	

port, "to carry"

de**port**	**port**er
ex**port**	re**port**
im**port**	sup**port**
im**port**ant	trans**port**
portable	

pose, "to put"

com**pose**	**pos**itive
de**pose**	**pos**ture
dis**pose**	pro**pose**
ex**pose**	re**pose**
op**pose**	sup**pose**
op**pos**ite	trans**pose**
position	

rupt, "to break"

ab**rupt**	e**rupt**
bank**rupt**	inter**rupt**
cor**rupt**	ir**rupt**
dis**rupt**	**rupt**ure

scribe or **script,** "to write"

circum**scribe**	de**script**ion
de**scribe**	de**script**ive
in**scribe**	in**script**ion
pre**scribe**	manu**script**
scribble	nonde**script**
scribe	pre**script**ion
sub**scribe**	sub**script**ion
tran**scribe**	tran**script**ion

sist, "to stand"

as**sist**	irre**sist**able
as**sist**ance	per**sist**
con**sist**	per**sist**ent
con**sist**ent	re**sist**
in**sist**	re**sist**ance
in**sist**ence	

sit(e), "place"

camp**site**	**sit**uation
site	**sit**us
situate	

spect, "to look"

a**spect**	re**spect**
circum**spect**	re**spect**able
in**spect**	**spect**acle
in**spect**ion	**spect**ator
in**spect**or	**spect**er
per**spect**ive	**spect**rum
pro**spect**	su**spect**
pro**spect**or	

tract, "to pull"

abs**tract**	ex**tract**
at**tract**	pro**tract**
at**tract**ion	re**tract**
at**tract**ive	sub**tract**
con**tract**	**tract**
de**tract**	**tract**ion
dis**tract**	**tract**or

vac, "to be empty"

e**vac**uate	**vac**ate
vacancy	**vac**uum
vacant	

ven(t), "to go; come"

ad**vent**	e**vent**
ad**vent**ure	inter**vene**
a**ven**ue	in**vent**
circum**vent**	pre**vent**
contra**vene**	re**ven**ue
con**vene**	sou**ven**ir
con**vent**	**ven**ue
con**vent**ion	

Spelling-Meaning Index

vid, "to see"

evident	video
provide	videotape

vis, "to see"

advise	visa
audio-visual	visible
improvise	vision
invisible	visit
provision	visor
revise	vista
supervise	visual
televise	visualize

Greek Word Parts

ast, "star"

aster	astronaut
asterisk	astronomer
asteroid	astronomy
astrology	disaster

phys, "nature"

physical	physics
physician	physique

poli, "city" or "government"

Acropolis	police
cosmopolitan	policy
megalopolis	politician
metropolis	politics
metropolitan	

tele, "far off; distant"

telecast	telescope
telegram	telethon
telegraph	televise
telepathy	television
telephone	

Spelling Dictionary

Spelling Table

This Spelling Table shows many of the letter combinations that spell the same sounds in different words. Use this table for help in looking up words that you do not know how to spell.

Sounds	Spellings	Sample Words	Sounds	Spellings	Sample Words
|ă|	a, au	bat, have, laugh	|ī|	ei, i, ie, igh, uy, y, ye	height, time, mind, pie, fight, buy, try, dye, type
|ā|	a, ai, ay, ea, ei, eigh, ey	made, later, rain, play, great, vein, eight, they	|îr|	ear, eer, eir, ere, ier	near, deer, weird, here, pier
|âr|	air, are, ear, eir, ere	fair, care, bear, their, where	|j|	dge, g, ge, j	judge, germ, orange, jump
|ä|	a, al	father, calm	|k|	c, cc, ch, ck, k, que	picnic, account, school, stick, keep, antique
|är|	ar, ear	art, heart	|kw|	qu	quick
|b|	b, bb	bus, rabbit	|l|	l, ll	last, all
|ch|	c, ch, tch, tu	cello, chin, match, culture	|m|	m, mb, mm, mn	mop, bomb, summer, column
|d|	d, dd	dark, sudden	|n|	gn, kn, n, nn, pn	sign, knee, nine, banner, pneumonia
|ĕ|	a, ai, ay, e, ea, ie	any, said, says, went, head, friend	|ng|	n, ng	think, ring
|ē|	e, ea, ee, ei, ey, i, ie, y	these, we, beast, fleet, receive, honey, chief, magazine, bumpy	|ŏ|	a, ho, o	was, honor, pond
			|ō|	ew, o, oa, oe, ou, ough, ow	sew, most, hope, float, toe, shoulder, though, row
|f|	f, ff, gh, ph	funny, off, enough, physical	|ô|	a, al, au, aw, o, ough	walk, talk, haunt, lawn, soft, brought
|g|	g, gg, gu	get, egg, guide			
|h|	h, wh	hat, who	|ôr|	oar, oor, or, ore, our	roar, door, storm, store, court
|hw|	wh	when			
|ĭ|	a, e, ee, i, ia, u, ui, y	cottage, before, been, mix, give, carriage, busy, build, gym	|oi|	oi, oy	join, toy

Sounds	Spellings	Sample Words	Sounds	Spellings	Sample Words
|ou|	ou, ough, ow	loud, bough, now	|th|	th	thin, teeth
|o͝o|	oo, ou, u	good, could, put	|ŭ|	o, oe, oo, ou, u	front, come, does, flood, tough, sun
|o͞o|	eu, ew, o, oe, oo, ou, ough, u, ue, ui	neutral, flew, do, lose, shoe, spoon, you, through, truth, blue, juice	|yo͞o|	eau, ew, iew, u, ue	beauty, few, view, use, cue
|p|	p, pp	paint, happen	|ûr|	ear, er, ir, or, our, ur	learn, herd, girl, word, journey, turn
|r|	r, rh, rr, wr	rub, rhyme, borrow, write	|v|	f, v	of, very
|s|	c, ce, ps, s, sc, ss	city, fence, psychology, same, scent, lesson	|w|	o, w	one, way
			|y|	i, y	million, yes
|sh|	ce, ch, ci, s, sh, ss, ti	ocean, machine, special, sure, sheep mission, nation	|z|	s, ss, x, z, zz	please, dessert, xylophone, zoo, blizzard
|t|	ed, t, tt	stopped, talk, button	|zh|	ge, s	garage, usual
|*th*|	th	they, other	|ə|	a, ai, e, eo, i, ie, o, ou, u	about, captain, silent, surgeon, pencil, ancient, lemon, famous, circus

How to Use a Dictionary

Finding an Entry Word

Guide Words

The word you want to find in a dictionary is listed in alphabetical order. To find it quickly, use the guide words at the top of each page. Guide words name the first and last entries on the page.

Base Words

To find a word ending in **-ed** or **-ing,** you usually must look up its base word. To find **accepted** or **accepting,** for example, look up the base word **accept.**

Homographs

Homographs have separate, numbered entries. For example, **content** meaning "the amount of a substance contained in something" is listed as **content¹. Content** meaning "happy with what one has" is **content².**

Reading an Entry

Read the dictionary entry below. Note the purpose of each part.

The **pronunciation** shows you how to say the entry word.

The **part of speech** (verb) is identified by an abbreviation (*v.*).

The **-ed** and **-ing** forms of a verb are often shown.

The **entry word** is shown, separated into syllables.

The **definition** tells you what the word means.

A **run-on entry** is shown in dark type at the end of the entry.

A **sample sentence** or phrase helps to make the meaning clear.

ac·cept |ăk sĕpt'| *v.* **ac·cept·ed, ac·cept·ing.** To take (something offered): *accept an award.* —**ac·cept'a·ble.** *adj.*

ac·ci·dent |ăk' sĭ dənt| *n.* **1.** Something that happens without being planned in advance: *Our meeting was an accident.* **2.** An

Spelling Dictionary

a·bil·i·ty |ə **bĭl′** ĭ tē| *n., pl.* **a·bil·i·ties.**
Talent; skill: *a person of great musical ability.*

-able. A suffix that forms adjectives and means: **1.** Capable or worthy of: **eatable; lovable. 2.** Tending toward: **sizable.**

a·bol·ish |ə **bŏl′** ĭsh| *v.* To put an end to: *The Thirteenth Amendment abolished slavery.*

a·brupt |ə **brŭpt′**| *adj.* **1.** Unexpected; sudden: *an abrupt change in temperature.* **2.** Very steep: *The path ends in an abrupt descent to the water.* **3.** Short and brief, suggesting rudeness or displeasure: *an abrupt answer made in anger.*

ab·sence |**ăb′** səns| *n.* The condition of being away from someone or from a place: *Absence can make you love someone more.*

ab·sent |**ăb′** sənt| *adj.* Not present; not on hand: *Two pupils are absent today.*

ab·surd |**ăb′ sûrd′**| *or* |**-zûrd′**| *adj.* Contrary to common sense; ridiculous.

a·buse |ə **byoōs′**| *n., pl.* **a·bus·es.**
1. Improper use; misuse: *the abuse of power.*
2. Mistreatment.

ac-. See **ad-.**

ac·cent |**ăk′** sĕnt| *n.* A mark showing the stress given to one or more syllables in pronouncing a word.

ac·cept |ăk **sĕpt′**| *v.* **ac·cept·ed, ac·cept·ing.** To take (something offered): *accept an award.* —**ac·cept′a·ble.** *adj.*

ac·ci·dent |**ăk′** sĭ dənt| *n.* **1.** Something that happens without being planned in advance: *Our meeting was an accident.* **2.** An unexpected and undesirable event; mishap: *a traffic accident.*

ac·ci·den·tal |**ăk′** sĭ **dĕn′** tl| *adj.*
Happening by mistake or without thinking.
—**ac′ci·den′tal·ly** *adv.: I accidentally poured orange juice on my cereal.*

ac·com·plish |ə **kŏm′** plĭsh| *v.* To carry out; achieve; complete: *accomplish an assignment.*

according to As stated or indicated by; on the authority of: *according to historians.*

ac·count |ə **kount′**| *n.* **1.** A written or spoken description of events; a narrative: *an exciting account of his adventures.* **2.** Often **accounts.** A record or written statement, especially of business dealings or money received or spent. ◊ *Idioms.* **call to account.** To demand an explanation from: *He was called to account for being late so often.* **on account of.** Because of: *We were late on account of traffic.* **on no account.** Under no conditions; never: *On no account should the live wires be touched.* **on that account.** For that reason: *He was very strong and was chosen as a guard on that account.* **take into account.** To take note of; consider: *In solving a problem, take everything into account.* **turn to good account.** To make good use of: *turn one's losses to good account.*

ac·count·ant |ə **koun′** tənt| *n.* A person who keeps or inspects the financial records of business concerns or individuals: *The accountant checked our tax records.*

ac·cu·mu·late |ə **kyoō′** myə lāt′| *v.*
ac·cu·mu·lat·ed, ac·cu·mu·lat·ing. To gather together; pile up; collect: *Snow has begun to accumulate on the sidewalk.*

ac·cu·rate |**ăk′** yər ĭt| *adj.* **1.** Free from errors or mistakes; correct: *accurate answers.* **2.** Exact; precise.

ac·cuse |ə **kyoōz′**| *v.* **ac·cused, ac·cus·ing. 1.** To charge (someone) formally with wrongdoing: *He was accused of the crime.* **2.** To blame.

ac·knowl·edge |ăk **nŏl′** ĭj| *v.*
ac·knowl·edged, ac·knowl·edg·ing. To recognize the standing or authority of: *He was acknowledged as supreme ruler.*

ac·quire |ə **kwīr′**| *v.* **ac·quired, ac·quir·ing.** To get to have; gain; obtain: *acquire new skills.*

a·cre |**ā′** kər| *n.* A unit of area equal to 43,560 square feet or 4,840 square yards, used in measuring land.

ac·tion |**ăk′** shən| *n.* The activity, process, or fact of doing something: *take action to improve the environment.*

ac·tor |**ăk′** tər| *n.* A performer, especially a person who acts a part in a play, motion picture, or other dramatic performance.

actor

ad-. A prefix meaning "toward" or "to": **adhere**.

ad·di·tion |ə **dĭsh′** ən| *n.* The process of finding the sum of two or more numbers.

ad·dress |ə **drĕs′**| *v.* To direct one's effort or attention toward.

ad·join |ə **join′**| *v.* **ad·joined, ad·join·ing.** **1.** To be next to: *The dining room adjoins the kitchen.* **2.** To lie side by side: *The rooms adjoin.*

ad·just |ə **jŭst′**| *v.* To change, set, or regulate in order to achieve a desired result: *adjust the volume control on a radio.*

ad·mi·ral |**ăd′** mər əl| *n.* The commander in chief of a navy or fleet.

ad·mi·ra·tion |ăd′ mə **rā′** shən| *n.* **1.** A high opinion; respect; esteem. **2.** Praise and approval.

ad·mire |ăd **mīr′**| *v.* **ad·mired, ad·mir·ing.** To have a high opinion of; feel respect for: *They admired her courage.*

ad·mit |ăd **mĭt′**| *v.* **ad·mit·ted, ad·mit·ting.** To confess as a fact.

a·dopt |ə **dŏpt′**| *v.* To accept and use: *adopt new methods.*

a·dor·a·ble |ə **dôr′** ə bəl| *or* |ə **dōr′**-| *adj.* *Informal.* Delightful; lovable; charming: *an adorable child.*

ad·o·ra·tion |ăd′ ə **rā′** shən| *n.* Great and devoted love.

a·dore |ə **dôr′**| *or* |ə **dōr′**| *v.* **a·dored, a·dor·ing.** *Informal:* To like very much.

ad·vance |ăd **văns′**| *v.* **ad·vanced, ad·vanc·ing.** To move forward, onward, or ahead: *Did the army advance or retreat?*

ad·vanced |ăd **vanst′**| *adj.* At a higher level than others: *an advanced student.*

ad·vance·ment |ăd **văns′** mənt| *or* |-**văns′**-| *n.* **1.** The act of advancing. **2.** A forward step; improvement: *new advancements in science.*

ad·van·tage |ăd **văn′** tĭj| *or* |-**vän′**-| *n.* A benefit that puts one in a favorable position: *Being tall is a real advantage in playing basketball.*

ad·ven·ture |ăd′ **vĕn′** chər| *n.* An unusual, exciting, or memorable experience: *the adventures of Marco Polo.*

ad·ver·tise |**ăd′** vər tīz′| *v.* **ad·ver·tised, ad·ver·tis·ing.** To call public attention to (a product), as by announcing on the radio or placing a notice in a newspaper: *Manufacturers advertise their products.*

ad·vice |ăd vīs′| *n.* An opinion about how to solve a problem; guidance: *Your advice helped me make a decision.*

ad·vise |ăd vīz′| *v.* **ad·vised, ad·vis·ing.** To give advice to or offer advice or guidance: *I advise you to go to the doctor.*

ad·vo·cate |ăd′ və kĭt′| *or* |-kāt| *n.* A person who supports or speaks in favor of a cause.

af·fair |ə fâr′| *n.* An occurrence, action, event, or procedure: *I have heard several versions of this affair.*

af·fect |ə fĕkt′| *v.* To influence; bring about a change in.

af·fec·tion |ə fĕk′ shən| *n.* A fond or tender feeling toward someone or something; fondness.

af·fil·i·ate |ə fĭl′ ē āt′| *v.* **af·fil·i·at·ed, af·fil·i·at·ing.** To associate or join, as with a larger or more important body: *Clare Dannatt is affiliated with the law firm of Richards and Dover.*

-age. A suffix that forms nouns and means: **1.** Collectively; in general: **mileage. 2.** Condition; state: **marriage.**

a·gen·cy |ā′ jən sē| *n., pl.* **a·gen·cies.** A governmental department of administration or regulation: *the agency for disease control.*

a·gen·da |ə jĕn′ də| *pl. n. (used with a singular verb).* A list of things to be done, as a program of business at a meeting: *What is the first issue to discuss on today's agenda?*

a·gent |ā′ jənt| *n.* **1.** Someone with the power or authority to act for another: *a railroad agent.* **2.** A representative of a government or a governmental department: *an FBI agent.*

ag·gres·sive |ə grĕs′ ĭv| *adj.* Vigorous; energetic; not timid: *a very aggressive salesperson.*

ag·ri·cul·ture |ăg′ rĭ kŭl′ chər| *n.* The science, art, and business of cultivating the soil in order to produce useful crops and livestock; farming. —**ag′ri·cul′tur·al** *adj.*

air |âr| *n.* **1.** The colorless, odorless, tasteless mixture of gases that surrounds the earth. **2.** The open space above the earth: *a view from the air.* **3.** Transportation by aircraft: *travel by air.* **4.** The appearance or manner of a person or thing: *The judge has a very dignified air.* **5.** A melody or tune. —*v.* **1.** To expose to the air so as to dry, cool, or freshen: *air a blanket.* **2.** To express publicly: *air one's views.*

-al¹. A suffix that forms adjectives from some nouns: **postal; medicinal.**

-al². A suffix that forms nouns from some verbs: **denial; arrival.**

a·lert |ə lûrt′| *adj.* **1.** Mentally quick; intelligent: *an alert child.* **2.** Watchful; attentive: *A good driver must remain constantly alert.*

al·low·ance |ə lou′ əns| *n.* An amount of money given at regular intervals or for a specific purpose: *a 25¢ weekly allowance; a travel allowance.*

al·ter·na·tive |ôl′ tûr′ nə tĭv| *or* |ăl-| *n.* A choice between two or more possibilities: *The alternative is between going to the movies tonight or tomorrow night.*

al·ti·tude |ăl′ tĭ tōōd′| *or* |-tyōōd′| *n.* A height measured in relation to a particular reference level such as sea level or the earth's surface.

al·to |ăl′ tō| *n., pl.* **al·tos. 1.** A low singing voice of a woman or boy or, sometimes, a high singing voice of a man, lower than a soprano and higher than a tenor. **2.** A person having such a voice.

am·bas·sa·dor |ăm băs′ ə dər| *n.* A diplomatic official of the highest rank who represents his or her government in another country.

am·bu·lance |ăm′ byə ləns| *n.* A large automobile especially equipped to rush sick and injured people to a hospital.

ambulance

a·muse·ment |ə **myōōz′** mənt| *n.*
Entertainment; diversion: *They performed music for their own amusement.*

a·nal·o·gy |ə **năl′** ə jē| *n., pl.* **a·nal·o·gies.**
An explanation of something by comparing it with something similar: *I use the analogy of a beehive to describe the city.*

an·ar·chy |**ăn′** ər kē| *n., pl.* **an·ar·chies.**
Disorder and confusion resulting from a lack of governmental authority.

-ance. A suffix that forms nouns from verbs: **resemblance.**

an·cient |**ān′** shənt| *adj.* Very old; aged: *The pyramids in Egypt are ancient.*

an·noy |ə **noi′**| *v.* To bother or irritate.

an·noy·ance |ə **noi′** əns| *n.* Irritation or displeasure.

an·swer |**ăn′** sər| *v.* **an·swered, an·swer·ing.** To reply to or respond in words or actions: *She answered him curtly.*

-ant. A suffix that forms nouns and adjectives: **occupant.**

an·to·nym |**ăn′** tə nǐm′| *n.* A word meaning the opposite of another word. For example, *dirty* is an antonym of *clean.*

ap·par·ent |ə **păr′** ənt| *or* |ə **pâr′-**| *adj.*
Readily understood or seen; obvious: *for no apparent reason.*

ap·peal |ə **pēl′**| *n.* An urgent or earnest request: *an appeal for help.*

ap·pear·ance |ə **pîr′** əns| *n.* The way something or someone looks or appears.

ap·plaud |ə **plôd′**| *v.* To express praise or approval, as by clapping the hands: *applaud the actors.*

ap·pli·cant |**ăp′** lǐ kənt| *n.* A person who applies for something: *a job applicant.*

ap·ply |ə **plī′**| *v.* **ap·plied, ap·ply·ing, ap·plies.** **1.** To put on: *apply glue to paper.*
2. To use: *apply what you have learned.* **3.** To request employment, acceptance, or admission: *apply for a job.*

ap·point |ə **point′**| *v.* To select or designate for an office, position, or duty: *We appointed a group leader.*

ap·pre·ci·ate |ə **prē′** shē āt′| *v.*
ap·pre·ci·at·ed, ap·pre·ci·at·ing. **1.** To recognize the worth, quality, or importance of; value highly. **2.** To be thankful for.

Pronunciation Key

ă	pat	îr	pier	ŭ	cut
ā	pay	ŏ	pot	ûr	urge
âr	care	ō	toe	th	thin
ä	father	ô	paw	*th*	this
ĕ	pet	oi	boy	hw	whoop
ē	be	ōō	took	zh	vision
ǐ	pit	ōō	boot	ə	about
ī	pie	ou	out		

---

ap·proach |ə **prōch′**| *n.* A way or method of dealing or working with someone or something: *a new approach to the problem.*

ap·pro·pri·ate |ə **prō′** prē ǐt| *adj.*
Suitable for a particular person, condition, occasion, or place; proper: *appropriate clothes.*

ap·prove |ə **prōōv′**| *v.* **ap·proved, ap·prov·ing.** To think of favorably; consider right or good.

ap·prox·i·mate |ə **prŏk′** sə mǐt| *adj.*
Almost exact or accurate: *the approximate height of a building.*

arch |ärch| *n.* Any of various curved structures of the body: *the arch of the foot.*

ar·chi·tect |**är′** kǐ tĕkt′| *n.* A person who designs and directs the construction of buildings and other large structures.

arc·tic |**ärk′** tǐk| *or* |**är′** tǐk| *adj.*
Extremely cold; frigid: *arctic weather.*

ar·rive |ə **rīv′**| *v.* **ar·rived, ar·riv·ing.** To reach a goal or objective: *They arrived at an understanding.*

as·par·a·gus |ə **spăr′** ə gəs| *n.* The young, tender stalks or spears of a cultivated plant, cooked and eaten as a vegetable.

as·pire |ə **spīr′**| *v.* **as·pired, as·pir·ing.**
To have a great ambition; desire strongly: *aspire to become a good player.*

as·sem·ble |ə **sĕm′** bəl| *v.* **as·sem·bled, as·sem·bling.** To perform the assembly of; put together: *The mechanic assembled the engine.*

as·sent |ə **sĕnt′**| *n.* Agreement, as to a proposal, especially in a formal or impersonal manner: *The prime minister desired the king's assent.*

as·set |ăs′ ĕt′| *n.* **1.** A valuable quality or possession: *Her smile is a real asset.* **2.** Often **assets.** Property, owned by a person or business, that has monetary value and may be used to pay debts.

as·sign |ə sīn′| *v.* **1.** To select for a duty or office; appoint: *assign a teacher to playground duty.* **2.** To give out as a task: *The teacher assigns homework every night.*

as·sign·ment |ə sīn′ mənt| *n.* Something set apart for a particular purpose, especially a task or job.

as·sist |ə sĭst′| *v.* To help; aid: *The whole community joined together to assist a family in distress.*

as·so·ci·ate |ə sō′ shē āt′| *or* |-sē-| *v.* **as·so·ci·at·ed, as·so·ci·at·ing.** To bring together in one's mind or imagination; connect: *We associate automobiles with Detroit.*

as·sume |ə soōm′| *v.* **as·sumed, as·sum·ing.** To take for granted; suppose: *Let's assume that everyone is going to the dance.*

as·sure |ə shoŏr′| *v.* **as·sured, as·sur·ing.** **1.** To inform positively: *I can assure you that we shall take appropriate action.* **2.** To make certain; guarantee; ensure.

as·tute |ə stoōt′| *or* |ə styoōt′| *adj.* Keen in judgment; shrewd: *an astute appraisal.*

-ate¹. A suffix that forms adjectives: **affectionate.**

-ate². A suffix that forms verbs: **pollinate.**

-atlas |ăt′ ləs| *n. pl* **at·las·es.** A book or bound collection of maps.

> ### History
> An **atlas** is a book of maps. Its name comes from Atlas, the Greek god who held the world on his shoulders.

---

at·ten·tion |ə tĕn′ shən| *n.* Concentration of the mental powers upon something or someone.

at·tract |ə trăkt′| *v.* To draw, pull, or direct to oneself or itself by some quality or action: *A magnet attracts nails.*

at·trac·tion |ə trăk′ shən| *n.* Something that draws or pulls people or things to itself by some quality or action: *The pyramids are some of Egypt's greatest attractions.*

at·trac·tive |ə trăk′ tĭv| *adj.* **1.** Capable of attracting or pulling toward: *the attractive force of magnetism.* **2.** Pleasing to the eye or mind; appealing: *an attractive offer.*

au·di·ble |ô′ də bəl| *adj.* Capable of being heard: *an audible whisper.*

au·di·ence |ô′ dē əns| *n.* The people gathered to see and hear a play, movie, lecture, or concert.

au·di·o |ô′ dē ō′| *adj.* Of or for reproduction or broadcasting of sound.

au·dit |ô′ dĭt| *n.* An official and thorough examination of financial records or accounts.

au·di·tion |ô dĭsh′ ən| *n.* A trial performance, as of a musician or actor who is applying for a job. —*v.* To perform in an audition: *Many musicians auditioned for a place in the orchestra.*

au·di·to·ri·um |ô′ dĭ tôr′ ē əm| *or* |-tōr′-| *n., pl.* **au·di·to·ri·ums** or **au·di·to·ri·a** |ô′ dĭ tôr′ ē ə| *or* |-tōr′-|. A large room or building designed for a big audience.

au·di·to·ry |ô′ dĭ tôr′ ē| *adj.* Of hearing or the organs of hearing: *the auditory canal of the ear.*

au·thor |ô′ thər| *n.* A person who writes a book, novel, or article.

a·void |ə void′| *v.* To keep away from; stay clear of; shun: *avoid crowds.* —**a·void′a·ble** *adj.* —**a·void′ance** *n.*

a·wake |ə wāk′| *v.* **a·woke** |ə wōk′|, **a·waked, a·wak·ing.** To rouse or emerge from sleep; wake up. —*adj.* Not asleep.

a·woke |ə wōk′| *v.* Past tense of **awake.**

B

ba·by-sit |bā′ bē sĭt′| *v.* **-sat** |-săt′|, **-sit·ting.** To care for a child or children when the parents are not at home.

back·ward |bǎk′ wərd| *adj.* Directed or moving toward the rear: *a backward glance; a backward tumble.* —*adv.* or **back·wards** |bǎk′ wərdz| **1.** To or toward the back or rear. **2.** With the back or rear first: *With its hind legs a toad can dig its way into the gound backward.* **3.** In reverse order or direction: *count backward from 100.* ◇ *Idiom.* **bend over backward** or **lean over backward.** To make an effort greater than is required: *They bent over backwards to be fair.*

bal·ance |bǎl′ əns| *n.* An equality between the debit and credit sides of an account: *A bookkeeper must achieve a balance at the end of the month.* —*v.* **bal·anced, bal·anc·ing.** To make or keep equal in weight or importance.

bal·let |bǎ lā′| *or* |bǎl′ ā′| *n.* A form of artistic dancing composed of jumps, turns, and poses, often done on the tips of the toes.

ballet

ban·ner |bǎn′ ər| *adj.* Unusually good; outstanding: *a banner year.*

ban·quet |bǎng′ kwĭt| *n.* A large, elaborate meal; a feast.

History

Banquet comes from the Old French word *banc,* meaning "bench." It seems that guests at the first banquets sat on benches.

---

ban·yan |bǎn′ yən| *n.* A tropical tree with large, oval leaves and spreading branches from which aerial roots grow downward to form new trunks: *A banyan looks like several trees.*

bare |bâr| *adj.* Without clothing or covering; exposed: *a bare hillside.* —*v.* **bared, bar·ing.** To make known: *bare your innermost feelings.*
♦ *These sound alike* **bare, bear.**

bare·foot |bâr′ fŏŏt′| *adj.* Also **bare·foot·ed** |bâr′ fŏŏt′ ĭd|. Without shoes or other covering on the feet. —*adv.*: *running barefoot over the grass.*

bare·ly |bâr′ lē| *adv.* Almost not; hardly; just: *We could barely see the shore in the dark.*

bar·on |bǎr′ ən| *n.* **1.** A nobleman. **2.** A businessman of great wealth and influence.
♦ *These sound alike* **baron, barren.**

bar·ren |bǎr′ ən| *adj.* **1.** Lacking or unable to produce growing plants or crops; without vegetation: *barren soil.* **2.** Unable to bear offspring or fruit.
♦ *These sound alike* **barren, baron.**

bar·ri·er |bǎr′ ē ər| *n.* A fence, wall, or other structure built to hold back or obstruct movement or passage: *The toddler could not climb over the barrier.*

bar·ter |bär′ tər| *v.* To trade in exchange for something else, without using money: *barter home-grown vegetables for clothing.*

base word |bās wôrd| *n.* A word to which other word parts may be added. For example, in *filled, refill,* and *filling,* **fill** is the base word.

bas·soon |bə sōōn′| *or* |bǎ′-| *n.* A low-pitched woodwind instrument having a long wooden body connected to a double reed by a bent metal tube.

beam |bēm| *n.* A long, rigid piece of wood or metal used to support or reinforce a structure or a part of a structure: *Tree trunks were used for beams in the old farmhouse.*

bear |bâr| *v.* **bore** |bôr| *or* |bōr|, **borne** |bôrn| *or* |bōrn|, **bear•ing.** **1.** To move while supporting; carry: *a train bearing freight.* **2.** To put up with: *bear the pain.*

♦ *These sound alike* **bear, bare.**

> ### History
> **Bear** comes from the Old English verb *beran*, meaning "to carry." **Bare** comes from the Old English adjective *baer*, meaning "naked."

bear•ing |bâr′ ĭng| *n.* Direction, especially angular direction as used in navigation: *The ship took a bearing on the distant lighthouse.*

be•gin•ning |bĭ gĭn′ ĭng| *n.* The time or point when something starts: *the beginning of the movie.*

be•lief |bĭ lēf′| *n.* Acceptance or conviction of the truth and existence of something; confidence, trust.

ben•e•fi•cial |bĕn′ ə fĭsh′ əl| *adj.* Bringing benefit; advantageous: *Many bacteria are beneficial to man.*

ber•ry |bĕr′ ē| *n., pl.* **ber•ries.** A usually small, juicy fruit with many seeds rather than a single stone.

♦ *These sound alike* **berry, bury.**

bev•er•age |bĕv′ ər ĭj| *or* |bĕv′ rĭj| *n.* Any of various drinks, such as milk, tea, or juice, usually excluding water.

be•ware |bĭ wâr′| *v.* To watch out for; be on guard against. Used chiefly in the imperative and infinitive: *Beware of pickpockets!*

bi•cy•cle |bī′ sĭ kəl| *or* |-sĭk′ əl| *n.* A light vehicle consisting of a metal frame on which two wheels are mounted, one behind the other. It has a seat for the rider, who steers the front wheel by means of handlebars and drives the rear wheel by means of pedals.

bill•board |bĭl′ bôrd′| *or* |-bōrd′| *n.* A large upright board for the display of advertisements in public places or alongside highways: *The amusement park is advertised on a huge billboard.*

birch |bûrch| *n.* Any of several trees with papery, easily peeled bark.

blame |blām| *v.* **blamed, blam•ing.** **1.** To hold (someone or something) at fault; to think of as guilty or responsible; to accuse: *Mom is always blaming the dog for digging up her garden.*

block•ade |blŏ kād′| *v.* **block•ad•ed, block•ad•ing.** To close off a city or harbor by troops or warships to prevent people and supplies from going in and out. *The fleet blockaded the enemy's harbors.*

bloom |bloōm| *n.* The flower or blossoms of a plant. —*v.* To bear flowers; blossom.

boast |bōst| *v.* To brag vainly or proudly about something relating to oneself.

bomb |bŏm| *n.* An explosive weapon constructed to go off upon striking a given object, area, or other target, or by another means, such as a timing mechanism.

bom•bard |bŏm bärd′| *v.* To attack with bombs or explosive shells.

bore |bôr| *v.* Past tense of **bear.**

bor•ough |bûr′ ō| *or* |bŭr′-| *n.* A self-governing incorporated town, as in certain U.S. states.

♦ *These sound alike* **borough, burro, burrow.**

both•er |bŏ*th*′ ər| *v.* **both•ered, both•er•ing.** **a.** To concern or worry: *bothered by financial problems.* **b.** To annoy, irritate, or pester: *The flies bothered the horse.*

boun•ti•ful |boun′ tə fəl| *adj.* Plentiful; abundant: *bountiful crops.*

brain |brān| *n.* The large mass of gray nerve tissue enclosed in the skull of a vertebrate. It interprets sensory impulses, coordinates and controls bodily activities and functions, and is the center of thought and feeling.

brake |brāk| *n.* Often **brakes.** A device for slowing or stopping motion, as of a vehicle or machine.

brand |brănd| *n.* A distinctive style or type: *a brand of shampoo.*

brass |brăs| *or* |bräs| *n.* **1.** A mixture that contains chiefly copper and zinc. **2.** Ornaments, objects, or utensils made of such metal: *polish the brass.*

break·neck |brāk′ nĕk′| *adj.* Dangerously fast: *The ambulance drove at breakneck speed.*

breath |brĕth| *n.* The air inhaled into and exhaled from the lungs.

breath·less |brĕth′ lĭs| *adj.* Out of breath; panting: *He was breathless after running.*

brief |brēf| *adj.* **brief·er, brief·est.** Short in time, duration, or length.

bril·liant |brĭl′ yənt| *adj.* **1.** Shining brightly; glittering: *A brilliant sun blazed in the sky.* **2.** Very vivid in color: *The sky was a brilliant blue.* **3.** Excellent; wonderful: *a brilliant performance.*

broad·cast |brôd′ kăst′| *or* |-käst′| *v.* **broad·cast** or **broad·cast·ed, broad·cast·ing.** To transmit over a wide area by radio or television. —**broad′cast′er** *n.: The broadcaster worked hard at the television station.*

bud·get |bŭj′ ĭt| *n.* An itemized list of probable expenditures and income for a given period, usually showing how the money available is going to be divided up and spent: *A monthly budget can help you save money.*

bull·doz·er |bŏŏl′ dō′ zər| *n.* A large, powerful tractor having a metal blade in front, which is used for moving and grading earth.

bul·let |bŏŏl′ ĭt| *n.* A metal object made to be fired from a pistol or other firearm.

bulletin board |bŏŏl′ ĭ tn bôrd| *n.* A board mounted on a wall, on which notices are posted.

bunch |bŭnch| *n.* **1.** A group of like things that are growing or placed together: *a bunch of grapes.* **2.** *Informal.* A small group of people.

bun·dle |bŭn′ dl| *n.* A number of objects tied or wrapped together; a package.

bur·den |bûr′ dn| *n.* Something that is carried; often a heavy load.

bur·ro |bûr′ ō| *or* |bŏŏr′-| *or* |bŭr′-| *n.* A small donkey, usually used for riding or for carrying loads: *She rode a burro down into the Grand Canyon.*

♦ *These sound alike* **burro, borough, burrow.**

bur·row |bûr′ ō| *or* |bŭr′ ō| *n.* A hole or tunnel dug in the ground by a small animal, such as a rabbit or mole: *a family of rabbits living in a burrow.*

♦ *These sound alike* **burrow, borough, burro.**

bur·y |bĕr′ ē| *v.* **bur·ied, bur·y·ing, bur·ies.** To place in the ground and cover with earth: *The dog buried its bone in the dirt.*

♦ *These sound alike* **bury, berry.**

cab·i·net |kăb′ ə nĭt| *n.* Often **Cabinet.** A group of people appointed by a head of state or prime minister to act as official advisers and to head the various departments of state: *The Cabinet met to discuss the national emergency.*

cal·en·dar |kăl′ ən dər| *n.* A chart showing the months, weeks, and days of a certain year: *I use my calendar to record family birthdays and anniversaries.*

calf |kăf| *or* |käf| *n., pl.* **calves** |kăvs| *or* |kävs|. A young cow or bull: *The newborn calf was unsteady on its feet.*

cam·paign |kăm **pān'**| *n.* Organized activity to attain some political, social, or commercial goal: *an advertising campaign to sell new cars.*

cam·pus |kăm' pəs| *n., pl.* **cam·pus·es.** The grounds of a school, especially of a college or university: *The college students enjoyed strolling across the campus.*

can·cel |kăn' səl| *v.* **can·celed** or **can·celled, can·cel·ing** or **can·cel·ling.** To call off or give up an idea or activity.

> ### History
> **Cancel** comes from the Latin word *cancer,* meaning "lattice." A latticework wall, like the choir screen in some churches, was called *cancellí.* The verb *cancellare* came to mean "to cross out."

ca·pa·ble |kā' pə bəl| *adj.* Able; skilled; competent: *a capable teacher.* —**ca'pa·bly** *adv.*

car·di·gan |kär' dĭ gən| *n.* A sweater or knitted jacket that buttons down the front.

care·free |kâr' frē'| *adj.* Without worries or responsibilities: *a carefree life.*

car·go |kär' gō| *n., pl.* **car·goes** or **car·gos.** The freight carried by a ship or airplane.

car·pen·try |kär' pən trē| *n.* The work or trade of someone who builds wooden objects or structures.

cat·a·log or **cat·a·logue** |kăt' l ôg'| *or* |-ŏg'| *n.* A book or pamphlet containing a list of items with a description of each.

catch |kăch| *v.* **caught** |kôt|, **catch·ing.** To get hold of or grasp something moving.

caught |kôt| *v.* Past tense and past participle of **catch.**

cau·li·flow·er |kô' lĭ flou' ər| *or* |kŏl' ĭ-| *n.* A plant closely related to the cabbage, having a rounded head of small, closely clustered whitish flowers, and eaten as a vegetable.

cau·tion |kô' shən| *n.* Care so as to avoid possible danger or trouble. —*v.* To warn against possible trouble or danger.

cav·al·ry |kăv' əl rē| *n., pl.* **cav·al·ries.** Troops trained to fight on horseback or, more recently, in armored vehicles.

ce·dar |sē' dər| *n.* Any of several evergreen trees related to the pines and firs, having reddish, pleasant-smelling wood.

ceil·ing |sē' lĭng| *n.* The inside upper surface of a room.

cel·e·brate |sĕl' ə brāt'| *v.* **cel·e·brat·ed, cel·e·brat·ing.** To mark (a special occasion) with festive activity.

cel·list, also **'cel·list** |chĕl' ĭst| *n.* A person who plays the cello.

cel·lo, also **'cel·lo** |chĕl' ō| *n., pl.* **cel·los.** A musical instrument of the violin family, having four strings and a pitch an octave below that of the viola.

Cel·si·us |sĕl' sē əs| *or* |-shəs| *adj.* Of the Celsius temperature scale on which the freezing point of water is 0° and the boiling point of water is 100°.

chan·cel·lor |chăn' sə lər| *or* |-slər| *or* |chän'-| *n.* The chief minister of state in some European countries: *The chancellor met with other heads of state.*

change |chānj| *v.* **changed, chang·ing.** To take, put, or use (something) in place of another, usually of the same kind; vary.

change·a·ble |chān' jə bəl| *adj.* Likely to change; variable: *Spring weather is often changeable.*

chan·nel |chăn' əl| *n.* **1.** A part of a harbor deep enough for ships. **2.** A broad strait: *the English Channel.* **3.** A passage for liquids. **4.** A way through which ideas may travel: *opening new channels of information.* **5.** A band of radio-wave frequencies for broadcasting: *a television channel.*

chart |chärt| *n.* Something written or drawn, as a table or graph, that presents information in an organized and easily viewed form.

cheap |chēp| *adj.* **cheap·er, cheap·est.** **1.** Low in price; inexpensive. **2.** Not spending or giving money generously; stingy.

check·book |chĕk′ bŏŏk′| *n.* A book or booklet containing blank checks, given by a bank to a depositor who has a checking account.

chief |chēf| *n., pl.* **chiefs.** A person with the highest rank or authority; a leader: *the chief of the fire department.*

chron·ic |krŏn′ ĭk| *adj.* Lasting for a long time; continuing.

cir·cum·stance |sûr′ kəm stăns′| *n.* Often **circumstances.** One of the conditions, facts, or events connected with and usually affecting another event, a person, or a course of action: *Write a few lines giving the circumstances of why the car stopped.*

cir·cum·vent |sûr′ kəm vĕnt′| *v.* **1.** To avoid or get around by cleverness or ingenuity: *They tried to circumvent the building code when remodeling the house.* **2.** To avoid by going around: *We took side roads to circumvent construction.* —**cir′·cum·ven′·tion** *n.*

cirque |sûrk| *n.* A steep or bowl-shaped hollow, often containing a small lake, that is at the upper end of some mountain valleys.

cirque

cite |sīt| *v.* **cit·ed, cit·ing.** To quote or mention as an authority or example: *Let me cite two cases of what I have in mind.*
◆ *These sound alike* **cite, site, sight.**

cit·i·zen |sĭt′ ĭ zən| *n., pl.* **cit·i·zens.** A resident of a city, town, or country.

civ·i·lize |sĭv′ ə līz′| *v.* **civ·i·lized, civ·i·liz·ing.** **1.** To bring to a more highly

ă	pat	îr	pier	ŭ	cut
ā	pay	ŏ	pot	ûr	urge
âr	care	ō	toe	th	thin
ä	father	ô	paw	th	this
ĕ	pet	oi	boy	hw	whoop
ē	be	ŏŏ	took	zh	vision
ĭ	pit	ōō	boot	ə	about
ī	pie	ou	out		

developed state of society and culture **2.** To refine by education and training.

clar·i·fy |klăr′ ə fī| *v.* **clar·i·fied, clar·i·fy·ing, clar·i·fies.** To make or become less vague or easier to understand.

clar·i·net |klăr′ ə nĕt′| *n.* A woodwind instrument with a single-reed mouthpiece, a cylindrical body, and a flaring bell. It has a hollow, reedy tone and is played by covering holes in its body and pressing keys with the fingers.

clause |klôz| *n.* In grammar, a sentence or part of a sentence containing its own subject and a verb or verb phrase.

clean |klēn| *v.* To get rid of dirt.

cleanse |klĕnz| *v.* **cleansed, cleans·ing.** To make clean or pure: *cleanse a wound.*

cli·ent |klī′ ənt| *n.* **1.** A person consulting a professional, such as a lawyer or an accountant. **2.** A customer or patron.

cliff |klĭf| *n.* A high, steep, or overhanging face of rock.

coax |kōks| *v.* To persuade or to try to persuade by gentle or persistent urging.

code |kōd| *n.* A system of words, symbols, or letters given arbitrary meaning, usually used to keep messages secret.

col·lapse |kə lăps′| *v.* **col·lapsed, col·laps·ing.** To fall down or inward suddenly; cave in: *Part of the roof collapsed under the weight of the snow.*

col·lege |kŏl′ ĭj| *n.* A school of higher learning, entered after high school, that grants a bachelor's degree.

colo·nel |kûr′ nəl| *n.* An officer in the U.S. Army, Air Force, or Marine Corps ranking below a brigadier general.
◆ *These sound alike* **colonel, kernel.**

com-. See **con-: compete.**

com·bi·na·tion |kŏm′ bə nā′ shən| *n.* Something that results from joining two or more things; a mixture.

com·bine |kəm bīn′| *v.* **com·bined, com·bin·ing.** To join or cause to join (two or more substances) to make one substance.

com·e·dy |kŏm′ ĭ dē| *n., pl.* **com·e·dies.** A play, movie, or other work that is meant to make people laugh and that ends happily: *We saw a hilarious comedy on TV.*

com·fort·a·ble |kŭmf′ tə bəl| *or* |kŭm′ fər tə bəl| *adj.* Giving a feeling of ease or well-being: *a comfortable home.*

com·ment |kŏm′ ĕnt| *n.* A written note or a remark that explains, interprets, or gives an opinion on something: *a critic's comment on a play.*

com·merce |kŏm′ ərs| *n.* The buying and selling of goods, especially on a large scale, as between nations; trade: *The nation halted all commerce with its enemy.*

com·mis·sion |kə mĭsh′ ən| *n.* **1.** The act of doing something. **2.** An assigned job or duty. **3.** A group of people officially authorized to perform certain duties. —*v.* To place an order for: *Did Erin commission an artist to paint that picture?*

com·mod·i·ty |kə mŏd′ ĭ tē| *n., pl.* **com·mod·i·ties.** An article of trade or commerce, as an agricultural or mining product: *Cotton was an important commodity of plantations.*

com·mo·tion |kə mō′ shən| *n.* Disturbance or tumult; agitation; violent motion.

com·mu·ni·ty |kə myōō′ nĭ tē| *n., pl.* **com·mu·ni·ties. a.** A group of people living in the same locality and under the same government. **b.** The district or locality in which they live.

com·pa·ny |kŭm′ pə nē| *n., pl.* **com·pa·nies. 1.** A business enterprise; a firm. **2.** A guest or guests.

com·pare |kəm pâr′| *v.* **com·pared, com·par·ing.** To examine so as to note the similarities and differences of: *compare the skills of an astronaut with those of an airplane pilot.*

com·pen·sate |kŏm′ pən sāt′| *v.* **com·pen·sat·ed, com·pen·sat·ing.** To act as or provide a balancing effect; make up: *A baseball player who is not a speedy runner can compensate by powerful hitting.*

com·pete |kəm pēt′| *v.* **com·pet·ed, com·pet·ing.** To strive against another or others to win something; take part in or as if in a contest; be a rival.

com·pe·ti·tion |kŏm pĭ tĭsh′ ən| *n.* Rivalry or struggle to win an advantage, success, or profit, from another or others.

com·plaint |kəm plānt′| *n.* A cause or reason for being dissatisfied, unhappy, or annoyed with something: *Several customers had complaints about the dishwashers.*

com·plex |kəm plĕks′| *adj.* Difficult to understand or figure out; complicated.

com·pli·ance |kəm plī′ əns| *n.* The act of complying; action or obedience in accordance with a rule, request, or command; conformity: *Compliance with a country's laws is expected of all citizens.*

com·pli·cate |kŏm′ plĭ kāt′| *v.* **com·pli·cat·ed, com·pli·cat·ing.** To make hard to understand, solve, or deal with; make confusing or perplexing: *The extra information only complicates the problem.*

com·po·si·tion |kŏm′ pə zĭsh′ ən| *n.* The putting together of parts or elements to form a whole; the act, process, or art of composing music or poetry.

com·pos·i·tor |kəm pŏz′ ĭ tər| *n.* A person who arranges or sets type for printing; a typesetter: *We sent the manuscript to the compositor.*

com·pound word |kŏm′ pound′ wôrd| *n.* A word made up of two or more smaller words. A compound word may be written as one word, as two words joined by a hyphen, or as two separate words.

com·pre·hen·sive |kŏm′ prĭ hĕn′ sĭv| *adj.* Including much; broad in scope; thorough: *This chapter ends with a comprehensive explanation of punctuation.*

com·put·er |kəm pyōō′ tər| *n.* A device that computes, especially an electronic device capable of processing information according to a set of instructions stored within the device.

con |kŏn| *n.* An argument or opinion against something. —*adv.* Against: *arguing pro and con.* —*adj.: the arguments pro and con.*

con-. A prefix meaning "together" or "with": **contain.**

con·ceit |kən sēt′| *n.* Too high an opinion of one's abilities or worth; vanity.

con·cen·tra·tion |kŏn′ sən trā′ shən| *n.* The act of fixing one's mind on something.

con·cern |kən sûrn′| *n.* A matter that relates to or affects someone or something.

con·cert |kŏn′ sûrt′| *or* |-sərt| *n.* A musical performance given by a number of singers or instrumentalists or a combination of both. ◇ *Idiom.* **In concert.** As a single unit or group; together: *work in concert.*

conch |kŏngk| *or* |kŏnch| *n., pl.* **conchs** |kŏngks| *or* **conch·es** |kŏn′ chĭz|. A tropical sea animal related to the snail, having a large, often brightly colored spiral shell.

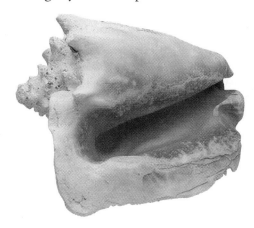

conch

con·clude |kən klōōd′| *v.* **con·clud·ed, con·clud·ing.** To bring or come to an end; close; finish.

con·clu·sion |kən klōō′ zhən| *n.* The close or closing part of something; end.

con·crete |kŏn′ krēt′| *or* |kŏn krēt′| *n.* A building or paving material made of sand, pebbles, and crushed stone, held together by a mass of cement or mortar.

con·di·tion |kən dĭsh′ ən| *n.* A state of being or existence; the way something or someone is: *They worked hard to restore the old house to its original condition.*

con·fed·er·a·cy |kən fĕd′ ər ə sē| *n., pl.* **con·fed·er·a·cies.** **The Confederacy.** The **Confederate States of America.** The eleven southern states that seceded from the United States (1860–1861).

con·fer·ence |kŏn′ fər əns| *or* |-frəns| *n.* A meeting to discuss a particular subject.

con·fes·sion |kən fĕsh′ ən| *n.* The act of confessing, revealing, or admitting; acknowledgment.

con·firm |kən fûrm′| *v.* To support or establish the truth of: *The news confirmed the rumors.*

con·flict |kŏn′ flĭkt′| *n.* **1.** Prolonged fighting; warfare. **2.** A clash of opposing ideas or interests.

con·form |kən fôrm′| *v.* **1.** To act in agreement with established customs, rules, or styles: *Many young people do not conform to the way older people dress.* **2.** To correspond in form or character; be similar: *The computer conforms to the manufacturer's advertising claims.*

con·for·ma·tion |kŏn′ fər mā′ shən| *n.* **1.** The way something is formed; shape or structure: *The conformation of a snake's skeleton is elongated.* **2.** The act of conforming or the state of being conformed.

con·form·ist |kən fôr′ mĭst| *n.* A person who conforms to current customs, rules, or styles.

con·front |kən frŭnt′| *v.* To come face to face with; stand before.

con·fuse |kən fyōōz′| *v.* **con·fused, con·fus·ing.** **1.** To mislead; mix up; baffle; puzzle. **2.** To fail to distinguish between; mistake for something else.

con·fu·sion |kən fyōō′ zhən| *n.* The condition of being confused; bewilderment.

con·nect |kə nĕkt′| *v.* To join or come together; link: *A new road connects these towns.*

con·nec·tion |kə nĕk′ shən| *n.* **1.** A relationship: *the connection between the sun and the seasons.* **2.** Something that connects or joins; a link: *a bad telephone connection.*

con·quer |kŏng′ kər| *v.* **1.** To win mastery over by war. **2.** To gain control over (a hostile environment or challenge).

con·sec·u·tive |kən sĕk′ yə tĭv| *adj.* Following in order without break or interruption; successive. —**con·sec′u·tive·ly** *adv.: It rained for five days consecutively.*

con·se·quence |kŏn′ sĭ kwĕns′| *or* |-kwəns| *n.* Something that follows from an action or condition; an effect or result: *Have you considered the consequences of your decision?*

con·sid·er |kən sĭd′ ər| *v.* To deliberate upon; to think over; examine.

con·sid·er·a·ble |kən sĭd′ ər ə bəl| *adj.* Fairly large or great in amount, extent, or degree: *a considerable income.* —**con·sid′er·a·bly** *adv.*

con·sid·er·ate |kən sĭd′ ər ĭt| *adj.* Taking into account others' feelings; thoughtful.

con·stant |kŏn′ stənt| *adj.* Happening all the time; persistent: *We were bothered by constant interruptions.*

con·sti·tu·tion |kŏn′ stĭ tōō′ shən| *or* |-tyōō′-| *n.* The basic law of a politically organized body, such as a nation or state.

con·struct |kən strŭkt′| *v.* To build; erect.

con·struc·tion |kən strŭk′ shən| *n.* The act or process of building something.

con·sum·er |kən sōō′ mər| *n.* Someone who buys and uses products and services. —*modifier: consumer goods.*

consumer

con·tact |kŏn′ tăkt′| *n.* The condition of touching or coming together: *physical contact.*

con·ta·gious |kən tā′ jəs| *adj.* Capable of being transmitted by direct or indirect contact: *a contagious disease.*

con·tain |kən tān′| *v.* To have within itself; hold: *Oranges contain vitamin C.*

con·tent¹ |kŏn′ tĕnt′| *n.* The amount of a substance contained in something: *Cream has a high fat content.*

con·tent² |kən tĕnt′| *adj.* Happy with what one has: *I am content with my life as it is.* —*v.* To make content or satisfied.

con·test |kŏn′ tĕst′| *n.* Any competition, usually between entrants who perform separately and are rated by a panel of judges: *a beauty contest; a skating contest.*

con·ti·nen·tal |kŏn′ tə nĕn′ tl| *adj.* Of or like a continent: *continental glacier.*

con·trac·tion |kən trăk′ shən| *n.* The shortened form of one or more words. An apostrophe replaces the missing letter or letters. For example, **shouldn't** is a contraction of *should not.*

con·tra·dict |kŏn′ trə dĭkt′| *v.* To assert or express the opposite of (a statement): *The witness seemed to contradict his previous testimony.*

con·trib·ute |kən trĭb′ yōōt| *v.* **con·trib·ut·ed, con·trib·ut·ing.** To give or supply in common with others: *contribute time and money.*

con·tri·bu·tion |kŏn′ trĭ byōō′ shən| *n.* Something given; a donation: *He gave a small contribution to the fund.*

con·trol |kən trōl′| *v.* **con·trolled, con·trol·ling.** To hold in check; restrain: *control one's temper.*

con·ven·tion |kən vĕn′ shən| *n.* **1. a.** A formal meeting of a group for a particular purpose: *a political convention for nominating candidates.* **b.** The group of persons attending such an assembly. **2. a.** General agreement on or acceptance of certain practices or attitudes: *Convention allows for much more casual dress today.* **b.** A widely accepted practice; a custom: *the convention of shaking hands.* **3.** A formal agreement or compact, as between nations.

con·ver·sa·tion |kŏn′ vər **sā′** shən| *n.* An informal talk in which people exchange thoughts and feelings.

con·vic·tion |kən **vĭk′** shən| *n.* A strong opinion or belief: *act according to one's true convictions.*

con·vince |kən **vĭns′**| *v.* **con·vinced, con·vinc·ing.** To cause (someone) to believe or feel certain; persuade.

co·op·er·ate |kō **ŏp′** ə rāt′| *v.* **co·op·er·at·ed, co·op·er·at·ing.** To work or act with another or others for a common purpose: *Everyone cooperated on the project.*

co·op·er·a·tion |kō ŏp′ ə **rā′** shən| *n.* Willingness to work with others for a common purpose.

co·or·di·nate |kō **ôr′** dn āt′| *v.* **co·or·di·nat·ed, co·or·di·nat·ing.** To work or cause to work together efficiently in a common cause or effort; harmonize: *An acrobat's muscles have to coordinate perfectly.*

cop·y·right |**kŏp′** ē rīt′| *n.* The legal right to exclusive publication, production, sale, or distribution of a literary, musical, dramatic, or artistic work: *The copyright on this book runs out in three years.*

cor·po·ral |**kôr′** pər əl| *or* |-prəl| *n.* A noncommissioned officer in the U.S. Army, Air Force, or Marine Corps ranking below a sergeant.

cor·po·ra·tion |kôr′ pə **rā′** shən| *n.* A group of persons acting under a legal charter as a separate organization with privileges and liabilities distinct from those of its members: *The small company was owned by a large corporation.*

cor·rect |kə **rĕkt′**| *v.* **a.** To remove the mistakes from. **b.** To indicate or mark the errors in. —*adj.* Free from error.

cor·rec·tion |kə **rĕk′** shən| *n.* The act or process of making something right.

cor·ri·dor |**kôr′** ĭ dər| *or* |-dôr′| *or* |**kŏr′**-| *n.* A narrow hallway or passageway with rooms opening onto it.

cor·rupt |kə **rŭpt′**| *adj.* Immoral; wicked: *the corrupt life of a swindler.* —*v.* **1.** To ruin morally: *Greed corrupts some people.* **2.** To taint, infect, spoil: *Several chemical spills corrupted the water supply.*

ă	pat	îr	pier	ŭ	cut
ā	pay	ŏ	pot	ûr	urge
âr	care	ō	toe	th	thin
ä	father	ô	paw	*th*	this
ĕ	pet	oi	boy	hw	whoop
ē	be	ŏŏ	took	zh	vision
ĭ	pit	ōō	boot	ə	about
ī	pie	ou	out		

Pronunciation Key

---

cos·mo·pol·i·tan |kŏz′ mə **pŏl′** ĭ tn| *adj.* Showing worldly experience, education, or cultivation; at home in all parts of the world: *a cosmopolitan person.*

coun·cil·or *also* **coun·cil·lor** |**koun′** sə lər| *or* |slər| *n.* A member of a council, either appointed or elected to make laws or rules governing something.

coun·try |**kŭn′** trē| *n., pl.* **coun·tries.** A nation or state: *all the countries of the world.*

cou·pon |**kōō′** pŏn| *or* |**kyōō′**-| *n.* A detachable part of a ticket or advertisement that entitles the bearer to certain benefits, such as a cash refund or a gift: *These coupons will save several dollars on the grocery bill this week.*

cour·age |**kûr′** ĭj| *or* |**kŭr′**-| *n.* The quality of mind or spirit that enables one to face danger or hardship with confidence, resolution, and firm control of oneself; bravery; fearlessness.

History

Courage comes from the Latin word *cor,* meaning "heart," which was thought to be the center of all feeling.

cour·i·er |**kûr′** ē ər| *or* |**kōōr′**-| *n.* A messenger, especially one on urgent or official diplomatic business: *The courier delivered important news about the peace talks.*

court |kôrt| *or* |kōrt| *n.* **1.** An area marked for tennis, basketball, and so on. **2.** A king or queen's governing body, including ministers and advisers.

craft |krăft| *or* |kräft| *n.* **1.** Skill or ability in something, especially in work done with the hands or in the arts. **2.** *pl.* **craft.** A boat, ship, aircraft, or spacecraft.

cre·a·tive |krē ā′ tĭv| *adj.* Having the ability or power to produce things; original and expressive: *a creative writer.*

cred·it |krĕd′ ĭt| *n.* A system of buying goods or services by charging the amount, with payment due at a later time: *buy on credit.* —**modifier:** *a credit card; a credit rating.*

cred·i·tor |krĕd′ ĭ tər| *n.* A person or company to whom money is owed.

crest·fall·en |krĕst′ fô′ lən| *adj.* Dejected; depressed.

cre·vasse |krə văs′| *n.* A deep crack, as in a glacier; a chasm: *a deep crevasse in the glacier.*

crevasse

crev·ice |krĕv′ ĭs| *n.* A narrow crack or opening; a fissure; cleft.

cri·sis |krī′ sĭs| *n., pl.* **cri·ses** |krī′ sēz′| A decisive, crucial point or situation in the course of anything; a turning point: *an environmental crisis.*

crit·ic |krĭt′ ĭk| *n.* A person whose job is judging and reporting on the worth of something intended as an artistic work or on its performance: *The book critic did not recommend the author's latest novel.*

crit·i·cal |krĭt′ ĭ kəl| *adj.* Inclined to judge severely; likely to find fault.

crit·i·cize |krĭt′ ĭ sīz′| *v.* **crit·i·cized, crit·i·ciz·ing. 1.** To judge the merits and faults of; evaluate. **2.** To judge severely; find fault with: *Dad will always criticize people who litter.*

crouch |krouch| *v.* To lower the body by bending or squatting; stoop.

crys·tal |krĭs′ təl| *n.* A clear, colorless glass of high quality.

cu·cum·ber |kyōō′ kŭm′ bər| *n.* A long vegetable with a green rind and white, watery flesh, eaten in salads and used for pickling.

cul·ture |kŭl′ chər| *n.* Intellectual and artistic activity and the works produced by this: *Our libraries and museums bring culture to the people.*

curb |kûrb| *n.* A concrete or stone rim along the edge of a sidewalk or street: *The car was parked next to the curb.*

cu·ri·ous |kyŏŏr′ ē əs| *adj.* Eager to acquire information or knowledge: *A scientist is always curious to learn more.*

cush·ion |kŏŏsh′ ən| *n.* A pad or pillow with a soft filling, used to sit, lie, or rest on.

cus·tom |kŭs′ təm| *n.* An accepted practice or convention followed by tradition: *Shaking hands when meeting someone is an ancient custom.*

cy·cle |sī′ kəl| v. **cy·cled, cy·cling.** To ride a bicycle or motorcycle.

cym·bal |sĭm′ bəl| n., pl. **cym·bals.** One of a pair of musical percussion instruments consisting of a dish-shaped sheet of brass that is sounded either by being struck with a drumstick or by being struck against another identical sheet of brass: *the clang of cymbals.*

D

dan·ger·ous |dān′ jər əs| adj. Full of risk or threat of harm; hazardous; unsafe: *a dangerous job.*

de-. A prefix meaning: **1.** Reversal: **decode.** **2.** Removal: **defrost.** **3.** Reduction: **demote.**

dead end |dĕd ĕnd| n. A street, alley, or other passage that is closed or blocked at one end.

deaf |dĕf| adj. Lacking the ability to hear, either completely or in part.

deal |dēl| v. **dealt** |dĕlt|, **deal·ing.** To do business; trade or bargain: *a merchant who deals in diamonds.* —n. *Informal.* An agreement.

de·bate |dĭ bāt′| n. A formal contest in which opponents argue for opposite sides of an issue. —v. **de·bat·ed, de·bat·ing.** To call into question; argue about; dispute: *He debated my decision.*

de·bris also **dé·bris** |də brē′| or |dā′ brē′| n. The scattered remains of something broken, destroyed, or discarded; rubble: *The glacier carries rock debris.*

dec·ade |dĕk′ ād′| n. A period of ten years.

de·cath·lon |dĭ kăth′ lən| or |dĭ kăth′ lŏn′| n. An athletic contest in which each contestant takes part in ten different track and field events.

de·cay |dĭ kā′| n. The breaking down of plant or animal matter by the action of bacteria or fungi: *Poor dental habits cause tooth decay.* —v. **1.** To rot or become rotten. **2.** To fall into ruin.

Pronunciation Key

ă	pat	îr	pier	ŭ	cut
ā	pay	ŏ	pot	ûr	urge
âr	care	ō	toe	th	thin
ä	father	ô	paw	th	this
ĕ	pet	oi	boy	hw	whoop
ē	be	ŏŏ	took	zh	vision
ĭ	pit	ōō	boot	ə	about
ī	pie	ou	out		

de·ceit |dĭ sēt′| n. The act or practice of deceiving; dishonesty.

de·ci·sion |dĭ sizh′ ən| n. A final or definite conclusion; a judgment: *made a decision about what should be done.*

de·cline |dĭ klīn′| v. **de·clined, de·clin·ing.** To refuse to accept or do: *decline an offer.*

dec·o·rate |dĕk′ ə rāt′| v. **dec·o·rat·ed, dec·o·rat·ing.** To furnish with something attractive, beautiful, or striking; adorn: *decorate a Christmas tree.*

de·crease |dĭ krēs′| v. **de·creased, de·creas·ing.** To make or become gradually less or smaller; diminish: *decrease one's speed.*

ded·i·cate |dĕd′ ĭ kāt′| v. **ded·i·cat·ed, ded·i·cat·ing.** To set apart for a special purpose; to give wholly; devote: *The scientists dedicated themselves to research.*

de·feat |dĭ fēt′| n. The condition of being defeated; failure to win: *Napoleon's defeat at Waterloo.*

de·fense |dĭ fĕns′| n. Something that protects or defends against attack, harm, or challenge: *An army is part of a country's national defense.* —**de·fense′less** adj.

de·fi·cient |dĭ fĭsh′ ənt| adj. Lacking an important element or elements; insufficient; inadequate: *a deficient diet.*

deft |dĕft| adj. Quick and skillful: *a deft motion; deft hands.*

de·lay |dĭ lā′| v. To cause to be late or slower than expected or desired: *A traffic jam delayed me in getting home.*

de·lete |dĭ lēt′| v. **de·let·ed, de·let·ing.** To strike out; remove; eliminate: *delete a name from a list.*

de·lib·er·ate |dĭ **lĭb′** ər ĭt| *adj.* Done or said on purpose; intentional: *Michael told a deliberate lie.*

de·light·ful |dĭ **līt′** fəl| *adj.* Giving joy; very pleasing: *We had a delightful time at the party.*

de·liv·er·y |dĭ **lĭv′** ə rē| *n., pl.* **de·liv·er·ies.** A person's manner of speaking or singing in public: *The content of his speech was good, but his delivery was poor.*

de·mand |dĭ **mănd′**| *or* |-mänd| *n.* An insistent request: *wage demands.*

de·moc·ra·cy |dĭ **mŏk′** rə sē| *n., pl.* **de·moc·ra·cies.** **1. a.** A form of government in which power belongs to the people, who express their will through elected representatives. **b.** A country with this form of government. **2.** Respect for the rights of every individual in a society.

dem·o·crat·ic |dĕm′ ə **krăt′** ĭk| *adj.* Based on the principle of equal rights for all.

dem·on·strate |dĕm′ ən strāt′| *v.* **dem·on·strat·ed, dem·on·strat·ing.** To display, operate, or explain (a product): *demonstrate a new washing machine.*

den·tist |dĕn′ tĭst| *n.* A doctor who treats people's teeth.

de·ny |dĭ **nī′**| *v.* **de·nied, de·ny·ing, de·nies. 1.** To declare untrue; contradict: *deny an accusation.* **2.** To refuse to give; withhold: *deny a request.*

de·par·ture |dĭ **pär′** chər| *n.* The act of going away or starting out.

de·pos·it |dĭ **pŏz′** ĭt| *n.* An account of money for or in a bank account.

de·pre·ci·ate |dĭ **prē′** shē āt′| *v.* **de·pre·ci·at·ed, de·pre·ci·at·ing.** To lower the worth of or go down in value: *A car depreciates in value each year.*

depth |dĕpth| *n.* A distance downward or inward from a surface: *The diver descended to a depth of 100 feet.*

de·scribe |dĭ **skrīb′**| *v.* **de·scribed, de·scrib·ing.** To transmit an impression or image of with words; picture verbally.

de·scrip·tive |dĭ **skrĭp′** tĭv| *adj.* Serving to describe; making a description of something, usually including many details: *descriptive words.*

de·sert¹ |dĭ **zûrt′**| *v.* **1.** To leave empty or alone; abandon: *Miners deserted the valley after the ore ran out.* **2.** To abandon (a military post, for example) in violation of orders: *The soldiers deserted their posts just before the attack.*

des·ert² |dĕz′ ərt| *n.* A dry barren region, often covered with sand, having little or no vegetation.

desert²

de·serve |dĭ **zûrv′**| *v.* **de·served, de·serv·ing.** To be worthy of; have a right to: *He deserved better treatment than he got.*

de·sire |dĭ **zīr′**| *v.* To wish or long for; want; crave: *anything your heart desires.*

des·per·ate |dĕs′ pər ĭt| *or* |-prĭt| *adj.* **1.** In a hopeless situation and thus ready to do anything; feeling despair: *a desperate criminal.* **2.** Having an urgent or overwhelming need for something: *desperate for food.*

des·ti·na·tion |dĕs′ tə **nā′** shən| *n.* The place to which someone or something is going or directed: *We reached our destination after traveling for three days.*

de·stroy |dĭ **stroi′**| *v.* To ruin completely; wipe out: *The storm destroyed his home.*

de·tail |dĭ **tāl′**| *or* |**dē′** tāl′| *n.* An individual or specific item; a particular: *No two people have fingerprints that are exactly alike in every detail.*

de·tec·tive |dĭ **tĕk′** tĭv| *n.* A person, usually a police officer, whose work is investigating and trying to solve crimes.

de·ter·mine |dĭ **tûr′** mĭn| *v.* **de·ter·mined, de·ter·min·ing.** To fix, settle, or decide: *Determine whether each of the following is true or false.*

de·tour |dē′ toor′| *or* |dĭ toor′| *n.* A deviation from a direct route or course.

de·vel·op·ment |dĭ vĕl′ əp mənt| *n.* **1.** The act or process of unfolding or revealing gradually. **2.** The act of growing or causing to grow.

dic·tate |dĭk′ tāt| *or* |dĭk tāt′| *v.* **dic·tat·ed, dic·tat·ing.** To say or read aloud so that another person may record or write down what is said: *The superintendent dictated the letter.*

dic·ta·tor·ship |dĭk tā′ tər shĭp′| *or* |dĭk′ tā′-| *n.* A form of government in which one person rules with absolute and often unjust authority.

dic·tion·ar·y |dĭk′ shə nĕr′ ē| *n., pl.* **dic·tion·ar·ies.** A book containing an alphabetical list of words with information given for each word.

died |dīd| *v.* **1.** Past tense and past participle of **die. 2.** Stopped living.
◆ *These sound alike* **died, dyed.**

die·sel |dē′ zəl| *n.* Something powered by a diesel engine, especially a locomotive. —*adj.* Powered by or intended for a diesel engine: *diesel locomotive; diesel fuel.*

di·e·ti·cian *also* **di·e·ti·tian** |dī′ ĭ tĭsh′ ən| *n.* A person who specializes in nutrition: *The school dietician plans nutritious meals that students like.*

dif·fer |dĭf′ ər| *v.* To be of a different opinion; disagree: *They differed over the amount to give their church.*

dif·fer·ence |dĭf′ ər əns| *or* |dĭf′ rəns| *n.* **1.** The condition of being unlike or different; variation. **2.** A degree or amount of variation: *a difference of 3 feet.*

dif·fer·ent |dĭf′ ər ənt| *or* |dĭf′ rənt| *adj.* Distinct; separate: *Different people like different things.*

dif·fi·cult |dĭf′ ĭ kŭlt′| *or* |-kəlt| *adj.* Hard to do, accomplish, or perform.

di·min·ish |dĭ mĭn′ ĭsh| *v.* To make or become smaller or less: *A drought diminished their food supply.*

di·no·saur |dī′ nə sôr′| *n.* Any of many kinds of often gigantic reptiles that lived millions of years ago and are now extinct.

Pronunciation Key

ă	pat	îr	pier	ŭ	cut
ā	pay	ŏ	pot	ûr	urge
âr	care	ō	toe	th	thin
ä	father	ô	paw	*th*	*this*
ĕ	pet	oi	boy	hw	whoop
ē	be	ŏŏ	took	zh	vision
ĭ	pit	ōō	boot	ə	about
ī	pie	ou	out		

di·o·ram·a |dī′ ə răm′ ə| *or* |-rä′ mə| *n.* A three-dimensional miniature scene with painted modeled figures and background: *the tiny model trains in the transportation diorama.*

di·rec·tion |dĭ rĕk′ shən| *or* |dī-| *n.* **1.** Management, supervision, or guidance of a performance: *The workers followed the foreman's direction.* **2.** Orientation or bearing in relation to surroundings: *The noise came from that direction.*

di·rec·tor |dĭ rĕk′ tər| *or* |dī-| *n.* **1.** A person who supervises, controls, or manages something. **2.** A person who supervises or guides the performers in a play, motion picture, opera, or television show: *I would rather be an actor than a director.*

dis-. A prefix that means: **1.** Not: **distrust.** **2.** Opposite of: **disapprove. 3.** Away: **discard.**

dis·a·ble |dĭs ā′ bəl| *v.* **dis·a·bled, dis·a·bling.** To weaken or destroy the normal capacity or abilities of; cripple; incapacitate: *The wound disabled him.*

dis·a·gree |dĭs′ ə grē′| *v.* **dis·a·greed, dis·a·gree·ing.** To dispute; quarrel.

dis·a·gree·ment |dĭs′ ə grē′ mənt| *n.* A dispute or quarrel caused by a difference of opinion.

dis·as·ter |dĭ zăs′ tər| *or* |-zä′ stər| *n.* Great destruction, distress, or misfortune.

dis·ci·pline |dĭs′ ə plĭn| *v.* **dis·ci·plined, dis·ci·plin·ing.** To train by instruction and control: *The dancers disciplined themselves by practicing daily.*

dis·cour·age |dĭ skûr′ ĭj| *or* |-skûr′-| *v.* **dis·cour·aged, dis·cour·ag·ing.** To make less hopeful or enthusiastic.

dis·cov·er·y |dĭ **skŭv′** ə rē| *n., pl.*
dis·cov·er·ies. Something newly found,
learned of, or observed.

dis·cuss |dĭ **skŭs′**| *v.* To speak together
about; converse; debate.

dis·cus·sion |dĭ **skŭsh′** ən| *n.* The
consideration of a subject by two or more
persons; a conversation in which ideas and
opinions are exchanged.

dis·ease |dĭ **zēz′**| *n.* Any condition of an
organism that makes it unable to function in
the normal, proper way, especially a condition
that results from infection, inherent weakness,
or pressures of the environment.

dis·grace·ful |dĭs **grās′** fəl| *adj.* Worthy
of or causing shame, dishonor, or disfavor;
embarassing: *a disgraceful secret that was kept
from the public.*

dis·guise |dĭs **gīz′**| *v.* **dis·guised,**
dis·guis·ing. **1.** To conceal the identity of,
as with clothes or other effects: *He disguised
himself.* **2.** To conceal: *He tried to disguise his
impatience.*

dis·hon·est |dĭs **ŏn′** ĭst| *adj.* Inclined to
lie, cheat, or deceive; untruthful.

dis·in·fec·tant |dĭs′ ĭn **fĕk′** tənt| *n.* A
substance that kills micro-organisms that cause
disease; antiseptic.

dis·miss |dĭs **mĭs′**| *v.* To direct or allow to
leave.

dis·rupt |dĭs **rŭpt′**| *v.* To throw into
confusion or disorder: *The noise from the
jackhammer disrupted the class.*

dis·tance |dĭs′ təns| *n.* The length of a
path, especially a straight line segment, that
joins two points.

dis·tant |dĭs′ tənt| *adj.* Far removed in
space or time.

dis·tinc·tion |dĭ **stĭngk′** shən| *n.*
The condition or fact of being different; a
difference; unlikeness: *a distinction between
capital letters and small ones.*

dis·tress |dĭ **strĕs′**| *n.* Pain or suffering of
mind or body resulting from worry, anxiety, or
sickness.

dis·trict |dĭs′ trĭkt| *n.* An area, especially
one having a particular characteristic or
function: *the theater district.*

dis·turb |dĭ **stûrb′**| *v.* To intrude upon;
bother: *The constant phone calls disturbed us.*

ditch |dĭch| *n.* A long, narrow trench dug in
the ground.

di·vide |dĭ **vīd′**| *v.* **di·vid·ed, di·vid·ing.**
1. To separate or become separated into parts
or groups; split: *divide a cake.* **2.** Disunite:
Bad feelings have divided the team.

div·i·dend |dĭv′ ĭ dĕnd′| *n.* A share of
profits paid to a stockholder.

doc·u·ment |dŏk′ yə mənt| *n.* An official
paper that can be used to furnish evidence or
information.

do·mes·tic |də **mĕs′** tĭk| *adj.* Of, within,
or originating within a particular country; not
foreign or imported.

doz·en |dŭz′ ən| *n., pl.* **dozen.** A set of
twelve: *How many eggs are there in two dozen?*

dra·mat·ic |drə **măt′** ĭk| *adj.* **1.** Of
drama or the theater: *dramatic performances.*
2. Striking in appearance or effect.

drift·wood |drĭft′ wŏod′| *n.* Wood
floating in or washed ashore by the water.

droop |drŏop| *v.* To bend or hang
downward; sag: *The flowers started to droop.*

dull |dŭl| *adj.* **dull·er, dull·est.** Not
brilliant or vivid; dim.

dune |dŏon| *or* |dyŏon| *n.* A hill or ridge
of wind-blown sand.

dune

du·ty |dŏo′ tē| *or* |dyŏo′-| *n., pl.* **du·ties.**
A task, assignment, or function; chores.

dyed |dīd| *v.* **1.** Past tense of **dye**.
2. Changed the color of.
♦ *These sound alike* **dyed, died.**
dy·nam·ic |dī **năm′** ĭk| *adj.* Energetic;
vigorous.

E

Pronunciation Key

ă	pat	îr	pier	ŭ	cut
ā	pay	ŏ	pot	ûr	urge
âr	care	ō	toe	th	thin
ä	father	ô	paw	*th*	*th*is
ě	pet	oi	boy	hw	whoop
ē	be	o͝o	took	zh	vision
ĭ	pit	o͞o	boot	ə	about
ī	pie	ou	out		

ear·nest |**ûr′** nĭst| *adj.* **1.** Showing or
expressing deep, sincere feeling: *The king knelt
in earnest prayer.* **2.** Serious and determined in
purpose: *groups of earnest students.*
earth |ûrth| *n.* **1.** Often **Earth.** The planet
on which human beings live. **2.** The surface of
the land; ground.
ebb tide |ěb tīd| *n.* **1.** The tide when it is
moving back after reaching its highest point.
2. The period between high tide and low tide.
ech·o |**ěk′** ō| *n., pl.* **ech·oes.** A sound
produced by reflected sound waves that can be
heard as a repetition of the original sound.
e·di·tion |ĭ **dĭsh′** ən| *n.* The entire number
of copies of a book or newspaper printed at
one time and having the same content: *A first
edition of that book is worth a lot of money.*
ed·u·cate |**ěj′** o͞o kāt′| *v.* **ed·u·cat·ed,
ed·u·cat·ing.** To provide with knowledge or
training, especially through formal schooling;
teach: *It is the responsibility of a community to
educate each child.*
ed·u·ca·tion |ěj′ o͞o **kā′** shən| *n.* **a.** The
process of imparting or obtaining knowledge
or skill; systematic instruction. **b.** The
knowledge or skill obtained by such a process;
learning.
ee·rie also **ee·ry** |**îr′** ē| *adj.* **ee·ri·er,
ee·ri·est.** Inspiring fear without being openly
threatening; strangely unsettling; weird: *The
entire countryside was bathed in an eerie,
crimson light.*
ef·fec·tive |ĭ **fěk′** tĭv| *adj.* Having or
producing the intended or desired effect;
serving the purpose: *There are two kinds of
vaccine effective against polio.*
ef·fi·cient |ĭ **fish′** ənt| *adj.* Acting or
producing effectively with a minimum of

waste, expense, or effort; capable: *She is an
efficient secretary.*
ef·fort |**ěf′** ərt| *n.* The use of physical or
mental energy to do something; exertion:
Doing it this way will save time and effort.
eight·y |**ā′** tē| *n., pl.* **eight·ies.** A number,
written 80 in Arabic numerals, that is equal to
the product of 8 X 10. —**eight′y** *adj. & pron.*
e·lab·o·rate |ĭ **lăb′** ər ĭt| *adj.* Planned or
made with great attention to numerous parts
or details; complicated but carefully wrought;
intricate: *elaborate scenery.*
el·e·men·ta·ry |ěl′ ə **měn′** tə rē| *or*
|trē| *adj.* Of, involving, or introducing the
fundamental or simplest aspects of a subject:
*Children learn elementary math skills in the first
years of school.*
el·e·va·tor |ěl′ ə **vā′** tər| *n.* A platform or
enclosure raised or lowered in a vertical shaft
to transport freight or people.
e·lim·i·na·tion |ĭ lĭm′ ə **nā′** shən| *n.* The
act or process of leaving something out: *Illegal
blocking resulted in the elimination of one player
from the game.*
else |ěls| *adj.* Other; different: *somebody else.*
e·man·ci·pa·tion |ĭ măn′ sə **pā′** shən| *n.*
Freedom.
em·bas·sy |**ěm′** bə sē| *n., pl.* **em·bas·sies.**
The official headquarters of an ambassador and
his or her staff.
em·i·grant |**ěm′** ĭ grənt| *n.* Someone who
leaves a native country or region to settle in
another: *wagons of emigrants from the East.*
em·pha·size |**ěm′** fə sīz| *v.*
em·pha·sized, em·pha·siz·ing. To stress
or accent something: *emphasize a word by
repeating it.*

em·ploy |ĕm **ploi′**| v. To engage the services of; provide with a job.

en·cour·age·ment |ĕn **kûr′** ĭj mənt| n. The act of giving hope or confidence to; support: *the encouragement of friends to enter a contest.*

en·deav·or |ĕn **dĕv′** ər| v. To make an effort; attempt; strive: *The duke endeavored to keep up some show of former wealth.*

en·dorse |ĕn **dôrs′**| v. **en·dorsed, en·dors·ing.** To write one's signature on the back of (a check) in order to receive or be credited with the money indicated on its front: *The bank requires each customer to endorse a check to cash it.*

en·e·my |ĕn′ ə mē| n., pl. **en·e·mies.** A person, animal, or group, that shows hostility toward, or is unfriendly toward, another; a foe.

en·gi·neer |ĕn′ jə **nîr′**| n. A person who plans and supervises the construction of roads and bridges.

en·hance |ĕn **hăns′**| or |-**häns′**| v. **en·hanced, en·hanc·ing.** To make greater; increase, as in value or beauty; heighten: *Beautiful colored illustrations enhance the book.*

en·joy·a·ble |ĕn **joi′** ə bəl| adj. Giving enjoyment; pleasant; agreeable: *We had a very enjoyable time.*

en·joy·ment |ĕn **joi′** mənt| n. Pleasure; joy: *He works in the garden for enjoyment.*

-ent. A suffix that forms adjectives and nouns: **resident.**

en·tire |ĕn **tīr′**| adj. Having no part missing or excepted; whole; complete: *the entire country.* —**en·tire′ly** adv.

en·trance |ĕn′ trəns| n. A door or passageway through which one enters: *the back entrance of a building.*

ep·i·dem·ic |ĕp′ ĭ **dĕm′** ĭk| n. A contagious disease that spreads rapidly: *an influenza epidemic.*

e·qual |ē′ kwəl| v. **e·qualed** or **e·qualled, e·qual·ing** or **e·qual·ling.** To be equal to, as in value; to have the same capability as another: *My ability equals his.*

e·qua·tion |ĭ **kwā′** zhən| or |-shən| n. A mathematical statement that two expressions are equal.

e·quip |ĭ **kwĭp′**| v. **e·quipped, e·quip·ping.** To supply or furnish with what is needed or wanted; provide: *We equipped ourselves with sleeping bags for the hike.*

e·rode |ĭ **rōd′**| v. **e·rod·ed, e·rod·ing.** To wear away or become worn away by or as if by rubbing or bombardment with small particles: *Wind eroded the hillside.*

er·ror |ĕr′ ər| n. Something that is incorrect or wrong; a mistake.

e·rupt |ĭ **rŭpt′**| v. **1.** To become violently active. **2.** To force out or release something with violence and suddenness: *The water heater erupted in a burst of steam.*

es·tab·lish |ĭ **stăb′** lĭsh| v. To begin to set up, as a business; found; create: *His grandfather established the company in 1889.*

eth·i·cal |ĕth′ ĭ kəl| adj. Conforming to accepted standards of right behavior or conduct; moral.

e·val·u·ate |ĭ **văl′** yōō āt′| v. **e·val·u·at·ed, e·val·u·at·ing.** To find out, judge, or estimate the value or worth of; examine and appraise: *evaluate a movie.*

ev·i·dent |ĕv′ ĭ dənt| adj. Obvious; clear; plain: *Although the story was predictable, the ending was not evident.*

ex-. A prefix meaning "out; out of": **exit.**

ex·ag·ger·ate |ĭg **zăj′** ə rāt′| v. **ex·ag·ger·at·ed, ex·ag·ger·at·ing.** To enlarge or magnify beyond the truth; overstate: *Often people will exaggerate a real story until it becomes a "tall tale."*

ex·am·i·na·tion |ĭg zăm′ ə **nā′** shən| n. **1.** Investigation; analysis. **2.** A set of written or oral questions or exercises designed to test knowledge or skills. **3.** An inspection of part or all of the body, as by a physician. **4.** A formal questioning.

ex·am·ine |ĭg **zăm′** ĭn| v. **ex·am·ined, ex·am·in·ing.** To investigate (someone or something) in detail; observe carefully: *She examined the plant cells under a microscope.*

ex·am·ple |ĭg **zăm′** pəl| or |-**zăm′**-| n. **1.** A problem or exercise shown with its solution to serve as a model: *This example illustrates multiplication with fractions.* **2.** One person or thing that is typical of a whole group.

ex·ca·vate |ĕks′ kə vāt′| *v.* **ex·ca·vat·ed, ex·ca·vat·ing.** **1.** To dig or dig out: *Archaeologists excavate for many years, trying to find ruins.* **2.** To uncover by digging.
ex·ca·va·tion |ĕks′ kə vā′ shən| *n.* The act or process of digging out.

History

Excavate and **excavation** come from the Latin word *excaváre*, meaning "to hollow out": *ex-*, out + *caváre*, to hollow.

excavation

ex·cel·lent |ĕk′ sə lənt| *adj.* Of the highest quality; very fine; superb: *an excellent reason.*
ex·cept |ĭk sĕpt′| *v.* To leave out, omit, or exclude.
ex·cep·tion |ĭk sĕp′ shən| *n.* A case that does not conform to normal rules.
ex·change |ĭks chānj′| *v.* **ex·changed, ex·chang·ing.** To replace with something else: *The store exchanged the tie for a belt.*
ex·cit·a·ble |ĭk sī′ tə bəl| *adj.* Easily excited: *We have an excitable cat.* —**ex·cit′·a·bly** *adv.*
ex·cite |ĭk sīt′| *v.* **ex·cit·ed, ex·cit·ing** To arouse strong feeling in: *The speaker excited the audience.*
ex·cite·ment |ĭk sīt′ mənt| *n.* The condition of being excited, stirred up, or stimulated; agitation: *the excitement of a first trip to Europe.*

ex·cit·ing |ĭk sī′ tĭng| *adj.* Creating or producing excitement: *an exciting rafting trip down the river.* —**ex·cit′ing·ly** *adv.*
ex·clude |ĭk sklo͞od′| *v.* **ex·clud·ed, ex·clud·ing.** To leave out; omit; reject: *Let's not exclude the possibility of rain during the weekend.*
ex·clu·sion |ĭk sklo͞o′ zhən| *n.* The act of leaving out or not including; omission; elimination.
ex·cuse |ĭk skyo͞oz′| *v.* **ex·cused, ex·cus·ing.** To pardon; forgive: *I beg you to excuse me for what I did yesterday.*
ex·ec·u·tive |ĭg zĕk′ yə tĭv| *n.* A person or group that has administrative or managerial authority in an organization, especially in a corporation.
ex·er·cise |ĕk′ sər sīz′| *n.* An activity requiring physical exertion, usually done to maintain or develop physical fitness.
ex·haust |ĭg zôst′| *n.* The escape or release of waste gases, fumes, or vapors, as from a car. —*v.* To wear out completely; tire: *Moving the heavy furniture exhausted us all.*
ex·hib·it |ĭg zĭb′ ĭt| *n.* Something demonstrated or displayed: *a museum exhibit.*
ex·pand |ĭk spănd′| *v.* To increase in one or more physical dimensions, as length or volume; enlarge. —**ex·pand′a·ble** *adj.*
ex·pe·di·tion |ĕk′ spĭ dĭsh′ ən| *n.* A trip made by an organized group of people with a definite purpose: *a map-making expedition.*
ex·pen·sive |ĭk spĕn′ sĭv| *adj.* High-priced; costly: *an expensive dress.*

ex·pe·ri·ence |ĭk spîr′ ē əns| *n.* **1.** An event or series of events participated in or lived through: *the experience of being in a flood. He had an exciting experience at the fair.* **2.** Knowledge or skill gained through direct activity: *He gained experience on the job.*

ex·per·i·ment |ĭk spĕr′ ə mənt| *or* |-mĕnt| *n.* Something done to demonstrate a known fact, check the correctness of a theory, or see how well a new thing works; a test. —*v.* To conduct an experiment or experiments; make tests or trials.

ex·per·tise |ĕk′ spər tēz′| *n.* Expert skill or knowledge.

ex·plain |ĭk splān′| *v.* To make plain or clear; clarify: *explain the rules of a game.*

ex·plode |ĭk splōd′| *v.* **ex·plod·ed, ex·plod·ing.** To burst forth or break out suddenly; erupt.

ex·plo·ra·tion |ĕk′ splə rā′ shən| *n.* The act of investigating something: *Spain began the exploration of the New World.*

ex·plore |ĭk splôr′| *or* |-splōr′| *v.* **ex·plored, ex·plor·ing.** To look into; investigate; to try out.

ex·plo·sion |ĭk splō′ zhən| *n.* A sudden, violent release of energy from a confined space, especially with the production of a shock wave and a loud, sharp sound, as well as heat, light, flames, and flying debris.

ex·port |ĭk spôrt′| *or* |-spōrt′| *or* |ĕk′ spôrt′| *or* |-spōrt′| *v.* To send or carry (goods or products) to another country for trade or sale: *America exports to many lands.*

ex·po·sure |ĭk spō′ zhər| *n.* The condition of being exposed or subjected to: *a child's exposure to measles.*

ex·press |ĭk sprĕs′| *v.* To make known; show; reveal.

ex·pres·sion |ĭk sprĕsh′ ən| *n.* A particular word, phrase, or saying: *"As dry as a bone" is a familiar expression.*

ex·tent |ĭk stĕnt′| *n.* The scope or range of something: *The extent of scientific knowledge has increased vastly since Benjamin Franklin's time.*

ex·te·ri·or |ĭk stîr′ ē ər| *n.* A part or surface that is outside: *the exterior of a house.*

ex·treme |ĭk strēm′| *adj.* Very great or intense; utmost: *suffer from the extreme cold.*

F

fac·ul·ty |făk′ əl tē| *n., pl.* **fac·ul·ties.** The teaching staff of a school, college, or university.

fa·mil·iar |fə mĭl′ yər| *adj.* Well-known; common: *the familiar voice of the radio announcer.* —*n.* A close friend or associate. — **fa·mil′iar·ly** *adv.*

fan·tas·tic |făn tăs′ tĭk| *adj.* **1.** Imagined or invented; unreal: *a fantastic story.* **2.** Weird; bizarre: *all sorts of fantastic figures and designs.* **3.** *Informal.* Remarkable; outstanding; superb.

fan·ta·sy |făn′ tə sē| *or* |-zē| *n., pl.* **fan·ta·sies.** Creative imagination; make-believe: *Modern technology has turned fantasy into fact.*

fath·om |făth′ əm| *n., pl.* **fath·oms** or **fath·om.** A unit of length equal to six feet, used mainly in measuring and expressing depths in the ocean.

fa·vor |fā′ vər| *v.* **fa·vored, fa·vor·ing.** To be for; support: *I favor Harris for the job of director.* ◊ *Idiom.* **in favor of. 1.** in support of: *All those in favor of the motion say "aye."* **2.** To the advantage of: *The judge decided in favor of the defendant.*

fea·ture |fē′ chər| *n.* A prominent part, quality, or characteristic: *Jagged rocks were a feature of the landscape.*

fierce |fîrs| *adj.* **fierc·er, fierc·est. 1.** Wild and savage; ferocious: *a fierce beast.* **2.** Extremely severe or violent: *a fierce snowstorm.* **3.** Extremely intense or ardent: *fierce loyalty.*

fier·y |fîr′ ē| *or* |fī′ ə rē| *adj.* **fier·i·er, fier·i·est. 1.** Very hot: *the fiery pavements of the city.* **2.** Glowing; gleaming.

file |fīl| *n.* A collection of papers arranged in order: *an office file.*

film |fĭlm| *n.* **1.** A thin sheet or strip of flexible cellulose coated with materials that are sensitive to light, used in recording photographic images. **2.** A motion picture; movie.

fin·ish |fĭn′ ĭsh| *v.* To bring to an end; complete.

fir |fûr| *n.* Any of several cone-bearing evergreen trees with rather flat needles.
♦ *These sound alike* **fir, fur.**

fire escape |fīr ĭ skāp′| *n.* A structure, such as an outside stairway attached to a building, used as an emergency exit in case of a fire.

fire extinguisher |fīr ĭk stĭng′ gwĭ shər| *n.* A portable device containing chemicals that can be sprayed on a fire to put it out.

fire·place |fīr′ plās′| *n.* A hollow space for holding a fire at the base of a chimney.

fire·proof |fīr′ prōōf′| *adj.* Made of material or materials that do not burn or that do not crack or break when exposed to heat or fire. —*v.* To make fireproof.

fire station |fīr′ stā′ shən| *n.* A building for firefighting equipment and firefighters.

fire·wood |fīr′ wōōd′| *n.* Wood used as fuel.

first aid |fûrst ād| *n.* Emergency care given to an injured or sick person before professional medical care is available.

fit |fĭt| *v.* **fit·ted** or **fit, fit·ting.** To be the proper size and shape for: *The clothes won't fit in my closet.* —*adj.* **fit·ting.** Suitable; appropriate: *fitting behavior.*

fjord |fyôrd| *or* |fyōrd| *n.* A long, narrow inlet from the sea between steep cliffs or slopes.

ă	pat	îr	pier	ŭ	cut
ā	pay	ŏ	pot	ûr	urge
âr	care	ō	toe	th	thin
ä	father	ô	paw	*th*	this
ĕ	pet	oi	boy	hw	whoop
ē	be	ŏŏ	took	zh	vision
ĭ	pit	ōō	boot	ə	about
ī	pie	ou	out		

flo·rist |flôr′ ĭst| *or* |flōr′-| *or* |flŏr′-| *n.* A person whose business is the raising, arranging, or selling of flowers.

flour·ish |flûr′ ĭsh| *or* |flŭr′-| *n.* An added decorative touch: *Her handwriting has many flourishes.* —*v.* To grow well; thrive: *While your flowers flourish, mine wither.*

force·ful |fôrs′ fəl| *or* |fōrs′-| *adj.* Full of force; strong; powerful.

fore·head |fôr′ ĭd| *or* |fŏr′-| *or* |fôr′ hĕd′| *or* |fōr′-| *n.* The top part of the face above the eyes.

for·eign |fôr′ ĭn| *or* |fŏr′-| *adj.* Of, from, by, with, or for another country or other countries: *a foreign language.*

for·feit |fôr′ fĭt| *n.* Something lost, given up, or paid as a penalty or fine: *pay a forfeit.*

for·get |fər gĕt′| *v.* **for·got** |fər gŏt′|, **for·got·ten** |fər gŏt′ n| or **for·got, for·get·ting.** To be unable to remember or fail to remember: *I sometimes forget her telephone number.* ◊ *Idiom.* **forget oneself.** To lose one's reserve, temper, or self-restraint: *The bystanders forgot themselves and ran to shake the President's hand.*

for·give·ness |fər gĭv′ nĭs| *n.* The act of excusing for a fault, injury, or offense; pardon.

for·got |fər gŏt′| *or* |fôr gŏt′| *v.* Past tense and a past participle of **forget.**

for·tu·nate |fôr′ chə nĭt| *adj.* Having, bringing, or brought by good fortune; lucky.

foul |foul| *adj.* **foul·er, foul·est. 1.** Dirty; filthy. **2.** Unpleasant; bad: *foul weather.* **3.** Offensive to the taste or smell. —*n.* In sports, a violation of the rules of play.
♦ *These sound alike* **foul, fowl.**

fjord

Spelling Dictionary

foun·da·tion |foun dā′ shən| *n.* The base on which a structure stands: *the foundation of a building.*

fowl |foul| *n., pl.* **fowl** or **fowls.** A bird such as a chicken, duck, turkey, or pheasant, that is raised or hunted for food.
♦ *These sound alike* **fowl, foul.**

fra·grant |frā′ grənt| *adj.* Having a pleasant odor; sweet-smelling: *a fragrant rose.*

frame |frām| *n.* An open structure or rim used to encase, hold, or border: *a door frame; a picture frame.*

fraud |frôd| *n.* A deliberate deception, often unlawful: *protecting the consumer against fraud.*

freight |frāt| *n.* Goods carried by a vessel or vehicle, especially goods transported as cargo.
—*modifier: a freight car.*

fright·en |frīt′ n| *v.* To make or become suddenly afraid; alarm or startle.

-ful. A suffix that forms adjectives and means: **1.** Full of: **eventful**. **2.** Characterized by: **boastful.**

fume |fyoom| *n.* Any smoke, vapor, or gas, especially one that is irritating or has an unpleasant odor: *the fumes from a smokestack.*

fur |fûr| *n.* The thick, soft hair covering the body of certain animals, such as a cat or fox.
♦ *These sound alike* **fur, fir.**

fu·ri·ous |fyoor′ ē əs| *adj.* Full of or marked by extreme anger; raging.

fu·ture |fyoo′ chər| *n.* The indefinite period of time yet to be; time that is to come: *plans for the future.*

G

gal·lant |găl′ ənt| *adj.* Brave and noble; courageous; valorous: *a gallant try.*

gal·le·on |găl′ ē ən| *or* |găl′ yən| *n.* A large three-masted sailing ship of the type much used by Spain in the 16th century.

gal·ley |găl′ ē| *n., pl.* **gal·leys.** A printer's proof taken from composed type before page composition to allow for the detection and correction of errors: *The editor checked the galley for errors.*

gal·lon |găl′ ən| *n.* A unit of liquid volume or capacity equal to 4 quarts or 23 cubic inches: *a gallon of orange juice.*

ga·rage |gə räzh′| *or* |-räj′| *n.* A shed or building in which to park cars.

gath·er |găth′ ər| *v.* **gath·ered, gath·er·ing.** To bring or come together in a group; assemble: *He gathered all his books.*

gaze |gāz| *v.* **gazed, gaz·ing.** To look intently, as with wonder or curiosity; stare. —*n.* An intent, steady look: *I could tell by her gaze that Mother was serious.*

gen·er·al |jěn′ ər əl| *adj.* Applicable to or involving the whole or every member of a class or category: *a general meeting.*

gen·er·al·i·ty |jěn′ ə răl′ ĭ tē| *n., pl.* **gen·er·al·i·ties.** A statement or idea that is general and imprecise rather than specific and to the point.

gen·er·ous |jěn′ ər əs| *adj.* Willing to give or share; unselfish: *a generous contributor to worthy causes.*

ges·ture |jěs′ chər| *n.* A motion of the hands, arms, head, or body used while speaking or in place of speech to help to express a feeling or an idea. —*v.* **ges·tured, ges·tur·ing.** To express or signal by gesture.

gi·gan·tic |jī găn′ tĭk| *adj.* Of extraordinary strength, size, or power; enormous; huge: *gigantic rocks.*

gink·go |gĭng′ kō| *n., pl.* **gink·goes.** A tree with straight branches and fan-shaped leaves, originally from China and often planted in city streets and parks.

gla·cier |glā′ shər| *n.* A large mass of slowly moving ice, formed from snow packed together by the weight of snow above it.

gloom |gloom| *n.* Lowness of spirit; sadness; depression.

gov·ern·ment |gŭv′ ərn mənt| *n.* A system by which a political unit is directed or managed: *democratic government.*

grace |grās| *n.* Seemingly effortless beauty of movement, form, or manner: *the grace of a swan swimming across a lake.* —*v.* **graced, grac·ing, grac·es. 1.** To honor; favor: *The governor's presence graced the meeting.* **2.** To give beauty, elegance, or charm to: *A bouquet of fresh flowers graced the mantelpiece.*

grace·ful |grās′ fəl| *adj.* Showing grace of movement or form: *a graceful dancer.* —**grace′ful·ly** *adv.* —**grace′ful·ness** *n.*

grace·less |grās′ lĭs| *adj.* **1.** Lacking grace; clumsy: *a graceless fall.* **2.** Without a sense of propriety or decency: *a rude and graceless remark.* —**grace′less·ly** *adv.* —**grace′less·ness** *n.*

grad·u·ate |grăj′ ōō āt′| *v.* **grad·u·at·ed, grad·u·at·ing.** To receive an academic degree or diploma.

grad·u·a·tion |grăj′ ōō ā′ shən| *n.* **a.** The act of completing a required phase of formal education and receiving an academic degree or a diploma. **b.** A ceremony during which academic degrees are awarded.

gram·mar |grăm′ ər| *n.* **1.** The system of rules used by the speakers of a language for making sentences in that language. **2.** Study of these rules or theory about them, especially as a school subject.

grand·child |grănd′ chīld′| *or* |grăn′ chīld′| *n., pl.* **grand·chil·dren** |grănd′ chĭl′ drən| *or* |grăn′ chĭl′ drən|. A child of one's son's or daughter's.

grasp |grăsp| *or* |gräsp| *v.* To seize and hold firmly with or as if with the hands.

grease |grēs| *n.* Animal fat when melted or soft.

greet |grēt| *v.* To address in a friendly way; welcome: *a hostess greeting her guests.*

grief |grēf| *n.* Intense sorrow; mental anguish.

grill |grĭl| *n.* A cooking utensil with parallel thin metal bars on which meat or fish may be broiled. —*v.* **1.** To cook on a grill. **2.** *Informal.* To question closely and relentlessly.

groove |grōōv| *n.* A narrow furrow or channel: *a drawer that moves in and out on grooves.*

group |grōōp| *n.* **1.** A number of persons or things gathered or located together: *a group of men on a street corner.* **2.** A number of things classed together because of similar qualities: *a singing group.*

guil·ty |gĭl′ tē| *adj.* **guilt·i·er, guilt·i·est.** **1.** Responsible for wrongdoing or a crime. **2.** Burdened with or showing a sense of guilt.

Pronunciation Key

ă	pat	îr	pier	ŭ	cut
ā	pay	ŏ	pot	ûr	urge
âr	care	ō	toe	th	thin
ä	father	ô	paw	th	this
ĕ	pet	oi	boy	hw	whoop
ē	be	ōō	took	zh	vision
ĭ	pit	ōō	boot	ə	about
ī	pie	ou	out		

gui·tar |gĭ tär′| *n.* A musical instrument having a long fretted neck and a large, pear-shaped sound box with a flat back. It has six strings that are played by plucking or strumming.

gup·py |gŭp′ ē| *n., pl.* **gup·pies.** A small, brightly colored tropical freshwater fish that is often kept in home aquariums.

guppy

H

hab·i·tat |hăb′ ĭ tăt′| *n.* The area, dwelling, or natural environment in which an animal or plant normally lives or grows.

hair·cut |hâr′ kŭt′| *n.* A shortening or shaping of the hair by cutting it.

half |hăf| *or* |häf| *n., pl.* **halves** |hăvz| *or* |hävz|. Either of two equal parts into which a thing can be divided.

han·gar |hăng′ ər| *n.* A building used for housing or repairing aircraft.
◆ *These sound alike* **hangar, hanger.**

hang·er |hăng′ ər| *n.* A frame or hook on which an article of clothing can be hung.
♦ *These sound alike* **hanger, hangar.**

haul |hôl| *v.* To pull, drag, or carry; tug.

hawk |hôk| *n.* Any of several birds with a short, hooked bill and strong claws.

hawk

haz·ard |hăz′ ərd| *n.* Something that is likely to cause harm; a possible source of danger: *a fire hazard.*

head·ache |hĕd′ āk′| *n.* **1.** A pain in the head. **2.** *Informal.* Something that causes trouble.

heir·loom |âr′ lōōm′| *n.* A possession valued by members of a family and passed down through succeeding generations.

he·ro |hîr′ ō| *n., pl.* **he·roes. 1.** A man noted for his courage or special achievements. **2.** The main male character in a novel, poem, or movie.

her·o·ine |hĕr′ ō ĭn| *n.* **1.** A woman noted for her courage or special achievements. **2.** The main female character in a novel, poem, or movie.

hes·i·tant |hĕz′ ĭ tənt| *adj.* Inclined to be slow to act, speak, or decide; uncertain.

hoist |hoist| *v.* To raise or haul up, often with the help of some mechanical apparatus: *Hoist the sails!*

home·made |hōm′ mād′| *adj.* Crudely or simply made, as if made at home: *homemade furniture.*

hom·o·graph |hŏm′ ə grăf′| *or* |hō′ mə grăf′| *n.* A word that has the same spelling as another word but differs in meaning, origin,

and sometimes in pronunciation. For example, **ring** (circle) and **ring** (sound).

hom·o·phone |hŏm′ ə fōn′| *or* |hō′ mə fōn′| *n.* A word that has the same sound as another word but differs in spelling, meaning, and origin. For example, **steel** and **steal.**

hor·ror |hôr′ ər| *or* |hŏr′-| *n.* A feeling of repugnance and fear; dread.

hy·giene |hī′ jēn| *n.* Practices that promote good health and the prevention of disease.

I

-ible. A form of the suffix **-able.**

-ic. A suffix that forms adjectives and means "of" or "characteristic of": **allergic.**

ice·berg |īs′ bûrg′| *n.* A huge body of floating ice that has broken away from a glacier.

i·dle |īd′ l| *adj.* **i·dler, i·dlest.** Avoiding work; lazy.
♦ *These sound alike* **idle, idol.**

i·dol |īd′ l| *n.* A person or thing that is adored or greatly admired.
♦ *These sound alike* **idol, idle.**

ig·no·rant |ĭg′ nər ənt| *adj.* Without education or knowledge; uninformed.

ig·nore |ĭg nôr′| *or* |-nōr′| *v.* **ig·nored, ig·nor·ing.** To pay no attention to.

il·lu·mi·nate |ĭ lōō′ mə nāt′| *v.* **il·lu·mi·nat·ed, il·lu·mi·nat·ing.** To provide with light; turn or focus light on.

im·age |ĭm′ ĭj| *n.* **1.** A picture or reproduction of an object, especially by reflection in a mirror or refraction through a lens. **2.** A general impression of a person or thing.

im·i·tate |ĭm′ ĭ tāt′| *v.* **im·i·tat·ed, im·i·tat·ing.** To copy the actions, appearance, function, or sounds of; imitate bird calls.

im·me·di·ate |ĭ mē′ dē ĭt| *adj.* **1.** Occurring without delay: *needing immediate care.* **2.** Coming next or very soon: *the immediate future.*

im·mense |ĭ mĕns′| *adj.* Of great, often immeasurable, size, extent, or degree; huge.

im·mi·grant |ĭm′ ĭ grənt| *n.* A person who leaves his native country or region to settle in another.

im·mov·a·ble |ĭ mōo′ və bəl| *adj.* Not capable of moving or of being moved; not portable.

im·mu·nize |ĭm′ yə nīz′| *v.* **im·mu·nized, im·mu·niz·ing.** To produce immunity, or resistance to disease, in, as by vaccination or inoculation.

im·par·tial |ĭm pär′ shəl| *adj.* Not favoring either side; fair; unprejudiced: *an impartial witness.*

im·ply |ĭm plī′| *v.* **im·plied, im·ply·ing, im·plies.** To say or convey indirectly; suggest without stating: *He turned down our request but implied that he might change his mind later.*

im·po·lite |ĭm′ pə līt′| *adj.* Not polite; discourteous; rude: *an impolite remark.*

im·port |ĭm pôrt′| *or* |-pōrt′| *or* |ĭm′ pôrt′| *or* |-pōrt′| *v.* To bring or carry in from an outside source, especially to bring in (goods) from another country for trade, sale, or use.

im·por·tance |ĭm pôr′ tns| *n.* The condition of being important; significance.

im·pose |ĭm pōz′| *v.* **im·posed, im·pos·ing.** To place (something burdensome) on someone; inflict: *long hours of work that imposed a great strain on us.*

im·pos·si·ble |ĭm pŏs′ ə bəl| *adj.* Not likely to happen or be done: *It will be impossible to get there today.*

im·prac·ti·cal |ĭm prăk′ tĭ kəl| *adj.* Not practical; unwise; foolish: *an impractical plan.*

im·press |ĭm prĕs′| *v.* To seem remarkable to: *His performance impressed me.*

im·pris·on |ĭm prĭz′ ən| *v.* **1.** To put in prison. **2.** To enclose or confine. —**im·pris′on·ment** *n. His life of crime led to years of imprisonment.*

im·prob·a·ble |ĭm prŏb′ ə bəl| *adj.* Unlikely: *an improbable tale.*

im·prop·er |ĭm prŏp′ ər| *adj.* Not proper; incorrect: *improper behavior.*

im·prove |ĭm prōov′| *v.* **im·proved, im·prov·ing.** To make or become better: *She improved her tennis serve by practicing.*

im·prove·ment |ĭm prōov′ mənt| *n.* **1.** A change or addition that improves something: *improvements in the wireless telegraph.* **2.** The

act or process of improving: *The student's homework shows great improvement.*

im·pro·vise |ĭm′ prə vīz′| *v.* **im·pro·vised, im·pro·vis·ing.** To invent or compose without preparation: *improvise a skit.*

in-¹. A prefix meaning "without" or "not": **inaccurate.**

in-². A prefix meaning "in," "within," or "into": **inbound.**

in·ac·tive |ĭn ăk′ tĭv| *adj.* Not active or not tending to be active; idle: *an inactive life.*

in·ad·e·quate |ĭn ăd′ ĭ kwĭt| *adj.* Not adequate; insufficient; not enough: *an inadequate amount of paint to cover the walls.*

in·clined |ĭn klīnd′| *adj.* **1.** Deviating from horizontal or vertical; slanting. **2.** Having a preference or tendency; disposed: *We are inclined to believe people we respect.*

in·clude |ĭn klōod′| *v.* **in·clud·ed, in·clud·ing.** To be made up of, at least in part; contain: *The collection includes some of her paintings.*

in·com·plete |ĭn′ kəm plēt′| *adj.* Not finished: *an incomplete project.*

in·crease |ĭn krēs′| *v.* **in·creased, in·creas·ing.** To make or become greater or larger: *increase one's knowledge.*

in·dent |ĭn dĕnt′| *v.* To set the first line of a paragraph in from the margin.

in·di·rect |ĭn′ də rĕkt′| *or* |-dī-| *adj.* Not taking a direct or straightforward course; roundabout: *an indirect route.*

in·di·vid·u·al |ĭn də vĭj′ ōo əl| *adj.* Single; separate: *for each individual child.* —*n.* A single person considered separately from a group.

Pronunciation Key

ă	pat	îr	pier	ŭ	cut
ā	pay	ŏ	pot	ûr	urge
âr	care	ō	toe	th	thin
ä	father	ô	paw	*th*	this
ĕ	pet	oi	boy	hw	whoop
ē	be	ŏŏ	took	zh	vision
ĭ	pit	ōō	boot	ə	about
ī	pie	ou	out		

in·di·vid·u·al·i·ty |ĭn′ də vĭj′ ōō ăl′ ĭ tē|
n., pl. **in·di·vid·u·al·i·ties.** The qualities
that make a person or thing different from
others; distinctiveness.

in·dus·try |ĭn′ də strē| *n., pl.* **in·dus·tries.**
a. The manufacture or production of goods
on a large scale. **b.** A specific branch of such
activity: *the motion-picture industry.*

in·ev·i·ta·ble |ĭn ĕv′ ĭ tə bəl| *adj.* Not
capable of being avoided or prevented: *an
inevitable outcome.*

in·fec·tion |ĭn fĕk′ shən| *n.* **1.** The entry
of germs into the body, where they multiply
and damage tissue or cause disease. **2.** A
disease caused or spread by infection.

in·fer |ĭn fûr′| *v.* **in·ferred, in·fer·ring.**
To conclude from evidence; deduce: *I infer
from your tears that you're sad.*

in·flex·i·ble |ĭn flĕk′ sə bəl| *adj.* **1.** Not
flexible; rigid. **2.** Not subject to change.

in·flu·ence |ĭn′ flōō əns| *v.* **in·flu·enced,
in·flu·enc·ing.** To have an effect or impact
upon: *The moon influences the tides.*

in·for·mal |ĭn fôr′ məl| *adj.* **1.** Casual;
relaxed: *an informal party.* **2.** Performed without
set rules; unofficial: *an informal agreement.*

in·for·ma·tion |ĭn′ fər mā′ shən| *n.* Facts
or data about a certain event or subject; data: *a
good source of general information.*

in·form·er |ĭn fôr′ mər| *n.* A person who
notifies authorities of secret and often illegal
activities.

in·hab·i·tant |ĭn′ hăb′ ĭ tənt| *n., pl.*
in·hab·i·tants. A permanent resident of a
particular place: *the inhabitants of the island.*

in·ner |ĭn′ ər| *adj.* Located farther inside:
the inner core of the earth.

in·no·cent |ĭn′ ə sənt| *adj.* Not guilty of
a specific crime or fault: *The jury found him
innocent.*

in·quire |ĭn kwīr′| *v.* **in·quired,
in·quir·ing.** To ask in order to find out.

in·scribe |ĭn skrīb′| *v.* **in·scribed,
in·scrib·ing.** To write, print, carve, or engrave
(words or letters) on or in a surface.

in·scrip·tion |ĭn skrĭp′ shən| *n.* The act
or example of signing or writing a brief
message in or on (a book or picture) when
giving it as a gift.

in·sist |ĭn sĭst′| *v.* To be firm in one's
demand: *I insist on watching the ball game.*

in·spect |ĭn spĕkt′| *v.* To examine carefully
and critically, especially for flaws.

in·spec·tion |ĭn spĕk′ shən| *n.* The act or
an example of inspecting: *An inspection of the
wiring uncovered the source of the power failure.*

in·stance |ĭn′ stəns| *n.* A case or example:
many instances of success.

in·stant |ĭn′ stənt| *adj.* Immediate: *an
instant success.*

in·struct |ĭn strŭkt′| *v.* To convey
knowledge or skill to; teach.

in·struc·tion |ĭn strŭk′ shən| *n.*
1. Something that is taught; a lesson or series
of lessons. **2.** The act or profession of
teaching; education.

in·stru·ment |ĭn′ strə mənt| *n.* **1.** A
device used by a musician in making music.
2. A means by which something is done:
*Education can be used as an instrument for
social change.*

in·su·late |ĭn′ sə lāt′| *or* |ĭns′ yə-| *v.*
in·su·lat·ed, in·su·lat·ing. To prevent the
passage of heat, electricity, or sound into or
out of, especially by surrounding or lining
with something that blocks such a flow:
Northerners insulate their houses well.

in·su·la·tion |ĭn′ sə lā′ shən| *or* |ĭns′ yə-|
n. Material that is used to prevent heat loss.

History

Insulate and **insulation** probably come from
the Latin word *īnsula,* meaning "island."

in·sult |ĭn sŭlt′| *v.* To speak to or treat with
contempt; offend.

in·tact |ĭn tăkt′| *adj.* Not impaired,
injured, or damaged; whole.

inter-. A prefix meaning: **1.** Between;
among: **international.** **2.** Mutually; together:
interact.

in·ter·act |ĭn′ tər ăkt′| *v.* To act on or
affect each other: *people who interact peacefully.*
—**in′ter·ac′tion** *n.* —**in′ter·ac′tive** *adj.*:
an interactive video program.

in·ter·de·pend·ent |ĭn′ tər dĭ pĕn′ dənt|
adj. Mutually dependent.

in·ter·est |ĭn′ trĭst| *or* |-tər ĭst| *n.*
a. Money a bank adds to a customer's account in return for the use of the money in that account: *My savings account earns 5 percent interest yearly.* **b.** A charge paid for borrowing money, usually a percentage of the amount borrowed: *She paid 10 percent interest on her bank loan.*

in·ter·fere |ĭn′ tər **fîr′**| *v.* **in·ter·fered, in·ter·fer·ing.** To intrude in the affairs of others; meddle.

in·te·ri·or |ĭn **tîr′** ē ər| *n.* The inner part of something; the inside: *the interior of a house.*

in·ter·mis·sion |ĭn′ tər **mĭsh′** ən| *n.* An interruption or recess, as between the acts of a play.

in·tern |ĭn′ tûrn′| *n.* A recent graduate, often of a medical school, who is undergoing supervised practical training.

in·ter·na·tion·al |ĭn′ tər **năsh′** ə nəl| *adj.* Of or between two or more nations or nationalities: *international trade.*

in·ter·rupt |ĭn′ tə **rŭpt′**| *v.* To stop the conversation, speech, or action of (someone) by breaking in.

in·ter·vene |ĭn′ tər **vēn′**| *v.* **in·ter·vened, in·ter·ven·ing.** To enter a course of events so as to hinder or change it: *The governor intervened to delay the execution.*

in·ter·ven·tion |ĭn tər **vĕn′** shən| *n.*
1. The act of intervening: *The governor's intervention saved the park from development.*
2. Interference in the affairs of another nation, usually with force.

in·ter·view |ĭn′ tər vyoo′| *n.* A face-to-face meeting, especially to obtain information: *an interview for a job.*

in·tol·er·a·ble |ĭn **tŏl′** ər ə bəl| *adj.* Not capable of being endured; unbearable: *an intolerable life of poverty.*

in·vent |ĭn **vĕnt′**| *v.* To think up and make, create, or devise (something that did not exist before): *invent new products.*

in·ven·tion |ĭn **vĕn′** shən| *n.* Something invented, as a device, system, or process that did not exist before: *Eli Whitney's cotton gin was an important invention.*

ă	pat	îr	pier	ŭ	cut
ā	pay	ŏ	pot	ûr	urge
âr	care	ō	toe	th	thin
ä	father	ô	paw	*th*	this
ĕ	pet	oi	boy	hw	whoop
ē	be	ŏŏ	took	zh	vision
ĭ	pit	ōō	boot	ə	about
ī	pie	ou	out		

invention

in·ven·tive |ĭn **vĕn′** tĭv| *adj.* Skillful at inventing; creative: *An inventive writer is able to keep the reader's attention.*

in·ven·tor |ĭn **vĕn′** tər| *n.* A person who invents things.

in·vest·ment |ĭn **vĕst′** mənt| *n.* A sum of money placed into something, such as stocks or property, in order to make a profit: *money earned on an investment.*

in·voice |ĭn′ vois′| *n.* A detailed list of goods shipped to a buyer, with an account of all costs and charges due.

in·volve |ĭn **vŏlv′**| *v.* **in·volved, in·volv·ing.** To take in; include.

-ion. A suffix that forms nouns and means:
1. a. Action or process: **oxidization. b.** Result of an action or process: **indention. 2.** State or condition: **hydration.**

ir·re·sist·i·ble |ĭr′ ĭ **zĭs′** tə bəl| *adj.* Too strong, powerful, or compelling to be refused or resisted; overwhelming: *irresistible forces.*

i·so·la·tion |ī′ sə **lā′** shən| *n.* The act or process of keeping someone with a contagious disease from having contact with others who are not infected: *I was kept in isolation when I had chicken pox.*

i·tal·ic |ĭ tăl′ ĭk| *or* |ī tăl′-| *adj.* Being a style of printing type with the letters slanting to the right, used chiefly to set off a word or passage within a text of roman print: *This is italic print.* —*n.* Often **italics.** Italic print or typeface.

i·tem |ī′ təm| *n.* A single article or unit: *an item of clothing.*

-ive. A suffix that forms adjectives and means "tending toward, performing, or accomplishing something": **disruptive.**

J

jazz |jăz| *n.* A type of music that was first played by black musicians in the southern United States. It has a strong rhythmic structure and although it has evolved a great deal with passing time, the music retains a characteristic style of melody and harmony.

jeal·ous |jĕl′ əs| *adj.* Resenting another's success or advantages; envious: *She was always jealous of her older sister.*

jel·ly·fish |jĕl′ ē fĭsh′| *n.* Any of numerous sea animals having a soft, often umbrella-shaped body. Many jellyfish have tentacles that can cause a sting.

jet·ty |jĕt′ ē| *n., pl.* **jet·ties.** **1.** A wharf or landing pier. **2.** A breakwater: *The jetty protected the ships in the harbor from the stormy sea.*

jetty

jour·ney |jûr′ nē| *n.* A trip, especially one over a great distance: *the long journey home.*

jun·ior |jōōn′ yər| *adj.* **1.** Of or for younger or smaller persons: *the junior skating championship.* **2.** Of lower rank or shorter length of service: *a junior partner.* **3.** Of the third year of a four-year high school or college. —*n.* A student in his or her third year at a four-year high school or college.

ju·ni·per |jōō′ nə pər| *n.* An evergreen tree or shrub related to the pines, having small scale-like or prickly leaves and bluish, aromatic berries: *The berries of the juniper tree are used as a flavoring.*

K

kelp |kĕlp| *n.* Any of several brown, often very large seaweeds.

ker·nel |kûr′ nəl| *n.* A grain or seed, especially of corn, wheat, or a similar cereal plant.

◆ *These sound alike* **kernel, colonel.**

kil·o·me·ter |kĭl′ ə mē′ tər| *or* |kĭ lŏm′ ĭ tər| *n., pl.* **kil·o·me·ters.** A unit of length equal to 1,000 meters or about 0.6214 mile.

king·dom |kĭng′ dəm| *n.* A country that is ruled or headed by a king or queen.

kitch·en |kĭch′ ən| *n.* A room where food is cooked or prepared, and sometimes eaten.

knit·ting |nĭt′ ĭng| *n.* The art or process of making a fabric or garment by interlocking yarn or thread in connected loops with special needles.

L

land·mark |lănd′ märk′| *n.* **1.** A fixed object used to indicate a position for travelers or surveyors. **2.** A familiar or easily recognized object or feature of the landscape.

lan·guage |lăng′ gwĭj| *n.* Any system of sounds, signs, symbols, or gestures for conveying information: *How many languages can you speak?*

late·ly |lāt′ lē| *adv.* Not long ago; recently: *She has been traveling a lot lately.*

lat·i·tude |lăt′ ĭ tōōd′| *or* |-tyōōd′| *n.*
1. Distance north or south of the equator measured in degrees. A degree of latitude is about 69 statute miles or 60 nautical miles.
2. A region of the earth indicated by its approximate latitude: *Some of the coldest temperatures on Earth occur in the polar latitudes.*

laun·dry |lôn′ drē| *or* |län′-| *n., pl.* **laun·dries.** A place or business establishment where clothes and linens are washed.

law·yer |lô′ yər| *or* |loi′ ər| *n.* A person who is trained and qualified to give legal advice to clients and represent them in court.

league |lēg| *n.* An association or group of sports teams or clubs that compete chiefly among themselves: *the major baseball leagues.*

leath·er |lĕth′ ər| *n.* A material made by cleaning and tanning the skin or hide of an animal and preparing it for use.

leg·end |lĕj′ ənd| *n.* A story of uncertain truthfulness handed down from earlier times.

lei·sure |lē′ zhər| *or* |lĕzh′ ər| *n.* Freedom from work or time-consuming tasks; time in which to do as one pleases: *devoting his leisure to stamp collecting. —modifier: leisure time.*

length |lĕngkth| *or* |lĕngth| *n.* The measured distance from one end of a thing to the other along its greatest dimension: *A ruler measures length.*

le·o·tard |lē′ ə tärd′| *n.* Often leotards. A tight-fitting, stretchy garment, originally worn by dancers and acrobats: *The dancers wore leotards at their rehearsals.*

-less. A suffix that forms adjectives and means "without; free of": **nameless.**

let·tuce |lĕt′ ĭs| *n.* A plant cultivated for its edible light-green leaves, eaten as salad.

lev·er |lĕv′ ər| *or* |lē′ vər| *n.* A projecting handle used to control, adjust, or operate a device or machine.

li·a·bil·i·ty |lī′ ə bĭl′ ĭ tē| *n., pl.* **li·a·bil·i·ties.** Something that one owes; an obligation; debt.

life·less |līf′ lĭs| *adj.* **1.** Without life; dead or inanimate. **2.** Lacking brightness; dull: *lifeless colors.*

Pronunciation Key

ă	pat	îr	pier	ŭ	cut
ā	pay	ŏ	pot	ûr	urge
âr	care	ō	toe	th	thin
ä	father	ô	paw	*th*	*th*is
ĕ	pet	oi	boy	hw	whoop
ē	be	ŏŏ	took	zh	vision
ĭ	pit	ōō	boot	ə	about
ī	pie	ou	out		

lil·y |lĭl′ ē| *n., pl.* **lil·ies.** Any of several related plants with showy, trumpet-shaped flowers.

lim·ber |lĭm′ bər| *adj.* Moving easily and nimbly; agile: *a limber athlete.*

lim·it·ed |lĭm′ ĭ tĭd| *adj.* Confined to a certain area, size, or amount; restricted: *a limited number of people.*

lin·en |lĭn′ ən| *n.* **1.** Strong, lustrous cloth made of flax fibers. **2.** Often **linens.** Cloth articles or garments, such as sheets, tablecloths, and shirts, made of or once made of linen.

lis·ten |lĭs′ ən| *v.* **lis·tened, lis·ten·ing.** To make an effort to hear something: *If you listen carefully, you can hear the wind.*

lit·ter |lĭt′ ər| *n.* **1.** Carelessly scattered scraps of paper or other waste material; rubbish. **2.** The young born to a mammal at a single time: *a litter of puppies.* **3.** Material, such as straw or hay, spread for animals to sleep on: *a horse asleep on its litter of straw.* **4.** A stretcher used to carry a sick or wounded person. **5.** A couch mounted on framework covered with curtains and used to carry a person from place to place.

loaf |lōf| *n., pl.* **loaves** |lōvz|. A shaped mass of bread baked in one piece.

lo·cate |lō′ kāt| *or* |lō kāt′| *v.* **lo·cat·ed, lo·cat·ing.** To determine and show the position or boundaries of: *Locate Austria on a map.*

lo·ca·tion |lō kā′ shən| *n.* A place where something is located; a site or position: *the location of the hospital.*

log·i·cal |lŏj′ ĭ kəl| *adj.* **1.** Of, using, or agreeing with the principles of logic: *a logical explanation.* **2.** Able to reason clearly and rationally.

lo·go |lō′ gō′| *n., pl.* **lo·gos.** The name, symbol, or trademark of a company, group, or publication: *Our team used a green helmet as its logo on our sweatshirts.*

lon·gi·tude |lŏn′ jĭ tōōd′| *or* |-tyōōd′| *n.* Distance east or west on the earth's surface, measured in degrees from a certain meridian, usually the meridian at Greenwich, England: *The ship is at the same longitude as this island chain.*

loose |lōōs| *adj.* **loos·er, loos·est.** **1.** Free from confinement: *The stallion was loose in the field.* **2.** Not tightly packed: *loose sand.*

lov·a·ble |lŭv′ ə bəl| *adj.* Having qualities that attract affection; adorable: *Otters are smart, lovable animals.*

loy·al |loi′ əl| *adj.* Faithful to a person, country, idea or custom; trustworthy.

-ly¹ A suffix that forms adjectives and means: **1.** Characteristic of: **sisterly. 2.** Appearing or occurring at specified intervals: **weekly.**

-ly² A suffix that forms adverbs and means: **1.** In a specified manner: **gradually. 2.** At a specified interval: **hourly.**

M

maes·tro |mī′ strō| *n., pl.* **maes·tros.** A master in an art, especially a famous conductor, composer, or music teacher.

mag·net·ic |măg nĕt′ ĭk| *adj.* **1.** Of or relative to the magnetic poles of the earth. **2.** Having the power to attract or charm: *That movie star has a magnetic personality.*

mag·nif·i·cent |măg nĭf′ ĭ sənt| *adj.* Splendid in appearance; grand; extraordinary: *a magnificent cathedral.*

mag·no·lia |măg nōl′ yə| *or* |-nō′ lē ə| *n.* A tree or shrub with large, showy, usually white or pink flowers: *Large magnolias lined the streets of the capital.*

ma·hog·a·ny |mə hŏg′ ə nē| *n., pl.* **ma·hog·a·nies.** A tropical American tree with hard, reddish-brown wood used for making furniture.

main·te·nance |mān′ tə nəns| *n.* The work involved in the care or upkeep of something.

ma·jor |mā′ jər| *adj.* Large and important; significant; considerable.

man·age·ment |măn′ ĭj mənt| *n.* The managers or supervisors of a business or organization.

ma·neu·ver |mə nōō′ vər| *or* |-nyōō′-| *v.* To make or cause to make one or more changes in course or position: *The Nautilus had to maneuver very carefully to avoid the icebergs.*

man·ner |măn′ ər| *n.* **1.** A way or style of doing things. **2.** A style of personal behavior. ♦ *These sound alike* **manner, manor.**

man·or |măn′ ər| *n.* **1.** The estate of a feudal lord or wealthy landowner. **2.** A house. ♦ *These sound alike* **manor, manner.**

man·u·script |măn′ yə skrĭpt′| *n.* A handwritten or typewritten book, paper, or article as distinguished from a printed copy: *submit a manuscript to a publisher.*

map |măp| *v.* **mapped, map·ping.** To plan in detail: *mapped out the day's activities.*

mass |măs| *n.* A unified body of matter with no specific shape: *a mass of clay.*

mat·ter |măt′ ər| *n.* The substance of which the physical bodies of the universe are made.

mav·er·ick |măv′ ər ĭk| *or* |măv′ rĭk| *n.* A person who refuses to go along with the policies or views of his or her group.

max·i·mum |măk′ sə məm| *adj.* Of or having the greatest number, measure, quantity, or degree that has been reached or can be reached: *The train has a maximum speed of 80 miles per hour.*

may·or |mā′ ər| *or* |mâr| *n.* The chief government official of a city or town.

mead·ow |mĕd′ ō| *n.* A stretch of grassy ground, such as one used as a pasture or for growing hay.

mean |mēn| *v.* **meant** |mĕnt|, **mean·ing.** To intend or say: *What did you mean by that look?*

meant |mĕnt| *v.* Past tense and past participle of **mean.**

meas·ure |mĕzh′ ər| *v.* **meas·ured, meas·ur·ing.** To find the size, amount, capacity, or degree of something.

me·di·a |mē′ dē ə| *n.* The various means used to convey information in a society, including magazines, newspapers, radio, and television: *the mass media.*

meg·a·lop·o·lis |mĕg′ ə lŏp′ ə lĭs| *n.* A region containing several large cities that are close enough together for their suburbs to merge and make the region one enormous city.

mel·o·dra·ma |mĕl′ ə drä mə| *or* |-drăm′ ə| *n.* A play full of suspense, romance, and exciting scenes, with the heroes defeating the villains in the end.

me·men·to |mə mĕn′ tō| *n., pl.* **me·men·tos** *or* **me·men·toes.** A reminder of the past; a keepsake or souvenir.

mem·o |mĕm′ ō| *n., pl.* **mem·os.** A memorandum or written communication circulated in an office.

mem·o·ra·ble |mĕm′ ər ə bəl| *adj.* Remarkable; unforgettable: *Memorable events are pictured on stamps.*

-ment. A suffix that forms nouns and means: **1.** An action or process: **attachment; government. 2.** A condition: **amazement. 3.** The product, means, or result of an action: **entanglement.**

men·tal |mĕn′ tl| *adj.* Occurring in or done by the mind: *a mental image.*

men·tal·i·ty |mĕn tăl′ ĭ tē| *n., pl.* **men·tal·i·ties.** A frame of mind; mental tendency: *the kind of cautious mentality that insists on reading everything twice.*

men·tion |mĕn′ shən| *v.* To speak or write about briefly; to refer to incidentally: *An index lists all the pages on which a subject is mentioned.*

mer·chan·dise |mûr′ chən dīz′| *or* |-dīs′| *n.* Things that may be bought or sold; commercial goods.

mer·chant |mûr′ chənt| *n.* A person who buys and sells goods for profit.

mes·mer·ize |mĕz′ mə rīz′| *or* |mĕs′ mə rīz′| *v.* **mes·mer·ized, mes·mer·iz·ing. 1.** To hypnotize. **2.** To fascinate or enthrall: *They know that the performance will mesmerize the audience.*

Pronunciation Key

ă	pat	îr	pier	ŭ	cut
ā	pay	ŏ	pot	ûr	urge
âr	care	ō	toe	th	thin
ä	father	ô	paw	*th*	this
ĕ	pet	oi	boy	hw	whoop
ē	be	ŏŏ	took	zh	vision
ĭ	pit	ōō	boot	ə	about
ī	pie	ou	out		

mes·sage |mĕs′ ĭj| *n.* Spoken or written words or signals sent from one person or group to another.

mes·sen·ger |mĕs′ ən jər| *n.* A person who carries messages or does similar tasks.

meth·od |mĕth′ əd| *n.* A regular or deliberate way of doing something: *Three methods of purifying water are to filter it, to distill it, and to add chemicals to it.*

me·thod·i·cal |mə thŏd′ ĭ kəl| *adj.* Arranged or done according to a clear plan; systematic.

me·trop·o·lis |mə trŏp′ ə lĭs| *n., pl.* **me·trop·o·lis·es. 1.** A large busy city. **2.** The largest or most important city of a country, state, or region.

met·ro·pol·i·tan |mĕt′ rə pŏl′ ĭ tən| *adj.* **1.** Of, from, or characteristic of a major city with its suburbs: *metropolitan daily newspapers.* **2.** Including a major city and the surrounding heavily populated area.

mi·cro·phone |mī′ krə fōn′| *n.* A device used to send sound over a distance.

mi·gra·tion |mī grā′ shən| *n.* The act of moving regularly to a different region at particular times of the year: *Many birds practice southern migration in the fall.*

mile·age |mī′ lĭj| *n.* Length or distance as measured or expressed in miles.

min·i·mum |mĭn′ ə məm| *adj.* Representing the least possible or allowed: *taking a minimum number of shirts.*

min·is·ter |mĭn′ ĭ stər| *n.* A clergyman; pastor of a church.

mi·nor |mī′ nər| *adj.* Smaller in amount, size, or extent: *a minor change.*

mi·nus |mī′ nəs| *prep.* **1.** Reduced by the subtraction of: *Seven minus four equals three.* **2.** *Informal.* Without; lacking: *arrived minus his wallet.*

mirth |mûrth| *n.* Gaiety or merriment: *shouts of mirth.*

mis·chief |mĭs′ chĭf| *n.* **a.** Naughty or improper behavior. **b.** Trouble resulting from such behavior: *Hardly a day goes by that he doesn't get into some mischief.*

mis·quote |mis kwōt′| *v.* **mis·quo·ted, mis·quo·ting** To quote incorrectly.

mis·sile |mĭs′ əl| *or* |-īl′| *n.* Any object or weapon that is thrown, fired, dropped, or otherwise launched at a target.

mis·sion |mĭsh′ ən| *n.* An assignment that a person or group of persons is sent to carry out; a task: *a rescue mission.*

mis·sion·ar·y |mĭsh′ ə nĕr ē| *n., pl.* **mis·sion·ar·ies.** A person sent to do religious or charitable work in some territory or foreign country.

mod·el |mŏd′ l| *v.* **mod·eled** or **mod·elled, mod·el·ing** or **mod·el·ling.** **1.** To make or construct out of clay, wax, or other material: *model animals in clay.* **2.** To pose for an artist or photographer.

mod·er·a·tor |mŏd′ ə rā′ tər| *n.* The person who presides over a meeting or panel discussion.

mod·ern·ize |mŏd′ ər nīz′| *v.* **mod·ern·ized, mod·ern·iz·ing.** To alter or bring up-to-date so as to meet current needs: *modernize a kitchen.*

moist |moist| *adj.* Slightly wet; damp.

mon·ar·chy |mŏn′ ər kē| *n., pl.* **mon·ar·chies.** Government headed by a king or a queen.

mon·o·logue |mŏn′ ə lôg′| *or* |-lŏg′| *n.* A long speech delivered by one actor on the stage or a character in a story or poem: *Hamlet's monologue is well known.*

mo·nop·o·ly |mə nŏp′ ə lē| *n., pl.* **mo·nop·o·lies.** Complete control by one group of the means of producing or selling a product or service: *The early railroads had almost a monopoly on freight and passenger transportation.*

mor·al |môr′ əl| *or* |mŏr′-| *adj.* Of or concerned with the judgment of the goodness and badness of human action: *moral principles.* —*n.* The principle, or lesson, taught by a fable, story, or event.

mo·rale |mə răl′| *n.* The state of a person's or group's spirits, as shown in confidence, cheerfulness, and willingness to work toward a goal.

mo·ral·i·ty |mə răl′ ĭ tē| *or* |mô-| *n., pl.* **mor·al·i·ties.** The quality of being moral; goodness or rightness: *questioned the morality of selling firearms to the public.*

mort·gage |môr′ gĭj| *n.* A legal pledge of property to a creditor as security for the payment of a loan or debt: *We make payments on our home mortgage every month.*

mo·tion |mō′ shən| *n.* **a.** The process of moving; change of position. **b.** An act of moving; a movement.

mo·ti·vate |mō′ tə vāt′| *v.* **mo·ti·vat·ed, mo·ti·vat·ing.** To instill with desire to study or perform well; inspire.

mound |mound| *n.* **1.** A pile of earth or rocks heaped up. **2.** A pile or mass of anything. —*v.* To heap into a pile.

mourn |môrn| *or* |mōrn| *v.* To express or feel sorrow for (a death or loss); grieve.

mu·se·um |myoo zē′ əm| *n.* A building in which works of artistic, historical, or scientific interest are exhibited.

mu·si·cian |myoo zĭsh′ ən| *n.* Someone who is skilled or talented in performing or composing music, especially someone involved in music as a profession.

mus·sel |mŭs′ əl| *n.* Any of several saltwater or freshwater mollusks having a pair of narrow, often dark-blue shells.

mussels

mute |myo͞ot| *adj.* **1.** Not having the power of speech. **2.** Silent.

mut·ter |mŭt′ ər| *v.* To say or speak in a low, unclear tone.

myth |mĭth| *n.* A traditional story dealing with ancestors, heroes, or supernatural beings and usually trying to explain some belief, practice, or natural occurrence: *The myth told how thunder was made by the gods.*

N

na·tive |nā′ tĭv| *adj.* **1.** Belonging to one by nature; inborn; natural; native ability. **2.** Being such by birth or origin: *a native of New England.*

naugh·ty |nô′ tē| *adj.* **naugh·ti·er, naugh·ti·est.** Disobedient; mischievous.

nav·i·gate |năv′ ĭ gāt′| *v.* **nav·i·gat·ed, nav·i·gat·ing.** To plot and control the course of (a ship or aircraft): *It is difficult to navigate in a heavy storm.*

nei·ther |nē′ thər| *or* |nī′-| *adj.* Not either; not one nor the other: *Neither shoe fits comfortably.* —*pron.* Not either one; not the one nor the other: *Neither of them fits.*

nerv·ous |nûr′ vəs| *adj.* **1.** High-strung; jittery: *a nervous person.* **2.** Uneasy; anxious.

-ness. A suffix that forms nouns and means "a state, condition, or quality": **rudeness.**

neu·tral |no͞o′ trəl| *or* |nyo͞o′-| *adj.* Not allied with, supporting, or favoring any side in a war, dispute, contest, or struggle for power: *a neutral nation.*

nev·er·the·less |nĕv′ ər thə lĕs′| *adv.* All the same; anyway: *The plan may fail, but we must try it nevertheless.*

niece |nēs| *n.* A daughter of one's brother or sister or one's spouse's brother or sister.

no·tice·a·ble |nō′ tĭ sə bəl| *adj.* Easily observed; evident: *a noticeable difference in their ages.*

noun |noun| *n.* In grammar, a word used to name a person, place, thing, or idea.

nov·el |nŏv′ əl| *n.* A book-length piece of writing that tells an invented story.

no·where |nō′ wâr′| *adv.* Not anywhere: *The screwdriver was nowhere to be found.* —*n.* A remote or unknown place, especially a wilderness: *a cabin in the middle of nowhere.*

nu·mer·ous |no͞o′ mər əs| *or* |nyo͞o′-| *adj.* Existing or occurring in large numbers; many: *numerous items for sale.*

ob-. A prefix meaning "toward, in front of, against": **obstacle.**

ob·ject |ŏb′ jĭkt| *or* |-jĕkt′| *n.* A thing that has shape and can be seen or otherwise perceived; a material thing.

ob·jec·tion |əb jĕk′ shən| *n.* **1.** The expression of an opposing view or argument: *made no objection when the idea first came up.* **2.** A feeling of disapproval: *had no objection to the boy as his son-in-law.*

o·blige |ə blīj′| *v.* **o·bliged, o·blig·ing.** To satisfy the wishes of; do a service or favor for; please: *The singer obliged the fans with another number.*

o·boe |ō′ bō| *n.* A woodwind instrument having a high range and a piercing, rather nasal tone. It is basically conical in shape and is played with a double reed.

ob·scure |əb skyo͞or′| *adj.* **ob·scur·er, ob·scur·est.** Difficult to understand; unclear; vague: *an obscure reference to a past incident.* —*v.* **ob·scured, ob·scur·ing.** To conceal from view; hide: *Clouds obscured the stars.*

ob·serve |əb **zûrv**ʹ| *v.* **ob·served,
ob·serv·ing.** To perceive, notice, or watch attentively: *She observed a bird on the ledge.*
—**ob·serv**ʹ**er** *n.*

ob·sta·cle |**ŏb**ʹ stə kəl| *n.* Something that opposes, retards, or stands in the way of progress toward a goal; a hindrance; a barrier.

ob·sti·nate |**ŏb**ʹ stə nĭt| *adj.* Stubborn; resistant to argument or reason; inflexible: *an obstinate old man.*

ob·struct |əb **strŭkt**ʹ| *v.* **ob·struct·ed,
ob·struct·ing.** To make impassable with obstacles; block: *Fallen stones obstructed the mountain pass.*

ob·tain |əb **tān**ʹ| *v.* To gain the possession of after planning or endeavor; get; acquire: *obtain an autograph.*

ob·vi·ous |**ŏb**ʹ vē əs| *adj.* Easily perceived or understood; evident: *The answer was obvious to me.* —**ob**ʹ**vi·ous·ly** *adv.*
—**ob**ʹ**vi·ous·ness** *n.*

oc·ca·sion |ə **kā**ʹ zhən| *n.* A significant event or happening: *Thanksgiving dinner was quite an occasion.*

oc·cu·pant |**ŏk**ʹ yə pənt| *n.* Someone or something occupying a place or position: *the occupants of a building.*

oc·cu·pa·tion |ŏk yə **pā**ʹ shən| *n.* A means of making a living; a profession or job: *Nursing is an occupation that requires specialized training.*

oc·cu·py |**ŏk**ʹ yə pīʹ| *v.* **oc·cu·pied,
oc·cu·py·ing, oc·cu·pies.** To dwell in; inhabit.

oc·cur |ə **kûr**ʹ| *v.* **oc·curred, oc·cur·ring.**
To take place; come about; happen: *Many accidents occur in the home.*

oc·cur·rence |ə **kûr**ʹ əns| *n.* The act or condition of occurring, taking place, or appearing: *the occurrence of an accident.*

o·cean·og·ra·pher |ōʹ shə **nŏg**ʹ rə fər| *n.*
A scientist who studies the ocean.

oc·tet |ŏk **tĕt**ʹ| *n.* **1.** A musical composition for eight voices or instruments.
2. Eight singers or instrumentalists. **3.** A group of eight.

oc·to·pus |**ŏk**ʹ tə pəs| *n., pl.* **oc·to·pus·es**
or **oc·to·pi** |**ŏk**ʹ tə pīʹ|. Any of numerous sea mollusks having a soft rounded body and eight tentacles bearing suckers used for grasping and holding.

octopus

o·dor |**ō**ʹ dər| *n.* The quality of a thing that affects the sense of smell; scent: *Onions have a pungent odor.*

of·fend |ə **fĕnd**ʹ| *v.* To cause anger, resentment, or annoyance in; insult or affront.

of·fer |**ô**ʹ fər| *or* |**ôf**ʹ ər| *v.* To present for acceptance or refusal.

of·fi·cial |ə **fĭsh**ʹ əl| *adj.* Arising from authority: *an official document.*

old-fash·ioned |**ōld**ʹ **făsh**ʹ ənd| *adj.*
1. Belonging to or typical of an earlier time and no longer in style. **2.** Sticking to, preferring, or in keeping with ways or ideas of an earlier time.

o·pin·ion |ō **pĭn**ʹ yən| *n.* A belief or conclusion held with confidence but not supported by positive knowledge or proof: *She is quick with an opinion on every topic.*

op·po·nent |ə **pō**ʹ nənt| *n.* A person or group that opposes another in a battle, contest, controversy, or debate: *Our opponents in the debate will be from the next county.*

op·por·tu·ni·ty |ŏpʹ ər **tōō**ʹ nĭ tē| *or*
|-tyōōʹ-| *n., pl* **op·por·tu·ni·ties.** A time or occasion that is suitable for a certain purpose; a favorable combination of circumstances.

op·pose |ə **pōz**ʹ| *v.* **op·posed, op·pos·ing.**
1. To fight or resist: *oppose the enemy.* **2.** To disagree with.

op·po·site |ŏp′ ə zǐt| *or* |-sǐt| *adj.*
Contrary in nature or tendency; altogether
different.

op·po·si·tion |ŏp′ ə zǐsh′ ən| *n.* The act
or condition of being against something;
resistance or antagonism: *joined in opposition to
the President's program.*

or·a·tor |ôr′ ə tər| *n.* A person who
delivers a speech.

or·der |ôr′ dər| *v.* **or·dered, or·der·ing.**
To issue a command or an instruction to:
ordered the dog to sit.

or·gan·ize |ôr′ gə nīz′| *v.* **or·gan·ized,
or·gan·iz·ing.** To arrange in an orderly,
systematic way: *organize one's cassettes.*

ox·y·gen |ŏk′ sǐ jən| *n.* One of the
elements, a colorless, odorless, tasteless gas
which is essential for breathing.

P

pace |pās| *n.* A step made in walking; a
stride. —*v.* **paced, pac·ing.** To set or
regulate the speed of an activity.

History

Pace comes from the Latin word *pandere,*
meaning "to stretch." The Latin word
passus, which developed from *pandere,*
meant "step." Romans saw a step as a
"stretch of the leg."

---

page |pāj| *n.* One side of a leaf of a book,
letter, or newspaper.

pag·i·nate |păj′ ə nāt′| *v.* **pag·i·nat·ed,
pag·i·nat·ing.** To number the pages of.

pains·tak·ing |pānz′ tā kǐng| *adj.*
Involving or showing great care or
thoroughness; careful: *painstaking research.*

pale |pāl| *adj.* Whitish or lighter than
normal in complexion.

pal·lid |păl′ ǐd| *adj.* Lacking healthy color;
pale.

Pronunciation Key

ă	pat	îr	pier	ŭ	cut
ā	pay	ŏ	pot	ûr	urge
âr	care	ō	toe	th	thin
ä	father	ô	paw	*th*	*th*is
ĕ	pet	oi	boy	hw	whoop
ē	be	ŏŏ	took	zh	vision
ĭ	pit	ōō	boot	ə	about
ī	pie	ou	out		

pan·el |păn′ əl| *n.* A flat piece, such as a
wooden board, forming part of a surface or
wall.

pan·ic |păn′ ĭk| *n.* A sudden,
overwhelming terror.

pan·to·mime |păn′ tə mīm′| *n.* Acting
that consists mostly of gestures and other body
movement without speech: *Actors often learn
the art of pantomime.*

pants |pănts| *n.* Trousers.

par·al·lel |păr′ ə lĕl′| *adj.* Having
corresponding points always separated by the
same distance: *parallel to the highway.*

par·don |pär′ dn| *v.* **par·doned,
par·don·ing.** To release (a person) from
punishment or disfavor; forgive.

par·lia·ment |pär′ lə mənt| *n.* An
assembly of persons that makes the laws for a
nation.

pars·ley |pär′ slē| *n.* A plant with
feathery, often curled leaves used to flavor or
decorate food.

part |pärt| *n.* Something that along with
other things make a whole; a portion or
division of a larger thing.

par·tial |pär′ shəl| *adj.* Not total;
incomplete: *partial success.*

par·tic·i·pate |pär tǐs′ ə pāt′| *v.*
par·tic·i·pat·ed, par·tic·i·pat·ing. To join
with others in being active; take part.

par·tic·u·lar |pər tǐk′ yə lər| *adj.* **1.** Of
or for a single person, group, or thing.
2. Distinct from others; specific; certain.

part·ner |pärt′ nər| *n.* One of two or
more persons associated in some common
activity: *a business partner.*

pass |păs| *or* |päs| *v.* To go from one place or position to another.

pass·a·ble |păs′ ə bəl| *or* |pä′ sə-| *adj.* **1.** Capable of being passed or crossed; not blocked: *a passable street.* **2.** Satisfactory but not outstanding; adequate: *a passable job of acting.*

pas·sen·ger |păs′ ən jər| *n.* A person riding in, but not driving, a train, airplane, ship, bus, car, or other vehicle.

pa·tri·ot·ic |pā′ trē ŏt′ ĭk| *adj.* Feeling or expressing love for one's country.

pearl |pûrl| *n.* A smooth, slightly iridescent white or grayish rounded growth formed inside the shells of some kinds of oysters and valued as a gem.

pel·i·can |pĕl′ ĭ kən| *n.* A large, long-billed, web-footed bird of warm regions, having under its lower bill a large pouch used for holding the fish it has caught.

pelican

per-. A prefix meaning "thoroughly; completely; intensely": **persist.**

per·cent·age |pər sĕn′ tĭj| *n.* **1.** A fraction that is understood to have 100 as its denominator; a fraction expressed by using the word *percent.* **2.** A portion or share in relation to the whole.

per·cep·tion |pər sĕp′ shən| *n.* **1.** The act or process of becoming aware of something through any of the senses, especially sight and hearing. **2.** The ability to perceive: *depth perception.*

per·form·ance |pər fôr′ məns| *n.* The act of presenting a musical or dramatic work before an audience.

per·fume |pûr′ fyōōm′| *or* |pər fyōōm′| *n.* A fragrant liquid distilled from flowers or prepared by synthetic means.

per·haps |pər hăps′| *adv.* Maybe; possibly: *Perhaps he'll come with us.*

per·il·ous |pĕr′ ə ləs| *adj.* Dangerous; hazardous: *The canoe trip down the rapids was a perilous journey.*

per·ma·nence |pûr′ mə nəns| *n.* The quality or condition of being permanent.

per·ma·nent |pûr′ mə nənt| *adj.* Lasting or meant to last indefinitely; enduring.

per·mis·sion |pər mĭsh′ ən| *n.* Consent, especially formal consent; authorization.

per·mit |pər mĭt′| *v.* **per·mit·ted, per·mit·ting.** To give consent or permission to; allow; authorize.

per·sist |pər sĭst′| *v.* To insist or repeat obstinately; continue: *She persisted in denying her guilt.*

per·son·al |pûr′ sə nəl| *adj.* Of a particular person; private; one's own: *a personal experience.*

per·son·al·i·ty |pûr sə năl′ ĭ tē| *n., pl.* **per·son·al·i·ties.** The totality of qualities and traits, as of character and behavior, that are peculiar to each person: *a pleasing personality.*

per·son·nel |pûr′ sə nĕl′| *n.* The body of persons employed by or active in an organization, business, or service.

per·spec·tive |pər spĕk′ tĭv| *n.* **1.** The technique of representing objects on a flat surface so that they have the three dimensional quality they have when seen with the eye. **2.** A view or vista: *the perspective from the top floor.*

per·suade |pər swād′| *v.* **per·suad·ed, per·suad·ing.** To cause (someone) to do or believe something by arguing, pleading, or reasoning; convince: *He tried to persuade them to come with us.*

per·tain |pər tān′| *v.* **1.** To have reference; relate: *a discussion pertaining to art.* **2.** To belong to.

phar·ma·cist |**fär′** mə sĭst| *n.* Someone who specializes in preparing and dispensing medicines: *The pharmacist prepared the medicine the doctor prescribed.*

phys·i·cal |**fĭz′** ĭ kəl| *adj.* Of the body rather than the mind or emotions.

phy·si·cian |fĭ **zĭsh′** ən| *n.* A person licensed to practice medicine; a doctor.

pi·an·o |pē **ăn′** ō| *n., pl.* **pi·an·os.** A keyboard musical instrument with black and white keys, in which the movement of a key by the player's finger actuates a felt-covered hammer that strikes a metal string and produces a tone.

pic·co·lo |**pĭk′** ə lō′| *n., pl.* **pic·co·los.** A small flute with a hard, brilliant tone and a range about an octave above that of an ordinary flute.

piece |pēs| *n.* A part of a set: *sixty pieces in a set of china.*

pier |pîr| *n.* A platform extending from a shore over water, used to secure, protect, and provide access to ships or boats.

pierce |pîrs| *v.* **pierced, pierc·ing.** To stab or puncture with a sharp instrument.

pi·lot |**pī′** lət| *v.* **pi·lot·ed, pi·lot·ing.** To operate and set the course of (a plane, ship, or vehicle).

pi·rate |**pī′** rĭt| *n.* An outlaw who robs ships at sea or plunders the land from the sea.

pitch |pĭch| *n.* A throw of a baseball or a softball by a pitcher to a batter.

plan |plăn| *v.* **planned, plan·ning.** To think out (what to do or how to do it) ahead of time: *plan one's vacation.*

plan·e·tar·i·um |plăn′ ĭ **târ′** ē əm| *n., pl.* **plan·e·tar·i·ums** or **plan·e·tar·i·a.** |plăn′ ĭ **târ′** ē ə| A building housing an optical device for projecting images of celestial bodies, such as stars, onto the ceiling of a dome.

plan·ta·tion |plăn **tā′** shən| *n., pl.* **plan·ta·tions.** A large farm or estate on which crops such as cotton, sugar, or rubber are tended and gathered by workers who often live on the same property.

pleas·ant |**plĕz′** ənt| *adj.* **pleas·ant·er, pleas·ant·est.** **1.** Pleasing: *a pleasant climate.* **2.** Pleasing or favorable in manner; amiable: *a pleasant person.*

Pronunciation Key

ă	pat	îr	pier	ŭ	cut
ā	pay	ŏ	pot	ûr	urge
âr	care	ō	toe	th	thin
ä	father	ô	paw	*th*	*th*is
ĕ	pet	oi	boy	hw	whoop
ē	be	ŏŏ	took	zh	vision
ĭ	pit	ōō	boot	ə	about
ī	pie	ou	out		

pledge |plĕj| *n.* A formal vow; a solemn promise: *made a pledge to do their duty.*

plumb·ing |**plŭm′** ĭng| *n.* The pipes, fixtures, and other equipment used in a system through which a liquid or gas flows.

plump |plŭmp| *adj.* Rounded and full in form: *a plump peach.*

plunge |plŭnj| *v.* **plunged, plung·ing.** To dive suddenly, as into a body of water or a place.

po·di·um |**pō′** dē əm| *n., pl.* **po·di·a** |**pō′** dē ə| or **po·di·ums.** An elevated platform on which an orchestra conductor or speaker stands.

poise |poiz| *n.* Dignity and self-possession of manner; composure.

poi·son |**poi′** zən| *n.* Any substance that

History

Poison is from the Latin word *potáre* meaning "to drink." In Middle English, the word *poysoun* was used to mean "a drink that is poisonous."

causes injury, sickness, or death, especially by chemical means.

po·lice |pə **lēs′**| *n., pl.* **po·lice.** The department of government established to maintain order, enforce the law, and prevent and detect crime.

pol·i·cy¹ |**pŏl′** ĭ sē| *n., pl.* **pol·i·cies.** A general management plan, principle, outlook, or course of action followed by a government, individual, or business.

pol·i·cy² |pŏl′ ĭ sē| *n., pl.* **pol·i·cies.**
A written contract of insurance between a company and an individual, specifying the premiums to be paid and the money awarded in the event of damage, injury, or death.

pol·ish |pŏl′ ĭsh| *v.* To make or become smooth and shiny, as by abrasion, chemical action, or both. —*n.* A substance containing chemicals or an abrasive material for smoothing or shining a surface.

pol·i·ti·cian |pŏl′ ĭ tĭsh′ ən| *n.* A person active in politics, especially one holding a political office.

pol·i·tics |pŏl′ ĭ tĭks| *n.* The activities or affairs of a government, politician, or political party.

pop·u·lar |pŏp′ yə lər| *adj.* Well-liked; having many friends or admirers.

pore |pôr| *or* |pōr| *n.* A tiny opening in an animal's skin or on a leaf.
♦ *These sound alike* **pore, pour.**

port·a·ble |pôr′ tə bəl| *or* |pōr′-| *adj.* Easily or conveniently carried.

por·tion |pôr′ shən| *or* |pōr′-| *n.* A part of a whole; a section or quantity of a larger thing: *the solid portion of a design.*

po·si·tion |pə zĭsh′ ən| *n.* The place where someone or something is located: *the position of the sun in the sky.*

pos·i·tive |pŏz′ ĭ tĭv| *adj.* Absolutely certain: *I'm positive about that.*

pos·ture |pŏs′ chər| *n.* The way in which a person holds or carries his body; carriage: *a person who has good posture.*

po·ta·to |pə tā′ tō| *n., pl.* **po·ta·toes.**
The starchy tuber, or enlarged underground stem, of a widely grown plant, eaten as a vegetable.

po·ten·tial |pə tĕn′ shəl| *adj.* Possible or future, though not yet actual, definite, or real: *potential buyers; potential problems.* —*n.* Capacity for further growth, development, or progress; promise: *students with high potential.*

pour |pôr| *or* |pōr| *v.* To cause (a fluid or loose particles) to flow in a steady stream.
♦ *These sound alike* **pour, pore.**

pra·line |prä′ lēn| *n.* A crisp candy made of nut kernels and sugar.

pre-. A prefix meaning "before" or "earlier": **prepaid.**

preach |prēch| *v.* To teach and urge others to accept or follow.

pre·cip·i·ta·tion |prĭ sĭp′ ĭ tā′ shən| *n.* Any form of water that condenses from the atmosphere and passes to the surface of the earth, including rain, snow, and sleet.

pre·cis·ion |prĭ sĭzh′ ən| *n.* The condition or quality of being precise; accurate; exactness: *the precision of a chemist's scales.*

pre·dict |prĭ dĭkt′| *v.* To tell about or make known in advance, especially on the basis of present knowledge; foretell: *predicted showers for this evening.*

pre·dom·i·nant |prĭ dŏm′ ə nənt| *adj.*
1. Greater than all others in strength, authority, or importance; dominant: *the predominant nation of the Middle East.*
2. Most common or noticeable; main.

pre·fer |prĭ fûr′| *v.* **pre·ferred, pre·fer·ring.** To choose as more desirable; like better: *I prefer to stay at home tonight.*

pre·fix |prē′ fĭks′| *n.* A word part added to the beginning of a base word to change the meaning of the word. For example, the word parts *dis-* in *dislike, re-* in *repeat,* and *un-* in *unable* are prefixes.

pre·his·tor·ic |prē′ hĭ stôr′ ĭk| *or* |-stŏr′-| *adj.* Of or belonging to the time before history or events were recorded in writing.

prehistoric

pre·paid |prē′ **pād′**| *adj.* Paid or paid for in advance: *a prepaid vacation tour.*

prep·a·ra·tion |prĕp′ ə rā′ shən| *n.* **1.** The act or process of preparing: *the preparation of dinner for six persons.* **2.** The condition of having been made ready beforehand; readiness: *a ship in good preparation for a voyage.*

pre·pare |prĭ **pâr′**| *v.* **pre·pared, pre·par·ing.** To make ready for some purpose, task, or event: *Prepare for a quiz.*

pre·scribe |prĭ **skrīb′**| *v.* **pre·scribed, pre·scrib·ing.** To order or recommend the use of (a drug, diet, or remedy).

pre·scrip·tion |prĭ **skrĭp′** shən| *n.* **1.** The act or process of prescribing. **2.** Something that is prescribed; a medicine ordered by a doctor.

pres·er·va·tion |prĕz′ ər vā′ shən| *n.* The act of preserving or the state of being preserved.

pre·serve |prĭ **zûrv′**| *v.* **pre·served, pre·serv·ing.** To protect, as from injury or peril; maintain in safety: *concerned with preserving wildlife.*

pres·i·dent |prĕz′ ĭ dənt| *n.* **1.** Often **President.** The chief executive of a republic, such as the United States. **2.** The chief officer of an organization or institution, such as a club, corporation, or university.

pres·sure |prĕsh′ ər| *n.* The application of a continuous force on one thing by another with which it is in contact.

pre·vent |prĭ **vĕnt′**| *v.* To keep from happening. —**pre·vent′a·ble** *adj.*

pre·ven·tion |prĭ **vĕn′** shən| *n.* The act or an example of keeping something from happening: *the prevention of illness.*

pre·ven·tive |prĭ **vĕn′** tĭv| *adj.* Designed to prevent or hinder: *They took preventive steps against accidents.*

pre·view |prē′ **vyo͞o′**| *n.* An advance showing of a motion picture, art exhibition, or play to an invited audience, prior to presentation to the general public: *The actor attended a preview of his new movie.*

pre·vi·ous |prē′ vē əs| *adj.* Existing or occurring prior to something else; earlier: *in the previous chapter.*

Pronunciation Key

ă	pat	îr	pier	ŭ	cut
ā	pay	ŏ	pot	ûr	urge
âr	care	ō	toe	th	thin
ä	father	ô	paw	*th*	this
ĕ	pet	oi	boy	hw	whoop
ē	be	o͝o	took	zh	vision
ĭ	pit	o͞o	boot	ə	about
ī	pie	ou	out		

prin·ci·pal |prĭn′ sə pəl| *adj.* Most important; chief. —*n.* A person who holds a leading position, especially the head of an elementary, junior high, or high school.
♦ *These sound alike* **principal, principle.**

prin·ci·ple |prĭn′ sə pəl| *n.* **1.** A basic or fundamental truth or law: *the principles of Christianity.* **2.** A rule or standard of behavior: *a woman of dedicated political principles.*
♦ *These sound alike* **principle, principal.**

History

Principle comes from the Latin word *princeps,* meaning "first." Later, the Old French word *principe* was used to mean "a first or basic truth."

pri·vate |prī′ vĭt| *adj.* Intimate; secret: *a private workroom in the house.* —**pri′vate·ly** *adv.*

pro |prō| *n.* An argument in favor of something. —*adv.* In favor of: *argue pro and con.* —*adj.* Supporting: *the arguments pro and con.*

pro-¹. A prefix meaning: **1.** Favor or support: **prorevolutionary.** **2.** Acting as; substituting for: **pronoun.**

pro-². A prefix meaning "before, in front of": **prologue.**

prob·lem |prŏb′ ləm| *n.* Any question or situation that presents uncertainty, confusion, or difficulty: *traffic problems.*

Spelling Dictionary

pro·ceed |prə **sēd′**| *v.* To go forward or onward, especially after an interruption: *Proceed with caution.*

proc·ess |**prŏs′** ĕs′| *or* |**prō′** sĕs′| *n.* A series of steps, actions, or operations used in making something or bringing about a desired result: *a manufacturing process.*

pro·cure |prō kyoŏr′| *v.* **pro·cured, pro·cur·ing.** To obtain; acquire: *procured tickets for the circus.*

prod·uct |**prŏd′** əkt| *n.* Something produced, as by nature or manufacturing: *industrial products.*

pro·fes·sion |prə **fĕsh′** ən| *n.* A kind of regular work, especially an occupation that requires training and specialized study: *the profession of medicine.*

pro·fes·sor |prə **fĕs′** ər| *n.* A teacher of the highest rank in a college or university.

prof·it |**prŏf′** ĭt| *v.* **prof·it·ed, pro·fit·ting.** To gain an advantage; benefit: *profited from the experience of others.*

pro·gram |**prō′** grăm| *or* |-grəm| *n.* A performance, presentation, or entertainment; a show before an audience: *The senior class planned and gave a program of folk music.*

pro·gram·mer |**prō′** grăm ər| *n.* Someone who prepares instructions, or programs, for computers: *Many businesses hire programmers to develop new programs.*

prog·ress |**prŏg′** rĕs′| *n.* Steady improvement, as in a civilization or individual: *a baby who was making progress in learning how to talk.*

pro·hib·it |prō **hĭb′** ĭt| *v.* To make unlawful; forbid by law or authority: *Stock-car racing rules prohibit the use of more than one carburetor.*

proj·ect |**prŏj′** ĕkt′| *or* |-ĭkt| *n.* A special study or experiment undertaken by a student or group of students: *For her science project, she decided to build an ant colony.*

prom·i·nence |**prŏm′** ə nəns| *n.* The quality or condition of being prominent; importance.

prom·i·nent |**prŏm′** ə nənt| *adj.* Well-known; leading: *a prominent politician.*

prom·ise |**prŏm′** ĭs| *v.* To make a vow; offer assurance: *promise to come home early.*

pro·mote |prə **mōt′**| *v.* **pro·mot·ed, pro·mot·ing.** **1.** To aid the progress or growth of; advance; further: *promoting the general welfare.* **2.** To urge the adoption or use of; advocate: *promote a measure in Congress.*

prompt |prŏmpt| *adj.* **prompt·er, prompt·est.** **1.** On time; punctual. **2.** Done without delay; immediate. —*v.* To urge (someone) to some action.

proof·read |**proōf′** rēd′| *v.* **proof·read** |**proōf′** rĕd|, **proof·read·ing.** To read and mark corrections in (printed, typed, or written material): *to proofread a story for spelling errors.*

prop |prŏp| *n.* A stage property: *Chaplin's props were a bowler hat and an umbrella.*

pro·pel |prə **pĕl′**| *v.* **pro·pelled, pro·pel·ling.** **1.** To cause (a vehicle, rocket, or body) to move or continue in motion: *the rearward thrust that propels a jet airplane.* **2.** To push or throw forcefully; hurl: *The sailor leaned back and propelled the harpoon.*

pro·pos·al |prə **pō′** zəl| *n.* A plan or scheme offered for consideration.

pros·pect |**prŏs′** pĕkt′| *n.* Something expected or foreseen; an expectation: *hurried home with the prospect of a good dinner.*

pro·tect |prə **tĕkt′**| *v.* To keep from harm, attack, or injury; guard.

pro·tec·tive |prə **tĕk′** tĭv| *adj.* Serving to protect: *a protective coat of shellac.*

pro·vide |prə **vīd′**| *v.* **pro·vid·ed, pro·vid·ing.** To give (something needed or useful); supply: *generators that provide electrical energy.*

pub·lish·er |**pŭb′** lĭsh ər| *n.* A person or company that produces and distributes printed matter, such as books, magazines, or newspapers.

punc·tu·al |**pŭngk′** choō əl| *adj.* Acting or arriving on time; prompt: *Teachers expect you to be punctual at school.*

punc·ture |**pŭngk′** chər| *v.* **punc·tured, punc·tur·ing.** To cause to collapse or deflate by or as if by piercing with something sharp: *I punctured the balloon with a pin.* —*n.* A hole or wound made by something sharp, especially such a hole in a tire.

pur·pose |**pûr′** pəs| *n.* The intended or desired result; a goal; aim; intent.

purse |pûrs| *n.* **1.** A small bag or pouch, used to carry money. **2.** A woman's handbag or pocketbook.

History

Purse began as the Greek word *bursa,* meaning "leather." Later the Romans adopted the word. As a Latin word, *bursa* meant "bag."

---

pur·suit |pər **soot′**| *n.* The act of striving to achieve or gain: *dedicated to the pursuit of happiness.*

Q

quad·ru·ped |**kwŏd′** rə pĕd′| *n.* A four-footed animal.

quad·ru·plet |kwŏ **drŭp′** lĭt| *or* |kwŏ **droo′** plĭt| *n.* **1.** One of four offspring born in a single birth. **2.** A group or combination of four things of one kind: *a quadruplet of apples.*

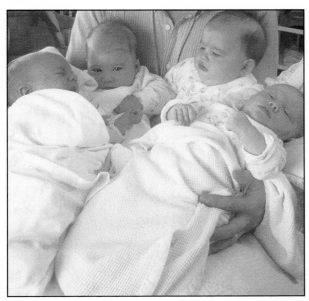

quadruplets

Pronunciation Key

ă	pat	îr	pier	ŭ	cut
ā	pay	ŏ	pot	ûr	urge
âr	care	ō	toe	th	thin
ä	father	ô	paw	*th*	this
ĕ	pet	oi	boy	hw	whoop
ē	be	oo	took	zh	vision
ĭ	pit	oo	boot	ə	about
ī	pie	ou	out		

qual·i·ty |**kwŏl′** ĭ tē| *n., pl.* **qual·i·ties.** Any property or feature that makes something what it is: *the good quality of the expensive fabric.*

quar·rel |**kwôr′** əl| *or* |**kwŏr′-**| *n.* An angry argument or dispute. —*v.* **quar·reled** or **quar·relled, quar·rel·ing** or **quar·rel·ling.** To engage in a disagreement; argue or dispute angrily.

quest |kwĕst| *n.* In stories of the Middle Ages, an expedition undertaken by a knight in order to find something: *the quest for the Holy Grail.*

quiz |kwĭz| *n., pl.* **quiz·zes.** A short oral or written examination.

quot·a·ble |**kwō′** tə bl| *adj.* Suitable or worthy of quoting.

quot·a·tion |kwō′ **tā′** shən| *n.* **1.** The act of quoting: *These remarks are not for direct quotation.* **2.** A passage that is quoted: *read a quotation from Shakespeare.*

quote |kwōt| *v.* **quo·ted, quot·ing.** To repeat a passage in something or a statement by someone: *quote the Bible; quote the mayor.* —*n.* A passage that is repeated: *Ken read his favorite quote to me.*

R

ra·dar |**rā′** där′| *n.* A method of detecting distant objects and determining their position, speed, and size by causing radio waves to be reflected from them and analyzing the reflected waves: *The airport used radar to track the approaching aircraft.*

rad·ish |răd′ ĭsh| *n.* A plant grown for its strong-tasting red-skinned or white root.

radish

rat·ing |rā′ tĭng| *n.* A classification assigned according to quality, performance, or skill: *I gave that restaurant an excellent rating.*

ra·tio |rā′ shō| *or* |-shē ō′| *n., pl.* **ra·tios.**
1. An indicated quotient of a pair of numbers, often used as a means of comparing them.
2. A relationship between the amounts or sizes of two things, expressed as such a quotient; proportion: *mixed flour and water in the ratio of five to two.* A ratio can be written as 3:1.

rave |rāv| *v.* **raved, rav·ing.** To speak about with wild enthusiasm or praise. —*n. Informal.* An opinion, description, or review full of enthusiastic praise. —*modifier: rave reviews.*

ra·vine |rə vēn′| *n.* A deep, narrow cut, similar to a canyon or gorge, in the earth's surface.

re-. A prefix meaning: **1.** Again; anew: **reassemble. 2.** Back; backward: **recall.**

re·ac·tion |rē ăk′ shən| *n.* **1.** An action, feeling, or attitude aroused by something; response. **2.** The response of a living thing to a stimulus.

re·al·ize |rē′ ə līz′| *v.* **re·al·ized, re·al·iz·ing.** To be fully aware of: *I did not realize that the play was two hours long.*

realm |rĕlm| *n.* A kingdom.

rea·son |rē′ zən| *n.* **1.** A statement or fact that justifies or explains an action, a decision, a conviction: *I have reason to believe that he is wrong.* **2.** A fact or cause that explains why something exists or occurs: *reasons for being late.* ◊ *Idioms.* **by reason of.** Because of. **stands to reason.** Makes sense.

rea·son·ing |rē′ zə nĭng| *n.* The process of thinking in an orderly way to form conclusions or judgments; the use of reason.

re·bel |rĭ bĕl′| *v.* **re·belled, re·bel·ling.** To resist or oppose openly any authority based on law, custom, or convention; disobey: *The boys rebelled against the unfair rules.*

re·but·tal |rĭ bŭt′ l| *n.* The act of proving (something) false by presenting opposing evidence or arguments.

re·ceipt |rĭ sēt′| *n.* A written acknowledgment that a sum of money has been paid or received or that a certain article or a delivery of merchandise has been received.

re·cent |rē′ sənt| *adj.* Of a time immediately before the present.

re·cep·tion |rĭ sĕp′ shən| *n.* The act or process of receiving something.

re·ces·sion |rĭ sĕsh′ ən| *n.* **1.** The act of withdrawing or going back. **2.** A moderate decline in economic activity.

re·cit·al |rĭ sīt′ l| *n.* A performance of music or dance, especially one by a solo performer: *We attended a dance recital.*

rec·og·nize |rĕk′ əg nīz′| *v.* **rec·og·nized, rec·og·niz·ing. 1.** To know or identify from past experience or knowledge. **2.** To know, understand, or realize: *recognized the value of virtue.*

rec·om·mend |rĕk′ ə mĕnd′| *v.* To praise or commend to another or others as being worthy or desirable: *recommend a woman for the job.*

re·cruit |rĭ krōōt′| *v.* To enroll or enlist (persons) in military service.

re·cur |rĭ kûr′| *v.* **re·curred, re·cur·ring.** To happen, come up, or show up again or repeatedly; return; reappear: *an area where earthquakes recur.*

re·fer |rĭ fûr′| *v.* **re·ferred, re·fer·ring. 1.** To direct to a person or thing for help or information: *refer a patient to a heart specialist.* **2.** To turn to, as for information or authority: *refer to the chart on the page opposite the text.*

re·fine·ment |rĭ fīn′ mənt| *n.* **1.** A small change or addition intended to improve something: *Our new car has computerized instruments and other refinements.* **2.** Elegance: *people of refinement.*

re·flec·tor |rĭ flĕk′ tər| *n.* Something that throws back light from a surface: *The bicycle's reflector helped the car driver see the rider.*

re·form |rĭ fôrm′| *v.* **1.** To improve, as by correcting errors. **2.** To cause to give up harmful ways: *work designed to reform criminals.* —**re·form′a·ble** *adj.* —**re·form′er** *n.*

ref·or·ma·tion |rĕf′ ər mā′ shən| *n.* The act of reforming or the condition of being reformed: *The governor ordered a total reformation of the school system.*

re·fund |rĭ fŭnd′| *v.* To pay back (money): *The store refunded the full price of the television set.* —*n.* |rē′ fŭnd′| A repayment of funds.

re·fute |rĭ fyo͞ot′| *v.* **re·fut·ed, re·fut·ing.** To prove (a person or idea) to be wrong; disprove: *refuted their statements.*

re·gard·less |rĭ gärd′ lĭs| *adj.* Heedless; unmindful: *I'll take the job, regardless of the pay.* —*adv.* In spite of everything; anyway: *She still loved him, regardless.*

reg·u·lar |rĕg′ yə lər| *adj.* Usual; normal.

re·hearse |rĭ hûrs′| *v.* **re·hearsed, re·hears·ing.** To practice (all or part of a program) in preparation for a performance: *The boys rehearsed their skit.*

reign |rān| *n.* The exercise of real or symbolic political power by a monarch. —*v.* **1.** To exercise the power of a monarch. **2.** To be widespread: *A stillness reigned after the storm.*

re·ject |rĭ jĕkt′| *v.* To throw out; discard: *Dad rejected my plea for a bigger weekly allowance.*

re·lease |rĭ lēs′| *v.* **re·leased, re·leas·ing.** To set free; liberate: *release prisoners.*

re·lief |rĭ lēf′| *n.* Ease from or lessening of pain, discomfort, or anxiety.

re·lieve |rĭ lēv′| *v.* **re·lieved, re·liev·ing.** To lessen or reduce (pain, discomfort, or anxiety); ease.

re·ly |rĭ lī′| *v.* **re·lied, re·ly·ing, re·lies.** —**rely on** (or **upon**). To depend on; trust confidently.

re·mark·a·ble |rĭ märk′ kə bəl| *adj.* Worthy of notice; extraordinary; uncommon: *a remarkable achievement.*

re·mind |rĭ mīnd′| *v.* To cause (someone) to remember or think of something: *Remind her to water the plants.*

Pronunciation Key

ă	pat	îr	pier	ŭ	cut
ā	pay	ŏ	pot	ûr	urge
âr	care	ō	toe	th	thin
ä	father	ô	paw	*th*	this
ĕ	pet	oi	boy	hw	whoop
ē	be	o͝o	took	zh	vision
ĭ	pit	o͞o	boot	ə	about
ī	pie	ou	out		

---

rep·e·ti·tion |rĕp′ ĭ tĭsh′ ən| *n.* The act or process of saying or doing something again: *the repetition of a word.*

re·place·ment |rĭ plās′ mənt| *n.* Something that takes the place of; substitution.

re·ply |rĭ plī′| *v.* **re·plied, re·ply·ing, re·plies.** To say or give an answer.

re·port |rĭ pôrt′| *or* |-pōrt′| *n.* An oral or written account containing information, often prepared or delivered in organized form: *a news report.*

re·pub·lic |rĭ pŭb′ lĭk| *n.* A country governed by the elected representatives of the people.

rep·u·ta·tion |rĕp′ yə tā′ shən| *n.* **1.** The general esteem in which a person is held by others or by the general public. **2.** Public recognition: *The novel established his reputation as a writer.*

re·quire |rĭ kwīr′| *v.* **re·quired, re·quir·ing.** To need; demand; call for: *Tightrope walking requires considerable practice.*

res·cue |rĕs′ kyo͞o| *v.* **res·cued, res·cu·ing.** To save from danger, harm, capture, or evil.

re·search |rĭ sûrch′| *or* |rē′ sûrch′| *n.* Systematic study of a given subject, field, or problem: *medical research.*

re·sem·blance |rĭ zĕm′ bləns| *n.* Similarity in appearance; likeness: *He bears a certain resemblance to your brother.*

res·o·lu·tion |rĕz′ ə lo͞o′ shən| *n.* A formal statement or expression of opinion adopted by an assembly, legislature, or other organization: *Our class adopted a resolution to conserve energy.*

Spelling Dictionary

re·source |rĭ **sôrs′**| *or* |-sōrs′| *or* |rē′ sôrs′| *or* |-sōrs′| *n.* Often **re·sourc·es.** Something that is a source of wealth to a country; assets: *Wheat is one of our country's most important resources.*

re·spect·ful |rĭ **spĕkt′** fəl| *adj.* Showing proper respect; honor, or esteem; polite; courteous: *I replied to his questions in a respectful tone of voice.*

re·spon·si·ble |rĭ **spŏn′** sə bəl| *adj.* Dependable; reliable; trustworthy: *a mature and responsible man.*

re·tail |rē′ **tāl′**| *adj.* Relating to the sale of goods in small quantities directly to the consumers: *Prices at a retail store are often higher than at a wholesale store.*

re·tire |rĭ **tīr′**| *v.* **re·tired, re·tir·ing.** To give up one's work, business, or career, usually because of advancing age. —**re·tire′ment** *n.* *My grandfather started his retirement when he turned sixty-five.*

re·trieve |rĭ **trēv′**| *v.* **re·trieved, re·triev·ing.** **1.** To locate (data or information) in a file, library, or storage system, and make it available for use, especially by means of a computer. **2.** To find and carry back; fetch.

retrieve

rev·e·nue |rĕv′ ə nōō′| *or* |-nyōō′| *n.* Yield from property or investment; income.

re·view |rĭ **vyōō′**| *v.* To look over; examine again: *Review Chapter 5.* —*n.* A report or essay that discusses something and attempts to judge its worth: *I read an enthusiastic review about a new play.*

re·vise |rĭ **vīz′**| *v.* **re·vised, re·vis·ing.** To edit in order to improve or bring up to date: *revise a paragraph.*

rhyme |rīm| *n.* A poem having a regular repetition of sounds at the ends of lines. —*v.* **rhymed, rhym·ing.** To correspond in sound: *"hour" rhymes with "flour."*

rhythm |rĭ*th*′ əm| *n.* **1.** A regular repeating of beats, movements, actions, or sounds. **2.** A pattern of stressed syllables or beats in poetry or music.

roam |rōm| *v.* To travel over or through (an area) without a fixed goal; wander.

ro·man·tic |rō **măn′** tĭk| *adj.* Full of the quality or spirit of romance; suggesting adventure, heroism, or love: *a soft romantic light.*

room·mate |rōōm′ māt′| *or* |rōōm′-| *n.* A person with whom one shares a room or apartment.

roost |rōōst| *n.* A branch, rod, or similar resting place on which birds perch.

rou·tine |rōō **tēn′**| *n.* A series of activities performed regularly. —*adj.* Not special; ordinary.

run·ner-up |rŭn′ ər ŭp′| *n.* A contestant who finishes a competition in second place.

ru·ral |rōōr′ əl| *adj.* Of or in the country: *rural areas.*

S

sal·a·ry |săl′ ə rē| *n., pl.* **sal·a·ries.** A set sum of money or other compensation paid to a person on a regular basis for doing a job.

sal·vage |săl′ vĭj| *v.* **1.** To save (a wrecked, damaged, or sunken ship or its cargo or parts) from total loss or ruin. **2.** To save endangered property from loss.

sam·ple |săm′ pəl| *or* |säm′-| *v.* **sam·pled, sam·pling.** To test by trying a little of, as in tasting. —*n.* A part, piece, amount, or selection that is considered to represent or to be typical of the whole; an example.

sand·bar |sănd′ bär′| *n.* Also **sand bar**. A mass of sand built up in the water near a shore or beach by the action of waves or currents shifting pebbles and dirt: *We walked out on a sandbar far from the beach.*

sandbar

sas·sa·fras |săs′ ə frăs′| *n.* A North American tree with irregularly shaped leaves. Its bark, roots, and leaves have a spicy odor and taste.

sau·sage |sô′ sĭj| *n.* Chopped and seasoned meat stuffed into a prepared animal intestine or other casing and cooked or cured.

sax·o·phone |săk′ sə fōn′| *n.* A wind instrument with a reed mouthpiece, a curved, conical body made of metal, and keys operated by the player's fingers.

scal·lion |skăl′ yən| *n.* A young onion with a small, narrow white bulb and long, narrow green leaves, both of which are eaten raw as a relish or used in cooking.

scar |skär| *n.* A mark left on the skin after a wound or injury has healed: *Bill hoped his cut would not leave a scar.*

scarce |skârs| *adj.* Not enough to meet a demand: *scarce rainfall.*

scarce·ly |skârs′ lē| *adv.* Almost not at all; barely; hardly: *I could scarcely see through the fog.*

scarf |skärf| *n., pl.* **scarfs** or **scarves** |skärvz|. A rectangular or triangular piece of cloth worn about the neck or head.

scene |sēn| *n.* **1.** A place or area as seen by a viewer; a view from a particular point: *a winter scene; the scene from my window.*

Pronunciation Key

ă	pat	îr	pier	ŭ	cut
ā	pay	ŏ	pot	ûr	urge
âr	care	ō	toe	th	thin
ä	father	ô	paw	*th*	this
ĕ	pet	oi	boy	hw	whoop
ē	be	o͝o	took	zh	vision
ĭ	pit	o͞o	boot	ə	about
ī	pie	ou	out		

2. The place in which the action of a story or play occurs.
♦ *These sound alike* **scene, seen.**

scen·er·y |sē′ nə rē| *n.* **1.** The landscape. **2.** The structures or curtains on the stage of a theater, designed and painted to represent the place where the action occurs.

sce·nic |sē′ nĭk| *adj.* Of natural scenery, especially attractive landscapes: *a scenic route.*

scent |sĕnt| *n.* **1.** A distinctive odor: *the scent of pine.* **2.** A perfume: *a woman wearing a strong scent.*
♦ *These sound alike* **scent, sent.**

schwa |shwä| *n.* A weak vowel sound found in unstressed syllables in words. The symbol for the schwa sound is |ə|. Different vowel letters can spell the schwa sound.

scheme |skēm| *n.* **1.** A plan of action. **2.** An underhanded or secret plan; a plot: *The robbers had a scheme for robbing the bank.*

sci·ence |sī′ əns| *n.* **a.** The study and theoretical explanation of natural phenomena. **b.** Such activity applied to a particular class of phenomena: *the science of living things.*

sci·en·tif·ic |sī′ ən tĭf′ ĭk| *adj.* **1.** Of or used in science. **2.** Appearing or considered in general to have a factual, logical, or systematic basis.

scoop |sko͞op| *n.* A small, shovellike utensil with a short handle, used to take up sugar, flour, and so on.

scorn |skôrn| *v.* To reject someone or something. —*n.* A feeling that someone or something is inferior or unworthy.

scraw·ny |skrô′ nē| *adj.* **scraw·ni·er, scraw·ni·est.** Thin and bony; skinny.

Spelling Dictionary

scrub |skrŭb| *v.* **scrubbed, scrub·bing.** To clean by rubbing, as with a brush and soap and water.

sea gull |sē′ gŭl′| *n.* A bird that usually lives along seacoasts.

se·cede |sĭ sēd′| *v.* **se·ced·ed, se·ced·ing.** To withdraw formally from membership in an organization or union: *Southern states that seceded at the outset of the Civil War.*

sec·on·dar·y |sĕk′ ən dĕr′ ē| *adj.* Of or relating to education between the elementary school and college: *Madison High is the best secondary school in the area.*

se·cure |sĭ kyŏŏr′| *adj.* **se·cur·er, se·cur·est.** Free from danger or risk of loss; safe: *a secure castle.* —*v.* **se·cured, se·cur·ing.** **1.** Fasten: *Secure the lock.* **2.** To get possession of; acquire: *I hope to secure a job.*

seek |sēk| *v.* **sought** |sôt|, **seek·ing.** To try to locate or discover; search for.

seen |sēn| *v.* Past participle of **see.** Viewed; visible.
♦ *These sound alike* **seen, scene.**

seize |sēz| *v.* **seized, seiz·ing.** To grasp suddenly and forcibly; lay hold of; take or grab.
♦ *These sound alike* **seize, sees.**

self-con·fi·dence |sĕlf′ kŏn′ fĭ dəns| *n.* Confidence in oneself; self-assurance. —**self′-con′fi·dent** *adj. Her self-confident manner helped her get the job.*

self·ish |sĕl′ fĭsh| *adj.* Showing lack of regard for others; greedy.

sen·a·tor or **Sen·a·tor** |sĕn′ ə tər| *n.* A member of Congress, elected by the people of a state.

send |sĕnd| *v.* **sent** |sĕnt|, **send·ing.** To dispatch (a letter or message) as by mail or telegraph; transmit.

sen·ior |sēn′ yər| *adj.* **1.** Older or oldest. **2.** Of or for older members: *a senior scout troop.* —*n.* A student in the fourth or last year of a high school or college.

sen·si·tive |sĕn′ sĭ tĭv| *adj.* Responsive to or affected by something: *Children are sensitive to criticism.*

sent |sĕnt| *v.* Past tense and past participle of **send.**
♦ *These sound alike* **sent, scent.**

sen·tence |sĕn′ təns| *n.* A group of words or, rarely, a single word that states a complete thought and that contains a finite verb or verb phrase and usually a subject and its predicate. For example, *It's almost midnight.* and *Stop!* are sentences.

sep·a·rate |sĕp′ ə rāt′| *v.* **sep·a·rat·ed, sep·a·rat·ing.** To put or keep apart: *separated the rolls in the pan.* —*adj.* |sĕp′ ər ĭt| *or* |sĕp′ rĭt|. Distinct from others; individual or independent.

se·quel |sē′ kwəl| *n.* A novel or movie complete in itself but continuing the story of an earlier work: *The sequel was even better than the first story.*

se·ri·ous |sîr′ ē əs| *adj.* **1.** Grave, sober: *Mike wondered what was wrong when his father looked so serious.* **2.** Not joking or silly; in earnest: *serious about quitting school.*

ses·sion |sĕsh′ ən| *n.* A meeting of a school class, a club, or any other group assembled to do or discuss something of common interest: *a recording session.*

shal·low |shăl′ ō| *adj.* **shal·low·er, shal·low·est.** Measuring little from the bottom to the top or surface; not deep: *a shallow lake.*

shelf |shĕlf| *n., pl.* **shelves** |shĕlvz|. A flat, usually rectangular piece of wood, metal, or glass, fastened at right angles to a wall and used to hold or store things.

shield |shēld| *n.* A piece of armor carried on the arm in olden times by knights or warriors to protect them from an opponent's blows.

shove |shŭv| *v.* **shoved, shov·ing.** To prod, thrust, or push roughly or rudely.

shov·el |shŭv′ əl| *v.* **shov·eled** or **shov·elled, shov·eling** or **shov·el·ling.** To remove with a shovel; dig: *shovel snow.*

side·burns |sīd′ bûrnz′| *n.* Growths of hair down the sides of a man's face in front of the ears, especially when worn with the rest of the beard shaved off.

sig·na·ture |sĭg′ nə chər| The name of a person as written by him- or herself.

sig·nif·i·cance |sĭg′ nĭf′ ĭ kəns| *n.* The state and quality of being meaningful; importance: *the significance of the rare books.*

si·lence |sī′ ləns| *n.* The absence of sound or noise; stillness.

si·lent |sī′ lənt| *adj.* **1.** Making or having no sound or noise; quiet: *the silent night.* **2.** Without speech; saying nothing: *remained respectfully silent.* **3.** Not disposed to speak; taciturn: *a person who is silent by nature.*

sil·hou·ette |sĭl′ ōō ĕt′| *v.* **sil·hou·et·ted,** **sil·hou·et·ting.** To cause to be seen as a silhouette. —*n.* A drawing consisting of the outline of something, especially a human profile, filled in with a solid color.

sim·i·lar |sĭm′ ə lər| *adj.* Related in appearance or nature; alike though not the same: *a wild cat similar to but smaller than a lion.*

sim·i·lar·i·ty |sĭm′ ə lăr′ ĭ tē| *n., pl.* **sim·i·lar·i·ties.** A feature or property shared by two or more things; a way in which things are alike.

sin·cere |sĭn′ sîr′| *adj.* **sin·cer·er,** **sin·cer·est.** Without false appearance or nature; honest; truthful. —*adv.* **sin·cere·ly.**

sink |sĭngk| *v.* **sank** |săngk| or **sunk** |sŭngk|, **sunk** or **sunk·en** |sŭng′ kən|, **sink·ing.** To cause to go beneath the surface or to the bottom of liquid or a soft substance: *The sled sank into the deep snow.*

site |sīt| *n.* **1.** The place where something was, is, or is to be located. **2.** The place or setting of an event.

♦ *These sound alike* **site, cite, sight.**

History

Site comes from the Latin word *situs,* meaning "place." **Cite** comes from the Latin word *citare,* meaning "to call." **Sight** comes from the Old English word *gesiht,* meaning "something seen."

---

sit·u·ate |sĭch′ ōō āt′| *v.* **sit·u·at·ed,** **sit·u·at·ing.** To place in a certain spot or position; locate.

sit·u·a·tion |sĭch′ ōō ā′ shən| *n.* **1.** A combination of circumstances at a given moment: *FBI agents face many dangerous situations.* **2.** The way in which something is placed in relation to its environment.

skel·e·ton |skĕl′ ĭ tən| *n.* The internal supporting structure of a vertebrate, composed of bone and cartilage and serving also to protect some of the more delicate body tissues.

skeleton

skirt |skûrt| *n.* A separate garment that hangs from the waist and is not divided between the legs, worn by women and girls.

sleeve |slēv| *n.* The part of a garment that covers all or part of the arm.

slen·der |slĕn′ dər| *adj.* **slen·der·er, slen·der·est.** Long and thin.

slip |slĭp| *v.* **slipped, slip·ping.** **1.** To move smoothly and easily: *She slipped into her seat.* **2.** To lose one's balance or foothold: *I slipped on a banana peel.*

slo·gan |slō′ gən| *n.* A phrase used to advertise a commercial product or service: *a slogan for a new soap product.*

History

Slogan comes from the Gaelic phrase *sluaghairm,* originally a battle cry of the Scottish clans. The word *sluagh* means "host" and *ghairm* means "shout."

---

smug·gle |smŭg′ əl| *v.* **smug·gled, smug·gling.** To import or export without paying lawful customs, or taxes: *smuggled cars into the U.S. and sold them at low prices.*

snarl |snärl| *v.* To growl angrily or threateningly, especially with the teeth bared.

soak |sōk| *v.* To make thoroughly wet by immersing in a liquid; drench.

soar |sôr| *or* |sōr| *v.* To rise, fly, or glide high, moving with little apparent effort, as eagles and hawks do.
♦ *These sound alike* **soar, sore.**

sol·dier |sōl′ jər| *n.* A person who serves in an army.

so·lo |sō′ lō| *n., pl.* **so·los.** A musical composition or passage for a single voice or instrument.

some·bod·y |sŭm′ bŏd′ ē| *or* |-bŭd′ ē| *or* |-bə dē| *pron.* An unspecified or unknown person; someone.

so·nar |sō′ när| *n.* A system, similar in principle to radar, that uses reflected sound waves to detect and locate underwater objects.

so·pran·o |sə prăn′ ō| *or* |-prä′ nō| *n., pl.* **so·pran·os.** **1.** A high singing voice of a woman or boy; a singing voice of the highest range. **2.** A person having such a voice.

sor·cer·er |sôr′ sər ər| *n.* A person who practices sorcery; a wizard: *The sorcerer made a potion to cast a spell.*

sore |sôr| *or* |sōr| *adj.* **sor·er, sor·est.** Painful or tender.
♦ *These sound alike* **sore, soar.**

sought |sôt| *v.* Past tense and past participle of **seek.**

sparse |spärs| *adj.* **spars·er, spars·est.** Not dense or crowded: *sparse vegetation.*

spe·ci·fic |spĭ sĭf′ ĭk′| *adj.* Explicitly set forth; exact; definite: *specific questions.*

spec·i·men |spĕs′ ə mən| *n.* An individual, item, or part taken as representative of the entire set or the whole; sample: *a fossil specimen.*

spir·it |spĭr′ ĭt| *n.* A particular mood marked by vigor, courage, or liveliness: *a team that showed a lot of spirit.*

sponge |spŭnj| *n.* Something that absorbs and holds liquids.

spot |spŏt| *v.* **spot·ted, spot·ting.** To become or cause to become marked with spots or stains: *a dress that spots easily.*

sprang |sprăng| *v.* Past tense of **spring.**

spring |sprĭng| *v.* **sprang** |sprăng| *or* **sprung** |sprŭng|, **sprung, spring·ing, springs.** To move upward or forward in a single quick motion or a series of such motions; leap: *springing up from her chair.*

sprint |sprĭnt| *n.* A short race run at top speed.

sprout |sprout| *v.* To begin to grow. —*n.* A young plant growth, such as a bud or shoot.

squawk |skwôk| *n.* A loud, harsh, screeching sound, as made by a parrot, chicken, or other bird.

staff |stăf| *or* |stäf| *n.* **1.** *pl.* **staffs.** Any organized group of employees working together. **2.** *pl.* **staves** or **staffs.** The set of horizontal lines and the spaces between them on which musical notes are written.

stam·i·na |stăm′ ə nə| *n.* The power to resist fatigue or illness while working hard; endurance: *Runners need stamina to compete in marathons.*

stan·dard |stăn′ dərd| *n.* A rule or model used to judge the quality, value, or rightness of something.

starch |stärch| *n.* Any of various products used to stiffen fabrics.

stare |stâr| *v.* **stared, staring.** To look at steadily and directly, often with a wide-eyed gaze.

sta·tion |stā′ shən| *n.* A stopping place along a route for taking on and letting off passengers: *a bus station.*

stat·ure |stăch′ ər| *n.* The natural height or size of a person or animal when upright.

ste·re·o |stĕr′ ē ō| *or* |stîr′-| *n., pl.* **ste·re·os.** Audio equipment having stereophonic sound.

sting |stĭng| *v.* **stung** |stŭng| **1.** To pierce or wound with a sharp-pointed part, as that of certain insects, such as bees or wasps. **2.** To cause to feel keen unhappiness or suffering: *Her angry words stung him bitterly.*

stir |stûr| *v.* **stirred, stir·ring.** To mix (a liquid or something in a liquid) by passing an implement through it in circular motions: *Stir the soup.*

stor·age |stôr′ ĭj| *or* |stōr′-| *n.* A space where something is put away for future use: *We have storage in the attic.*

strain |strān| *v.* To exert or tax to the utmost; strive hard: *Reading in low light may strain your eyes.*

stra·te·gic |strə tē′ jĭk| *adj.* Having a plan of action: *The chess player made a strategic move and won the game.*

strat·e·gy |străt′ ə jē| *n.* A plan of action intended to accomplish a specific goal: *The general planned a special strategy for the peacetime forces.*

stress |strĕs| *n.* The emphasis placed upon the syllable spoken with the most force in a word.

strict |strĭkt| *adj.* **strict·er, strict·est.** Demanding strong discipline.

strive |strīv| *v.* **strove** |strōv|, **striv·en** |strĭv′ ən|, *or* **strived, striv·ing.** To exert much effort or energy: *strive to improve working conditions.*

strove |strōv| *v.* A past tense of **strive.**

struc·ture |strŭk′ chər| *n.* **1.** The way in which parts are arranged or put together to form a whole. **2.** Something constructed, as a building or a bridge.

strug·gle |strŭg′ əl| *v.* **strug·gled, strug·gling.** To make a great effort or strive

against or as if against a great force. —*n.* A battle.

stu·dent |stōōd′ nt| *or* |styōōd′-| *n.* A person who is attending a school, college, or university.

stu·di·o |stōō′ dē ō′| *or* |styōō′-| *n., pl.* **stu·di·os.** An artist's workroom.

stum·ble |stŭm′ bəl| *v.* **stum·bled, stum·bling.** To trip and almost fall; falter.

stung |stŭng| *v.* Past tense and past participle of **sting.**

stu·pid |stōō′ pĭd| *or* |styōō′-| *adj.* Not sensible or clever; unintelligent.

sub·ma·rine |sŭb′ mə rēn′| *or* |sŭb′ mə rēn′| n. A ship capable of operating underwater.

submarine

sub·merge |səb mûrj′| *v.* **sub·merged, sub·merg·ing.** To place or go under water or another liquid: *The swimmer was submerged in the pool.* —**sub·merged** *adj.*: *a submerged reef.*

sub·mis·sion |səb mĭsh′ ən| *n.* **1.** The act of offering something for consideration: *the submission of a story to a publisher.* **2.** Something submitted for consideration: *The publisher rejected my submission.*

sub·scribe |səb skrīb′| *v.* **sub·scribed, sub·scrib·ing.** To contract or receive and pay for a certain number of issues of a periodical: *subscribe to a magazine.*

sub·scrip·tion |səb skrĭp′ shən| *n.* A purchase made by a signed order, as for issues of a periodical or a series of theatrical performances: *a subscription to the opera.*

sub·sti·tute |sŭb′ stĭ tōōt′| *or* |-tyōōt′| *v.* **sub·sti·tut·ed, sub·sti·tut·ing.** To take the place of another; replace; exchange.

sub·sti·tu·tion |sŭb stĭ tōō′ shən| *or* |-tyōō′-| *n.* The act of replacing; replacement; alternate.

suc·cess |sək sĕs′| *n.* The achievement of something desired or attempted: *the success of the experiment.*

suf·fix |sŭf′ ĭks| *n.* A word part added to the end of a base word to form a new word. The word part *less* in *careless* is a suffix.

sug·gest |səg jĕst′| *or* |sə-| *v.* To offer for consideration or action; bring up.

sug·ges·tion |səg jĕs′ chən| *or* |sə-| *n.* Something offered for consideration; an idea.

sum·ma·ry |sŭm′ ə rē| *n., pl.* **sum·ma·ries.** A retelling of the substance of something larger: *a summary of our findings.*

sunk |sŭngk| *v.* A past tense and a past participle of **sink.**

su·pe·ri·or |sə pîr′ ē ər| *or* |sōō-| *adj.* High or higher in quality: *A superior product is better than an inferior one.*

su·per·vise |sōō′ pər vīz′| *v.* **su·per·vised, su·per·vis·ing.** To direct and inspect the action, work, or performance of: *Managers supervise the work of others.*

sup·ply |sə plī′| *v.* **sup·plied, sup·ply·ing, sup·plies.** To make available for use; provide: *Vast forests supply trees for lumber.*

sur·face |sûr′ fəs| *n.* The outermost layer or boundary of an object.

sur·geon |sûr′ jən| *n.* A doctor specializing in performing operations on parts of the body.

sur·prise |sər prīz′| *n.* Something sudden and unexpected.

sur·ren·der |sə rĕn′ dər| *v.* To give oneself up, as to a pursuer or enemy; submit.

sweat |swĕt| *v.* **sweat·ed** or **sweat, sweat·ing.** To give out a salty liquid through the pores in the skin; perspire. —*n.* The liquid itself.

swift |swĭft| *adj.* Moving with great speed; fast.

swirl |swûrl| *v.* To rotate or spin.

switch |swĭch| *v.* To exchange: *The teams switched sides at halftime.*

sword |sôrd| *or* |sōrd| *n.* A hand weapon consisting of a long, pointed blade set in a handle or hilt.

syc·a·more |sĭk′ ə môr′| *or* |-mōr′| *n.* A North American tree with ball-shaped seed clusters, which frequently grows along streams: *The huge sycamore shaded the side of the house.*

sym·bol·ic |sĭm bŏl′ ĭk| *adj.* Serving as something representative of something else.

syl·la·ble |sĭl′ ə bəl| *n.* A word or a word part that has one vowel sound.

syn·o·nym |sĭn′ ə nĭm| *n.* A word having the same or similar meaning as that of another word.

sys·tem |sĭs′ təm| *n.* Something formed of a set of elements or parts that function together: *the nervous system.*

T

tack |tăk| *n., pl.* **tacks.** A small nail with a sharp point and a flat head.
♦ *These sound alike* **tacks, tax.**

tam·bou·rine |tăm′ bə rēn′| *n.* A percussion instrument consisting of a small drumhead stretched over a narrow rim that is fitted with small metal disks that jingle when the drumhead is struck or when the instrument is shaken.

tan·dem |tăn′ dəm| *n.* A bicycle built for two.

tar·dy |tär′ dē| *adj.* **tar·di·er, tar·di·est.** Occurring, arriving, or acting later than expected; delayed: *My brother was tardy yesterday because he missed the bus.*

tar·iff |tăr′ ĭf| *n.* A system of taxes imposed by a government on imported or exported goods: *The tariffs protected local industry.*

taut |tôt| *adj.* **taut·er, taut·est.** Pulled or drawn tight; not loose.

tax |tăks| *n.* Money that people must pay to support the government. —*v.* To strain.
♦ *These sound alike* **tax, tacks.**

team·mate |tēm′ māt′| *n.* A fellow member of a team.

tease |tēz| *v.* **teased, teas·ing.** To annoy or pester by making fun of or taunting: *I tease my dad by calling him my ancestor.*

tech·ni·cian |tĕk nĭsh′ ən| *n.* A person skilled in certain scientific techniques.

tel·e·vise |tĕl′ ə vīz′| *v.* **tel·e·vised, tel·e·vis·ing.** To broadcast by television.

tell·er |tĕl′ ər| *n.* A bank employee who receives and pays out money: *The teller gave me a receipt for my deposit.*

tem·per·a·ture |tĕm′ pər ə chər| *or* |-prə chər| *n.* A numerical measure of hotness or coldness referred to a standard scale.

ten·nis |tĕn′ ĭs| *n.* A sport played between two persons (singles) or two pairs of persons (doubles) on a court divided in two by a net. A player strikes a ball with a racket, the object being to make the ball bounce in the opposing half of the court in such a way that the opposition cannot return it.

tense |tĕns| Nerve-racking; suspenseful: *a tense situation.*

tep·id |tĕp′ ĭd| *adj.* Moderately warm; lukewarm: *tepid water.*

tern |tûrn| *n.* Any of several sea birds related to and resembling the gulls, but generally smaller and with a forked tail.

tern

ter·rain |tə rān′| *or* |tĕ-| *n.* A tract of land, especially when considered with respect to its physical features: *hilly terrain.*

ter·ri·ble |tĕr′ ə bəl| *adj.* **1.** Causing terror or fear; dreadful: *a terrible storm.* **2.** Very bad.

ter·ri·fic |tə rĭf′ ĭk| *adj.* **1.** *Informal.* Very good; splendid: *a terrific party.* **2.** Very great; intense: *working under terrific pressure from his boss.*

text·book |tĕkst′ bŏŏk′| *n.* A book used for the study of a particular subject.

theme |thēm| *n.* The subject or topic of a talk or a piece of writing.

thief |thēf| *n., pl.* **thieves.** |thēvz| A person who steals, especially stealthily when the victim is not present.

thorn |thôrn| *n.* A sharp, woody spine growing from the stem of a plant such as a rosebush.

thread |thrĕd| *n.* A length of fine, thin cord made of two or more strands of fiber twisted together.

threat |thrĕt| *n.* Something regarded as a possible danger.

thrift·y |thrĭf′ tē| *adj.* **thrift·i·er, thrift·i·est.** Practicing thrift; economical and frugal.

throne |thrōn| *n.* The chair occupied by a king, queen, pope, or bishop on ceremonial occasions.

ti·ny |tī′ nē| *adj.* **ti·ni·er, ti·ni·est.** Extremely small.

toast |tōst| *n.* Sliced bread heated and browned: *French toast is my favorite breakfast.*

tooth·brush |tōōth′ brŭsh′| *n.* A small brush used in cleaning the teeth.

torch |tôrch| *n.* A portable light produced by the flame of an inflammable material wound about the end of a stick of wood.

tor·ture |tôr′ chər| *n.* Physical pain or mental anguish.

trac·tor |trăk′ tər| *n.* A small vehicle, powered by a gasoline or diesel engine, equipped with large tires, and used for pulling farm machinery.

trag·e·dy |trăj′ ĭ dē| *n., pl.* **trag·e·dies.** A serious play that ends with great misfortune or ruin for the main character or characters: *the tragedy of Hamlet.*

trag·ic |trăj′ ĭk| *adj.* Bringing or involving great misfortune, suffering, or sadness.

trait |trāt| *n.* A particular feature or characteristic: *Generosity is one of her best traits. Eye color is an inherited trait.*

tram·po·line |trăm′ pə lēn′| *or* |tram′ pə lĭn| *n.* A table-like device for performing acrobatic feats, consisting of a sheet of taut canvas attached with springs to a metal frame.

trans·fer |trăns fûr′| *or* |trăns′ fər| *v.* **trans·ferred, trans·fer·ring.** To move or shift from one place, person, or thing to another: *money transferred from a savings account to a checking account.*

trans·mit |trăns mĭt′| *or* |trănz-| *v.* **trans·mit·ted, trans·mit·ting.** To send from one person, place, or thing to another: *transmit a message.*

tril·o·gy |trĭl′ ə jē| *n., pl.* **tril·o·gies.** A group of three related dramatic or literary works.

tri·o |trē′ ō| *n.* **1.** A group of three people or things joined or associated. **2. a.** A musical composition for three performers. **b.** The group performing such a composition.

trom·bone |trŏm bōn′| *or* |trŏm′ bōn′| *n.* A brass wind instrument that is somewhat similar to the trumpet in construction and sound but larger and lower in pitch. Some trombones change pitch by using a slide that varies the length of the instrument, and some use valves similar to those of a trumpet.

trout |trout| *n., pl.* **trout.** Any of several chiefly freshwater fishes often having a speckled body and related to the salmon.

tur·moil |tûr′ moil′| *n.* A condition of great confusion or disturbance: *The 17th and 18th centuries saw Europe in religious turmoil.*

tur·quoise |tûr′ koiz′| *or* |-kwoiz′| *n.* A light bluish green mineral valued in some forms as a gem. —*adj.* Light bluish green.

tux·e·do |tŭk sē′ dō| *n., pl.* **tux·e·dos.** A man's formal or semiformal suit, usually black, including a dinner jacket, trousers, and a black bow tie.

tuxedo

typ·i·cal |tĭp′ ĭ kəl| *adj.* Having the traits or characteristics peculiar to a group or category; usual; representative: *a typical college campus.*

ty·rant |tī′ rənt| *n.* A ruler who exercises power in a harsh, cruel manner; an oppressor: *King John was known as a tyrant for taxing the starving poor.*

U

un-¹. A prefix meaning "not" or "contrary to": **unattached; unhappy.**

un-². A prefix meaning: **1.** Reversal of an action: **unbar. 2.** Release or removal from: **unburden. 3.** Intensified action: **unloose.**

u·nan·i·mous |yoō **năn′** ə məs| *adj.* Sharing the same opinion.

un·be·liev·a·ble |ŭn′ bĭ **lē′** və bəl| *adj.* Not to be believed; incredible; unconvincing: *an unbelievable tale.*

un·clear |ŭn **klîr′**| *adj.* Not clear; not sharp or explicit.

un·der·stud·y |ŭn′ dər stŭd′ ē| *n., pl.* **un·der·stud·ies.** An actor trained to substitute for the regular actor: *The understudy performed when the star had the flu.*

u·ni·corn |yoō′ nĭ kôrn′| *n.* A legendary animal resembling a horse and having a single long horn projecting from its forehead.

u·ni·form |yoō′ nə fôrm′| *adj.* **1.** Always the same; not changing or varying: *planks of uniform length.* **2.** Conforming to one principle, standard, or rule; consistent. —*n.* A suit of clothing that identifies the persons who wear it as members of a specific group.

u·nite |yoō nīt′| *v.* **u·nit·ed, u·nit·ing.** To bring together or join so as to form a whole: *Benjamin Franklin had a plan to unite the Colonies under one government.*

u·ni·ty |yoō′ nĭ tē| *n., pl.* **u·ni·ties.** The condition of being united into a single whole; oneness.

un·kind |ŭn **kīnd′**| *adj.* **un·kind·er, un·kind·est.** Not kind; harsh; thoughtless. —**un·kind′ly** *adv.* —**un·kind′ness** *n.*

un·re·li·a·ble |ŭn rĭ **lī′** ə bəl| *adj.* Not reliable or trustworthy.

un·skill·ful |ŭn **skĭl′** fəl| *adj.* Not skillful; clumsy; incompetent.

up·roar |ŭp′ rôr′| *or* |-rōr′| *n.* A condition of noisy excitement and confusion.

urge |ûrj| *v.* **urged, urg·ing. 1.** To push, force, or drive onward; encourage. **2.** To plead with.

ur·gen·cy |ûr′ jən sē| *n.* The condition of being urgent: *the urgency of their financial need.*

ur·gent |ûr′ jənt| *adj.* Calling for immediate attention; pressing: *an urgent situation.* —*adv.* **ur′gent·ly**

us·a·ble |yoō′ zə bəl| *adj.* Capable of being used.

Pronunciation Key

ă	pat	îr	pier	ŭ	cut		
ā	pay	ŏ	pot	ûr	urge		
âr	care	ō	toe	th	thin		
ä	father	ô	paw	*th*	this		
ĕ	pet	oi	boy	hw	whoop		
ē	be	ŏŏ	took	zh	vision		
ĭ	pit	ōō	boot	ə	about		
ī	pie	ou	out				

us·age |yoō′ sĭj| *or* |-zĭj| *n.* The act or manner of using something; use or employment: *The car was ruined by rough usage.*

V

vain |vān| *adj.* **vain·er, vain·est.**
1. Unsuccessful; fruitless: *a vain effort to regain her balance.* **2.** Showing undue preoccupation with one's appearance or accomplishments; not humble; conceited.
♦ *These sound alike* **vain, vein.**

val·or |văl′ ər| *n.* Courage; bravery; fearlessness.

val·u·a·ble |văl′ yoō ə bəl| *or* |-yə bəl| *adj.* Having high monetary or material value: *a valuable piece of jewelry.*

val·ue |văl′ yoō| *n.* Monetary or material worth: *the value of a rare stamp.*

van·ish |văn′ ĭsh| *v.* To pass out of existence: *Some animal species have vanished forever.*

vault¹ |vôlt| *n.* **1.** An arched structure forming a ceiling or roof. **2.** An underground storeroom. **3.** A safe for valuables. **4.** A burial chamber.

vault² |vôlt| *v.* **vault·ed, vault·ing.** To jump or leap over. —*n.* The act of vaulting; a leap.

veil |vāl| *n.* A piece of fine, sheer fabric, such as net, lace, or gauze, worn by women over the head or face.

337

vein |vān| *n.* **1.** A blood vessel through which blood returns to the heart. **2.** One of the narrow, usually branching tubes of supporting parts forming the framework of a leaf or an insect's wing.
◆ *These sound alike* **vein, vain.**

ve·to |vē′ tō| *n., pl.* **ve·toes.** Any authoritative prohibition or rejection of a proposed or intended act.

view·point |vyōō′ point′| *n.* A way of thinking about or regarding something.

vig·or |vĭg′ ər| *n.* Physical energy or strength.

vi·o·lence |vī′ ə ləns| *n.* Physical force exerted to cause damage or injury: *crimes of violence.*

vi·o·lin |vī′ ə lĭn′| *n.* The highest-pitched stringed instrument of the modern orchestra, played with a bow and having four strings tuned at intervals of a fifth: *The musicians tuned their violins.*

vi·rus |vī′ rəs| *n., pl.* **vi·rus·es.** A tiny particle of nucleic acid capable of invading living cells and destroying them, thus producing a disease: *a flue virus.*

vis·i·ble |vĭz′ ə bəl| *adj.* Capable of being seen; perceptible to the eye: *Only one ninth of an iceberg is visible above water.* —**vis′i·bly** *adv.*

vi·sion |vĭzh′ ən| *n.* The ability to sense light that enters the eye and make fine judgments about the color of the light and the directions from which the rays come; the sense of sight.

vis·it |vĭz′ ĭt| *v.* To go or come to see for reasons of business, duty, or pleasure.

vi·sor |vī′ zər| *or* |vīz′ ər| *n.* A projecting part, as on a cap or the windshield of a car, that protects the eyes from sun or wind.

vis·ta |vĭs′ tə| *n.* A distant view, especially seen through a passage or opening.

vis·u·al·ize |vĭzh′ ōō ə līz′| *v.* **vis·u·al·ized, vis·u·al·iz·ing.** To form a mental image or vision of: *It is difficult to visualize what scientists mean by light waves.*

vi·tal |vīt′ l| *adj.* Having great importance; necessary: *Irrigation was vital to early civilization.*

vol·ca·no |vŏl kā′ nō| *n., pl.* **vol·ca·noes** or **vol·ca·nos.** Any opening in the crust of the earth through which molten rock, dust, ash, and hot gases are thrown forth.

volcano

W

war·ran·ty |wôr′ ən tē| *or* |wŏr′-| *n., pl.* **war·ran·ties.** A guarantee given to a buyer, stating that the product sold is as represented and that repairs will be made without charge if certain defects are found within a stated period of time.

wash·a·ble |wŏsh′ ə bəl| *or* |wôsh′-| *adj.* Capable of being washed without fading, shrinking, or other injury.

wa·ter·re·pel·lent |wô′ tər rĭ pĕl′ ənt| *or* |wŏt′ ər-| *adj.* Resistant to water but not entirely waterproof.

watt |wŏt| *n.* A unit of electrical power equal to about 1/746 horsepower.

weap·on |wĕp′ ən| *n.* Any instrument or device used to attack another or to defend oneself from an attack: *The police officer surprised the thief and took his weapon.*

week·end |wēk′ ĕnd′| *n.* The end of the week, especially the period from Friday evening through Sunday evening.

where·as |hwâr ăz′| *or* |wâr-| *conj.* **1.** Because; since: *Whereas the accused has been found not guilty, he is released.* **2.** While on the contrary: *I like squash, whereas my brother prefers corn.*

whirl |hwûrl| *or* |wûrl| *v.* **whirled, whirl·ing.** To spin, twirl, or rotate: *whirl a baton.* —*n.* **1.** The act of whirling. **2.** *Informal.* A short trip or ride: *Let's go for a whirl in the automobile.* **3.** *Informal.* A brief try: *I've never skied before, but I'll give it a whirl.*

whis·per |hwĭs′ pər| *or* |wĭs′-| *v.* To speak or say very softly.

whole·sale |hōl′ sāl′| *adj.* Sold in large bulk or quantity, usually at a lower cost: *wholesale merchandise.*

who's |hōōz| **1.** Who is. **2.** Who has.
♦ *These sound alike* **who's, whose.**

whose |hōōz| *pron.* **1.** The possessive form of **who:** *Did you see the girl whose horse won the race?* **2.** The possessive form of **which:** *an old oak in whose branches I sat.*
♦ *These sound alike* **whose, who's.**

wield |wēld| *v.* To handle a weapon or a tool.

wild·life |wīld′ līf′| *n.* Wild plants and animals, especially wild animals living in their natural surroundings.

wind¹ |wĭnd| *n.* A current of air. —*v.* To cause to be out of or short of breath: *The long hill winded the runners.*

wind² |wīnd| *v.* **wound** |wound|, **winding, winds.** **1.** To wrap (something) around itself or around something else: *Wind the string into a ball; wind the line around the pole.* **2.** To turn (a crank, for example) in a series of circular motions: *Wind the crank and then release it.*

win·ning |wĭn′ ĭng| *adj.* Successful; victorious: *the winning entry.*

wolf |wŏolf| *n., pl.* **wolves** |wŏolvz|. An animal related to the dog, living chiefly in northern regions and feeding on the flesh of other animals.

won·der |wŭn′ dər| *v.* **won·dered, won·der·ing.** To have doubt or curiosity about: *I wonder what she is doing.* ◊ *Idiom.* **no wonder.** Not surprising: *It's no wonder that you slipped on this icy sidewalk.*

word root |wôrd rōōt| *or* |rŏot| *n.* A word part from which other words are formed. For example, *min* is the word root of *minus* and *minute.*

work·a·ble |wûr′ kə bəl| *adj.* Capable of being used or put into effect successfully; practical: *a workable idea.*

wound¹ |wōōnd| *n.* **1.** An injury, especially one in which skin or tissue is cut, pierced, or broken. **2.** An injury to one's feelings. —*v.* **1.** To inflict a wound or wounds on. **2.** To hurt the feelings of (someone).

wound² |wound| *v.* Past tense and past participle of **wind².**

wreck |rĕk| *n.* The remains of something that has been destroyed.

yarn |yärn| *n.* **1.** Wool or other natural or manmade fibers twisted or spun to form long strands used for weaving, knitting, or crocheting. **2.** *Informal.* An adventure tale or long story, often exaggerated or made-up.

yield |yēld| *v.* **1.** To give in; submit: *yielded to her arguments.* **2.** To provide as return for effort: *An investigation will yield answers.* **3.** To give over possession of; surrender: *Cars must yield the right of way to pedestrians.*

young·ster |yŭng′ stər| *n.* A child or a young person.

Z

zuc·chi·ni |zoō kē′ nē| *n., pl.* **zuc·chi·ni.** A type of long, narrow squash with a thin dark-green rind.

Content Index

Numbers in **boldface** indicate pages on which a skill is introduced as well as references to the Capitalization and Punctuation Guide.

Content Index

classifying. *See* first page of each Basic Unit. *See also* 19, 68, 78, 79, 116, 133, 150, 186, 188, 193, 218, 222, 230, 238, 241

comparing, 27, 51, 82–**83,** 154, 155, 158

contrasting, 27, 51, 62, 82–**83,** 212

creative thinking, 15, 16, 21, 27, 28, 33, 34, 35, 39, 40, 51, 52, 57, 63, 64, 70, 77, 87, 88, 93, 94, 99, 100, 107, 112, 123, 129, 130, 135, 141, 147, 148, 149, 159, 165, 171, 177, 183, 185, 195, 196, 201, 202, 207, 208, 213, 214, 215

critical thinking, 17, 23, 29, 41, 53, 59, 65, 71, 89, 95, 101, 113, 125, 131, 137, 143, 161, 167, 173, 179, 197, 203, 209, 221

distinguishing between facts and opinions, 226–**227**

making generalizations. *See* first page of each Basic Unit.

making inferences, 46, 55, 59, 61, 76, 82, 85, 109, 118, 125, 128, 139, 150, 154, 163, 169, 186, 190, 206, 212, 215, 222, 226, 232, 233, 239, 241, 242, 243, 244

persuasion, 21, 39, 63, 77, 93, 105, 107, 129, 141, 165, 190–**191,** 201, 215

predicting outcomes, 118

sequencing, 15, 123, 149, 159, 171, 185, 207

summarizing, 135, 177

using graphic organizers, 22, 28, 34, 40, 47, 58, 76, 94, 100, 112, 119, 142, 155, 160, 166, 172, 178, 191, 214, 220, 227

Vocabulary

See also Spelling and Meaning.

antonyms, **91,** 100, 103, 115–116, 148, 152, 187–188, 205, 224, 236–237, 240, 242

base words, **86,** 90, 94, 96, 110, 114–115, 140, 168, 169, 170, 181, 216–217, 220

building word families, 22, 40, 94, 160, 172, 178, 220

cloze activities, 13, 17, 20, 23, 29, 32, 35, 40, 41, 42, 43, 52, 53, 55, 58, 59, 61, 62, 65, 70, 71, 73, 76, 77, 78, 85, 89, 95, 101, 103, 107, 113, 114, 116, 121, 125, 130, 131, 137, 139, 143, 148, 149, 150, 151, 158, 160, 161, 164, 167, 169, 173, 179, 181, 184, 185, 187, 196, 197, 199, 202, 203, 209, 212, 215, 217, 221, 223, 224, 229–232, 235–239, 242, 245

compound words, **48**–51, 52, 78, 232

connotations, **214**

content area vocabulary, 17, 23, 29, 35, 41, 53, 59, 65, 71, 77, 89, 95, 101, 107, 113, 125, 131, 137, 143, 149, 161, 167, 173,

179, 185, 197, 203, 209, 215, 221

definitions, 13, 17, 19, 25, 26, 28–29, 31, 37–38, 42, 43, 45, 49–50, 55–56, 68, 73, 78, 80, 91, 92, 109, 115, 127, 133, 140, 152, 163, 186, 199, 205, 206, 217, 229–233, 238, 241, 244

easily confused words, 130, 184, 202

exact words, 16, 76, 112, 136, 154–155, 208

homographs, **34,** 134

homophones, **54**–57, 58, 78, **92,** 193, 232

idioms, **88,** 200

multiple-meaning words, 70, 124

prefixes, 91, **96**–99, 115, 121, 132–134, 151, 168, 169, 170, 180–181, 187, 188, 198–200, 210–211, 216–217, 222–225, 236, 239, 242–246

absorbed, 96–97, 115, 132–133, 151, 198–200, 210–211, 222–223, 225, 236, 239, 244–245, 275

rhyming words, 20, 31–32, 32, 42, 44, 85

suffixes, **90**–92, 97, 114, 120–121, 126–127, 144–146, 150, 152, 170, 174–176, 187, 204–205, 216–217, 224, 235, 238, 240, 242, 246

synonyms, **16,** 25, 37, 42, 44, 79, 85, 104, 114, 116, 121, 152, 157, 181, 187, 211, 223, 229, 231, 233–237, 240, 245–246

Content Index

Credits

Illustration **76** Rita Lascaro **94** Lehner & Whyte **134** Fred Schrier **106** Rita Lascaro **124** Annie Gusman **130** Jennifer Harris **148** Rita Lascaro **163** Rita Lascaro **172** Fred Schrier **178** Rita Lascaro **193** Rita Lascaro **200** Linda Davick **208** Fred Schrier **217** Rita Lascaro

Assignment Photography **16, 23, 45** (r), **55, 61, 68** (b), **94, 127** (m), **133, 141,145, 148** (bl), **153, 158, 163, 164, 170, 175, 176, 181, 184, 189, 193, 217, 202, 212, 214, 294, 328** Alan Landau **119, 225, 227** Parker/Boone Productions **13, 14, 20, 25, 32** (b), **38** (b), **74** (b), **97** (br), **128** (b), **129** (m, b), **136, 140, 146, 147, 149, 177, 182, 206, 207, 213, 220** Tony Scarpetta

Photography **10** Allan Landau **17** (m) Jack Deutsch/ Stock South/PNI; (bl) Corbis-Bettmann **19** (b) Image Copyright ©1997 PhotoDisc, Inc. **22** (bl) National Aeronautics and Space Administration; (br) Hulton Deutsch/PNI **25** (b) Image Copyright ©1997 PhotoDisc, Inc. **27** Jasmine/PNI **29** Joseph Sohm/Tony Stone Images/ PNI **35** The Granger Collection **41** The Granger Collection **50** (b) Image Copyright ©1997 PhotoDisc, Inc. **51** (br) Image Copyright ©1997 PhotoDisc, Inc. **53** (l) © CNES; Licensed by SPOT Image Corporation/Photo Researchers, Inc. **59** (mr) Mike Mazzaschi/Stock Boston/PNI **65** UN/DPI Photo **71** (t) Ron Testa/Northern Indiana Historical Society; (b) The Granger Collection **73** National Aeronautics and Space Administration **77** Corbis-Bettmann **81** Corbis-Bettmann **85** Jeffrey Aaronson/Network Aspen **88** (b) Brown Brothers **89** Archive Photos/PNI **95** The Granger Collection **101** (t) Julie Stone/City Year **107** (br) Kay Chernush/Black Star/PNI **113** Don Smetzer/Tony Stone Images **117** Erik Anderson/Stock Boston/PNI **121** Arkansas Archeological Survey **123** (t) David Barnes/Tony Stone Images/PNI **125** (b) Hugh Sitton/Tony Stone Images **131** (b) Brown Brothers; (tl, ml) United States Postal Service **137** Andy Sacks/Tony Stone Images **149** (b) Don Smetzer/Tony Stone Images **157** Gordon Wiltsie/APA/Black Star/PNI **161** (b) Arnulf Husmo/Tony Stone Images **167** (b) The Granger Collection **171** (t, br) Image Copyright ©1997 PhotoDisc, Inc. **173** (b) A. Wolf/Explorer/Photo Researchers, Inc. **179** (tl) Image Copyright ©1997 PhotoDisc, Inc.; (b) John Heimlich/Stock South/PNI **185** Corbis-Bettmann/Reuters **195** Larry Gilpin/Tony Stone Images/PNI **196** (l) Robert Pickett/Corbis **199** (b) Image Copyright ©1997 PhotoDisc, Inc. **205** Culver Pictures/PNI **209** (b) The Granger Collection **215** (b) The Granger Collection **221** The Granger Collection **283** Chen Juanmci/New China Pictures/Eastfoto/PNI **284** Mitch Kezar/Phototake/PNI **287** Gunter Marx/Corbis **289** Vince Streano/Tony Stone Images **291** Philip & Karen Smith/Tony Stone Images **296** Michael S. Yamashita/Corbis **298** Nick Gunderson/Tony Stone Images/PNI **300** Stephen Frisch/Stock Boston/PNI **303** Ann Purcell; Carl Purcell/ Words & Pictures/PNI **305** Arnulf Husmo/Tony Stone Images **307** Robert Pickett/Corbis **308** Lynda Richardson/ Corbis **311** Smithsonian Institution **312** Peter Newton/ Tony Stone Images **318** Hal Beral/Photo Network/PNI **320** Robert E. Schwerzel/Stock Boston/PNI **322** Francois Gohier/Photo Researchers, Inc. **325** Milkie Studio, Inc./ Tony Stone Images **326** Image Copyright ©1997 PhotoDisc, Inc. **329** Grandadam/Tony Stone Images **331** Phil Degginger/Tony Stone Images **333** Joe Towers/ Check Six/PNI **335** Robert Franz/Corbis **336** Darlene Hammond/Archive Photos/PNI **338** Nicholas DeVore/Tony Stone Images

Handwriting Models

a b c d e f g h i
j k l m n o p q r
s t u v w x y z

A B C D E F G H I
J K L M N O P Q R
S T U V W X Y Z

Words Often Misspelled

You probably use many of the words on this list when you write. If you cannot think of the spelling of a word, you can always check this list. The words are in alphabetical order.

A

again
all right
a lot
always
another
anyone
anything
anyway

B

basketball
beautiful
because
before
believe
brought

C

cannot
can't
captain
caught
clothes
coming
cousin

D

didn't
different
don't

E

eighth
enough
everybody
everyone
everything
everywhere

F

family
favorite
field
finally
friend

G

getting
going
guess
guy

H

happened
happily
haven't
heard
here

I

instead
its
it's

K

knew
know

M

might
millimeter
morning

O

o'clock
once

P

people
pretty
probably

R

really
received
right

S

Saturday
school
someone
sometimes
stopped
stretch
suppose
swimming

T

that's
their
there
there's
they
they're
thought
through
to
tonight
too
two

U

usually

W

weird
we're
whole
would
wouldn't
write
writing

Y

your
you're